T. EDGAR LYON

A TEACHER IN ZION

Biographies in Latter-day Saint History

An imprint of BYU Studies and the
Joseph Fielding Smith Institute for Latter-day Saint History

Brigham Young University
Provo, Utah

T. EDGAR LYON

A Teacher in Zion

T. Edgar Lyon Jr.

Brigham Young University Press
Provo, Utah

This is the inaugural volume of the Smith Institute and BYU Studies series
Biographies in Latter-day Saint History.

© 2002 Brigham Young University Press and T. Edgar Lyon Jr.

Cover portrait by Lynnette Moench Perkes
Cover design by Nichole Klein

ISBN 0-8425-2499-1
ISBN 0-8425-2500-9
For Library of Congress
Cataloging-in-Publication Data visit
http://ByuStudies.byu.edu/Lyoncip

Printed in the United States of America
10 9 8 7 6 5 4 3 2 1

Contents

Illustrations

Preface

I hope this book is enjoyable and easy to read; it has not been easy to write. Each time I began research for a new chapter, I felt overwhelmed: "this is too big to handle," I thought, or "there is simply too much life here to ever condense it into a single chapter," or "he was so great that my meager writing can't begin to capture that greatness." Besides these hesitations that might apply to any biography, T. Edgar Lyon was my father, and I admired, respected, and loved him. This made me often wonder, "How can I be objective enough when I am so close to my subject?" The book was not easy to write, but it was enjoyable to do so. May you, too, find delight in it.

One may question, as I have, the need for a biography of a man who already left many written documents on his life. For example, over a three-month period in 1974 and 1975, Assistant Church Historian Davis Bitton conducted nine interviews of fifteen total hours duration with Ed. These interviews formed part of the Oral History Program of The Church of Jesus Christ of Latter-day Saints' Archives Division; Church Historian Leonard J. Arrington and his associates considered Ed a "probable candidate . . . [to interview because of his] vast experiences" in the Church.[1] The result of these interviews is nearly three hundred pages of Lyon's recollections and insights into his own life. Unfortunately, this document is not readily available to the public, but more important, it is very incomplete. This oral history covers several major events in great detail, but leaves out many others; those other events appear in the biography you hold in your hands. Further, as Ed recognized, interviews and oral histories conducted many years after the fact are not always accurate accounts of the past. I have used Ed's oral history, but have supplemented it with original documents from the time of the various events.

From 1923 to 1975, Ed kept datebooks and sketchy diaries. He also wrote thousands of letters and usually retained a copy of each. After his death, his children donated these letters, datebooks, files, and manuscripts to the Church Archives. Ron Barney and Jay G. Burrup catalogued the miscellaneous files into seventy-two organized boxes. They later filmed all the items on fifty reels of microfilm, which are openly available in the Church Archives. Copies of the fifty microfilm reels have been donated to the L. Tom Perry Special Collections in the Harold B. Lee Library at Brigham Young University. I have relied heavily on these materials for the history of T. Edgar Lyon's life, and I thank the Church Archives' staff for their excellent work in organizing this collection.

My intent in writing this book has been to make the life of T. Edgar Lyon available to some of his former students from the Salt Lake institute (ten to twelve thousand in number); to his 128 living posterity (as of 2002); to those interested in Church history in general and in the history of the twentieth century in particular; and to young and old "Nauvooers." For scholars who desire more depth, I have included endnotes with additional information or sources on the subject matter of the text. The appendices also provide additional historical information about Ed's experiences. Unless otherwise noted, pictures are from the Lyon family.

I have attempted to write an accurate history of T. Edgar Lyon. Recognizing my own difficulty in being objective, I have tried to make this biography a faithful representation of his life. I have tried not to exaggerate, distort, eulogize, or ignore conflicts. Ed would have appreciated that.

It has been difficult to be fully objective; my father's presence still looms large in my life. I bear his name, his temperament, his passion for history, and even his hairline. Throughout the chapters, I have provided considerable historical and cultural background, especially during his early years when the Church was in a more formative period.

My personal association with my father and my research on his life have led me to conclude that he generally projected a positive, even optimistic outlook on life. His views on history and how to communicate it, however, did occasionally place him in conflict with authorities and Church Educational System leaders, as well as in disagreement with other academicians on historical issues. Much of Lyon's greatness was his ability to harmonize his own passionate conviction for historical thoroughness and unbiased scholarship with an equally firm desire to serve his church and sincerely preserve the faith of its brightest minds. The complex method and unique experiences with which he achieved this synthesis hopefully become evident in the following chapters.

I thank many. The Brigham Young University Religious Studies Center kindly provided a necessary start-up grant. The BYU Department of Spanish and Portuguese along with the Kennedy Center for International Studies provided time and encouragement as well as excellent secretarial help. Many research and editing assistants, especially Heather

Seferovich, Melinda Silver, Trent Lyon, Derek Howell, and Kristi Smith have improved the text greatly. Ron Watt, Ron Barney, Bill Slaughter, and Linda Haslam in the Church Archives have given many hours of thoughtful help. The staff at BYU Studies, particularly Heather Seferovich, Kimberly Yi-Jiun Pace, Marny K. Parkin, and John W. Welch, guided the entire manuscript through publication with patience and efficiency. I thank Lynnette Moench Perkes for permission to use her portrait of T. Edgar Lyon on the cover. My brothers have encouraged and supplied much information; Jamie and Lynn rewrote parts of two chapters. My wife, Cheryl, has read the manuscript in many versions and provided both sincere support and frequent encouragement, especially at times when discouragement and fatigue overcame enthusiasm. Thank you.

When Ed's grandfather, the poet John Lyon, died in 1889, the *Millennial Star* observed: "It is rare that Death lays his hand upon one who, without special official position in the Church, was so widely known."[2] The same eulogy could be given to his grandson. As a teacher, T. Edgar Lyon influenced thousands to examine history honestly and to thoughtfully maintain the faith of their fathers.

Notes

1. T. Edgar Lyon, Oral History, preface, Church Archives, Family and Church History Department, The Church of Jesus Christ of Latter-day Saints, Salt Lake City.

2. "Death of Elder John Lyon: A Faithful Veteran Passes to His Rest," *Deseret News* (November 29, 1889): 3.

1

A Living Pioneer Legacy

The birth of a baby—even an eight-pound one—had become routine for Mary Cairns Lyon. She had given birth to seven other children at two- or three-year intervals over the last sixteen years. Like most of her contemporaries, she saw no need to go to St. Mark's or Holy Cross Hospital. So on the hot summer day when she knew she was close, Mary asked her oldest son to summon midwife Rachel Simmons, affectionately called "Granny Simmons" by the family. After a brief but intense labor, Mary (and Rachel) delivered a son, the seventh. Rachel cleaned up, repeated some standard advice about confinement and care, and promised to return in the morning. The baby's father, David Ross Lyon, thanked Rachel and paid five dollars for her tender, efficient services.[1]

Thus Thomas Edgar Lyon was born on Sunday afternoon, August 9, 1903, in a simple, white-frame home in the Avenues, a prosperous section of Salt Lake City northeast of the city's center. No official record was made of this rather routine birth.

A few weeks later, the baby's father performed his accustomed ecclesiastical duties. On Sunday, November 1, 1903, in the Salt Lake Twentieth Ward chapel, David Lyon blessed his son and christened him with the name Thomas Edgar Lyon.[2] Mary and David may have chosen the name "Thomas" to honor David's righteous but short-lived brother Thomas;[3] or Mary's younger brother Thomas, still in Scotland; or her mother's brother, Thomas Edgar Johnstone. Or perhaps they chose to dignify a whole string of Scottish great-grandfathers with the same name.

"Edgar" definitely came from Mary's side. It was her grandmother's maiden surname, also from Scotland. The baby's only sister, ten-year-old Carol, soon created the affectionate nickname "Teddy," borrowing the "T" from Thomas, the "Ed" from Edgar, and adding the diminutive "-dy" for childish endearment. In adolescent and adult years, Teddy gave way to Edgar, and later to Ed.

Pioneers and Poetry

By 1903, Teddy's father, David Lyon, and his family considered themselves "Old Salt Lakers." His father, poet John Lyon, had emigrated from Scotland to Salt Lake City in 1853. John Lyon, born exactly one hundred years before his grandson Thomas Edgar, was raised in poverty in the slums of Glasgow and was unable to attend public or parish schools. While in his teens, John moved from Glasgow to Kilmarnock, Scotland; took up hand-loom weaving; married; learned to read and write in an adult literacy program; and began to write for local newspapers. He not only covered newsworthy activities, but also wrote poetry for local and regional journals (illus. 1-1).

In 1844, William Gibson baptized John Lyon into The Church of Jesus Christ of Latter-day Saints. John soon baptized his family and scores of townspeople. His wife, Janet, bore twelve children in Kilmarnock, and the family often hosted visiting Church leaders in their crowded home. In early 1853, the Church in Great Britain published 5,148 copies of *Harp of Zion*, a book of John's poems written after his baptism in 1844. It was the first book of poetry by a Latter-day Saint writer. Proceeds from the book's sales were to assist needy members in gathering to Utah under the auspices of the Perpetual Emigrating Fund (PEF). John, Janet, and their children, with assistance from friends and from the PEF, left Scotland in February 1853 and sailed to the United States. They later walked the 1,344 miles from Keokuk, Iowa, to Salt Lake City.[4]

Teddy's grandmother Carolyn Holland was born in Staffordshire, England, in

Illus. 1-1. Pioneer poet John Lyon, age 80, 1883.

1839. As a five-year-old, she journeyed with her parents to Nauvoo, Illinois, arriving just weeks before the 1844 martyrdom of Joseph Smith but in time to see and meet the Prophet. Her father died in August of that year, leaving the small family to struggle and survive in a new country and a new religion. Kind Nauvoo neighbors assisted the widow and her young children.

Carolyn left Nauvoo with her mother and siblings in the 1846 exodus and took up residence in Winter Quarters, Nebraska. There the death of her mother in 1847 left Carolyn an eight-year-old orphan. A newly married couple in the camp, Robert and Ann Crookston, took her in as a domestic helper and foster daughter. Carolyn lived for five years in Winter Quarters. By 1852 the Crookstons had scraped together enough money to gather to the mountains, and they took Carolyn with them.[5] They moved into Salt Lake City's intellectual Twentieth Ward in the same area of the city where John Lyon resided. Four years after her arrival in the valley, Carolyn, affectionately known as "Carrie," accepted John Lyon's marriage proposal and became his plural wife.[6]

John, his two wives, and his families enjoyed high status and visibility in pioneer Utah. John served as superintendent, or president, of the Endowment House and acted as the "preacher" in every sacred endowment session for nearly thirty years. For many years, he also greeted local, national, and international visitors as the Utah territorial librarian. He frequently published his poetry, prose, and theater reviews in Salt Lake City newspapers and periodicals. All these activities brought him renown with both Church leaders and lay members.

Between 1857 and 1872 Carolyn bore seven children (illus. 1-2).

In Carolyn's later years, she rose in nearly every ward testimony meeting to share her deep convictions, which had first taken root in Nauvoo. She continually felt an urgency to warm her children and grandchildren with the fire of her testimony of the Prophet Joseph Smith.

After John Lyon died in 1889 at age eighty-six, Carolyn continued living in her Salt Lake home on the corner of F Street and Second Avenue until 1910 and occasionally tended her grandson Teddy. She spent the last two years of her life at the home of her daughter Eliza in Holbrook, Idaho, where she died on May 2, 1912, at age seventy-three.

Scottish Strength

Teddy's mother and maternal grandmother also brought a British legacy to Utah. Maternal grandfather Joseph Cairns, though originally from Londonderry, Ireland, was a shipbuilder in Govan, Scotland, when he married Janet Edgar Johnstone in 1864. Five feet two inches tall with a small build and tiny feet, Janet had been a schoolteacher, and she and her mother ran a small, noisy boardinghouse for Govan's shipbuilders. Joseph lodged with the family, met Janet, and married her in 1863. They had two children: Mary (1866–1948) and Thomas (1868–1930). During the early 1860s, Latter-day Saint missionaries traveled the few miles from Glasgow to Govan and preached to the young Cairns family. Janet eagerly listened and joined, but Joseph remained loyal to his Irish Catholic traditions. Conflicts arose in the marriage.

In the normal course of receiving Church visitors, Janet hosted newly called Apostle Albert Carrington (1813–1889). Carrington preached the doctrine of the gathering to her and suggested that if Janet's husband would not gather to Zion, she should go without him. Carrington also apparently promised, or strongly implied, that in Utah he would marry her and care for her as his plural wife. So in October 1871, twenty-nine-year-old Janet left her husband and two young children, journeyed alone to Liverpool, and booked passage for New York on the steamship *Nevada*. Carrington was the Church agent who chartered the ship. Janet paid part of her own fare, and the PEF picked up the balance. Once in the United States, she traveled from New York to Ogden, Utah, on the recently completed transcontinental rail line. Back in Scotland, Joseph

Illus. 1-2. Carolyn Holland Lyon and her children, c. 1873. David R. is second from the left.

Cairns was furious and, according to family tradition, severed all ties with his now-departed wife.

In Salt Lake City, Janet experienced only poverty and loneliness. The expected marriage to the Apostle did not take place until 1889 when Carrington was on his deathbed.[7] During the 1870s, Janet took in sewing and washing to survive, receiving no support from Carrington. Not surprisingly, alone and in poverty, she missed her children greatly. She finally arranged to smuggle her daughter Mary out of Scotland and bring her to Utah. This she planned with the help of Elder Carrington and her mother. Mary, then nine years old, left Govan in early October 1875 on the pretense of visiting her grandmother Johnstone in White Inch, a few miles down the Clyde River. In reality, she was taken to Liverpool, where she boarded a ship.

Rumors reached Mary's father that she was joining with a company of Mormons bound for the United States. Joseph Cairns rushed to Liverpool and found the ship *Dakota* filled with Latter-day Saints ready to sail. He summoned the police and demanded his daughter, but some passengers had hidden her in a large coil of rope, having warned her to be quiet or she would never see her mother again. Joseph searched the steamship for hours but never found his concealed daughter. The ship sailed the next day, on October 14, 1875, with Mary in the charge of caring British Saints. Church records list her fare as "chgd [charged] to Church." After just ten days at sea, she and the other 120 Church members landed in New York, then quickly left for the Salt Lake Valley by train. After enduring four long years of separation, mother and daughter were joyously reunited.

For a time, Janet and Mary resided in Salt Lake's Thirteenth Ward, near the center of town. During the 1870s, they frequently attended church services in the Tabernacle on Temple Square. To save the soles of their shoes, they often walked barefooted along South Temple Street to Eagle Gate. There they would wade across City Creek, dry their feet, then put on their shoes to walk the final block to the Tabernacle in high style, dry and comfortable in the knowledge that they had saved some wear on their shoes. They reversed the process when they returned home.[8]

In January 1882, Janet accepted a position as housekeeper in the Gardo House to work with President John Taylor's sister, Agnes Swartz, who functioned as matron in the mansion. Janet helped serve the two thousand guests who called on January 2, 1882, at the open house for the president's quarters. She continued serving in the house even after 1885, when President Taylor "preached his last public sermon, and . . . went into retirement" because of polygamy raids.[9] In late 1882, Janet and Mary moved into the fashionable mansion, ending their financial woes and feeling grateful for their association with the families of the Church President. After her long-awaited sealing and the death of Elder Carrington, Janet was known as "Granny" Carrington. Unfortunately, Teddy never really knew this warm-hearted grandmother—she died just a year and a half after his birth.

Self-Taught Man

Teddy's father, David Ross Lyon, was born August 16, 1864, the fourth of seven children in the Caroline and John Lyon family. Growing up the son of a celebrated poet, he enjoyed certain advantages: as a boy, he often met Brigham Young; he was baptized and confirmed in the Endowment House by Joseph F. Smith; and he frequently visited the home of John Taylor. For part of a year, David attended Karl G. Maeser's school in the Twentieth Ward, an experience that sparked his lifelong desire for learning coupled with spirituality. In his adult years, David fondly recalled Maeser lamenting, "You vill drive me crazy."[10] David's father, John, discouraged formal schooling for his sons, perhaps viewing his own success in Scotland as a self-taught poet and writer as a pattern for his children. David only participated in parts of four or five years of formal school, withdrawing completely at age twelve. Many years later, on March 4, 1937, he sadly noted in his diary: "Father took me out of school to go to work. At that time I did not realize what school meant. I know now that it was a great mistake, as I might have had a different story to tell as to what I might have accomplished in life."[11]

At age twelve, David began full-time work as a "printer's devil," an errand boy for the Salt Lake *Herald*. A year later, in 1877, he was apprenticed as a typesetter. He studied on his own time to ensure proper spelling and grammar of the printing he set. His experience as a typesetter allowed him to get better work with printer and entrepreneur Joseph Hyrum Parry in 1884. At that time, Parry published *Parry's Monthly Magazine,* which later became (the second) *Utah Magazine*. There, young David gained valuable insight into journal publication that helped set the pattern for his life's work.

When Joseph Parry experienced financial difficulties and offered his business for sale, David borrowed five hundred dollars and bought a half interest. His friend and stake Sunday School missionary companion John R. Park bought in as the second owner and silent partner.[12] As the Church began publishing more periodicals in Utah, Lyon and Park bid on the contracts and soon began printing the *Women's Exponent* (1872–1914), the *Young Woman's Journal* (1889–1929), and the *Improvement Era* (1897–1970). On April 22, 1890, they officially changed the name of the establishment to the Magazine Printing Company (see illus. 1-3), since they were now publishing the Church's magazines. They also prepared organ recital programs and flyers for Church activities and bid on printed work for the University of Utah. As a result of Park's behind-the-scenes influence, the Magazine Printing Company received much of the university's business.

For sixty-one years, from 1876 to 1937, David actively worked in the printing business. For forty-seven of those years, he was the general manager and chief financial officer of the Magazine Printing Company. The business provided a stable income, but David worked hard—ten to fourteen hours each weekday and at least half a day on Saturday, averaging over sixty hours of work a week. After his official retirement from the Magazine Printing Company at age seventy-three, he continued as president of the company for three years, until his death in 1940. David's hard work ensured sufficient money so that his family never knew serious want. His journals and letters show that he was extremely generous with his means, often lending or giving money to his adult children and friends. David's comfortable income allowed him to build a large, second home on the corner of Ninth Avenue and E Street.

Illus. 1-3. David R. Lyon inside his Magazine Printing Company on Richards Street, May 15, 1902.

In 1908, Elder B. H. Roberts ordained David a Seventy. Shortly thereafter, David began service as the "Poor Man's Bishop" in the Twentieth Ward. This unofficial position resulted from the then-frequent practice of leaving bishops in office for life. During 1910, Bishop George Romney (bishop from 1887 to 1912) was ill and often away in California. One of his counselors had died, and the other was frequently ill. So as presiding Seventy in the ward, David called the meetings, organized and presided over them, and collected tithing from the twelve hundred members of the Twentieth Ward.

After at least two years as unofficial ward leader, David was called as bishop and served for just a year before the ward was divided in 1913. He was then called as the first bishop of the newly created Salt Lake Ensign Ward, a position he held for another twelve-and-a-half years. The new ward was a bit smaller, only 833 members when created. Since it was not the custom (or even permissible) to have more than one ward meet in the same chapel, the Ensign Ward's sacrament meetings were originally "held either on the back lawn of the LDS Hospital or in the basement of the nurses' home."[13] Bishop Lyon opened his two homes for Priesthood and Sunday School sessions. He was released in 1926 and soon thereafter was ordained stake patriarch, a position he held until his death in 1940.

One of David's most rewarding ecclesiastical associations was his participation in a prayer circle, namely the John Taylor Prayer Circle. This association of Church leaders began in 1858 and met every Thursday evening for seventy years. It first met in the Endowment House (where David's father was superintendent), later in the historian's office, and, after 1893, in the Salt Lake Temple. Prominent men of the valley comprised the membership, including George Q. Cannon, Franklin D. Richards, John W. Taylor, Orson F. Whitney, other members of the Quorum of the Twelve, and sixteen local bishops. In the informal group, David learned of developing activities in the Church and the gossip. He was a member of this group for forty-three years, having been invited to join in 1886 as a relatively young man of twenty-two. Growing out of the temple ceremony, the prayer circle provided brotherhood, testimony-bearing, and discussion of gospel doctrine.[14]

Teddy inherited from his father the vital need to stay actively involved in his faith. He admired his father's tenacity as a defender when a biased or negative article incorrectly criticized the Church. Teddy would fight similar misrepresentations later in his life as a student at the University of Chicago, as a mission president, and as an institute teacher. His father's financial generosity would not only help Teddy earn an advanced college

Illus. 1-4. David Ross Lyon and sons, c. 1912. *Back row, left to right:* Edgar, Kyle, Paul. *Front row, left to right:* David C., David R., Joseph.

degree, but also provide a model for his own generosity in helping his sons in their early married lives (illus. 1-4). Teddy held his father in awesome respect. He said, "Once at the BYU I was asked to write an essay describing the ideal Christian—and I wrote a description of Father as he was, and it was the best paper in the class."[15]

Tender but Feisty Woman

Mary Cairns, Teddy's mother, also received very little formal education, and throughout her life she expressed some shame at her limited writing ability. Teddy received only one letter from her during his entire mission. But in the latter years of her life, Mary wrote frequently, having studied and gained confidence as a result of literacy lessons from her youngest daughter, Janette, in the late 1920s. She even typed some letters during the 1940s. Mary's letters are accurate and insightful.

Like her mother, Mary was small, probably no more than five feet one inch tall. She was feisty and fun-loving. She met David Lyon at an occasion at the Gardo House. They courted and were married in the Logan Temple on September 30, 1885. Throughout her life, Mary defined her role as support-giver and mother. Over a twenty-one-year span, from 1887 through 1908, she bore ten children.[16] Sadly, three of her children died between 1905 and 1912. Their deaths saddened Mary but did not embitter her.

Mary was known as a wonderful cook and generous provider. In her large home at 435 E Street, she regularly received the homeless who were looking for a free meal. One of her sons once pointed out a small symbol that one of the "tramps" had marked on her home to indicate the possibility of a free meal. Her son painted over it, but it soon reappeared, and Mary refused to have it removed a second time. She insisted that the homeless needed food as much as anyone else and that she would feed them.

In later years, Mary traveled much, making annual week-long trips to Logan to complete temple work and to southern California to visit her married daughter Carol. A few of the letters she wrote to her husband during these trips are preserved in the Church Archives. Mary often signed her name affectionately as "Mamie," though her children always referred to her as "Mama." But "Papa" was the main figure in Mary's life. She supported him before she filled her own needs.

Teddy recalled that his "mother had an unusual memory and I guess I acquired something from her."[17] From his mother, he also learned the joy of service. During the deadly influenza epidemic of 1918, none of the members of the Lyon family came down with the flu, but many of their neighbors did. Mary was a Relief Society visiting teacher, and because her companion was bedridden with the flu, Mary took fifteen-year-old Teddy on her visits. He recalled that during a period of several weeks when school was dismissed, he and his mother would visit the sick. Teddy built fires while his mother prepared breakfast for the people. These tasks were repeated at each house.

> In the beginning I thought, "Gee, this is a lot of work. Why don't they do it themselves?" But they were in bed. Some way Mother got over to me the idea that this was some kind of a Christian service and these people couldn't do it. It was something they needed done or they would die. They needed to be fed. She had good luck because there wasn't a person as I remember on the whole block who died. It was quite a deadly disease and a lot of people died in that period of time.[18]

Mary wanted a garden in the sloping backyard of her home on E Street but recognized that it would need terracing to keep the sandy soil from washing away. She assured Teddy that he could build a rock wall terrace and sent him to City Creek Canyon to observe masons who were building rock pillars and bridge foundations. Teddy came back, gathered cobblestones left over from a water main excavation in front of their house, and built his mother a large rock wall. She praised his effort.

In 1934, Teddy wrote a Mother's Day letter to Mary, expressing gratitude and thanking her. The letter reveals the tone of the home as well as Mary's character.

> I must have tried your patience and nerves with my questions and pranks and streaks of mischief, as I have . . . sons who now do the same to me. I look back on the care-free years you gave to us. . . . I am thankful for the freedom you gave us, of the welcome we received at home, of the freedom with which we could bring our friends home, and the welcome you always gave them. I am thankful that you and Father lived in such a spirit of peace and harmony that we did not have to fear embarrassing outbursts of temper or petty quarrels, which mark so many homes. We never lived under a tension.[19]

Mary's example, lessons, and love largely formed the calm, optimistic, hardworking character of her youngest son.

In the year T. Edgar Lyon was born (1903), Church membership was 304,901, most of it concentrated in the stakes along the Wasatch Front.[20] The majority of the Church's general leadership came from the Salt Lake Valley, and Teddy's father and mother knew and associated with these leaders. Salt Lake City had been the home of the extended Lyon family since the early 1850s. Loving and concerned aunts and uncles honored family traditions, and Teddy had many cousins in the town. The pioneering spirit, with its optimistic, can-do attitude; love for his home in the mountains of Utah; physical labor; the urgent need and desire to give service, especially to the needy; and the intimate association with the Church's highest leaders all confirmed to Thomas Edgar Lyon that he was of faithful heritage, of real, living pioneer stock. He would carry on that legacy.

Notes

1. Much of the information for this biography is taken from the T. Edgar Lyon Collection in the Church Archives, Family and Church History Department, The Church of Jesus Christ of Latter-day Saints, Salt Lake City (hereafter cited as Church Archives). The collection consists of seventy-two boxes, mainly from T. Edgar Lyon's personal files, including diaries, daybooks, correspondence,

mission and mission president's files, Church Institute materials, and so forth. A detailed index to the collection is available in the Church Archives and in the L. Tom Perry Special Collections, Harold B. Lee Library, Brigham Young University, Provo, Utah (hereafter cited as Perry Special Collections).

2. Twentieth Ward Records, November 1, 1903, Church Archives.

3. Thomas Lyon, 1826–63, son of poet John Lyon.

4. See more specific details in T. Edgar Jr., *John Lyon: The Life of a Pioneer Poet*, Religious Studies Center Specialized Monograph Series, vol. 6 (Provo, Utah: Religious Study Center, Brigham Young University, 1989).

5. Robert Crookston, "Autobiography of Robert Crookston, Sr.," manuscript in author's possession.

6. He was fifty-three years old; she had just turned sixteen. The marriage caused some friction with John's first wife, Janet, who moved to Tooele for a time, allowing John to bond with his new, young bride.

7. Elder Carrington officially married just two wives, Rhoda Maria Woods (married December 6, 1836) and Mary Ann Rock (no date given on Church records). His deathbed marriage to Janet is nowhere recorded but is widely recognized.

8. T. Edgar Lyon, interview by Richard Crabb, tape recording, Salt Lake City, January 13–15, 1978, in author's possession.

9. Brigham H. Roberts, *The Life of John Taylor* (Salt Lake City: Bookcraft, 1989), 489.

10. T. Edgar Lyon, "Oral History," 8, bound typescript, Church Archives.

11. David R. Lyon, Diary, March 4, 1937, T. Edgar Lyon Collection.

12. Born May 7, 1833, in Ohio, John Rockey Park emigrated to Utah in 1861 and converted to The Church of Jesus Christ of Latter-day Saints in 1862. He taught school for seven years in Draper, Utah, until called to be president of the University of Deseret in 1869. After twenty-five years in this position, he was elected State Superintendent of Public Instruction. Although he never married, Park adopted and raised seven children. He died on September 30, 1900, at the age of fifty-seven. Andrew Jenson, *Latter-day Saint Biographical Encyclopedia: A Compilation of Biographical Sketches of Prominent Men and Women in The Church of Jesus Christ of Latter-day Saints*, 4 vols. (Salt Lake City: Andrew Jenson History, 1901–36) 1:785–86.

13. *Live Together in Love: A History of the Ensign Third Ward* (Salt Lake City: Printers, 1981), 2.

14. George S. Tate, "Prayer Circle," in *Encyclopedia of Mormonism*, ed. Daniel H. Ludlow, 4 vols. (New York: Macmillan, 1992), 3:1120–21. See also, Michael D. Quinn, "Latter-day Saint Prayer Circles," *BYU Studies* 19 (1978): 79–105. A more detailed account of the John Taylor Prayer Circle appears in chapters three and four of this volume.

> Although deriving in all instances from temple worship, some prayer circles were formally organized apart from the endowment ceremony. Membership in these special prayer circles, which began in 1851 and continued

until 1929, did not depend upon Church position. Other prayer circles were formed for priesthood groups: stake presidencies and high councils, priesthood quorums, ward bishoprics—all of them formed under the authority of the First Presidency and generally in response to specific requests. On May 3, 1978, the First Presidency announced that all prayer circles outside the temple were to be discontinued. Apart from the endowment ceremony, the only prayer circles still held are part of the weekly meeting of the First Presidency and Quorum of the Twelve and the monthly meeting of all General Authorities in the Salt Lake Temple. (Tate, "Prayer Circle," in *Encyclopedia of Mormonism*)

15. T. Edgar Lyon to Mary C. Lyon, June 22, 1940, Church Archives.
16. Children of David R. and Mary Cairns Lyon:
17. T. Edgar Lyon, "Oral History," 8.

Child	Birth	Death	Age at Death
David Cairns	January 6, 1887	October 18, 1971	84
John McArthur	September 23, 1888	March 20, 1907	18
Paul Cairns	January 4, 1891	May 20, 1974	83
Caroline Holland (Ash)	October 27, 1892	February 28, 1978	85
Joseph Valentine	February 14, 1895	December 18, 1970	75
Alan Ross	February 2, 1898	December 2, 1912	14
Kyle Arden	September 29, 1900	February 16, 1973	72
Thomas Edgar	August 9, 1903	September 20, 1978	75
Phillip	March 29, 1905	December 4, 1905	8 mos
Janette (Halton, Ermish)	February 7, 1908	July 22, 1994	86

18. T. Edgar Lyon, "Oral History," 28–29.
19. T. Edgar Lyon to Mary C. Lyon, April 28, 1934, Church Archives.
20. *1995-96 Church Almanac* (Salt Lake City: Deseret News, 1994), 419.

2

"Teddy Boy," 1903–23

The year of Teddy's birth, 1903, was a year of great prosperity in Utah. The state's population had grown to nearly three hundred thousand. Businessman Ezra Thompson was mayor of Salt Lake City, which numbered approximately seventy thousand residents. The city's "industrial establishments include[d] car shops, breweries, candy factories, a cocoa factory, shoe factories, foundries and machine shops, lime and cement works, saddlery and harness factories, a picture factory, tobacco, cigar and cigarette shops, and lumber mills."[1] Salt Lake historian John S. McCormick notes that in the early 1900s "Mormons made up approximately 50% of the population," that there were ninety-seven liquor or saloon dealers in the city, and that the "streets were not only dirty, they were also dusty in summer and muddy in winter. In 1880, there were no paved streets in the entire city. By 1904, only 4.05 miles had been paved."[2]

The depression following the Panic of 1893 was only a distant memory in 1903 as mining, railroad construction, and banking led Utah's return to prosperity. Mining in Park City, Mercur, and Bingham Canyon brought considerable capital into the city. Coal mining operations in Carbon County sported business headquarters in Salt Lake City. The entire first decade of the twentieth century was filled with optimistic expansion of city services, especially for the prosperous Avenues area, where nine new subdivisions were platted between 1888 and 1902.[3] Various civic groups pushed for improvements in the streetcar system; mandatory smallpox vaccinations; a new hospital; cleaner air; water and sewer service; paved sidewalks; public parks and libraries; and recreational facilities.[4]

David Lyon's printing business was also flourishing, and his house was now too small (illus. 2-1). The home on Seventh Avenue, in which all but his last child was born, was overcrowded. In 1905 the compact home held nine children, two adults, and a maid, all jammed into four rooms. It was time to build a new family dwelling. The family selected a lot just two blocks away, on the corner of Ninth Avenue and E Street. There were only a few scattered homes higher up the hill. Dave, the oldest son and an engineering student at the University of Utah, helped his mother design the family's new home. Mary had him place five large windows on the

Illus. 2-1. House where T. Edgar Lyon was born in 1903.

south wall so she could have a year-round indoor flower garden. She planned for three large fireplace grates in the home—one in the dining room, a second in the parlor, and a third in the master bedroom upstairs. The house would be built of light-yellow brick.[5] David and Mary contracted with several builders, including Bishop George Romney, whose lumber company supplied all the wood for the home. The large two-story, six-bedroom home was completed in October 1906, finally allowing the family ample room for sleeping and entertaining friends. David, Mary, and their children lived in this home until 1937 (illus. 2-2).

Early Years

With seven older siblings, little Teddy lacked no attention during childhood. Early family life for young "Teddy Boy"—an endearing term his sister Janette used all his life—was usually peaceful and happy. The principal task of caregiving fell to Mary, but Annie Russell, a hired girl who lived with the family, also assisted. Teddy's ten-year-old sister Carol often changed his diapers, put him to bed, read to him, sang soothing songs, and assumed the role of substitute mother. She had performed similar duties for Kyle three years earlier, but Kyle had been colicky, and Carol resented her mother for needing help again. Fortunately Teddy was a calm, contented child who slept well, enjoyed good health, and smiled early and often.

One of Teddy's earliest memories was his third birthday. "I had my picture taken," he later recalled (illus. 2-3). "I was bashful and they took off my clothes to get a picture of my bust, like cupid or something. I had long hair down to [my shoulders] and I remember having my head down and them coaxing me to get my head up."[6]

In a letter to his son Dave, dated July 31, 1907, David noted, "We are all well. Edgar always coaxes his pa to 'take a 'ittle walk' with him nearly every night."[7] The short hikes in the hills to the north of the house or

Illus. 2-2. David Ross Lyon with some of his children and neighbors at the new Lyon family home on Ninth Avenue and E Street. Edgar is seated at his father's right.

longer walks up City Creek Canyon were filled with David's inexhaustible explanations about snakes and insects, squirrels and birds. David taught his children to observe closely and engrave small details in their minds, a technique that characterized Teddy's later research and teaching. Teddy's sister Carol remembered:

> He was like the Pied Piper, with many children from the neighborhood following his lead. . . . Papa read and studied a lot, so he could tell us the names of all the wild flowers. He had us examine each very carefully: the sepals, stamen, pistils and leaves, counting each and noticing how the leaves were attached. . . . He identified all the wild birds we saw and had us try to imitate their calls. . . . Rocks always interested him and he told us how different kinds had probably come to be where they were.[8]

The Lyon house was filled with pets—dogs, cats, rabbits, and birds—largely because of Teddy's younger sister Janette's intense love for animals. The family kept a milk cow in a shed behind the house, and Teddy's brother Joe had a light buggy horse named Zeke that shared the small enclosure for a few years.[9]

Formal Education

Because of their own lack of schooling, Mary and David insisted on formal education for all their children. By 1909, when Teddy began first grade, his oldest brother, Dave, had already graduated as a mining engineer from the University of Utah and was working in the boomtown areas of Tintic and Bingham.

Teddy completed first grade in the Lowell School, a few blocks down the hill from his home. For the rest of his elementary education, he went to the newer Ensign School around the corner from home. He attended Bryant Junior High School, which was also within walking distance. After attending public elementary and junior high schools, Teddy enrolled in Latter-day Saint University (LDSU) to attend high school.

Illus. 2-3. Teddy at age three, in long curls and a dress, in photo studio.

Because of family sickness, Teddy missed most of second grade. His sister Carol and brother Paul came down with scarlet fever, so all the children at home were quarantined from December 1910 to June 1911. When Teddy returned to school in fall 1911, he began second grade for the second time. For several years, Teddy was a year behind his age-group. He had gotten his growth early and felt awkward, especially when he "was [placed] in the odd class that was made up usually of people that had failed or been held back."[10] But in seventh grade, a kindly teacher allowed him to take two "specials," a type of bypass exam. By doing well on these tests, he caught up with his own age group by the end of elementary school.

As an adult, Teddy rarely talked about his grade school teachers or experiences. He was more prone to reflect on the religious education he received in his home, at church, and at the Latter-day Saint high school. With the growth of public-supported education in Utah after 1890, many

Church leaders became concerned about the secularization of learning. Milton Bennion, professor of education at the University of Utah, observed that "the Latter-day Saints felt that to bar positive religious instruction from the schools would be tantamount to breeding infidelity in children." So in lieu of spending the hefty amount of money required to operate its own schools, the Church provided religion classes that met "immediately after school one day a week, often in the school building, and were generally conducted by the public school teacher, if he were a Mormon."[11] This forerunner of the Church's seminary program helped infuse the youth with faith. Such was the case with Teddy, who each Monday after school attended religion class in his own Twentieth Ward chapel, just a few steps from the Lowell School, and listened to his school teachers affirm gospel principles. Each Tuesday after school he also attended Primary, which supplemented his early religious preparation inside the home.

A proper education for a young boy meant more than just attending school; he also had to learn to work. David employed his children at his printing business. When he was just eight or nine years old, Teddy began work at the Magazine Printing Company, where he helped print labels for the Salt Lake–based J. G. McDonald Candy Company. To achieve a gold-colored effect, he would take candy bar wrappers printed in brown ink and dip them in bronze powder, rub them dry, and stack them. "I've done that by the hours," Teddy recalled. "We even put a piece of cloth around our nose so we wouldn't breath . . . in [the fumes]. . . . I would work there in the summertime till I thought there were enough bars to feed the world with McDonald's chocolate bars or almond bars."[12] In later years, Teddy observed that "seven of [my father's] sons grew up in that [printing] shop because there was a lot of hand work back in the days before automation."[13] It was in the printing shop, with its tedious, urgent chores, that Teddy learned to work hard, long, and happily. And it was there that he met respected historian and General Authority B. H. Roberts as well as other Church leaders who came to examine contracted work.

Summertime Ranch Hand

The year 1915 saw a major shift in Teddy's life and summer work. Much to the worry of his father, Teddy's older brother Paul had forsaken formal education and regular work in Salt Lake City and moved to Jackson Hole, Wyoming. He fell in love with the wildness of the place. He began working in a sawmill but soon, with considerable financial help from his

father, began buying and homesteading land. By 1915 he claimed
approximately twenty-five hundred
acres as his cattle ranch at the eastern
foot of the majestic Teton range.
Paul called it the Triangle P Ranch.[14]

At the young age of twenty-four,
Paul had become a minor land and
cattle baron, and he needed help
with his huge endeavor. So in June
1915, eleven-year-old Teddy, fourteen-year-old Kyle, and twenty-two-
year-old Carol spent the summer
on the ranch (illus. 2-4). Years later
Lyon reflected on the influence of
this wearisome summer work: "This
was a great experience in my life
because I was getting *pioneer* experience. This was the first chance I had
to do such a thing as drive horses
or [even] ride horses." With a large
piece of railroad iron borrowed from
a neighbor, Paul and Teddy

Illus. 2-4. Ed Lyon at his brother's
cabin near Jackson Hole, Wyoming.

hooked two teams of horses on it and . . . drove it through the sagebrush to break it loose.

Then we would take all the stuff [sagebrush] and throw it out
by hand and stack it in big piles and burn it. Then we would go
through the field with grubbing hoes and have to grub the roots of
the sagebrush out that hadn't been jerked up whole. . . . That was
quite a tedious job. I can remember we worked there for several
weeks and got [only] about two acres cleared. [Then] we had to
plow it and we had to follow along [after] the plow with a grubbing
hoe because even then we'd miss some that broke off.[15]

Besides grubbing sagebrush, Teddy mowed and raked hay with
pioneer-era equipment: "I learned to stack hay, cure hay, turn it over, and
irrigate. I learned to build log houses."[16] With his older brothers, Teddy
went into the Teton hills, selected the straightest trees, cut them, pulled
the timbers down to the flat with oxen, loaded them on the wagon, peeled
and squared the logs, laid them out, and began a new cabin.

In late August, Teddy left the ranch with his two brothers, his sister Carol, and her fiancé in a covered wagon to explore nearby Yellowstone Park. The group spent nearly three weeks visiting the tourist attractions. They entered from the south and proceeded north to the Thumb area, around the loop, and over Mt. Wasburn, finally leaving the park at West Yellowstone. They lived on crayfish, fresh water clams, trout, and flour and beans they had brought from the ranch. Teddy loved these pioneer-type experiences and the natural wonders of the park.

Illus. 2-5. T. Edgar Lyon, his sister, and brother in a covered wagon near Jackson Hole, Wyoming, 1915.

My sister slept in [the] covered wagon at night and the four of us [men and boys] slept on the ground. We simply made a bed . . . with blankets. We had no tent. We had [only] a wagon cover. We'd put one post up in the middle, stake it down on the four corners and get shelter, but it didn't always hold [out the] water. . . .

We walked, my brother and I, a good deal of the way through the park. We could walk faster than the horses and we would walk ahead and come to something and watch geysers work and then they'd catch up with us.[17]

Yellowstone Park had been created as the nation's first national park in 1872, but in 1915 it was still in early development and had few modern amenities (illus. 2-5). While in Yellowstone, Teddy witnessed the first automobile, a Wite, that had ever come into the park. Up to that time, travel had always been by personal covered wagon or by horse-drawn stage-coach. While the Lyons "were plodding along with a team of old crowbaits about three miles an hour," four or six white horses drew the yellow stage-coaches, often at a gallop.[18] At West Yellowstone, the group separated. Paul drove the wagon back to the ranch, while the others caught a train to Salt Lake City. Teddy returned from the romance and danger of "pioneer life" to the necessary but mundane tasks of school and home life.

For each of the next seven summers, from 1916 through 1922, Teddy spent three months in the outdoor wonders of Wyoming. He received a

Illus. 2-6. T. Edgar, with axe, and Paul Lyon splitting timber for fences, 1920.

Illus. 2-7. T. Edgar and David Lyon fishing at Yellowstone National Park, c. 1920.

minuscule salary for his hard work, but the outdoor life gave him the opportunity to fall in love with the land, camping, and mountains. He often drove teams of horses westward over Teton Pass to the trail head in Victor, Idaho, where he picked up barbed wire, a new plow, a fanning mill, harrows, wheat, and other commodities not available in remote Jackson. He smoked moose and elk meat for Paul's winter supply. He built seemingly endless fences to separate pastures and establish property lines (illus. 2-6). He irrigated the potatoes and grain, which would be stored for the long, cold winters. He rode a favorite horse while helping to bring some of the cattle off the mountains for early fall sale. He fished for huge, nearly tame trout in Lake Creek, right on his brother's property, often pulling them out with his hands (illus. 2-7). He built crude rafts of logs and poled around the shores of Phelp's Lake.[19] On one occasion, Teddy mowed a large field of hay, starting at the outside perimeter and mowing the field into ever-smaller squares. As he prgressed, he noticed numerous pheasants flying into the small, unmowed center. He called the team to a halt, took out a pitchfork and speared several pheasants for the evening meal.

Teddy frequently slept outside the cabin, studying the brilliant stars in the transparent sky. In Wyoming, Teddy found a new freedom, an escape from his shyer city self. He easily associated with the other ranch hands, especially with Paul's one-time partner Thaddeus Kaufmann, who had no trouble convincing all that he had not bathed in seventeen years! The Jackson summers helped shape Teddy into a more confident individual, a lover of nature and mountain beauty, and a dedicated, hard worker. Even his older brothers praised his endurance and energy on the ranch.

Despite the bucolic joys of ranching, Paul could not make a good living from the land. Antirancher sentiment had grown in the area, and Paul saw that he would never expand the ranch.[20] When cattle prices became severely depressed following World War I, Paul had to resort to selling insurance during the winters so he could afford ranching in the summers. Because his new wife disliked the Wyoming winters, she and Paul frequently spent October through March or April with his parents in Salt Lake City.

In 1926 the sons of oil tycoon John D. Rockefeller began quietly buying up much of the area around the Tetons (they would later donate most of it to Yellowstone National Park). Finally in 1927, Paul sold his entire spread to the local agent acting for the Rockefellers. Workers burned down most of the cabins on the ranch, but the Rockefellers did not deed all Paul's land to the Teton National Park—they retained a large section of it for their own private estate.[21]

Bishop's Son

While in Salt Lake City during his grade school and junior high school years, Teddy naturally associated mostly with his parents and closest siblings.

Sibling relationships were generally good, but Teddy's closest family friend was his younger sister Janette. Although separated by four-and-a-half years, the pair established a close bond that lasted Teddy's entire life.[22]

Shortly after his father was called to serve as bishop of the Ensign Ward, Teddy received the nickname "Bish," a term that stuck with him until his mission. Why Teddy and not one of his older brothers got this label is unclear. Perhaps it was because he frequently joined his father on Church and other charitable visits. Young Teddy knew just how much time and energy his father and mother devoted to community and Church service because he was often in their company as they served:

"I remember a time or two walking to work [with my father] . . . and President Smith just happened to be coming out of the Beehive House . . . and he would say, 'Hello, David,' and Father would say, 'Hello, Joseph.' I was shocked. He was *President* Joseph F. Smith and Father called him Joseph!"[23] David had selected one of President Smith's sons, Willard R., as his counselor in the bishopric; consequently the Church President often visited and spoke to the ward. He spoke at the ground breaking, the cornerstone laying, and the dedication of the new Ensign meetinghouse.[24]

At age sixteen, Teddy had a direct encounter with President Grant and his family:

> The first ward teaching district to which I was assigned after having been ordained a Priest, included the home of President Heber J. Grant. My senior companion was a recent[ly returned] missionary who lived at President Grant's home while attending the University of Utah. The first evening that we started to do our teaching, I met my companion by appointment and we made our first call. I sat quietly while my partner delivered the scheduled message and I marveled at his ability to explain the Gospel.

> Our second house was that of our church President. While waiting on the front porch to be admitted, my companion said, "I live here. I can't teach the message here, so you'll have to take over." This remark so astonished me that as the door was opened by Sister Grant and we were invited to come in, I was speechless. President Grant had just come from a long day at the office and was in the kitchen eating a late dinner. Upon being informed of our presence, he summoned the other members of the household and came into the living room. Then he said, "Here we are. What is your message for us? We need to be taught the same as any members of the Church."

> While the family had been assembling I had experienced fear and embarrassment and sensed my own inability to teach the President of the Church any thing pertaining to the Gospel. However, the example he set in being willing to hear us, and the humble spirit in which he encouraged us soon dispelled my fear and embarrassment. When I tried to speak the words came easily and I was soon interested in the presentation of the teacher's message.

> At the conclusion of a short discussion that followed the delivery of the message, we were invited to kneel in prayer with the family. We were then thanked for our visit and departed for the next house.

> I've never forgotten the humility and kindness of President Grant in listening to a young, inexperienced Priest who came to his house as a Ward Teacher. I've never experienced a finer example of hospitality to Ward Teachers.[25]

"Old Nauvooers"

As a youth, Teddy not only made acquaintance with the living prophets of the Church but also came to appreciate Joseph Smith through the testimonies and stories of those who had associated with the Prophet during his lifetime. In the Twentieth Ward, Teddy remembered "twenty or twenty-five people who seemed very old to me . . . women in black dresses trimmed with white collars and cuffs. They wore small black bonnets tied under their chins with black silk ribbons. The men were dressed in black suits and ties, and practically all had full beards and gray or white hair."[26] These people were known as the "Old Nauvooers." Teddy's own grandmother Carolyn Holland Lyon was among them. They had all lived in Nauvoo as children or youth and carried pioneer zeal to every testimony meeting. Teddy felt their power as they testified, and in his youthful naiveté informed his mother

> it seemed if one had not known Joseph Smith personally and lived in Nauvoo, one did not have a [real] testimony. . . . Her reply was that there appeared to be an unwritten law in the Twentieth Ward that if you had not lived in Nauvoo and known Joseph Smith, you could not bear your testimony until all the Old Nauvooers had first borne theirs.[27]

Since there were so many "Old Nauvooers," very few other people ever got the chance to bear their testimonies. When they did, however, Teddy felt as though the other testimonies were somewhat less dynamic and convincing than those of the Old Nauvooers.

Growing up around those who had personally known the Prophet, Teddy sensed the dramatic impact that Joseph had on them. Joseph Smith was a living heritage for them, not a dead and distant prophet. Teddy began to realize that he too should know Joseph intimately.

> Young as I was, I was impressed by the love and respect these people had for Joseph Smith, based on an intimate relationship with him and a closeness to him. Although these people had known Brigham Young, John Taylor, Wilford Woodruff, Lorenzo Snow, and Joseph F. Smith, who was then president, these leaders were referred to as "president of the Church," while the Old Nauvooers referred to Joseph Smith with two more endearing names: "The Prophet," or "Brother Joseph." What impressed my young mind about Joseph Smith from their talks was his concern for people and their problems, and the personal contacts they had experienced with him.[28]

In his adult years, Teddy frequently recounted the incidents he had heard told in his youth by the Old Nauvooers, whose own youth had been profoundly enhanced by the human tenderness of Brother Joseph. Their testimonies inspired Teddy to study history, gain a conviction of Joseph's divine manifestations, and later bring Joseph to life for thousands of his institute students. Teddy retold some of these stories, especially those involving Joseph and children, in his 1978 article "Recollections of 'Old Nauvooers': Memories from Oral History."

> Such were the components of my first meaningful introduction to Joseph Smith—a very human being, engaged in doing the kinds of things which would appeal to children, young people, and those of mature years and thinking. I'm certain these Old Nauvooers bore testimonies to the divinity of Joseph Smith's work as a spiritual leader. Although I was not old enough at that time to understand the meaning of abstract faith and principles of the gospel, I did learn to love and admire him, as many of those testimony-bearing Saints of my childhood years had done, as a very much alive and alert and loveable and human person.[29]

Student at LDSU

In 1915, President Joseph F. Smith warned against secularism and reaffirmed the Church's commitment to spiritually based education: "Religion is excluded from it . . . we have to establish Church schools or institutions of education of our own, . . . that our children may have the advantages of moral training in their youth."[30]

In September 1917, at age fourteen, Edgar—no longer going by "Teddy" in public—began high school (ninth grade) at LDSU. The buildings of this Church-sponsored combination high school and university stood right in the heart of the city, in the area now occupied by the Church Office Building. The school had been founded in 1886 as the Salt Lake Stake Academy and moved through the years to various locations in Salt Lake City. The "university" consisted of a high school, a business school, and a fledgling music education program (illus. 2-8).

In 1917, under progressive President Guy C. Wilson, the school abandoned a restrictive admissions policy and "enrollment shot up to nearly two thousand, including night school and the missionary class."[31] The year Edgar began the tenth grade (1918), work began on the new Joseph F. Smith Memorial Science Building. Elder James E. Talmage, of the Quorum of the Twelve, traveled to Europe and purchased a thousand

Illus. 2-8. Latter-day Saint University campus, 1920s.

dollars' worth of the most up-to-date scientific equipment for the labora-
tories. The university's Deseret Scientific Museum housed specimens
and exhibits that had previously appeared in smaller Church museums.[32]

The Church-sponsored high school competed with East, West, and
Granite High Schools in Salt Lake. It drew most of its students from the
valley, although a few came from Morgan, Payson, Mendon, or Aurora,
Utah, and boarded with friends or relatives to attend the spiritually oriented
high school. Although LDSU enrolled only approximately 5 percent of
the high school students in the state of Utah in 1919,[33] that dynamic 5 percent
included many future state and Church leaders. The Church kept tuition
fees at a minimum by subsidizing the school.

As fourteen-year-old Edgar entered the imposing red-brick buildings
of the combination high school and university, he walked among some of
the city's elite, including children of the Cannons, Smiths, Youngs,
Woodruffs, Romneys, Talmages, and Kimballs as well as children of the
emerging social and business elite of the valley. High school was not an
easy transition for Edgar, but the stimulating teachers personalized and
spiritualized the instruction and quickly fostered enthusiasm for learning.
Many teachers already "know a lot of us and know our parents and our
parents know them. . . . When I went to school some would say, 'Oh yes,
I knew your father, I know your mother. I used to dance with your mother
before your father married her,' and so on."[34]

Well-known Church musician Alexander Schreiner was the organist
for Edgar's required choir class; B. Cecil Gates was the conductor. The
school's president, or headmaster, was Guy C. Wilson, son-in-law of
Anthony W. Ivins, counselor in the First Presidency. Wilson had written
exciting, innovative manuals for the Mutual Improvement Association
(MIA) and lent an open spirit to the school. I. O. Horsfall sparked Edgar's
interest in math. Edgar also remembered learning math from "Emily Grant,
President Grant's daughter, who later married Truman Madsen's father."[35]
Gerrit de Jong taught Edgar Spanish for two years. And the always popular James (Jimmy) E. Moss excited the students with the need for physical education in his classes at the nearby Deseret Gym.

Four days a week, approximately nine hundred high school students
met in devotionals with the headmaster, who quickly dispensed with the
announcements and then taught religion—Old Testament, New Testament, Book of Mormon, and Church history. Often, Church President
Heber J. Grant spoke and charmed the students with his wit and personal
stories of dogged perseverance. Other General Authorities also spoke in
these near-daily devotionals. One of Edgar's classmates, Fielding Kimball

Smith, son of Joseph Fielding Smith, often exercised his drawing talents during these assemblies and irreverently caricatured each religious speaker in "ludicrous situations—in crap games, in bars having a beer. . . . Not all seriousness but there was a lot of fun."[36]

When asked if he was a good student, Edgar replied, "Oh, normally. I never failed any classes."[37] But he also told of his difficulties studying foreign languages, possibly, he believed, because he skipped grades in elementary school and did not get a proper base in English grammar. His grades did not distinguish him as an unusually bright student, nor did Edgar find a singular academic interest in high school. Although he began to enjoy the study of history, he never considered it as a profession at that time.

Edgar was relatively shy during his years at LDSU. Only in his senior year (1921) does the yearbook note that Edgar was a member of Ciceronia, the debating society, but he is not pictured among the other twenty-nine students in the club; he was likely on the apprentice or practice team. In later years, Edgar told his family that he had played football in high school, but his yearbook does not list him as a member of the varsity squad, and he did not receive a letter in any sport. Because he was large for his age, he played guard, but likely on the second- or third-string team. During Edgar's junior year, Church officials had reinstated football at LDSU as well as Brigham Young University and Ricks College. Edgar and others on the team made their high school field by tearing down an old wall on Brigham Young's former estate. They hauled topsoil from Ensign Flat and then smoothed and planted grass on their freshly groomed field. During this first year of football, the team truly struggled, losing to East High School 148 to 0. Edgar later confessed, "I just warmed up the bench that year but did get in one game. . . . I'm not fast enough on some things . . . I was never quick enough on focusing my eyes to watch something moving."[38]

In Edgar's senior yearbook, each of the 220 graduating seniors is characterized by a motto, maxim, or phrase. Many of these are quotes from Shakespeare or the Bible. Others are original rhymes or ditties. Whether these quotes were selected by the individual or by the yearbook staff is unclear. Alongside Lyon's photo appears the terse caption, "A sense of humor is valuable." It is impossible to know whether Edgar made this suggestion to himself or whether it was advice to the shy, serious senior from peers. Edgar was definitely not the school clown of LDSU.

The Odean dance hall stood across the street from the school. Every Friday afternoon, LDSU dismissed classes early and held a huge dance.

Edgar reasoned, "I was never a dancer so I seldom went."[39] Nor did he attend the junior proms or the "sophomore step." Once again, his insecurity with music and dancing kept him from mixing in the social activities of the majority. Edgar did not date much in the sense of one boy courting one girl. He did engage, however, in group activities with his high school friends, which included many young women. Among the group was sophisticated Peg Partridge, who took a shine to tall, dark-haired Edgar. Their friendship continued into the first few months of his mission.

Fortunately, Edgar forged close friendships during high school with two ward members: James (Jim) Armstrong and Jesse Robinson (Bob) Smith. Jim Armstrong was a big lad. He lettered in football and track and actively participated in the debate society, encouraging his quieter friend into these same activities. Jim's father owned a large fruit and vegetable farm at the mouth of Big Cottonwood Canyon. Edgar and Jim helped harvest potatoes, onions, apples, and peaches. "We used to take the old streetcar downtown and get on the Holladay street car . . . and then walk five miles up to work."[40] The two boys built a bond that continued through college and beyond. Edgar's friend Bob Smith was a year younger and more academically oriented than the other two boys. The three young men all served missions in Europe and nurtured lifelong friendships.

On May 25, 1921, Edgar graduated from LDSU at age seventeen. The commencement ceremony was held in the Assembly Hall on Temple Square. Apostle Richard R. Lyman addressed the graduates, and the Church's First Presidency presented diplomas to the seniors. Graduation from high school was not required by law, and few young people attained it. Only 16.6 percent of Utah eighteen-year-olds in that year graduated, compared to 12.7 percent nationally.[41] Immediately after the ceremony, Edgar and his friend Jim left for Paul's ranch near Jackson for another summer of frontier life and teenage friendship. Like most high school graduates, they undoubtedly experienced some feelings of nostalgia as an important era in their lives came to an end.

Career Search

Upon returning to Salt Lake City in the fall, Edgar entered the University of Utah (illus. 2-9). The "U" enrolled approximately twenty-two hundred students that year, just slightly more than Edgar's high school. During the 1920s, Utah led the country in the percentage of eligible eighteen- and nineteen-year-olds entering college.[42] Edgar paid $39.50 in tuition and fees. His older brother Dave and his sister Carol had already

preceded him at the U. His
brother Kyle had quit high school
in 1917 to work full-time on Paul's
ranch in Wyoming, but when Kyle
realized that his younger brother
would attend college, he decided
to matriculate as an over-age freshman with only one semester of
high school credit. Edgar remembered that when he and Kyle
"stood in line to register that first
day, the dean of the college looked
at his almost blank high school
record, looked at the dates, and
asked, 'What kept you out of
school?' Kyle, who was never a
person of many words, replied
simply, 'Ignorance.'"[43]

Illus. 2-9. T. Edgar Lyon in 1922.
Photograph by Armstrong Photo,
Salt Lake City.

One of Edgar's high school
teachers had encouraged him to
study political science and become an international lawyer. Another
thought he ought to become a scientist, specializing in botany. His
mother suggested he study medicine, "but I didn't get too excited about
that."[44] In short, Edgar was struggling with the same dilemma that faces
most freshmen: "Now that I'm here, what do I become?"

For two years, Edgar took general education courses as he struggled
to find a niche. His grades were not outstanding, but they were adequate
for continuance from one quarter to the next. Edgar struggled in physical
education classes and avoided mathematics classes during his first college
years. He received a C in public speaking, likely due to his nonassertive,
quiet demeanor. A two-credit general history class also resulted in a C
during his first year, as did courses in physics, English, and philosophy
in his second year. These mediocre grades left him still pondering, after
two years, what his academic forte might be.

During his freshman year, he met and took classes from forty-seven-
year-old Levi Edgar Young, professor of western American history and
one of the seven Presidents of the Seventies. Young had received academic
training at Harvard and Columbia Universities and was popular with the
students. As a freshman, Edgar took three classes from Young, beginning an

association that lasted until Young's death in 1963. But Young, the professor, was an enigma.

> Nobody could figure it out but he was the most powerful figure on that campus except the president. He was the only professor that had an office in the Park Building. The deans were there but he had his office and he was head of the Western History Department, which consisted of Levi Edgar Young and nobody else. . . .
>
> Now I was intrigued by the spirit of the man, but his information was not always the most reliable. He sort of took a liking to me. He used to have me do chores for him such as haul examination papers into his office. . . . He didn't like to carry things because he wasn't too strong and so when term papers were due he would have a big stack of them and would give them to me and I would carry them over in his office. "Put them down in the corner, Brother Lyon." (He'd always call me Brother Lyon.)
>
> He encouraged me to go into history but I wasn't too excited about it. I'd say, "Well, why? What could you do with it?"[45]

Edgar recognized that he "was just sort of flopping around here and there."[46] He found nothing that sparked his academic fire. Because of Professor Andrew Kerr's excitement for the discipline, archaeology had been "one of [Edgar's] early loves. [He] would get interested in American and Egyptian archeology and for a while toyed with that idea but dropped it."[47] Edgar knew that school was the right place to be, but he lacked a direction in his studies.[48]

Mission Call

While college attendance had become a family tradition by the time Edgar was of age, missionary work had not. Only his oldest brother, Dave, had filled a mission, from 1909 to 1912 in the Netherlands. Three other brothers and a sister had not chosen to serve, but this was not uncommon. Only about 8 percent of available young Latter-day Saint men in 1923 were in the mission field.[49] On November 8, 1922, at age nineteen, Edgar received his personal patriarchal blessing under the hands of Vernee L. Halliday, stake patriarch. In the blessing he was told that "your desire to preach the gospel to your fellowmen will be granted to you in time."[50] Edgar had talked about the possibility of serving a mission but had not yet made any specific plans. His training, teachers, and peers at LDSU School had reinforced his parents' desire that he serve.

Edgar's father, who was also his bishop, had been priming his youngest son for missionary work for years. The generally accepted age for young men to serve was twenty, although some were called at a younger age, and many served in their mid- and upper-twenties. Edgar did not go through any formal application process of filling out mission papers or interviewing with his bishop. Bishop Lyon simply certified his son's worthiness and willingness to serve a mission to President Heber J. Grant and Harold G. Reynolds, the mission secretary, both members of the Ensign Ward.

A letter from Church headquarters arrived at the Lyon home on E Street on May 19, 1923 (illus. 2-10). Edgar's mother, Mary, already knew what was in it. The day before, her husband had called from work to report a conversation he had just had with Harold Reynolds. Edgar had been selected to serve in the Netherlands Mission. Mary was not happy with the choice of country: she harbored a deep desire for one of her sons to serve in her native Scotland, and her youngest son, Edgar, was her last hope. Mary hid the letter for three days while she cajoled her husband to use his influence with the many General Authorities he knew and have the call changed. Edgar recalled,

> I came home in the afternoon [of May 23, 1923]. Mother handed me a letter from 47 East South Temple. It hadn't been opened, but she handed it to me and said, "I know what's inside it." I opened it and read it and it was a letter from President Grant calling me to serve a mission in the Netherlands Mission and if I were willing to accept the call, to reply to him or the missionary department . . .
>
> Mother said, "You're not going, are you?" I said, "Well, why not?" She said, "I don't want you to go. You're the last of my sons to be going on a mission and your older brother went to Holland and that's enough. Nobody in our family has been on a mission to Scotland and England where my folks and your grandparents came from, your father's mother, and it's time one of you went over there. One of you ought to go and you're the last son to be going." I said, "Now Mother, you've taught me all my life I was supposed to obey the authorities and the first time I get a chance you tell me not to do it." She said, "I'm sure that Daddy can have it changed. I think he should just talk to the mission secretary and they can do it." I said, "Well, I don't think you ought to do it."
>
> So I wrote back and said I was going. I did want to go, but I was full of fear and trembling because I had had a year of Latin in junior high and two years of Spanish in high school and I was no good at it. Languages just floored me. But I figured, "Well, I'll go and I'll try and do something anyway."[51]

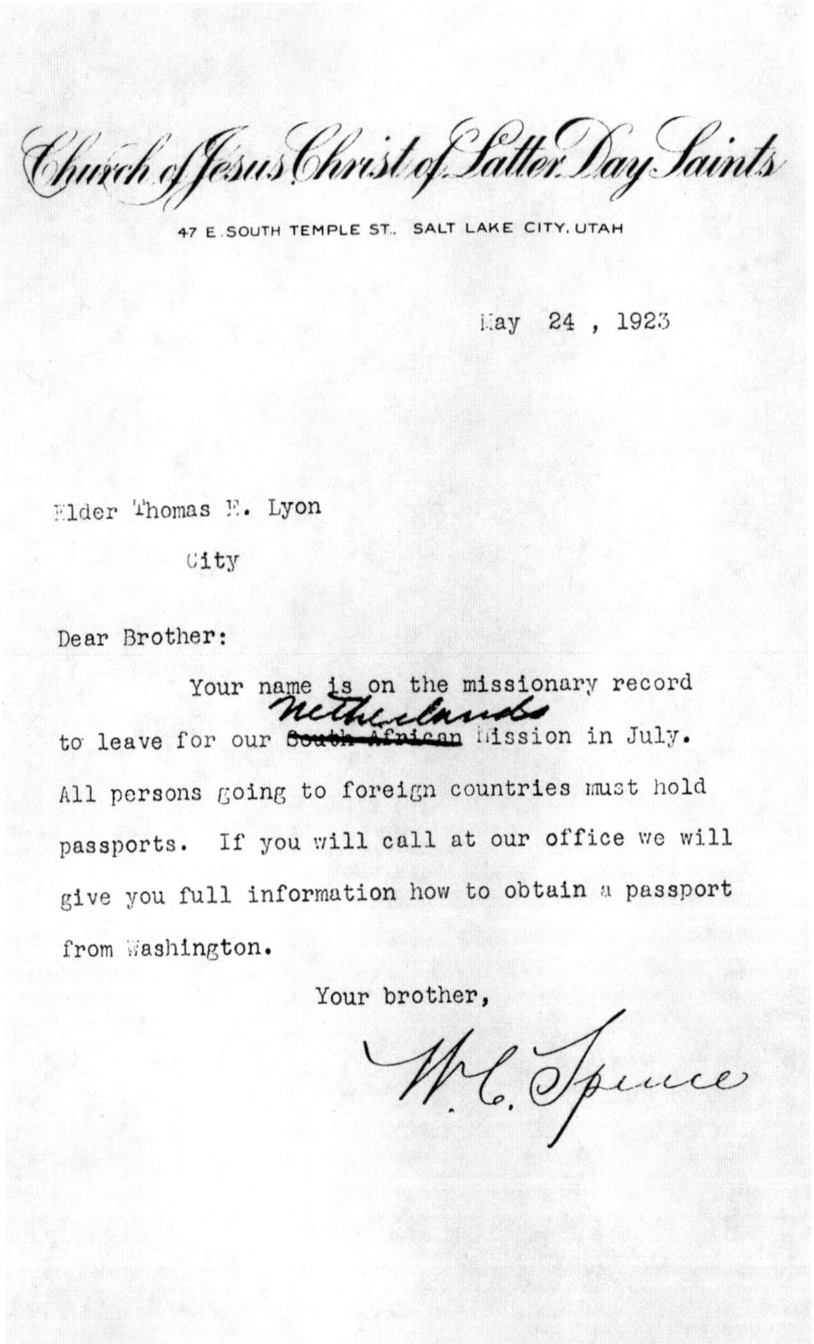

Church of Jesus Christ of Latter Day Saints

47 E. SOUTH TEMPLE ST., SALT LAKE CITY, UTAH

May 24 , 1923

Elder Thomas E. Lyon

City

Dear Brother:

Your name is on the missionary record to leave for our ~~South African~~ Netherlands Mission in July. All persons going to foreign countries must hold passports. If you will call at our office we will give you full information how to obtain a passport from Washington.

Your brother,

W. C. Spence

Illus. 2-10. A second letter relating to Lyon's mission call showing his mission assignment.

Though Edgar was prepared to go to the Netherlands, some musing persisted regarding the place of his service. A May 24th letter from the Church Office Building instructed Edgar that "your name is on the missionary record to leave for our ~~South African~~ Netherlands Mission in July."[52] The word "Netherlands" was handwritten above the typed and crossed-out "South African." A third letter, dated May 28, instructed Edgar to report to Church headquarters on July 13.

Preparations began immediately. On May 27, 1923, Bishop Lyon ordained his son an elder. A "farewell" was arranged in the ward. Because Sunday sacrament meetings were reserved for serious preaching by older, more experienced adults, missionary farewells were held during the week, usually on a Friday night, with a party or dance afterward. Edgar's farewell took place on Tuesday, July 10, just three days before he was to report to 47 East South Temple. The first entry in Edgar's missionary diary, on July 10, notes, "My farewell. The largest in the [Ensign] ward. $205.00 [collected]. E. Wilson read 'If.'"[53] Following a long-established Church custom, those attending the farewell contributed money directly to the missionary to aid with his expenses. The $205, given by generous friends, would pay his transportation to the Netherlands and help support him for the first few months.

The printed program from the farewell illustrates its entertaining nature. There was music, a poetry recitation, and a demonstration of magic, billiards, and mind reading. President Heber J. Grant was among the hundreds of ward members, high school and college mates, and family friends who attended the gala gathering. But another attendee may have been even more important: the third number on the program featured a dramatic prose recitation by an attractive, artistic seventeen-year-old ward member named Hermana Forsberg.

At age nineteen, almost twenty, Edgar was a handsome young man. His five-foot-eleven-inch frame and dark curly hair attracted attention. He considered himself shy and insecure, but he had acquired sufficient experience to give him more assurance than he would admit. From Wyoming summers, he had gained confidence in his ability to work hard, to deal with people of differing social and economic status, and to love the world of nature. He had picked up practical knowledge of frontier life, of tools, and of homesteading. With his father, he had learned bookkeeping and financial management. In school, he had been serious and studious. And although his first two years of college had lacked focus, Edgar had taken a wide variety of classes, which had stimulated his intellect and introduced many avenues for future study.

With his father and mother, he had enjoyed regular service. Further, he had experienced a relatively small, personal church, where he was known by name. He knew most of the Church leaders through his parents, and the Church leaders' children through his schooling. His direct experience with two prophets had taught him that in human relations, feelings and friendships are more important than rigid rules. He had lived in an intimate, somewhat informal church, and Joseph Smith was almost as real to him as Heber J. Grant. Now he was going to devote at least two and a half years of his life to sharing the gospel with others.

Notes

1. Albert L. Fisher, *Geography of Utah* (Salt Lake City: University of Utah, 1987), 32, 33.

2. John S. McCormick, *Salt Lake City: The Gathering Place* (Woodland Hills, Calif.: Windsor Publications, 1980), 47.

3. Thomas G. Alexander, *Mormons and Gentiles: A History of Salt Lake City* (Boulder, Colo.: Pruett Publishing, 1984), 152.

4. Alexander, *Mormons and Gentiles*, 125–61. See especially chapter 5.

5. T. Edgar Lyon, "Personal Recollections: The Family of David Ross Lyon," July 1976, in author's possession.

6. T. Edgar Lyon, "Oral History," bound typescript, 8, Church Archives, Family and Church History Department, The Church of Jesus Christ of Latter-day Saints, Salt Lake City (hereafter cited as Church Archives).

7. David R. Lyon to David C. Lyon, July 31, 1907, T. Edgar Lyon Collection, Church Archives.

8. Carol Lyon Ash, "Life Story of David Ross Lyon," in author's possession.

9. T. Edgar Lyon, "Oral History," 12–32.

10. T. Edgar Lyon, "Oral History," 12.

11. Milton Lynn Bennion, *Mormonism and Education* (Salt Lake City: Department of Education of The Church of Jesus Christ of Latter-day Saints, 1939), 132, 135.

12. T. Edgar Lyon, "Oral History," 11, 12.

13. T. Edgar Lyon, "Church Historians I Have Known," *Dialogue: A Journal of Mormon Thought* 11, no. 4 (1978): 14–22.

14. T. Edgar Lyon, "Oral History," 18–20.

15. T. Edgar Lyon, "Oral History," 19.

16. T. Edgar Lyon, "Oral History," 20.

17. T. Edgar Lyon, "Oral History," 20, 21.

18. T. Edgar Lyon, "Oral History," 20.

19. T. Edgar Lyon, "Oral History," 18–20.

20. See Margaret Sanborn, *The Grand Tetons: The Story of the Men Who Tamed the Western Wilderness* (New York: G. P. Putnam and Sons, 1978), 254–59.

21. T. Edgar Lyon, "Oral History," 19.
22. Teddy wrote to her regularly over a period of fifty-five years. She saved many of these letters (at least 280), which show a devoted older brother sharing his feelings and time with his sister, even when separated by thousands of miles.
23. T. Edgar Lyon, "Oral History," 34; italics added.
24. *Live Together in Love: A History of the Ensign Third Ward* (Salt Lake City: Printers, 1981), 2–14.
25. T. Edgar Lyon, "Ward Teaching at the Home of the President," in author's possession.
26. T. Edgar Lyon, "Recollections of 'Old Nauvooers': Memories from Oral History," *BYU Studies* 18, no. 2 (1978): 143.
27. T. Edgar Lyon, "Recollections of 'Old Nauvooers,'" 144.
28. T. Edgar Lyon, "Recollections of 'Old Nauvooers,'" 144.
29. T. Edgar Lyon, "Recollections of 'Old Nauvooers,'" 150.
30. Joseph F. Smith, "General View of Church Conditions," *Improvement Era* 19 (November 1915): 73, cited in James B. Allen and Richard O. Cowan, *Mormonism in the Twentieth Century* (Provo, Utah: Brigham Young University, 1964), 102.
31. John Henry Evans, "The History of L.D.S.U.," in *Gold and Blue Yearbook* (Salt Lake City: n.p., 1919), 24–28.
32. Thomas Howells, "Our New Building," in *Gold and Blue Yearbook*.
33. Bennion, *Mormonism and Education*, 281.
34. T. Edgar Lyon, "Oral History," 13.
35. T. Edgar Lyon, "Oral History," 16. For more information on Alexander Schreiner, see Daniel Frederick Burghout, "Alexander Schreiner: Mormon Tabernacle Organist" (Ph.D. diss., University of Kansas, 1999), reprinted as *Alexander Schreiner: Mormon Tabernacle Organist*, Dissertations in Latter-day Saint History series (Provo: Joseph Fielding Smith Institute for Latter-day Saint History and BYU Studies), 2001.
36. T. Edgar Lyon, "Oral History," 18.
37. T. Edgar Lyon, "Oral History," 15.
38. T. Edgar Lyon, "Oral History," 14.
39. T. Edgar Lyon, "Oral History," 17.
40. T. Edgar Lyon, "Oral History," 28.
41. *Biennial Survey of Education, 1918–1920*, Bulletin no. 29 (Washington, D.C.: Government Printing Office, 1923), 40.
42. *Survey of Education in Utah*, Bulletin no. 18 (Washington, D.C: Government Printing Office, 1926), 233.
43. T. Edgar Lyon, "Personal Recollections."
44. T. Edgar Lyon, "Oral History," 35.
45. T. Edgar Lyon, "Oral History," 35.
46. T. Edgar Lyon, "Oral History," 36.
47. T. Edgar Lyon, "Oral History," 38.
48. A year or two later, while contemplating these early college years from the perspective of the mission field, Edgar disclosed to his parents that "I did not study as hard as I should have done. . . . I promise I shall make more of my schooling than

I have done in the past." T. Edgar Lyon to David R. Lyon, December 7, 1923, Church Archives. In another letter, written to his mother on May 10, 1924, he avowed that he was stubborn and had "squandered [his] youth" (Church Archives). In a birthday letter to his father, Edgar acknowledged the "wasted time of my youth. At times I feel like kicking myself because of the time I have wasted at your expense—four years of high school which I squandered, as well as about a year of my time at the university." T. Edgar Lyon to parents, August 9, 1924, Church Archives. These confessions of wasted time likely sprung from the zeal for wise stewardship of time and energy generated by Edgar's missionary activities; his grades indicate that he was at least working better than the average student.

49. Richard O. Cowan, *The Church in the Twentieth Century* (Salt Lake City: Bookcraft, 1985), 277.

50. Patriarchal Blessing of T. Edgar Lyon, in author's possession.

51. T. Edgar Lyon, "Oral History," 42–43.

52. LDS Missionary Committee to T. Edgar Lyon, May 24, 1923, in author's possession.

53. T. Edgar Lyon, Diary, July 10, 1923, Church Archives.

3

Mission to the Netherlands, 1923–26

Before he left for Europe, Lyon wanted to experience the "hills of home" one more time. Hiking in the mountains and sleeping outdoors had become a vital part of his life. The ward planned a fathers and sons' outing for Wednesday, July 11, 1923. David, as bishop and father, took nearly two full days away from the Magazine Printing Company and accompanied the boys and their fathers to City Creek Canyon (illus. 3-1). Upon returning home Thursday evening, Edgar continued preparations for his mission at a frantic pace. He was to go through the Salt Lake Temple the next morning, but his endowment ceremony would prove rather unusual.

Until that time, all Latter-day Saints who had participated in the endowment ceremony wore garments that extended to the wrists and ankles. No Church outlet or store sold a ready-made garment. Each individual bought the proper size of "long-handled" underwear and took it with him or her to the temple. There, as part of the ceremony, the authorized officiator altered the clothing. Things began to change, however, when comrades of endowed servicemen in World War I misunderstood the "old-fashioned underwear" that seemed out of uniform and especially inappropriate during the muggy European summers. Later, fashion exerted an even greater pressure on the Church when the loose, open styles of women's clothing in the 1920s further separated devout Mormons from mainstream America. George F. Richards of the First Presidency recorded considerable discussion and reflection in Church councils over the styling of the garment. Which features had been divinely inspired and which had simply evolved over the years? Finally, a First Presidency letter dated June 14, 1923, announced a new option to endowed Latter-day Saints: outside the temple they would now be authorized to wear a shorter-sleeved, one-piece garment.[1]

Because of his privileged position in the John Taylor Prayer Circle,[2] David Lyon learned of this policy change the night before Edgar was to receive his endowment, but this new information moved more slowly to other Church members. Mary Lyon bought two pairs of one-piece long

Illus. 3-1. Father and sons' outing in 1923, just before T. Edgar Lyon left for his mission. Ed is standing, brother Kyle is seated on the far left, David Lyon is kneeling, in rear.

underwear at ZCMI the morning of the ceremony and cut off the long sleeves and legs. Early Friday morning, July 13, 1923, in company with his parents, Edgar entered the temple. After the lengthy endowment session, Edgar took his new-fangled garments and presented himself before the temple officiator, who viewed him as an impudent new missionary in short-sleeved underwear. The officiator thought that all devoted missionaries should wear the old, authorized style. Edgar pleaded for understanding and finally got his experienced father to come and explain the new policy and authorized design. Official written instructions had simply not gotten to all temple workers; General Authorities were planning to announce the policy when they visited quarterly conferences.[3]

Despite David's insistence, the temple worker still refused to accept Edgar's shortened garments. Finally, the senior Lyon put on his street clothes, went to the temple office, and brought President Richards to the dressing room. Richards sternly reminded the worker: "You know this morning when we met . . . I told you that there had been a change made yesterday. . . . The decision has been made and it's all right. Let's hear no more about it."⁴ Even after this rebuke, the officiator remained upset. With a large pair of scissors, hand still shaking after having been proved wrong, he took measure of the appropriate spot and snipped decisively, cutting through the material and carelessly into Edgar's skin. Another temple worker quickly acquired a bandage, and the ceremony proceeded normally. "As far as I know, I am the first person . . . that ever wore the modified garment," Lyon observed.⁵

Departure with a Blessing

Immediately after the temple ceremony, Edgar reported to Church headquarters, where thirteen new missionaries—the total outgoing force for the month—nervously greeted each other. Within just a few hours, the young representatives of their church would board trains for the East Coast. Each missionary had already secured a passport and visa, since all were going to European missions. At this time, the Church provided no formalized language training or intense spiritual schooling. Those going to foreign-speaking missions would have to learn the new language on their own. The Church expected the missionary to have been instructed in spiritual matters by his family and home ward. No Church authorities conducted worthiness interviews. Several years later, as Edgar reflected on his call to serve in the Netherlands, he confided that

> I was very disappointed and frightened. I had desired to go to England and work among the people from whom I was descended. Furthermore, I feared to go to the Netherlands, because of the language I should have to learn . . . my efforts in school to learn foreign languages having convinced both me and my teachers that languages was not my forte.⁶

Edgar's fears were addressed later that day. As he recalled, "[Elder] Melvin J. Ballard had been designated to set us apart. . . . Now I didn't know Brother Ballard and I don't think Father knew him [either]."⁷ After the formal setting apart, Elder Ballard blessed Edgar to

> have no fear concerning the call that has come to you; you have been called to the land where the Lord has need of you. Have no fear concerning the language . . . for the Lord will bless you with both the gift of interpretation of the language and the gift of speaking it.⁸

Elder Ballard (illus. 3-2) gave no similar promises to any of the other twelve missionaries, and Edgar was assuredly calmed by this apostolic blessing. Elder Ballard also promised the gift of healing to the eager elder.

After all were set apart, the secretary of the mission committee, Harold Reynolds, put Edgar, now Elder Lyon, in charge of the elders who would be departing the next morning.[9]

Elders Nibley, Mollinet, and Lyon left Salt Lake City together at 8:30 A.M. on July 14. At the station, Lyon exchanged goodbyes with family members and with friends Jim Armstrong and Bob Smith. In Ogden the three elders met Elders Skeen, Parkinson, and Perkins and continued on. The group stopped in Chicago to spend the night and do some sight-seeing in the morning. The following day found them in Buffalo, New York, where they visited Niagara Falls. Lyon had never previously been east of western Wyoming; in Niagara, he was shocked. "I have never seen so many impudent taxi drivers, railway men, etc. in my life."[10] The group next moved on to Toronto and finally to Montreal. There, Lyon booked passage on the ship *Montclare*. In Montreal the group of elders met the seven other new missionaries who had taken a slightly different route. Among the newcomers was Elder Franklin J. Murdock, also called to serve in the Netherlands. Lyon was now in charge of all thirteen missionaries. This leadership calling belies his self-image of a quiet youth who lacked confidence.

The *Montclare* left Montreal on July 20, taking eight days to cover the three thousand miles to Liverpool. With much free time on board the luxurious, slow-moving ship, Lyon had the opportunity to ponder, wander, and write. He penned a detailed letter to his parents in which he seemed to count everything. The ship was 640 feet long; thirteen and then seventy icebergs slowed the ship's progress; the ship was nine months old; there were "seven priests, two nuns and four Methodist missionaries aboard."[11]

Elder Lyon also wrote home that "on Saturday night three of the Elders went into the bar and got a few drinks. I caught them at it, and called a meeting in our room, where I gave a lecture to them." Up to this point in his life, Lyon would never have characterized himself as a take-charge person, but when this human and public relations

Courtesy Church Archives

Illus. 3-2. Melvin J. Ballard set Edgar apart for his mission.

conflict loomed, he called a meeting in which he forcefully extracted promises of conformity. The Word of Wisdom was not yet entrenched as a distinguishing standard for all Latter-day Saints, but it was a requirement for all missionaries. After the meeting, Lyon noted, "they all agreed to stay away from the bar and smoking room, and not to dance."[12] In the two weeks since leaving Salt Lake City, Lyon had already grown in confidence and leadership.

On July 28, the eighth day on board, Lyon saw the Scottish coast and wished that "mother were here to see the land of her birth."[13] A few hours later, the ship arrived in Liverpool, but the port authority had already closed for the night. They would have to wait until morning to disembark. Many of the returning Scots and Englishmen aboard celebrated their confinement to the ship by partying all night. One man drank himself into a stupor, fell overboard, and was retrieved in a noisy rescue. Others sang, danced, and boisterously jumped rope. Lyon slept very little. In his private contemplations, he might have recalled that his grandfather John Lyon had spent nights in the same harbor waiting for favorable winds to carry him to America exactly seventy years earlier. John, a successful missionary himself, had left a comfortable life and business and sailed for Zion in 1853. Now the grandson was returning to the land of his grandfather's birth.[14]

Early Saturday morning, British elders met the thirteen exhausted but eager missionaries and took them to the headquarters of the European Mission, where they met Elder David O. McKay (illus. 3-3). Elder McKay not only served as president of the British Mission but also supervised "eight other large missions—Swiss-German, French, Swedish, Norwegian, Danish, Netherlands, Armenian, and South African—with the responsibility to train and motivate their leaders, missionaries, and members."[15]

In 1923, Lyon was one of 981 new missionaries who joined the approximately twenty-three hundred others serving in five world areas. The majority, 64 percent, labored in the United States and Canada. Twenty-five percent fulfilled their missions in Europe.[16] The European missionary force had diminished drastically during World War I and had been slow to rebound, but by 1923 the Church deemed Europe a fertile area, with fields "white and ready to harvest."[17]

During the few hours in Liverpool, Elder McKay instructed Lyon and his traveling companions in their duties.[18] Lyon recalls that the summary of the rules was quite simple: "Leave the women alone . . . we were over there not to play but to work and not to sightsee but to preach the gospel."[19] Lyon

Courtesy Church Archives

Illus. 3-3. Edgar met British Mission president David O. McKay in 1923.

and his traveling companions also met a twenty-four-year-old elder named Ezra Taft Benson, who presided over the Newcastle Conference (district) but was in the mission office that day. In the afternoon, the three elders bound for the Netherlands—Lyon, Murdock, and Perkins—boarded a train to cross England to the port of Harwich. A heavy rainstorm washed out a bridge, and they had to wait several hours for a temporary repair. When the very late train arrived, the signal for the ship to depart had already been given. The missionaries' large trunks, which had gone on an earlier train, were already on board.

The train just pulled right along the quay and they pulled the boat back. They didn't put out a plank. They just said "jump." [We were about four feet away]. We gave a jump and got over. [But] they had given our berths away . . . because they thought we weren't coming. . . . So we tried to find a place to settle and we ended up on the floor of a big lounge, a dining room type of thing, on a night boat for Holland. There was a terrible storm at sea that night. The ship was rolling and lurching and we laid down on the carpeted floor and put our legs around the table legs . . . trying to keep from rolling around.[20]

The elders slept very little, enduring their second night of almost complete sleeplessness. Exhausted, bewildered, and frightened, and deep in language and culture shock, they arrived at the docks in Rotterdam early Sunday morning, July 29.

Divine Help with the Language

Seasoned Dutch missionaries met the three new elders and helped them with their trunks as they tiredly made their way to the mission home and office in Rotterdam. There they gulped a hurried breakfast and then were whisked away to a 9:00 A.M. church service. The sleep-deprived elders sought inconspicuous seats in the audience but were honored with a place on the stand. Though bone weary, Lyon had no trouble staying awake for the events that followed.

There was a song and prayer, "none of which we could understand." At the request of the branch president,

> one of the local brethren . . . address[ed] the meeting. Coming to the stand he commenced to speak, and before I was aware of the fact, I suddenly found myself sitting on the edge of my chair, listening to his sermon, while my two companions had fallen asleep.

Lyon did not yet know Dutch, "yet [he] understood what he was saying." The man "discussed the organization of the primitive Church, the place of Apostles and prophets in the Church, and the beginning of the apostasy in the first centuries of the Christian era, as shown by the absence of these divinely constituted authorities."

After this brother finished, the branch president then called on another man to speak,

> and he carried the same thread of thought through to its logical conclusion, namely, the condition of the Church in the Middle Ages, the Reformation, and then told the story of the restoration of the Gospel in this dispensation, and the value of living Apostles and prophets.

A third speaker arose. However, "of his entire sermon I understood only the 'amen' at the end. . . . the gift of interpretation that had so suddenly come to me and removed all traces of drowsiness had left me as quickly as it came." At that point, "the three newly arrived missionaries were then asked to make a few remarks. Through an interpreter I stated that I had been blessed that morning with the gift of interpretation, as I had understood the remarks of the first two speakers."[21] This experience fulfilled part of Elder Ballard's promise to Lyon. It gave the new missionary, at least temporarily, confirmation that he would have divine help in mastering the unfamiliar Dutch language.

The Netherlands already had a long history of Latter-day Saint missionary activity. In 1840 Orson Hyde traveled through the country and preached, principally to the Jewish population. In 1861 the first full-time elders, called from among the European Saints, began labors in the tiny country, which was part of the Swiss, Italian, and German Mission. In 1864 the Netherlands became a separate mission.[22] In early 1923, Orson Hyde's grandson thirty-five-year-old Charles Stanford Hyde (illus. 3-4) was called to serve as president, and his wife and three children accompanied him to the Netherlands. His term as mission

Improvement Era, 26:540.

Illus. 3-4. Charles S. Hyde, Netherlands Mission president in 1923.

president corresponded almost
exactly with Lyon's mission. President Hyde spoke good Dutch, having
completed a mission in the Netherlands between 1907 and 1909.[23] He
had known Lyon's older brother
Dave during this earlier mission,
and Dave had set high standards
for his younger brother to follow.
Lyon later recalled President Hyde's
positive influence:

> [Charles Hyde] was very con-
> siderate. . . . He would let you
> know that we weren't over
> there to fool around; he was
> sincere. He was a fellow with
> a good sense of humor. . . . He
> was continually impressing
> upon us the obligation of the
> great mass of people . . . that

didn't know a thing about the gospel. . . . He would stress to us the
idea of trying to get as much as we could in contact with better grades
[classes] of people. I had a great respect for President Hyde.[24]

In 1923 the Netherlands, often called Holland (although technically
the name "Holland" referred to only one part of the country), had a population of just over seven million. The Netherlands was a small country
(illus. 3-5), just 15,722 square miles, only one-sixth the size of Lyon's home
state of Utah. The highest elevation barely reached one thousand feet, and
much of the country, diked and reclaimed from the ocean, was actually a
few feet below sea level, quite different from the ten-thousand foot peaks
that circled Lyon's Salt Lake Valley. Annual rainfall rarely exceeded thirty
inches, but for the boy fresh from Utah's dry, hot summer, the frequent
light showers, humidity, mist, and fog from the nearby ocean created a
dreary environment. Notes about food and the gloomy gray weather were
frequent in Edgar's mission diary.

Queen Wilhelmina, forty-three years old in 1923, ruled the country
from her regal seat in the capital, Amsterdam. She had deftly managed
to keep the Netherlands neutral during World War I, but the country
was now experiencing social and economic problems. The Netherlands was not nearly as prosperous as the United States in the 1920s,

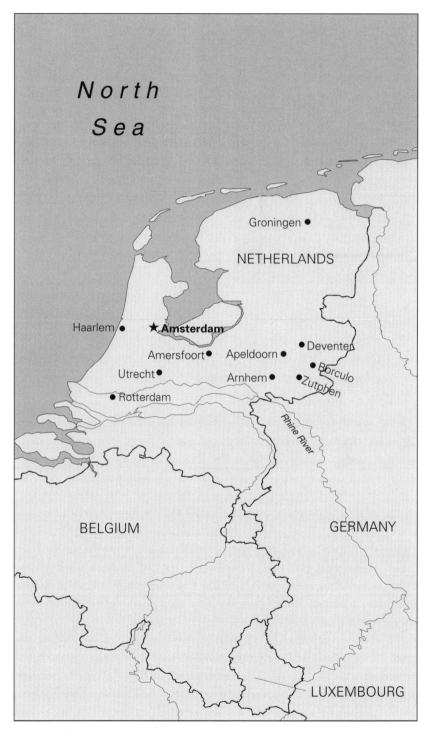

Illus. 3-5. Cities in the Netherlands where missionaries labored.

but Latter-day Saints were faring sufficiently well, and they occasionally received clothing and foodstuffs sent by Church leaders in Utah.[25]

The Netherlands Mission prospered greatly at this time. By the end of 1923, sixty-eight American missionaries and at least four local brethren were serving as full-time missionaries,[26] and the Saints in the Netherlands numbered approximately three thousand, a figure that had remained constant since 1909. Each year the number of new converts approximately equaled the number of Saints who emigrated to America. This trend changed during Lyon's mission, as more members stayed in their homeland.[27] From mission reports, historian Keith C. Warner counted 306 baptisms in 1923, the most productive year to that date in the mission and the most baptisms until 1950.[28] The Netherlands mission held a very favorable position: it could boast the second highest rate of converts per missionary in the European area and fourth highest among the twenty-two missions of the Church. The year 1923 was an optimistic time for Lyon to enter the Netherlands Mission.

Netherlands Mission Statistics, 1921–25[29]

1. Members (yearly average)	3,087
2. Missionaries (average)	50
3. Branches (average)	18
4. Converts (yearly average)	188
5. Converts per missionary (during total mission time)	3.73
6. Monthly cost per missionary	$29.42
7. Cost per convert	$95.00
8. Hours worked daily by each missionary (average; includes personal gospel study and visits to the homes of members)	11.7
9. Proselyting hours per convert	460

Missionary Tracting in Amsterdam

Just twenty-four hours after Lyon's arrival, President Hyde assigned him to temporarily work in the Amsterdam area with LeRoy T. Ostler from Nephi, Utah. The very next day, after just a few hours of exposure to the Dutch language, Lyon made a note in his diary that "this language is certainly abominable. Bro. Ostler is giving me lessons in pronunciation."[30] Apparently the joy of the previous Sunday's gift of tongues had rapidly faded into the realization that language mastery would come only by prolonged study. But the next day, after the customary registration with police as a minister, he observed:

I'm beginning to like this country of canals, boats, tile roofs, dogcarts, funny looking automobiles, brick paved streets, and smoking children. The people appear to be big-hearted, broad-minded, and honest. . . . I never saw so many people smoking in my life. I haven't seen any men who showed respect for women since I left America.[31]

Lyon grew up in a home where his mother was honored and spoken to respectfully; gender relations in the Netherlands did not meet his high expectations.

Lyon's diary and letters of the first eight weeks in Amsterdam detail his first visit to a public bath, visits to museums, language lessons from his companions, his first experience bearing his testimony in testimony meeting, and his reactions to the strange foods. He notes simply, "[I] ate my first horse-meat."[32] He admitted to his diary that he was covered with welts from itching flea bites and suffered from the common "missionary itch," which he attributed to the strange food and humid climate. On August 25, Lyon counted "143 sores on my left leg below the knee."[33] A few weeks later, there were three hundred sores on his lower body. He did not include these negative details in his letters home, however. His letters portray a more positive view of Dutch life. Obviously he did not want to worry his already fretful mother, so he continually assured her that all was well. His diary is much more revealing of his personal discomforts, anguish, and reactions to the foreign food.

As part of their proselyting activity in Amsterdam, Ostler and Lyon began tracting in the poorer areas of town. Lyon's diary entry for August 12, 1923, records:

> Tracted with Bro. Ostler for 2½ hours. Fully half the people do not believe in God or the Bible. I can account for it if the spirit of God will not dwell in an unclean place because they certainly are living in filth. At night we went to Classfen's and ate horse meat. A mission would be an ideal thing for a sociologist. It would enable him to study real slum life, and here in Holland he could also study the germination and growth of revolution, starting with the poverty-stricken tenement dwellers.

He observed that Holland was divided into "five social classes; we only work with the lowest two."[34] Later he wrote, "We tried the rich part of town, but without success, so went into the poverty stricken district [again] . . . where we sold all the booklets that we had."[35]

The mission's yearly report confirms Lyon's observations:

> Thousands parade the streets without work and several of our saints are among these unfortunates . . . . Labor conditions are really serious

> in Holland at the present time and prices for food and clothing . . . are
> extortionally high and are beyond the reach of these poor people . . . .
> [These conditions turn] many people from religion to seek a temporal
> salvation in some of the numerous political organizations.[36]

Lyon began noticing signs and parades that advocated Communism as a solution to the social and economic problems of the country. His diary frequently mentions Communist demonstrations and his opposition to this brand of social idealism. But he understood its appeal among the poor: "Ate supper in a dirty attic, that we reached by climbing up three flights of ladders. Horse meat, grease, and red cabbage. Oh Boy!"[37] In a letter home, he informed his parents that "Half of our saints are 'Reds' and I do not blame them."[38]

Lyon contrasted the grime of poverty in his tracting areas with the royal pomp of Amsterdam. In the late 1600s, Amsterdam had been the richest city in Europe, a prosperous center of world trade. Wealthy merchants built elegant canal houses along the waterways. Philosophy, art, and theology thrived there. Dutch masters including Vermeer, Rembrandt, Rubens, and van Gogh memorialized Holland, and their paintings made Amsterdam's Rijksmuseum one of the greatest art galleries in the world. Jews from Spain and Portugal took refuge in the cosmopolitan city during the war. The tragic contrasts between pomp and poverty overwhelmed Lyon. For more than a week in late August and early September, the country celebrated Queen Wilhelmina's birthday in opulently grand style. Royal orange was everywhere in Amsterdam during those days, but it clashed with the red banners in the poorer sections of town. It was in these slums that people were willing to admit two well-dressed Americans to their homes.

The rapport between the two young men helped the work. Lyon especially enjoyed Ostler's sense of fun, his teasing, and his love of horse-play. Forty-three years after they served as companions, Lyon and Ostler still maintained contact. Lyon often expressed his appreciation for Ostler: "No missionary was ever more fortunate than I was, to have had such a good missionary break me in."[39] Ostler helped Lyon loosen up a bit and learn to enjoy the place and the people. Lyon and Ostler worked as a threesome with a new elder, Lafayette T. Hatch. Hatch slept in their apartment for a few days until he received a more permanent assignment in Apeldoorn. On September 25, 1923, however, Hatch died quite suddenly from a complication of diabetes.[40] The unexpected death of a young man with whom they had so recently shared food and bed threw a temporary panic into the elders as they sensed a new vulnerability.

Although they considered themselves to be especially blessed and watched over by angels, they questioned how one so near to them could have died so unexpectedly. Were they giving all that they should in service to God?

A further source of anguish for Lyon was his struggle with the Dutch language. After his first thrilling experience speaking in tongues, his slow progress caused him great frustration. Lyon and Ostler practiced reading the Book of Mormon in both English and Dutch and soon progressed to reading in Dutch only.[41] But Lyon's spoken Dutch did not develop as quickly as his ability to read a familiar text. Lyon later confessed, "A lot of people told me I [spoke] Book of Mormon Dutch."[42] About all Lyon could do at first was memorize a prayer for a Church meeting and the few words needed for passing out tracts—memorization came easily for him. Once his companion left him alone with some members, and Lyon proudly noted that "for about three hours I never said anything in English. I used every Dutch word I had ever heard, a dozen times, and a whole lot that I nor anyone else had ever heard."[43]

Fortunately for Lyon, missionary work of the era did not require regular conversations with all contacts. The elders passed out tracts with little or no engaging dialogue during the first encounter. Then they returned a few weeks later to see if the recipients had read the tract or had questions. If need for discussion arose, the senior missionary would handle it. Rather than spending long hours tracting, the elders spent many of their missionary hours with the patient members, who were used to nurturing and teaching the struggling elders.

Lyon and his companion in Amsterdam often took advantage of opportunities to sightsee with the mission president. They attended a play, rode their bicycles out of town on infrequent sunny days, taught English classes to members, attended parties with members and investigators, and visited many museums, including the Rijksmuseum, where Lyon established a lifelong love for the Dutch master painters Rembrandt and Vandermeer.

The typical day, as noted in Lyon's diary, consisted of one and a half or two hours of passing out tracts in the morning and a shorter session of the same in the afternoon. But heavy rain, high winds, and snow would cancel tracting altogether. There was only minor pressure to reach a specified number of baptisms, contact hours, or lessons taught. Studying took up more of the missionaries' time than any other activity. They studied the gospel and the Dutch language, often for five or more hours a day. As Lyon studied, he fell in love with the history of Christianity and

Improvement Era, 26 :847.

Illus. 3-6. Hilbertus Noorda was Edgar's mission companion.

read many volumes on the subject. The long study sessions confirmed his growing love for history and convinced him even more deeply of the truths he was trying to teach in his halting Dutch. He also grew in confidence. "I am developing enough nerve to sell life insurance," he noted.[44]

Fulfillment of Blessings in Amersfoort

While struggling to learn Dutch, Lyon received his first permanent assignment. Teamed with seasoned and enthusiastic Elder Hilbertus Noorda (illus. 3-6), he was assigned to open a new area in the small medieval town (about forty-five hundred people) of Amersfoort. Noorda had been born in the Netherlands, where he had lived until age seven, when his family emigrated to Utah. Lyon's relationship with his new companion was pleasant, relaxed, and positive. In his diary, Lyon praised the Dutch-born elder and expressed deep love for him.

On September 23, 1923, Lyon delivered his farewell speech to the Amsterdam branch: "I talked for about four minutes (my first public offense as a speaker) saying 342 words."[45] Four days later, on September 27, Lyon and Noorda took the short train ride to Amersfoort and quickly fell in love with the ancient Hanseatic League town. The slums of old Amsterdam gave way to a smaller, more manageable town of many trees, a nearby friendly stream, and general cleanliness. Here, Lyon opened up and enjoyed himself more than in the large, bustling city. In a meeting with investigators, he even sang a solo, "Rock in the Cradle of the Deep." He began enjoying the Dutch food, including eel, much more. Newly arrived elders from Utah brought him packages from home, and he thrilled at the sight and taste of Maxfield's chocolates, dried dates, some withered Jonathan apples, and even his own personalized, two-month-old, moldy birthday cake.

While the Dutch language still posed a struggle, on October 11, 1923, Lyon had another miraculous experience.

> After arranging to hold cottage meetings at the home of our one member in the city, we stamped some tracts [with the branch address] (No. 1 of the Rays of Living Light series), and then my companion taught me to say one sentence ("Good day, lady, will

you please read this tract?") and we set out tracting. My companion assigned me to one side of the street, while he took the other. Being able to converse, he moved slowly along the way, having frequent discussions, while my work consisted of ringing a bell, speaking my one sentence, handing the lady a tract, and going to the next door. I had soon left my companion far behind, and had come to the outskirts of the city. There were four more dwellings remaining on my side of the road. I thought to myself, "I'll leave tracts at these houses and return to find Brother Noorda," at the same time looking at my watch and noticing that it was 3:50 P.M.

These houses before me had no front doors, so I was obliged to go to the rear to contact the inhabitants. As I went into the yard at the rear of the first house I noticed a man raking refuse together and burning it. I walked up to him, said my sentence (even calling him a lady, as I could not think of the word for a man) and he refused my proffered tract. I left him, but in my heart I was saying, "Oh, if only I had the ability to speak, I would so like to tell him our message!" Having gone about 15 feet, something took hold of me, turned me about, and I returned to him. I offered him a tract for the second time. He took it, crumpled it up, and threw it in the fire, I walked away, but upon reaching the same spot, I was again turned about by some strange power, and returned and made an offer of a tract for the third time, with the same experience that had met my second offer. Again I walked away, and again I was forcibly wheeled about and returned for the fourth time. The man, apparently annoyed by my conduct, commenced to speak in a loud tone, and by the evident display of anger, I was certain that he was provoked by my insistence. Then suddenly I commenced to speak, and he became silent and listened. I did not know what I was saying. I was conscious of standing before him. I was conscious of speaking, but beyond that I was unaware of my message to him. After a few minutes I had apparently completed my talk because I handed him a tract which he kindly accepted, and I returned to the street. There I met my companion. He had been hunting for me, as he could not see me and decided I had met some opposition or had become involved in some difficulty because of my inability to speak Dutch.

Elder Noorda said to me, "What have you been doing?" "I have been having a Gospel conversation with a man," I answered.

"Did you find someone who spoke English?" he asked. Upon being answered in the negative, he said, "But you cannot speak Dutch."

"I know I can't," was my reply, "but the Spirit of the Lord has been speaking through me." I felt weak and trembling when the experience had passed. Brother Noorda doubted my story, told me to make a special note of the address, and the following week he would return with me when we came with the second tract in the series. The entire experience had lasted ten minutes.

The following week my companion knocked at the door and met the man whom I had encountered the foregoing week. He commenced to tell the man something concerning our message, but the man replied that I had told him that the preceding week. Elder Noorda then told him of the Restoration, and the man made the same reply. He then commenced to discuss baptism, but the man said I had told him of that. Elder Noorda said, "That is impossible. He cannot speak Dutch."

The man then replied, "All I know is that he talked to me for about ten minutes last week, and he spoke in perfect Dutch, without a foreign accent." The conversation ended here.

Returning to the street, Elder Noorda said, "Companion, you win." He then told me what had happened (I had been unable to understand it, of course).[46]

Often skeptical of supernatural stories or mythical oral tradition, Lyon was not one to hang a testimony on a single miraculous event. Yet this incident fulfilled the promise Elder Ballard had made three months earlier. Lyon said the experience "gave me the feeling [that] 'I can learn it. I am going to try.' I worked and worked and worked hard."[47]

On November 29, 1923, Thanksgiving Day in the United States, Lyon expressed gratitude for "my parents, the gospel, my body, health, strength, and the privilege of coming to Holland to preach. I would be much more thankful if I could speak the language so I could do real missionary work."[48] On New Year's Day 1924, he reflected, "I have been in Holland for 5 months, and unable to speak Dutch. Hope next year at this time I shall be able to."[49] His all-encompassing concern about his language inadequacies dominated his diary and letters for months.

In March the anguish abated slightly, and by April 1924, Lyon began to make regular notations in Dutch in his diary. After eight months, he could communicate sufficiently well, but still he yearned and studied for more perfection. "I have been promised the gift of languages," he wrote, "but it won't come to me unless I work for it. The Lord never lifted up any skull and dropped brains in while they were resting."[50]

Lyon wrote home at least once a week during his entire mission. He set aside Saturday mornings for letter writing, first to his parents, then to his siblings, and finally to his friends. He often penned short notes to the Dutch Saints who had treated him so kindly. He used an old typewriter whenever it was available, rapidly turning out very accurate, lengthy letters with the two-fingered "hunt and peck" method, a technique he would employ all his life. He also kept a detailed daily journal, often a bit formal and stiff, for every day of his mission. His letters to family members reveal his feelings and insights more than most of his diary entries.

After Lyon and Noorda had worked together for five and a half months, the mission president carried out transfers, and Karl Fife from Logan, Utah, replaced Elder Noorda as Lyon's companion. A short time later, Elder Fife received a letter from an aunt informing him that his father had been killed two weeks earlier. Lyon lamented, "I seem to be a poor comforter [to him]."[51] The grieving elder stayed in the mission field but did not work diligently. A month later, Lyon wrote that "Bro. Fife was [still] tired, so [he] stayed home. I started out for a walk, ending up at Heinings . . . . came home [at 9:30 P.M.], but Bro. Fife had already gone to bed."[52] Lyon regularly functioned at a high energy level, usually not going to bed until 11:30 or 12:00 each night, but Fife wanted more sleep.

Whatever the relationship between "partners," the term Lyon usually employed for his companions, the missionary work went very well. When Lyon and Noorda first arrived in Amersfoort, just two Mormon families lived in the town. The elders scheduled meetings and invited those who accepted tracts to come to the Sunday preaching meeting. After just a few weeks of tracting and teaching, Lyon noted that the Sunday service often had twenty-five people, usually less than half of which were members.

Nevertheless, baptisms could not be rushed. Investigators had to feel the spirit, gain a firm testimony, and demonstrate commitment by personal study and regular attendance at meetings for several months before being baptized. At one point, Lyon noted that he and his companion engaged a good family who participated every week for three months, "though of course we will not baptize anyone until they have been investigating the gospel six or eight months."[53] This waiting period before baptism was a general Church practice, a matter not left to the discretion of the individual missionary or mission. Gone were the days of Wilford Woodruff, who baptized scores of people after just one night of preaching. Missionaries carefully nurtured their contacts for months, gave them many reading assignments, and attentively shepherded their progress. Because Amersfoort was a new missionary area, Lyon and his companions did not expect to baptize new converts for many months. From the standpoint of the number of participating investigators, Elder Lyon and his two companions in Amersfoort were successful; the baptisms, however, came much later, after Lyon had been reassigned to other branches.

In Amersfoort and throughout most of the country, missionaries encountered regular opposition to their work, usually from ministers of other faiths and often in the press. The biggest single issue that provoked opposition was plural marriage. In 1909 an official government publication, the *Staats Courant,* had printed an article that equated Latter-day Saint polygamy with white slavery. Most of the country's newspapers reprinted the article.[54] Despite retractions and denials, the idea caught hold of the public imagination, and Lyon heard references to polygamy and white slavery nearly every day.

In 1921 a former clergyman of the Dutch Reformed Church, M. H. A. van der Valk, published a combative book on Joseph Smith. The book was widely reviewed and hailed as the best text on Mormonism in Dutch. In 1924, van der Valk published another book critical not only of the origins of the Church and its prophets, but also of the temple and its sacred ordinances. Pamphlets on "Temple Secrets" and other topics were extracted from the chapters of the book and sold to counter the efforts of the young missionaries.[55] Despite this intense opposition, missionary work in Amersfoort prospered.

To counter such claims against the Church, Lyon placed his whole body and soul into missionary work. He awoke early, usually before his companions, studied the scriptures with discipline and excitement, and found that he thoroughly enjoyed tracting. He spent money frugally, learned to love the members and their language, and generally stayed up reading late into the night. This passionate energy for life, people, work, and reading, which also characterized his later years, sprang from decisions made and discipline developed during his nine months in Amersfoort.

Inexperienced Branch President in Haarlem

Among Lyon's greatest joys in the mission field were the regular missionary and member conferences held at least each January and June. When all the missionaries gathered, Lyon could converse in easy English with his original traveling companions to the Netherlands and old buddies from the Ensign Ward. Missionaries journeyed by train (and sometimes by bike) to mission headquarters in Rotterdam (illus. 3-7), where they lodged with members for three nights. Each day was filled with meetings containing instruction and testimony. One such meeting lasted eleven hours, and Lyon loved it, wishing it would not end.[56]

During these conferences, Lyon came to the attention of President Charles S. Hyde as a hardworking, serious young man given wholly to missionary labors. Here, too, he rubbed shoulders with the Apostles. At his second mission conference, "Apostle McKay stood up, and in that wonderful manner that he has, with his commanding personality, made me sit up and take notice. . . . I was sorry when he sat down, after having talked for three and one half hours!"[57] Elder McKay, as president of the European Mission, spoke of a new missionary program he had introduced in Great Britain: "Every Member a Missionary." He advised the elders to use the local priesthood and Church membership to influence people to investigate the Church.[58] Elder McKay also urged the Saints to stay in the Netherlands and build the Church there, having seen the debilitating effects of constant emigration from the European branches.[59] In meetings with members, he spoke on families and the duties of parents. Lyon's letters portrayed President McKay as both an inspiring and a practical leader who spoke on the effective use of time and how to best use auxiliary organizations in missionary efforts.

In these conferences with President Hyde, President McKay, and later with President James E. Talmage, each elder reported on his mission. The lengthy oral reports by each of the sixty-seven elders in attendance reassured Lyon that, in comparison to most other missionaries, he was progressing very well, except possibly with his language skills.

Illus. 3-7. Netherlands Mission conference in 1924. T. Edgar Lyon, wearing a bow ties, is seated on the front row in the middle.

Others noticed Elder Lyon's growth also. In fact, during his second conference, on June 23, 1924, the mission president surprised him with a call to leave Amersfoort immediately to serve as branch president and senior companion in Haarlem, a branch known among the elders as the "battlefield of the mission."[60]

Lyon's older brother Dave had labored in Haarlem fourteen years earlier and was still revered there as a model missionary. Lyon found Dave's picture framed and prominently displayed in the homes of many members and even a few long-standing investigators. He felt deeply inferior to his older brother: "I can see that I'll never live up to the ideals and standards that [Dave] set while here in Holland."[61] Dave had also worked in Arnhem and Utrecht, Lyon's next two branches, and there, too, he felt inferior by comparison to the "saintly elder" loved by so many. These feelings were reinforced in December 1924 when Lyon received word that Dave, at the relatively young age of thirty-seven, had been named bishop in the rough mining town of Bingham, Utah. For the remainder of his mission, Lyon worked under the shadow of an older brother who appeared to be much more successful than he.

Reflecting on the call to serve as Haarlem Branch president, Lyon humbly noted: "I had not expected such a thing. . . . Oh! Boy. I think Pres. Hyde's inspiration is off of its track. I feel so weak, so incompetent and insufficient that I do not feel capable of the job, but I'll try, and do my best."[62] His new companion was Alfred Lindberg from Tooele, Utah, also an experienced elder. Lyon felt that Lindberg was "so far ahead of me in speaking . . . and is so full of the spirit of his mission that he makes me feel ashamed of myself for not having studied more."[63] These diary notations demonstrate Lyon's continued anxiety and insecurity over his language abilities after eleven months in the mission. Indeed, it was rather rare for such a "new" elder to be called as branch president. Elder Lyon's call was the result of his diligent work ethic in previous branches.

For missionaries to be called as branch presidents was not unusual. Young American elders presided over all twenty-six branches in the mission. This had been the custom since the first days of the Church in the Netherlands, with only a brief hiatus during World War I. According to tradition, local members were simply not ready to direct a branch or, much less, an entire conference or district. Yet the experience of forced self-governance during the war had given many of the local brethren the opportunity to develop leadership skills. When missionaries returned to the Netherlands after the war, they displaced the local leaders, causing some resentment, especially in Haarlem. Lyon entered a hostile situation in his first experience as a branch president, but the mission president obviously had more confidence in Lyon than the young man had in himself.

To give moral support, the Hydes and McKays accompanied Lyon to Haarlem. On the train, "both Sister McKay and Bro. McKay complimented me on the testimony that I gave in the meeting yesterday, and wished me God's speed and success in my labors."[64] And Lyon needed this blessing: Haarlem was rife with petty jealousies among members and squabbles with apostates who continued to cause troubles for both missionaries and members. In characteristic fashion, Lyon simply jumped into the fray. For eight months, he served in the divided branch, filling out all branch reports and tithing receipts as well as conducting all meetings, including choir practice, Relief Society, and Sunday School. He visited and discussed the gospel with apostates, tried to assuage one member who accused another of being a Freemason, and attempted to resolve petty but seriously divisive disputes over issues such as what songs the choir leader should be practicing.

And he spoke in just about every meeting, still not an easy or pleasant task for the twenty-year-old elder: "I hate speaking [in meetings] worse than any other phase of the work. I'd rather tract ten hours than speak ten minutes."[65] Even toward the end of his mission, Lyon believed that his Church talks remained weak: "I followed with a 23 minute [talk] on 'Christ and Resurrection and the 10 Virgins'—a rotten speech."[66] What irony for one who would later be hailed as one of the most engaging speakers in the Church.

After working in the Netherlands for a full year without baptizing a single person, Lyon had the privilege of baptizing Margaretha Scheen, age thirty, and Jannetje Nienhius, age sixty-five. These two women had been friendly to the Church for some time but had resisted official entrance until Lyon taught and helped them. Finally he saw the fruits of hundreds of hours of preaching. He performed the baptisms in a local bathhouse.[67]

From June 23, 1924, until February 26, 1925, Lyon continued as president of the sixty-member Haarlem Branch (illus. 3-8). In a November 28, 1924, letter to President Hyde, Lyon observed that "we are unable to find any investigators who are searching, but haven't given up hope yet. The bad spirit of the branch has driven all investigators away."[68] After a monthly priesthood meeting, Lyon mused over the negative spirit he felt: "Such hate and jealousy and haughtiness I never saw [before] . . . most are seeking for honor and position."[69] The small choir was causing a huge conflict that Lyon insightfully analyzed: "The whole trouble lies in the fact that the choir leader is an elder, and presided over the branch during the war. Now he finds it hard to step down and be in subjection to the missionaries."[70] Lyon felt trapped between Church rule and logical wisdom—he felt it might have been wiser to leave the branches in control of local leaders, as they had been during the war, but this option did not exist. Nevertheless, Lyon's experience in the strife-ridden Haarlem Branch prepared him for a major policy change when he returned ten years later as mission president.

In the midst of strife, Lyon and his companions found joy in the budding romance of the recently baptized Sister Margaretha Scheen and Brother Andries Meyer. The young branch president encouraged Meyer to further his romantic relationship with Sister Scheen. Lyon enjoyed the Cupid role. He likewise delighted in his association with the Mulder family during his eight months in Haarlem. He never mentioned a single conflict or problem with them, and he frequently wrote in his journal "Spent the evening at the Mulder's." Their home seemed to be a haven in the tempest of conflicts.

Lyon also enjoyed serving branch members. On St. Nick's Day (December 6) in 1924, he recorded:

I also played St. Nicholas for a poor family. The mother has been excommunicated but the 3 children are still faithful members. The mother is a widow, and also has consumption. I bought 3 gingerbread dolls, about 18 inches high, and took them to them. They were as happy as could be, because they were too poor to buy anything. I also gave her a dollar to buy potatoes and vegetables.[71]

Lyon and his companions continued to teach English lessons, especially to the young adults of the branch, many of whom desired to leave the Netherlands for the United States or Canada. As part of the MIA, the elders also taught a Bible class each Wednesday night.

Illus. 3-8. T. Edgar Lyon with a member in Haarlem spading a field in 1925. Ed's derby hat and wooden shoes were very practical in the wet climate.

By January 1925, Lyon felt better about the spirit in the branch, but he still felt anguish over the pettiness of many members. To President Hyde he wrote: "Yesterday the Verbruggen family wanted to start something and I told them to mind their own business, and I would lead the branch! If what I said was not enough, I'll tell them more."[72] This is strong talk for the formerly insecure, tongue-tied foreigner. Haarlem brought out boldness in Lyon's leadership. "I see that I have been too easy on the branch and I think I can control them now. . . . I realize that I have a man-sized job, although only a boy," he further confided to President Hyde.[73] Mixed with this new boldness, however, was ever-present humility and even a degree of self-effacement. After nineteen months, Lyon lamented: "I am becoming disgusted with myself because I have accomplished nothing. My Dutch grammar is very imperfect and my pronunciation is abominable."[74] Despite these occasional negative evaluations, however, Lyon had accomplished much in Haarlem. He would leave the branch in better peace than he found it.

Leadership in Arnhem and Utrecht

On February 26, 1925, President Hyde reassigned Lyon to serve as branch president in Arnhem, a small town in the eastern part of the country. His new companion was forty-nine-year-old Andries de Bruyn, a native Dutchman who had emigrated to Salt Lake City seven years earlier and had now returned to the Netherlands while his family remained in Utah. De Bruyn's fluency in the language benefited Lyon, who, with de Bruyn's help, worked on polishing his pronunciation. In contrast to Haarlem, the Arnhem Branch was calm, even pleasant. Lyon's letters and diary mention few conflicts among the members. Tracting went well, and the companions even found a well-prepared investigator whom they soon baptized.

In January 1925, scholar and writer Elder James E. Talmage replaced David O. McKay as president of the European Mission. President Talmage held his first Netherlands Mission meetings in March 1925. Every missionary in the country went to Amsterdam to report on the work and to meet the Apostle. At the meetings, President Talmage assigned all the missionaries in his charge to review the methods and materials used in proselyting.[75] Lyon was impressed by this man who was both a man of science and a man of God: "Bro. Talmage gave a wonderful sermon on obedience, using illustrations of electricity and the photographic plate, and from II Kings 4:1–7."[76]

In late April 1925, President Hyde notified Lyon that he was to leave Arnhem and travel to Utrecht to take on the duties of conference president. The conference, or district, included six branches in the central part of the Netherlands: Amersfoort, Apeldoorn, Arnhem, Deventer, Utrecht, and Zutphen. For some reason not explained to Lyon, the remote and tiny Groningen Conference (in the northernmost part of the country) was temporarily put under his supervision as well. Lyon was to exercise ecclesiastical authority over both areas, acting in much the same role as what were later called district or stake presidents. Lyon was to preside over nine hundred Church members as well as all the missionaries in the area. When the call came, Lyon observed, "I did not know whether to cry, or laugh, or feel disgusted with myself."[77] In his diary, he humbly confided that the call "was surely a surprise, and I felt like jumping in a hole and pulling it in after me."[78] This meekness and humility endeared him to both members and missionaries alike.

As conference president, Elder Lyon regularly traveled among the branches, studying and tracting with the elders and encouraging them to dedicate themselves to higher achievement. He visited a different branch each Sunday and was always called on to speak. At this stage in his mission, he quit complaining about speaking in meetings. He now had at least sufficient command of the language and sufficient knowledge of the gospel as well. He had studied diligently, and by the end of his mission had read at least thirty religious books. Although he probably would not have admitted to enjoying the weekly speaking assignments, Lyon had acquired the confidence to fulfill them successfully.

In addition to his speaking assignments, many of Lyon's conference duties were financial. He had to collect and write receipts for all tithing and other donations in the district, handle all subscriptions to the *Ster* (the *Star*—the Church's magazine in Dutch), check the financial records of each branch, and pay for each of the rented halls in which meetings were held. He found keeping track of his personal finances much easier than tending the conference records. He received between twenty-five and forty dollars each month from his father and dutifully recorded each month's allotment in the back of his diary as well as the amount spent in guilders and cents. In more than one letter, Lyon mildly boasts of his Scottish frugality and the fact that he was spending less than the mission average. The noncommitted elders, he felt, were the ones who spent too much and were always short of funds at month's end.

While in Utrecht, Lyon often ended up with two companions when the president found himself with an odd number of elders. This worked well—three missionaries could pass out tracts just as easily as two. President Hyde continued to express his confidence in Lyon, as evidenced by the companions he assigned to Lyon during the final months of his mission. Some worked very hard, while others wanted to be excused from the work entirely. One new arrival, a son of a former Church leader, refused to participate in the "emotional and psychological gimmicks" of the Church. When Lyon met him at the train station in Utrecht, he immediately said:

> Now Brother Lyon, I want to tell you something. I've come on this mission because of the pressure of my mother and family. I didn't want to come. I don't believe in the gospel, and I'm not interested. . . . I don't want you to call on me to pray because I don't believe in praying. And don't ask me to sing. . . . I can give speeches that don't necessarily need any testimony. . . . That I'll do, but I'm not going to get involved in these emotional things.[79]

Lyon was taken aback but not daunted. They left the elder's steamer trunk in the train station and hurried to the home of a member family who had requested an urgent blessing. Three days earlier, their three-year-old daughter had fallen from her uncle's arms and landed on some sharp bricks. As a result, she was paralyzed from the waist down. She was to be operated on the next day, and her distraught mother wanted her to have a priesthood blessing. Once in the house, Lyon

> handed the bottle [of consecrated oil] to this [new] young missionary. . . . He looked at me and said, "I told you I wasn't going to do anything like this." I said, "That isn't the point. They think you are a missionary, and you should do it." He said, "Well I can't speak Dutch anyway." And I said, "We assume God understands English [too]. That isn't going to make any difference. You go ahead."[80]

The new elder dutifully anointed the girl, and Lyon blessed her that "she would be healed without an operation. When I got through . . . she hopped off that couch and ran [out] in the hall and down in back. That's the first step she'd taken [in three days]."[81] This healing, near the end of his mission, fulfilled an additional promise given to Lyon by Elder Ballard two years earlier—that he would experience the power of miraculous healing. Equally importantly, the new elder, on his first full day in the Netherlands, had witnessed and participated in a power that he had previously denied. Within two or three months, he was also singing hymns and praying.[82]

The missionaries lived with the stalwart van Mondfrans family. Brother van Mondfrans helped Lyon calm and train the sometimes rowdy young elders, a cooperation between members and missionaries that was all too rare. In the van Mondfrans's home, Lyon and one companion, Thain, participated in a second miraculous healing when Brother van Mondfrans's daughter Marie recovered almost immediately following a priesthood blessing.[83]

Of an almost equally miraculous nature, to Lyon at least, was the receipt of a singular letter from Utah. To emphasize the event, Lyon underlined in his diary: "I received a letter from mother this day—the first that I have received from her since I have been on my mission."[84] Until then, all written communication from home had come from his father. Even the candy relief packages contained a mother's sweet love but no letter. After two years, his mother had finally gathered the courage to write. The five pages, in halting handwriting, expressed a mother's deep pride and joy in her youngest son's spiritual accomplishments. Alongside the expected maternal advice about bathing regularly and eating well, Mary apologized for not writing sooner. She had written several letters "but have not had the courage to send them. I write them in my crude way and am so ashamed of them that I destroy them."[85] The spelling and grammar of this letter were generally accurate, perhaps having been checked and corrected by her husband. Mary did not have sufficient confidence in her literacy to write freely—that would follow only in the next decade, after age sixty-five, and with the help of her daughter Janette. Lyon joyously responded to her letter, reporting that despite no showers or regular baths, his health was fine, he was not overweight, he was eating his vegetables, and he was looking forward to seeing her soon. In the back of his diary, Lyon meticulously marked a tick for each letter he wrote—391 of them during the two and a half years.

The Utrecht Branch had uproars similar to those in Haarlem. Lyon successfully instituted the new program of block (home) teaching to the members, but in other matters he met resistance. As conference president, Lyon had the duty to choose the leaders in each branch, in consultation with the missionary branch president. After one such decision, an entire family left the Church because the wife and mother had not been put in the Relief Society presidency.[86] A week later, the conflict continued. In a letter home, Lyon explained that "a big fight ensued and about half of the Saints want to apostatize. At times I become so disgusted with their childish fights and jealousies that I feel like letting them all go to h_ _l." For the second time in his mission, Lyon and two other elders held a Church disciplinary counsel and after hours of anguished discussion and debate "excommunicated the four people for apostasy. . . . I was sorry to do it but it was the only thing to do."[87] These events gave Lyon vital ecclesiastical experience but also a type of negative human experience he would have preferred to forgo.

Lyon also participated in more uplifting activities during his assignment in the Utrecht Conference. Missionaries generally did not render social service at the time, but one experience with the local Saints allowed Lyon to feel the joy of assisting with temporal problems. While returning from a branch picnic one Saturday in August, he and his companions fearfully observed the blackest, lowest cloud he had ever seen, moving from west to east. The lamplighters began to light the street lamps during daylight hours. Lyon recounted, "Suddenly there arose the most violent wind I had ever experienced, soon accompanied by the most terrific downpour of rain I had ever seen. . . . The water began running one and two feet deep in the street."[88] The storm's center turned into a tornado as it rushed through the nearby village of Borculo, destroying homes and public buildings and leaving not a single roof on a house. That year (1925), the queen decided to cancel her normal birthday celebration and urged all to contribute to the reconstruction of the town. From among the Church members, most of them quite poor, the Utrecht Branch raised 66 guilders (about $40 U.S.). Lyon felt the joy of rendering service to the needy when he personally delivered the money to the town council in Borculo.[89]

On Tuesday, May 26, 1925, Lyon baptized Dirk Schuurman in the Rhine River. Dirk, who then lived in Utrecht, was a mature man Lyon had "tracted out" nearly twenty months earlier in Amersfoort. The conversion process had been slow, but Schuurman had become fully committed to the gospel. In July, Lyon performed the baptism of eight-year-old Johanna Miermet, daughter of a member family. The ceremony took place in a local canal. Four weeks later, he again saw the fruits of his earlier work in Amersfoort when the van den Hazel family was baptized. During the twenty-seven and a half months of his mission Lyon baptized four people, but he participated in the conversion process and confirmation of many more.

While Lyon was serving as conference president in Utrecht, he attended a special mission conference in Rotterdam with European Mission President James E. Talmage (illus. 3-9). After the conference, Lyon escorted Sister May Booth Talmage on a three-hour tour through the Rijksmuseum and National Art Gallery.[90] After the Apostle and his wife returned to England, Elder Talmage wrote a full-page letter to Lyon's

Courtesy Church Archives

Illus. 3-9. Elder James E. Talmage, president of the European Mission in 1926.

father in Salt Lake City, extolling the work of his son. Talmage's unsolicited praise provides insight into the character of the now-mature missionary.

> My Dear Brother [David R. Lyon]:
>
> I am happy, indeed, whenever I am able to say good words about any missionary, and I am able so to do in most cases; and in speaking of your son I can speak in the happiest way possible.
>
> Your boy has made a record, according to my own observation and the report of his Mission President, of which you may be justly proud. . . .
>
> Extend my congratulations to Sister Lyon and your entire family. With all of you I rejoice in the work of your boy. May he come back to you, in due time, rejoicing in the consciousness of having continued to the end of his mission in honorable and devoted service, and counting the memory of his mission as one of the treasures of his life.
>
> Sincerely your brother,
>
> James E. Talmage
>
> President European Missions[91]

Elder Talmage mentioned that Lyon would come home "in due time." Although mission calls in the 1920s mentioned no specific length of tenure, it was generally understood that a missionary serving in a foreign country would remain in the mission field approximately two and a half years. Most mission presidents deemed a week or two sufficient notice to prepare for release. The mystery of his release date became a minor concern in Lyon's letters after the two-year mark, but he often expressed his willingness to continue working until the president suggested release. His parents apparently pushed to know when he would return to Utah, but Lyon kept urging their patience. Finally, in late October 1925, President Hyde informed Lyon that he and the two elders with whom he came to Holland would be released after a mission conference on November 15.

Postmission Travel

During his final months in the Netherlands, Lyon occasionally contemplated postmission travel in Europe, especially to France and Great Britain. He also wanted to visit several friends who were serving missions in England and search for his mother's birth records in Scotland.

Extended travel after a mission was common for Latter-day Saint elders in Europe during this era. Lyon's mission diaries show that he hosted several Salt Lake City friends as they passed through the Netherlands from Germany, Scandinavia, and Belgium. Elder Rudger Clawson, acting for the Quorum of the Twelve Apostles, also approved, noting that "if there is opportunity for [postmission] sightseeing, it should be enjoyed in the spirit of learning and righteous pleasure." The phrase "righteous pleasure" is not defined, but Elder Clawson did warn against "witnessing evil sights."[92]

Lyon was officially released from his mission duties on Monday, November 16, 1925. Alone, he boarded a train to France. In the giddy freedom following his discharge from dedicated missionary work, Lyon concocted an ambitious plan to see as many tourist sites as possible in and around the City of Lights. On his first evening in Paris, he ventured into the Casino de Paris but found the entertainment too titilating for his returned missionary tastes and walked out at intermission. The next day he began the usual tourist swing—Notre Dame, the Eiffel Tower, L'Opera, and, of course, the Louvre, where he "spent much time among the Greek, Roman, Egyptian, Assyrian, and Babylonian divisions [of the museum], as that sort of archeological work is very interesting to me."[93] The famous paintings and sculptures held much less excitement for him. He was already becoming a historian. On a third day he visited Rheims and several World War I battlefield sites, names made familiar by his brother Dave's participation in that conflict. Upon his return to Paris he censured, "If this is Paris, I'm glad that I was born in Salt Lake. Taxis, feminine men; and masculine women. . . . Haven't seen a good looking woman yet. . . . Kissing and loving on the streets. . . . Paris is no place for me. But I'll confess it's beautiful."[94]

The Three Wise Fools

In Paris, Lyon met up with Frank Murdock and Walter Perkins, the missionaries with whom he had come to the Netherlands. They finalized their grand plans to go all the way to Egypt and Palestine. This ambitious threesome then journeyed south by train to the city of Lyon and on to

Marseilles. There, they sadly discovered that the ship for Egypt sailed only once a week, and they had missed it by just a few hours. They each paid eighty dollars for the next week's departure on the steamer *General Metzinger*, and accepting their fate, they booked a cheap hotel for a week and visited tourist sites in the warmth of southern France. The three young men, in a country where they couldn't speak the language, started to doubt their abilities to complete their gigantic adventure and began calling themselves the "three wise fools" on a pilgrimage to the Holy Land.

On November 30, a stormy, windy day, they boarded ship and within a few hours reached calmer waters as they sailed past Corsica, Sardenia, and Crete. The ship arrived in Alexandria, Egypt, on the warm morning of December 5. Within minutes the three North Americans were running the gauntlet through hundreds of overly aggressive cab drivers, beggars, porters, travel agents, guides, and bootblacks.

After seeing sites in ancient Alexandria, they caught a noon train for a dusty, three-hour ride to Cairo. Again they were plagued by porters and would-be guides, but, Lyon commented, "we learned to plead innocent at understanding English, and [we] spoke Dutch. As no one could understand us, we learned a secret which was worth much. . . . We ignored them and it worked like a charm."[95] They spent three packed days in and around Cairo (illus. 3-10) in relative anonymity, avoiding tipping cab drivers, and disregarding insistent guides. They wandered and pondered for a full day at the three pyramids of Giza, visited the Great Mosque in Cairo, strolled through the bustle of outdoor bazaars, and spent much of one

Illus. 3-10. The "three wise fools" wearing new fezes on their postmission tour.

day in Cairo's famous museum mentally recording the glory of its statu-
ary and ancient papyri; the original tomb of King Tut, transported from
Luxor; and a cast of the Rosetta Stone.[96]

The "wise fools" boarded a train on December 8 and arrived in
Jerusalem the next morning. While trying to create their sight-seeing
agenda, a young man approached them:

> "Are you fellows Mormon missionaries?" We looked at him and
> said, "Why do you think so?" . . . And he said, "Well, you all look
> alike. . . . I've been showing them around over here for quite a
> number of years. I've got a proposition. I know you don't have
> much money, and you want to see the most for the least money. I'll
> tell you how you can do it."[97]

The young man was Fareed J. Imam, the son of one of the Arab leaders
(Mufti) of Palestine. He had indeed assisted many previous missionaries,
and in good English he proposed, "[I'll] charge you [only] fifty-five dollars
apiece. I'll provide [all] the transportation and the hotels and the sight-
seeing for [ten] days. That's [about] five dollars a day apiece."[98] The
elders quickly counted the cost, accepted the offer, and were whisked off
to a pension house just outside the walls of the old city.

For the next six days, the four saw numerous sites in and around
Jerusalem, including the Garden of Gethsemane, the Mount of Olives,
Mt. Scopus, the purported Tomb of Christ and supposed room of the
Last Supper, Calvary, and the Wailing Wall. They rode donkeys to nearby
Bethlehem, Siloam, and Emmaus. Fareed rented an old Oakland automobile and drove them to the Dead Sea, where they complained of the
heat and oppressive air pressure. They continued to the tiny town
(approximately four hundred inhabitants) of Jericho. They also traveled
to the River Jordan, where they saw the supposed exact spot where
Christ was baptized (illus. 3-11 map of travels). In his diary, Lyon frequently expressed skepticism about the authenticity of many of the places
shown to tourists. Things were simply too convenient, too easy to identify; guides were too sure about places such as a pillar where Jesus sat, a
pool where he washed the disciples' feet. The three missionaries read
from the Bible each night about the places they were to see the next day,
then discussed the importance and meaning of each. They also studied
Baedeker's guidebook, but Lyon noted that "Talmage's *Jesus the Christ*
was better than all of them. It's amazing how good that book is."[99]

On Tuesday, December 15, they left by car for northern Palestine,
driving through ancient Arab villages and new Jewish settlements. The
contrast emphasized the tensions in Palestine. There had been riots and

major disturbances in 1920 and 1921, but 1925 was a year of relative calm and peaceful acceptance. Lyon praised the order that the British seemed to maintain yet saw firsthand the conflicts in the country and the people.

The four traveled from Samaria to Nazareth, a town of about seventy-five hundred people, Lyon recorded. They then traveled to the Sea of Galilee and spent the night in a hotel in Tiberias. On subsequent days, they explored the surrounding towns of Capernaum, Bethsaida, and Cana, returning to Nazareth for more detailed study. The landscape excited them; Lyon compared it to places he'd known around St. Anthony, Idaho, or Canyon Creek in the Teton Basin. They "all agreed that Christ had [good] reason for loving the Galilee country."[100] The skepticism of hectic, touristy Jerusalem disappeared. Galilee felt much more authentic, natural, and true; here they felt Christ's presence.

Despite not being Christian, Fareed gave an honest, even spiritual depiction of Christ's life in Galilee. As a result, the three young Americans learned not only to admire Fareed, but also to appreciate his Arab faith and point of view. This friendship lasted a lifetime. Lyon and Fareed exchanged Christmas cards annually, and Murdock used Fareed's services regularly from the 1950s to the 1980s on his tours in Israel.

From Galilee, Fareed accompanied the enthusiastic missionaries to Haifa where he said good-bye and arranged for a driver to take them into French-controlled Syria, passing through Tyre and Sidon, and eventually into Beirut. In Beirut they made arrangements for their cruise back west through the Mediterranean. They also visited the American University, founded in 1866, where Lyon confessed that "I almost became homesick for the old U[niversity] of U[tah] and the student life."[101]

Although his thoughts might have drifted to his formal education, this trip itself was the most comprehensive and condensed learning he had ever experienced. In one short month since leaving the Netherlands, he had experienced life in four countries, read several books dealing with the ancient world, and observed firsthand the suffering of the masses in Egypt. He had studied the first World War to understand the roles of Britain and France in "protecting" and "mandating" Palestine and Syria, and though his biblical knowledge helped him grasp the concept of and need for a Jewish homeland, he felt a deep sympathy for the displaced Arabs who had occupied the land for so long. He had come to realize how much other nationalities and cultures could teach Americans, yet he was still sometimes critical of too much deviation from his Mormon-American ways.

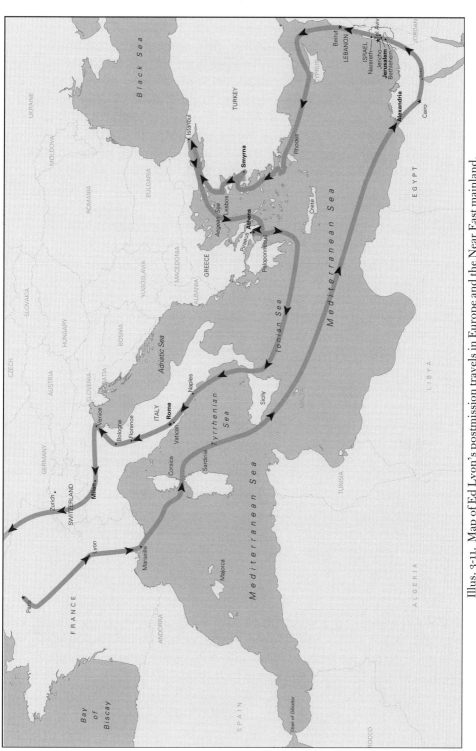

Illus. 3-11. Map of Ed Lyon's postmission travels in Europe and the Near East mainland.

Westward Passage

On Friday, December 18, the three now-wiser travelers were rowed from Beirut to the SS *Lamartine,* an old English-built steamer operated by a French line. The ensuing eleven-day trip through the Mediterranean Sea cost them each eighty dollars. The ship stopped briefly at the island of Cyprus, then cruised on to Rhodes, Ephesus, Smyrna, and through the narrow Dardanelles to Constantinople. Their pattern was to sleep— weather permitting—on the ship at night and go onshore during the day when the ship docked. This worked well until they arrived in Constan- tinople. Here, Turkish authorities insisted on visas, priced at five dollars apiece. Lyon, Murdock, and Perkins refused to pay—they were on a tight budget and felt they simply could not afford it. So for a full day and a half they lounged on the docked ship, observing the city from on deck.

They left the Turkish port on December 24, sailing smoothly through the Aegean Sea toward Greece. Lyon was elated; these were the seas and towns he'd heard about since his high school days, the places where Western civilization was born. At last he would visit Greece. On Christmas morning, still at sea, he jotted a terse entry at the top of his diary page—"(Third Christmas away from home)"—and in the next sentence, he mentioned that he hoped it would be the last one for some time.

The *Lamartine* docked in the port of Piraeus, and the awestruck young men rode a bus into Athens. Despite its being Christmas Day, they tried to see everything, running from one building to another—the Acropolis, the Temple of Athena, Mars Hill, and every other accessible site—eager to capture everything in a few short hours. At the end of the day, again aboard ship, Lyon proudly recorded, "We saw Piraeus and Athens on $2.00 and bought food and candy. Some Christmas, I'll say!" Indeed it had been some Christmas, a thrilling, hands-on excursion through classical history, mythology, and literature. Lyon contemplated: "It's easy to see where the ancient Greeks received their inspiration— these valleys and mountains are fountains of inspiration."[102]

They sailed on to the port of Naples; visited Pompeii and Mt. Vesuvius; and, on New Year's Eve, boarded a third-class train to Rome. Lyon's diary simply noted: "So ends 1925, a short one for me. And it finds me in the Eternal City." Then he pondered, "What will have happened by the end of 1926, and where shall I be?" For at least the first ten days of 1926 he was in Italy. Four full days were necessary just to see the sights of Rome. They climbed the hills, and visited the catacombs, the Sistine

Chapel, the Colosseum, the Vatican Library, and St. Peters. Lyon summarized: "The beauty of Rome exceeds my expectation."[103]

After a week in Rome, the three young men journeyed northward, parting company in Milan. Murdock and Perkins returned to Paris. Lyon bid them a temporary farewell and boarded a Swiss train for Basel. The train snaked between the snow-covered peaks of the Alps, hurried through broad glaciated valleys and past deep blue lakes, and rushed through noisy mountain tunnels. Lyon exulted in the landscape, which now reminded him of Utah, especially of "Little Zion Canyon, near La Verkin. I stood in the hallway [of the train] and sang hymns and church songs to my heart's content."[104]

After visiting friends in the mission office in Switzerland, Lyon boarded the train for his return to the Netherlands. When he arrived in Rotterdam, he "walked to the mission office and was royally received . . . and enjoyed a real, good Dutch meal again."[105] Two and a half years earlier when he had first arrived in the Netherlands, he never would have used the verb *enjoyed* to describe his response to a Dutch meal. But now he was "coming home," returning to the country and language he had learned to appreciate and love and to the people who loved him.

For thirteen days, he delighted in the rare opportunity to return to his field of labors as a nonmissionary, to stay with the members, to be a returning hero, lionized by those he had served. He slept in a different home each night and was still not able to satisfy the hospitality of many other offers. He gave forty-five-minute sermons on three occasions and basked in his newfound status as an "authority" on the Holy Land. Yet he expressed some insecurities to his parents:

> I might just as well start preparing you now for the terrible shock which you will receive when I get home. Do not expect too much of me, as I have changed very little, and am still the same old Ed, but I laugh less now. I am not a public speaker, and have lost much of my loud voice. And what is more I have a terrible time speaking English. So be prepared to receive your son as a common man, and not an orator or flashy speaker.[106]

To Great Britain

From Holland, he took an overnight ferryboat to England. He had at least three specific purposes in delaying his departure to the United States: to do genealogical studies in the land of his mother's birth, to visit old friends from Utah, and to see the important historical and cultural sites of the region.

After seeing the major attractions of London, Lyon headed north to Newcastle, where he visited with his LDSU friend Jim Armstrong, who was serving in the British Mission. They talked for eight hours straight, comparing experiences and recalling past teenage life in Utah. Two days later, Lyon entrained for Edinburgh, Scotland, and then went on to Glasgow. In both cities, he tried to research his mother's family but made no headway.

From Scotland, Lyon traveled south to Liverpool, where another dear friend from his home ward, Bob Smith, was carrying out missionary efforts. Elder Smith was a real "organizational man," now assigned to labor in the mission office. He suggested that Lyon come and visit President and Sister Talmage. The Talmages remembered the impressive young elder from their time in the Netherlands and insisted that he stay for dinner. President Talmage listened with fascination to Lyon's stories about the Holy Land and invited him to speak in a church meeting the next day, noting that despite writing his book *Jesus the Christ*, he had not been to Palestine. The next day, Lyon returned to London.

On February 10, Lyon and nine other returning missionaries—including President Hyde and his family—met in Southampton and boarded the *Aquitania* for the journey to America. It was the biggest ship Lyon had traveled on: a 901-foot-long four-stacker, with a capacity for 3,250 passengers and a crew of one thousand. They sailed across the channel to Cherbourg, France, where they picked up mail and additional passengers, and then headed out for the eight-day crossing to New York harbor. The wind blew, the swells rose, and the huge ship began nearly six days of constant swaying, bumping, and pitching. Sister Hyde was sick during the entire journey. Lyon admitted that once he was a bit "groggy" but never queasy enough to miss a meal. The days on the rough sea passed slowly with plenty of time for Lyon to read, talk, and reflect on the past thirty-one months away from home—and to anticipate his return to his loved ones in Utah. While in Europe and the Near East, Lyon had tried to see as much as possible, "because when I get back to Salt Lake, I don't think anyone will be able to get me to leave the West for some time."[107]

Home in America

In New York, elders from the Eastern States Mission office met the party of ten and took them to mission headquarters. Lyon felt that his reception in New York was rather cold in comparison to the way he had been received at mission offices in Basel, Rotterdam, and Liverpool. After taking rooms in a nearby boarding house, Lyon and the party returned to have dinner with President B. H. Roberts (illus. 3-12). Lyon wrote, "I'd known him in my father's print shop prior to that time, but this was as close as I ever came to him. He was a very dynamic, vigorous person. . . . He was idolized [by the missionaries] . . . because he had a tremendous impact upon them. He was no monkey business."[108] Lyon did not record any further observations about this scholar among the Seventies but later told stories of the very serious demeanor of the man and of the mission home he directed. One of Roberts's missionaries recalled, "He hated ignorance. . . .

Courtesy Church Archives

Illus. 3-12. B. H. Roberts, Eastern States Mission president, 1922–27.

He just loved anyone who would get in and work and produce and try to better himself."[109] The table talk was stimulating, innovative, exciting. At one point, Roberts proposed that effective missionaries be renamed "Ambassadors."[110] The brief visit was pivotal for Lyon's future career, where he would be faced with harmonizing faith and Church history.

From New York, the returning missionary traveled to Washington, D.C., to visit the tourist sites. Then he set off for Chicago, where he saw old friends and toured the University of Chicago's impressive campus, to which he would return in a few short years.

On February 22, the group loaded their travel-worn luggage aboard the Los Angeles Limited for the last train ride home. The train followed a route similar to that of the early Latter-day Saint pioneers: through Iowa to North Platte, Nebraska; then on to Cheyenne and Green River, Wyoming; down Echo Canyon, and into the Salt Lake Valley. The anticipation grew strong, especially after forty-three hours on the clickety-clack train. Finally, at 2:30 P.M. on Wednesday, February 24, 1926, the train braked to a stop in Salt Lake City's Union Pacific depot, where most of the Lyon family was waiting. Lyon's mother was at home, fixing a gigantic meal. The welcomes were teary. In a simple diary entry, too brief for the emotion of the moment, Lyon noted, "It certainly seems good to be home again."[111]

It was good to be home, but it had also been very good to travel. Lyon had been on the move for ninety-nine days. He had visited fourteen countries and toured many of the major cities of the world: Paris, Marseilles, Alexandria, Cairo, Jerusalem, Beirut, Smyrna, Constantinople, Athens, Naples, Rome, Venice, Milan, Basel, Brussels, Antwerp, Amsterdam, London, Edinburgh, Glasgow, Liverpool, New York, Washington, D.C., and Chicago.

Besides these twenty-four large, historical cities, he had also motored through villages and towns in Palestine, filling his eyes and imagination with scenes from the Old and New Testaments. He and his traveling companions had taken many pictures, purchased post cards, and behaved wisely and maturely most of the time. The whole adventure was bold and daring, an excursion into unfamiliar lands and languages, into cultures very different from Utah or the Netherlands. Most missionaries of the time did some touring on their return home, but few journeyed so far. The entire trip had covered approximately 12,500 miles.

The experience taught Lyon and his partners confidence in travel and enjoyment of diverse cultures and customs. It broadened their perspectives on life, on world conflicts, and on religion. The traveling even opened Frank Murdock's eyes to business possibilities in the tourism industry: years later he founded the Franklin J. Murdock Travel Agency. Most of all, the trip was an education, a chance for young men from the remote western United States to experience the world outside Utah. Lyon used his experiences as inspiration and background for hundreds of talks, lectures, and classes during the next fifty years of his life.

Lyon spent approximately $550.00 during the 99 traveling days—money well spent in terms of long-range return. When asked in later years how he regarded the trip, he affirmed:

> It was a real crowning glory to the mission because we'd been preaching the gospel and didn't know too much about it. To get over there [Palestine] and see the country and see the way the people lived . . . the shepherds still living in their tents, nomads with these old black wool tents. . . .
>
> You learn what they say in the Bible when Jesus went into a house to eat bread because you get bread, bread, bread, not too much meat. . . . And you see Elisha's fountain down there in Jerico and as far as it runs it's paradise. . . . It was a real eye opener to give you a sense of feeling for the Bible.[112]

Frank Murdock recalled that "we've used these experiences all during our lives. Whenever the three of us get together, we recall what a marvelous trip it was."[113] The trip was the crowning jewel of their experiences, the dessert after the main course of the mission.

The frightened, shy twenty-year-old who had arrived in the Netherlands in 1923 was now a very different man. In thirty-one months, he had
grown tremendously in confidence, knowledge, language abilities (in
both Dutch and English), personal dedication, testimony, love for
people, love for the gospel, and love for the Lord. An equal period of
time at a university or in a job would never have effected the dramatic
changes that occurred during his mission. Future confidence, teaching
skills, attitudes toward the less fortunate, general knowledge of peoples
and cultures, and a love for Christian and Latter-day Saint Church
history all found their origins in this mission experience. Lyon was
beginning to understand the great pioneer legacy of missionary work—
taking the gospel to all the world. Just as Elder Talmage had hoped and
suggested, Lyon did indeed count his mission as "one of the treasures
of his life."

Notes

1. Thomas Alexander, *Mormonism in Transition: A History of the Latter-day
Saints* (Urbana: University of Illinois Press, 1985), 301.

2. See note 13 in chapter 1.

3. T. Edgar Lyon, "Oral History," bound typescript, 250, T. Edgar Lyon Collection, Church Archives, Family and Church History Department, The Church of
Jesus Christ of Latter-day Saints, Salt Lake City (hereafter cited as Church
Archives). Unless otherwise noted, all citations for T. Edgar Lyon materials are
located in the Lyon Collection.

4. T. Edgar Lyon, "Oral History," 250.

5. T. Edgar Lyon, "Oral History," 250.

6. T. Edgar Lyon, "A Blessing and Its Fulfilment [*sic*]," *Millennial Star* 98
(1936): 613.

7. T. Edgar Lyon, "Oral History," 43.

8. T. Edgar Lyon, "A Blessing and Its Fulfilment," 613.

9. T. Edgar Lyon, Diary, July 13, 1923, Church Archives.

10. T. Edgar Lyon, Diary, July 18, 1923.

11. T. Edgar Lyon to parents, July 25, 1923, Church Archives.

12. T. Edgar Lyon to parents, July 25, 1923.

13. T. Edgar Lyon, Diary, July 28, 1923.

14. T. Edgar Lyon Jr., *John Lyon: The Life of a Pioneer Poet* (Provo: BYU Religious Studies Center, 1989), 173–74.

15. Francis M. Gibbons, *David O. McKay, Apostle to the World, Prophet of God*
(Salt Lake City: Deseret Book, 1986), 124.

16. The period from 1920 to 1924 was a boom time for missionaries, and it represented a 487 percent increase in the number of missionaries over the previous five-year span. Gordon Irving, "Numerical Strength and Geographical Distribution of the LDS Missionary Force, 1930–1974," Task Papers in LDS History no. 1 (Salt Lake City: Church Archives, 1975), tables 8, 9.

17. Richard O. Cowan, *The Church in the Twentieth Century* (Salt Lake City: Bookcraft, 1985), 277.

18. See "Rules for Missionaries" in appendix A.

19. T. Edgar Lyon, "Oral History," 44.

20. T. Edgar Lyon, "Oral History," 45.

21. T. Edgar Lyon, "A Blessing and Its Fulfilment," 614.

22. Keith C. Warner, "History of the Netherlands Mission of The Church of Jesus Christ of Latter-day Saints, 1861–1966" (master's thesis, Brigham Young University, 1967), 9, 21, 153.

23. Andrew Jenson, *Latter-day Saint Biographical Encyclopedia: A Compilation of Biographical Sketches of Prominent Men and Women in The Church of Jesus Christ of Latter-day Saints,* 4 vols. (Salt Lake City: Andrew Jenson History, 1901–36), 4:353.

24. T. Edgar Lyon, "Oral History," 50–51.

25. T. Edgar Lyon, "Oral History," 51, 55.

26. Warner, "History of the Netherlands Mission," 155. There were no female missionaries in the Netherlands at the time, although a few were serving in other European missions. Despite worldwide requests, there were relatively few women serving in any foreign countries. President Grant set the policy: "Lady missionaries, we want it understood, are called to labor in the United States. . . . We feel it is a mistake to send our sisters further away." Heber J. Grant, "President Heber J. Grant's Conference Message," *Improvement Era* 29 (May 1926): 684.

27. The 1924 Johnson-Reed National Origins Act made it much more difficult for Dutch citizens to enter the United States. Thomas A. Aleinikoff and David A. Martin, *Immigration: Process and Policy* (St. Paul, Minn.: West Publishing, 1985), 50; Jack P. Greene, ed., *Encyclopedia of American Political History,* 3 vols. (New York: Scribner's and Sons, 1983), 2:588. From 1924 to 1926 Dutch membership swelled from 2,985 to 3,770 as potential emigrants were forced to stay in the Netherlands. Warner, "History of the Netherlands Mission," 155.

28. Warner, "History of the Netherlands Mission," 155.

29. This chart is compiled from data provided by Warner, "History of the Netherlands Mission," 150.

30. T. Edgar Lyon, Diary, July 31, 1923.

31. T. Edgar Lyon, Diary, August 1, 1923.

32. T. Edgar Lyon, Diary, August 11, 1923.

33. T. Edgar Lyon, Diary, August 25, 1923.

34. T. Edgar Lyon to parents, August 31, 1923, Church Archives.

35. T. Edgar Lyon to parents, June 16, 1924, Church Archives.

36. Annual Report of the Netherlands Mission, 1921, Church Archives.

37. T. Edgar Lyon, Diary, August 28, 1923.

38. T. Edgar Lyon to parents, August 25, 1923, Church Archives.

39. In the following 1966 letter to Ostler, Lyon gives insight into the great start Ostler provided him:

Dear Roy,

For years I talked to the missionaries in the mission home. . . . I told them of going to the Helder with you on a boat—an 8 hour trip—but how you capitalized on it to preach the gospel to the people on the boat—they could not escape, and how you had me sell pamphlets "Wat is Het Evengelie?" Then, when you had done the first class, you went to the second class at the rear of the boat, and repeated the performance. As we were walking to the prow, an hour out of the Helder, you passed the open hatch of the engine room, and looked down at the engineer, and said "That isn't nearly as hot as the place you are going if you don't repent."

. . . Well, Roy I want to tell you that you captivated my heart, and set an example of what a missionary could do with his time, that I've never forgotten. And it wasn't all ultra serious, such as the laugh I had when you had Pres. Noorlander hunting for fleas, when in reality it was bits of hair from Cornelis Tellekamp's hair you had put under the sheet.

Ed

40. Warner, "History of the Netherlands Mission," 165.

41. Franklin J. Murdock, Oral History (Salt Lake City: Oral History Program, 1973), 24.

42. T. Edgar Lyon, "Oral History," 49.

43. T. Edgar Lyon to parents, September 7, 1923, Church Archives.

44. T. Edgar Lyon to parents, August 31, 1923.

45. T. Edgar Lyon, Diary, September 23, 1923.

46. T. Edgar Lyon, "A Blessing and Its Fulfilment," 614–15, 620.

47. T. Edgar Lyon, "Oral History," 48.

48. T. Edgar Lyon, Diary, November 29, 1923.

49. T. Edgar Lyon, Diary, January 1, 1924.

50. T. Edgar Lyon to parents, August 31, 1923.

51. T. Edgar Lyon, Diary, April, 29, 1924.

52. T. Edgar Lyon, Diary, May 29, 1924.

53. T. Edgar Lyon to parents, November 10, 1923, Church Archives.

54. Warner, "History of the Netherlands Mission," 37–38.

55. Warner, "History of the Netherlands Mission," 41–42.

56. T. Edgar Lyon, Diary, January 21, 1923.

57. T. Edgar Lyon to parents, June 24, 1924, Church Archives.

58. Gibbons, David O. McKay, 126.

59. James B. Allen, "David O. McKay," in *Encyclopedia of Mormonism,* 2:370–75.

60. T. Edgar Lyon to parents, June 24, 1924.

61. T. Edgar Lyon to parents, May 20, 1924, Church Archives.

62. T. Edgar Lyon to parents, June 23, 1924, Church Archives.
63. T. Edgar Lyon, Diary, June 24, 1924.
64. T. Edgar Lyon, Diary, June 24, 1924.
65. T. Edgar Lyon to parents, July 5, 1924, Church Archives.
66. T. Edgar Lyon, Diary, September 20, 1925.
67. T. Edgar Lyon, Diary, n.d.
68. T. Edgar Lyon to Charles S. Hyde, November 28, 1924, Church Archives.
69. T. Edgar Lyon to parents, July 26, 1924, Church Archives.
70. T. Edgar Lyon to parents, September 27, 1924, Church Archives.
71. T. Edgar Lyon to parents, December 6, 1924, Church Archives.
72. T. Edgar Lyon to Charles S. Hyde, January 26, 1925, Church Archives.
73. Lyon to Hyde, January 26, 1925.
74. T. Edgar Lyon to parents, February 14, 1925, Church Archives.
75. There was no unified teaching plan for the Church at the time. Each missionary determined his own teaching approach. Passing out tracts in Dutch was the usual method of introducing the gospel to would-be investigators. Missionaries in the Netherlands used:

1. *Rays of Living Light,* by Charles W. Penrose, twelve scripture-filled pamphlets on basic principles, authority, revelation, the Ten Tribes and so on.
2. *What is the Gospel,* a sixteen-page summary of the above twelve tracts, written by former mission president, John P. Lilywhite.
3. *Friendly Discussion,* a basic tract by Ben Rich.
4. *Voice of Warning,* by Parley P. Pratt.
5. *Key to Theology,* by Parley P. Pratt.
6. The Book of Mormon.
7. Other standard works. (Lyon, "Oral History," 67–69)

The *Key to Theology* fell from favor during Lyon's mission.

One of the Protestant ministers got hold of it and wrote an anti-Mormon book on the unchristian, Godless people who were worshipping a man and degrading God by making people almost vault into Godhood at the moment they died. . . . So President Hyde got word from Salt Lake to destroy all copies. All of them were destroyed, but I [kept] one. But as I remember it, they held the fire out in back of the mission home and burned them all. (Lyon, "Oral History," 67)

The Book of Mormon cost two guilders (nearly a dollar) and was too expensive for most investigators, who generally came from the poorer classes. At that time, the Book of Mormon was not thought of as an essential tool in missionary work, as it is now.

Lyon almost had an obsession with keeping accurate track of numbers. At the back of his mission diary several summary entries record tracts and books that he dispensed. Under the heading "Literature Distributed in Holland," he lists:

(1) Tracts   22,738

(2) Booklets

–given away	388	
–loaned	20	
–sold	353	

(3) Books of Mormon

–given away	5	
–loaned	5	
–sold	10	

(4) Standard Works

–given away	3	
–loaned	2	
–sold	9	

(5) Other Church works

–given away	2	
–loaned	15	
–sold	12	

76. T. Edgar Lyon, Diary, March 18, 1925.

77. T. Edgar Lyon to Charles S. Hyde, April 24, 1925, Church Archives.

78. T. Edgar Lyon, Diary, April 21, 1925.

79. T. Edgar Lyon, "Oral History," 59.

80. T. Edgar Lyon, "Oral History," 59.

81. T. Edgar Lyon, "Oral History," 60.

82. T. Edgar Lyon, "Oral History," 63.

83. T. Edgar Lyon, Diary, October 16, 1925.

84. T. Edgar Lyon, Diary, August 10, 1925.

85. Mary C. Lyon to T. Edgar Lyon, July 24, 1925, Church Archives.

86. T. Edgar Lyon to parents, September 12, 1925, Church Archives.

87. T. Edgar Lyon to parents, September 21, 1925, Church Archives.

88. T. Edgar Lyon, "Oral History," 56.

89. T. Edgar Lyon, Diary, October 11, 1925; also T. Edgar Lyon, "Oral History," 56.

90. T. Edgar Lyon, Diary, September 26, 1925.

91. James E. Talmage to David R. Lyon, November 5, 1925, Church Archives.

92. See item number 36 of appendix A, "Letter from Elder Rudger Clawson."

93. T. Edgar Lyon to parents, November 21, 1925, Church Archives.

94. T. Edgar Lyon, Diary, November 17, 1925, Church Archives.

95. T. Edgar Lyon, Diary, December 6, 1925.

96. T. Edgar Lyon, Diary, December 6–7, 1925.

97. T. Edgar Lyon, "Oral History," 73.

98. Murdock, "Oral History," 46.

99. T. Edgar Lyon, "Oral History," 72.

100. T. Edgar Lyon, Diary, December 16, 1925.

101. T. Edgar Lyon, Diary, December 17, 1925.

102. T. Edgar Lyon, Diary, December 25, 1925.

103. T. Edgar Lyon, Diary, January 1, 1926.

104. T. Edgar Lyon, Diary, January 10, 1926.

105. T. Edgar Lyon, Diary, January 13, 1926.

106. T. Edgar Lyon to parents, January 15, 1926, Church Archives.

107. T. Edgar Lyon to parents, February 16, 1926, Church Archives.

108. T. Edgar Lyon, "Oral History," 76–77.

109. Truman G. Madsen, *Defender of the Faith: The B. H. Roberts Story* (Salt Lake City: Bookcraft, 1980), 324.

110. Madsen, *Defender of the Faith*, 331.

111. T. Edgar Lyon, Diary, February 24, 1926.

112. T. Edgar Lyon, "Oral History," 75, 76.

113. Murdock, "Oral History," 47.

4

From Homecoming to Honeymoon, 1926–27

The life-changing and sacred experiences in the Netherlands, the eye-opening educational tour through seven European countries, and the spiritual thrill of the Holy Land were all gratifying and valuable memories for Ed Lyon. But they weren't quite as good as just being home in Utah, the arid West, among familiar mountains and friendly people. Bed sheets were flealess and dry, vegetables and fruits were plentiful, and every meal that Mary Lyon prepared was a feast. Despite the late February cold of Utah (illus. 4-1), so different from the bone-chilling dampness of the Netherlands, Lyon felt warm, the deep-down warmth of home.

Less than twenty-four hours after his arrival in Utah, Ed and his father walked to the Church's headquarters, where Ed reported on his missionary labors and travels to some of the Brethren. He then delivered carefully packed gifts sent by Dutch Saints to their relatives residing in Utah, and he took letters and greetings to the parents of Jim Armstrong, Bob Smith, and others. He gripped the armrests of a dentist's chair for two long hours while several cavities, brought from Europe, were drilled and washed down the drain. His mother put him to work scraping the varnish off the pine woodwork in the house, sanding it, and then painting it a soft ivory color. He enjoyed this restful physical labor. He renewed acquaintance with brothers and sisters and spent long hours weaving tales about life with the Hollanders and his lengthy travels, illustrating many of his stories with pictures, especially from the Holy Land. He thanked his father repeatedly for the abundant support during his mission and postmission trip. When asked later if he had had any troubles readjusting to civilian life, Lyon recalled, "I was too busy, just didn't have any time at all to worry about [that]."[1]

David Lyon had recently been released as bishop, after serving nearly fourteen years, and was immediately called to the spiritually challenging positions of stake patriarch and gospel doctrine teacher in his home ward. On his first Sunday home, Ed spoke and passed around his pictures in priesthood meeting and to the 452 people present in Sunday School.[2]

This talk impressed certain adults of the ward, especially Willard R. Smith, a former counselor to David and son of deceased Church President Joseph F. Smith. Willard suggested that young Ed be called as his second counselor in the Sunday School superintendency, a responsible administrative assignment almost always reserved for older adults. Ed accepted. During his mission, he had pondered on his life and penned his thoughts: "My ancestors had foresight enough to follow a prophet of God into the valleys of the mountains, and I owe a life of service to others for it."[3] He would serve in the Sunday School willingly and gratefully.

On Sunday, March 28, 1926, after Ed had been home a full month, the ward scheduled an official homecoming report. Ed wrote, "I occupied the entire time at the evening sacrament meeting (one full hour +). I told of my mission and trip to Palestine. Sort of bored 'em."[4] The speech was an early indication that history would be Ed's forte:

> I started by describing how way back . . . before the time of Christ people from the Rhine Valley and the Black Forest of Germany who were peace-loving people who didn't like the contention and the fighting and the quarreling . . . had floated down the Rhine River . . . had settled there [in lowland swamps] because they figured they'd be left alone. . . . Then I told about the growth of these people. They had always had this idea of an independence.[5]

He then discussed intellectual and political ideas that demonstrated how "Holland is more like America than it is like England" regarding deeds to

Illus. 4-1. Ed Lyon as a recently returned missionary shoveling snow in Salt Lake City.

property, free education, ridding itself of the idea of primogeniture, and the concept of a republic with two branches of government. He spoke of the artistic appreciation of the Dutch people and the closeness of Dutch families. Then he expressed his profound love for the people.[6] The hour-long talk appealed to the intellectual traditions of the large, 1,217-member ward. Ed was no longer "Bish," the bishop's son; he now had his own identity as a bright young man with a firm grasp of the gospel and an enduring testimony.

First Love

A shy, blond, seventeen-year-old girl had recited a poem at Ed's mission farewell. She was also present during his homecoming speech. Ed hardly knew her prior to his mission—she was two and a half years younger than he and ran with a different crowd. She was now twenty and during Ed's mission had attended the University of Utah, received a temporary teaching certificate, and taught fifth grade for a year in Sigurd, Utah. Her name, Laura Hermana Forsberg, first appeared in Ed's diary on April 16, 1926. They both attended a ward party that night, and surprisingly, Ed danced several numbers, some of them with Hermana. His diary casually notes, "Took Hermana Forsberg home."[7]

Laura Hermana Forsberg always went by her middle name, frequently explaining that it was not the Spanish word for "sister" but the Swedish feminization of Herman. Her family background was fully Swedish, springing from Hedstrom, Ockander, Stengard, and Forsberg stock. Her father, Gustave Forsberg, was born in Sweden but emigrated to Utah with his then non–Latter-day Saint parents in the early 1890s. In Utah the entire family joined the Church, and Gustave returned to Sweden as a missionary in 1900.

Hermana's independent-minded mother, Hermana Maria Christina Ockander, was also born in Sweden. She joined the Church there, emigrated to Utah, and served as a missionary in the Central United States Mission from 1903 to 1905. Gustave waited for her during her mission, and they were married on April 26, 1905. Their first child—Laura Hermana— was born ten months later, on February 14, 1906 (illus. 4-2). Three other children, including a set of twins, were born within three years. Hermana Maria died from tuberculosis just one day after Hermana's eighth birthday (illus. 4-3). Gustave remarried shortly after her death, but the four children from the first marriage never bonded closely with their stepmother and found their new home a difficult place to live.

Hermana Forsberg

Illus. 4-2. Laura Hermana Forsberg at six months old.

In 1913 the family moved from their tiny house on Pugsley Avenue in the Twenty-Second Ward to a much larger home in the Ensign Ward. There, Hermana attended Ensign Elementary School and then Bryant Junior High School, where she skipped a grade due to advanced skills in basic subjects (illus. 4-4). She served as valedictorian at the parting ceremonies from junior high school. Her father owned the prospering Wasatch Electric Company, which allowed Hermana to follow the pattern of many of the youth in the Ensign Ward and attend the private LDSU, where she graduated at age seventeen. Although her family had no tradition of higher education, she attended the University of Utah, preparing herself for an elementary education teaching certificate.[7]

After teaching for a year in Sigurd, Utah, twenty-year-old Hermana had returned to Salt Lake City and was taking classes at the U. She loved music, drama, and art, as evidenced by her poetic reading at Ed's 1923 farewell. While at the university, she acted in occasional dramatic productions. She described herself as shy and lacking in self-confidence, to some extent due to the discouragement and criticism she received from her stepmother. In the Ensign Ward, despite her youth, she served in the presidency of the Young Women's Mutual Improvement Association, where she taught dramatics and put on small theatrical

Illus. 4-3. Hermana's mother and father, Hermana age six, and her brother Norman, age four. Because Hermana's mother had tuberculosis, she spent winter 1912 sleeping in this tent.

productions. She also taught a children's class in the Sunday School. In later years, Lyon told his family that on the first Sunday back from his mission, he "saw her walking down the ramp in the Ensign Ward with her class, and knew [at that time] that he would marry her."[8] Hermana possessed physical beauty, with a clear and fair complexion, blonde hair trimmed around her ears, a soft smile, and glowing radiance.

Ed's diaries of this period (1926–27) are sketchy and irregular: he wrote only thirty-six entries from the time he returned from his mission until his marriage eighteen months later. Even those entries were usually brief and straightforward, merely recording the activities of the day. On

Illus. 4-4. Hermana, left, with a cousin, 1913.

the few occasions when he talked of his relationship with Hermana, he frequently glided into Dutch, worried, perhaps, that his younger sister might snoop in the diary. The second mention of Hermana occurred two months after the first, when on June 20, 1926, Ed recorded: "Walked with H. F. after meeting. A wonderful evening, *en wij hadden en mooi gesprek en belijdenis*" [and we had a pleasant conversation and pledged our love to each other].[9] The term *belijdenis* indicates a confession or a testimony of love, almost in the religious sense.

Hermana always viewed that day as the pivotal point of their relationship. She wrote: "On Sunday, June 20 Ed and I took a walk up City Creek Canyon. The world has been different ever since."[10] Hermana wrote only two diary entries in 1926. She likely had written about feelings and friendships prior to meeting Ed, but the first thirty-two pages of her journal have been torn out and thrown away. She had probably dated other young men and simply wanted to destroy the evidence once she became serious with Ed. Hermana's irregular diary entries portray her as a dreamy young romantic, recording sunsets and sunrises, watching the flowers bloom, and embracing every day with sentimental gusto. Ed brought her chocolates and flowers. They held hands as they walked to church together. Just four months after his return to Utah, the relationship was becoming serious.

Ed and Hermana had fallen in love in the spring. Ed gathered dogtooth violets from the hills and brought them to the young woman who gave him so much happiness. Daffodils and red tulips, smaller than the ones in the Netherlands, were next. In the summer, he gave roses. Even though he was attending summer school at the University of Utah, he created plenty of opportunities to be with Hermana and her family, especially on weekends or holidays.

On a Saturday, after a full day of work at his father's office, Ed "called on Hermana in the evening. Long talk, read a book, *Acres of Diamonds.* Wonderful talk with *bilooften en belydenissen van befde van beide partyen* [promises and assurances of our mutual love that were finally sealed with a beautiful and holy kiss—oh! how wonderful this was, coming from her! From now on life will become better, delightful]."[11] They had been seeing each other for three months and, finally, the ecstatic moment of the first kiss! Now the relationship picked up steam. *Acres of Diamonds,* by popular motivational speaker Russell H. Conwell, was first published in 1915. It reproduced a classic talk that Conwell delivered across the United States, stimulating young men and women to seize opportunity by finding the hidden treasures under their feet. Ed and Hermana were finding theirs, especially the small mountain flowers.

For three days over the long Pioneer Day weekend of July 24, the two of them and Hermana's siblings walked approximately sixteen miles up City Creek Canyon to Rotary Grove and over the summit to Morgan, Utah, to the home of Hermana's Uncle Charlie and Aunt Hilma Forsberg. They rode horses, visited with family members, and basked in acceptance and love. Ed records some emotion, noting, "Thus ended a never-to-be-forgotten trip."[12] Hermana exulted in the emotions caused by the beauty of this familiar place, now seen in the light of newfound love: "I shall never forget a glimpse I had of the sun going down in a little hollow, bathing the meadows and hills in gold. . . . It seemed like a glimpse of the infinite. It made me feel as if I could always live wisely and well."[13] They went to a dance and waltzed to the tune of "Always," singing, "I'll be loving you, *always,* with a love that's true, *always.*"

The next month they were in Brighton with Hermana's younger sister and brothers at the cabin of Nephi L. Morris. Over the Labor Day weekend, they took a long walk, gathering sticky piñon pinecones. Hermana twisted her ankle severely but stuck it out, despite pain and swelling. The couple loved to be outdoors together, and they loved each other.

Hermana loved the strength, the power, the wisdom of this returned missionary. His presence thrilled her as she studied his serene face, and his handsome, curly dark hair. She enjoyed the esteem the older adults of the ward held for him. She later told her children that she sensed a deep spirituality. She knew that he was intelligent and that, with her support, they would have a brilliant future. She loved his calm home, his accepting and sweet mother, and his saintly father.

Ed was swept away by Hermana's beauty, by her love of children and teaching, and by the confidence she had gained through dramatic art presentations. He had received a spiritual confirmation in the Ensign Ward hallway that she was the one for him, and he did not waver, even when she was unsure. He loved the confidence she had in him, more steady than his own.

Ed shared his feelings with a few others. His family saw and recognized the signs, but his two best friends were still serving their missions. He wrote to Bob Smith and Jim Armstrong, hesitantly but firmly admitting his love. The letter he received from Armstrong is a classic of male friendship, humor, and just plain clever writing:

September 11, 1926

Eddie, The Bold

Romance Street

Walled City

Dear Softie:

. . . . Wake up partner, shake the dust out of your whiskers. . . . . Are you not the same dumb-bell that was president of one "Woman Hater's Club"? Then how come you fall for the queen of Sheba without first asking the permission of the board of directors? To say that you are a first class numskull would be putting things mild. . . . let me call your attention to the probable headlines that will no doubt appear . . . when a reporter gets the story for the press.

–LYON'S ROAR TAMED TO WHISPER–

Local Sheba boasts of the deed.

or

-HERMIT OF FIVE POINTS FOUND

OFF CENTER-

Falls Like Ton of Lead For Skirt. . . .

Now that I have frightened you to death or nearly, let me implore you to impart the great secret to me when and where is the splicing to take place. If you procrastinate until Brother Smittie and I return, then I will do all I can to help you fix things up but on the other mit, if you choose to make this a hurry up affair and plan on excluding your partners in crime from your big bull-fest, then I am sure we will derive much and plenty pleasure out of exposing you.[14]

The letter continues for many paragraphs, needling the shy young man for getting serious with a young lady without consulting his old buddies.

Despite the advice and teasing, the romance continued. But the couple did indeed "procrastinate"; Ed was eager to marry, but his young girlfriend still had many obligations to fill. Hermana had returned to the University of Utah in fall 1925, and she also taught half-day kindergarten at Lafayette School. At the U, she took classes in elementary education, psychology, public speaking, English, and physical education. She graduated with a two-year Grammar Grade diploma on June 8, 1926. Before Ed's return, she had considered going back to teach in central Utah after graduating, but now the added complication of love would not allow the distance. Instead, she applied somewhat late but received a contract to teach third grade at Jackson Elementary School in Salt Lake City during the 1926–27 school year.[15]

Romantic Turmoil

Just three weeks after returning from Europe, Ed had begun the spring quarter at the University of Utah. The Lyon and Forsberg homes were just five blocks from each other, and Hermana and Ed often walked the two miles to school together. Largely as a result of his mission, Ed realized that he wanted to be a teacher: "I came home feeling that I believed I would like to teach. I had a sister [Carol] who was a teacher and she encouraged me. I . . . had made up my mind that I didn't want to become a lawyer, I wanted to teach."[16] Ed immediately began courses in secondary education, and he now knew that history would be his basic area of academic emphasis.

Ed attended the U for five quarters after his mission—spring, summer, and autumn 1926, and winter and spring 1927. School was not just academics and study time. During his first quarter he "pledged" and joined the Friars' Club, a campus social group for male returned missionaries. He was even selected as chairman of the "goats," the entering pledges. As part of their initiation into the fraternity they all participated in a spoof of *Cinderella*. Ed amused the group by twirling around in the role of the fairy godmother. The initiation was completed when "we were paddled, and hard, too."[17] This was truly a different Ed, a more confident, fun-loving, social student.

Ed took Hermana to Friars' parties and even attended a few dances: "I had never been a social lion. I have no sense of rhythm . . . I would dance but it was purely mechanical. The music doesn't mean anything. . . . I would rather do a day's work than dance but [Hermana] loves to dance."[18] He also attended plays with her, not because he loved the theater but because he loved Hermana. It was a magical time. Neither of them had previously experienced the joy of strong romantic commitment; life was now so exciting, promising, thrilling. But no date was set, no formal promises made.

Christmas 1926 provided an opportunity for romantic exchange—she gave him a black leather briefcase; he reciprocated with a subscription to *National Geographic* and a handsomely carved leather album that he had commissioned a Dutch member to complete. They took a sleigh ride that evening, zooming down the snowy road from Tenth to First. "The day was simply perfect. Words can't describe my happiness," Hermana recorded in her diary.[19]

Throughout her diary, Hermana often anguished over her inability to verbally express her feelings of love. For whatever reasons—Hermana blamed her unhappy home and hence an inability to risk sharing feelings—she had a hard time telling her beloved how deeply she felt about him. Even her few diary entries only obliquely express her deep feelings. Ed was much more vocal concerning his commitment to the relationship, and he often expressed his feelings to Hermana in poetry and poetic prose. The ecstasy of their first kiss was so vivid that Ed wrote about it several years later. Most of his extant poetry extols Hermana's beauty and virtue. (For examples of this poetry, see Appendix C.)

A second romantic holiday presented itself—Valentine's Day 1927, which was also Hermana's twenty-first birthday. After a silent movie at the Paramount Theater, Ed gave her a dozen red roses and his Friars' pin. Now they were "pinned," promised to each other, with vague plans to be engaged and married soon. Four days later, on February 18, Ed accompanied Hermana when she received her endowment in the Salt Lake Temple.[20]

Ed was doing well in his classes, and Hermana was working, able to save a small amount of money. However, despite the spiritual and emotional highs, doubts and problems crept in. The uncertainty about where Ed would find a job made Hermana hesitant about their future together. Ed confided to his datebook that he was eager to get married. On May 18, Ed began a diary notation in English but quickly switched to Dutch: "We have been talking of *en toe, van trowen. Wij hadden . . .* [getting married, from time to time. We had already decided to get married this summer]. But tonight she told me: 'It won't work, because it wouldn't be wise for us to do so. This is my decision, and it may not happen until next year.'" Hermana's doubts and her rational approach to major decisions had, at least momentarily, triumphed over the joy of a quick marriage—she apparently wanted to wait until they were more financially secure. Ward member and friend Nephi Morris had told her during the previous summer at Brighton that she was trying to "intellectualize her heart."[21]

Ed was distraught. But the next dawn brought yet another change: "This morning I met Hermana as she was going to [teach] school, and she said 'I have thought it over and have changed my mind—it will be this summer.' In the evening we took a walk, and decided . . . to go to Rigby [Idaho] together."[22] For several weeks, Ed had been considering a teaching job in Rigby but did not want to go without his sweetheart; now they could marry and go together. The next day, before Hermana could change her mind, Ed "asked Brother and Sister Forsberg if I might marry their daughter—they agreed. Then we came down here, and spoke to [my] father and mother about it. All seem to feel all right about it."[23] The following day, he and his mother hastily bought a small 0.31 carat diamond at Daynes Jewelry. Ed and Hermana walked to a favorite spot in Spring Hollow, where he built a fire and quickly slipped the ring on her slender finger. That night he wrote, in Dutch, that they had also made plans for their honeymoon in the mountains. But on May 24, Hermana still displayed some insecurity. Ed recorded a quote from Hermana: "'I don't believe this [marriage] will ever go through!' L.H.F." Within a few weeks, however, all was again calm as wedding plans resumed in the Forsberg and Lyon homes.[24]

History at the U

During the romantic turmoil of spring 1927, Hermana continued teaching at Jackson School, and Ed pursued his studies at the U (illus. 4-5). While on his mission, he had vowed to do much better in his studies, and he now followed through on this promise. He determined that besides his major in history, he would have a minor in philosophy. His grades reflect his dedication and purpose. He received only A's and

B's, achieving a 3.51 grade point average during his last two years. Among the teachers who encouraged the now eager student were the following:

Andrew Runni Anderson (ancient language)
Milton Bennion (education)
Herbert Bolton (history; visiting professor)
LeRoy Cowles (education)
E. E. Erickson (philosophy)
George E. Fellows (history)
James L. Gibson (English)
Andrew Kerr (archaeology)
Joseph F. Merrill (physics)
Dorothy Snow (education)
John T. Wahlquist (education)
Levi Edgar Young (history)

Joseph F. Merrill, who was ordained an Apostle in 1931 and later served as Ed's mentor in the Church Educational System, exerted a strong influence and was a role model and friend. Ed had taken three quarters of physics with Merrill in 1922. Milton Bennion, who served as General Sunday School Superintendent for the Church, encouraged

Courtesy Special Collections Dept., J. Willard Marriott Library, Universtiy of Utah

Illus. 4-5. Park Administration building at the U in the early 1920s.

Ed to be a teacher. E. E. Erickson, a highly respected and even feared professor of philosophy, taught courses in aesthetics and ethics of the scriptures to young Ed.[25]

Ed was keenly aware of campus conflicts that pitted Latter-day Saints against professors of other faiths; such conflicts often resulted in confusion and antagonism among the students. Ed had a class from Dean James L. Gibson, "one of the most cantankerous persons for a dean I've seen. He helped influence me to get out of this School of Arts and Sciences by his [anti-Mormon] nature and disposition."[26] Ed contrasted Gibson to the "kindly, loving Milton Bennion, who was a good administrator but had an understanding of students."[27] The conflicts over the role of religion in education were never resolved, but in Ed's time the Latter-day Saint view usually dominated at the U because of the predominance of Mormon faculty members and students.

Ed registered for heavy course loads, taking eighteen or nineteen hours each quarter. During his final two quarters, he served a type of apprenticeship as a student teacher in the old student training school, a junior high program that provided practical experience for both faculty and students. By the end of spring quarter, Ed had completed all the required classes, and he graduated with a Bachelor of Science degree on June 7, 1927. History was his major area of preparation; he took ten history courses (39 hours). Philosophy was an official minor, but Ed also emphasized political science. His grades in the required English classes had been his lowest in any subject, and he had avoided taking any foreign languages, still feeling a weakness in that area; hence, he received a Bachelor of Science rather than an "Arts" degree.

Ed's parents had good reason to attend and be proud at graduation— Ed and Kyle graduated on the same day, both receiving their degrees with honors. Kyle had begun courses during the same quarter as his younger brother in 1921. He had performed very well and was one of the twenty-two students who graduated with "high honors"; Ed received an "honors" designation with his diploma, putting him among the top ten percent of the 514 students in the graduating class but not quite as high as Kyle.[28]

The university hosted a commencement parade, followed by a sit-down ceremony at which the speaker, according to Ed, mouthed "45 minutes of incomprehensible bunk"[29] on the topic of "Some Problems of Life and Destiny." Afterward the two brothers paraded across the stand to receive degrees and perfunctory congratulations. Later, Ed and Hermana went to the graduation dinner at the elegant Hotel Utah and then danced at the ball.

Church Service and the Prayer Circle

Besides Hermana, classes, and work with the Friars, Ed filled his waking hours with several other activities. On Saturdays he worked with his father at the Magazine Printing Company collecting bills, delivering orders, carrying out basic accounting chores, and helping around the shop. He never became a full-fledged printer, but through close observation, he learned the processes and problems of the business. During his last quarter in school, he also took an after-hours job at the university cleaning a classroom building to save money for his approaching marriage.

Ed continued to grow spiritually. As counselor to successful banker Willard R. Smith, he faithfully carried out his Sunday School work. Perhaps he visited Hermana's class more than any other, but he also organized and conducted regular meetings of the Sunday School board and often spoke to its teachers. Smith was much older and allowed the younger, energetic Ed a major role in the superintendency. Once again Ed found himself in an unexpected leadership position. On December 26, 1926, he participated in the day-long Ensign Ward Sunday School conference, instructing the teachers in new techniques and pedagogical methods he had learned at the U. At the conference, the Second Intermediate Second Year Girl's class presented "Pages from Nephite History," an original dramatic sketch by Hermana. The conference program, printed at the Magazine Printing Company, lists Ed's father, who taught the gospel doctrine class, and two siblings—Janette and Paul—as teachers. The Lyons were becoming a family of teachers.[30]

Many neighboring wards requested Ed's speaking services. His trip to the Holy Land gave him status as an authority. For his part, Ed had developed a talent in narrating interesting anecdotes and tales, often passing around his snapshots as he spoke to Sunday School and MIA classes in Salt Lake City wards. He was even invited to judge ward speech contests. He generally felt nervous about his own speaking and insecure about judging others, but with encouragement from Hermana, he accepted many such assignments in 1926 and 1927.

Ed made such an impression in the Sunday School superintendency that on January 19, 1927, he was "recommended by W[illard] R. Smith to join Apostle Richard's [Prayer] Circle."[31] This was a continuation of the John Taylor Prayer Circle to which Ed's father, David, had belonged since 1886 and where he now served as secretary and second in command to Elder George F. Richards (illus. 4-6).[32] The invitation to join the Circle allowed Ed to become part of a group of eighteen select Church members.

He was by far the youngest and the only unmarried man in the group. Years later as a historian, Ed detailed the activities of this now-defunct brotherhood in an interview with Davis Bitton:

Courtesy Church Archives

Illus. 4-6. Elder George F. Richards, temple president and leader of the John Taylor prayer circle.

> Lyon: It appears that at an early date . . . each of the apostles had what was spoken of as a prayer circle. . . . Apparently the apostle selected those people who were to belong to it.
>
> As I grew up in the early part of this century I can remember my father coming home later one night in the week than all the rest . . . with a large leather-bound book. It had stamped on the back of it . . . "John Taylor's Prayer Circle." Of course John Taylor had been long since dead by the time I became acquainted with it. George F. Richards, the father of LeGrand Richards, was then the president of the circle.
>
> . . . Well, when I came home from my mission, there was a vacancy in the George F. Richards or John Taylor prayer circle. . . .
>
> Some time later I received official word that I had been invited and was to come to the temple. . . .
>
> Bitton: Men only?
>
> L: Men only. Just men, all the time. We gathered in the room where the Council of the Twelve met. . . .
>
> Then we gathered and sat down and any instructions that might be given would be given by President Richards.
>
> Then after business had been taken care of and any particular announcements about new changes in the Church policy, we went through the regular prayer circle, surrounding an altar where the list of the ill that we had brought from the gatehouse up with us would be placed on the altar. . . .
>
> B: Well, did they do anything besides just the ceremonial part of it?
>
> L: . . . George F. Richards would discuss something about maybe a conference he had been to, just sort of [some] interest[ing thing] that he had been doing. . . .

B: Did you feel a very close affinity and comradeship with these people in the prayer circle?

L: Every time, every time. They would go out of their way to be nice to you. We felt it. They were very, very fine, devout Latter-day Saints, good people, good-living people, and they really tried to make you feel welcome; they felt a real brotherhood there.[33]

He was now in a circle of friends, with his father, that allowed him access to many of the city's and Church's highest authorities.

Marriage for Eternity

During summer 1927, Ed and Hermana continued their talks and dreams of marriage. Finally, in mid-July, they decided to get married on August 16, 1927—it might be more accurate to say that Hermana finally agreed to the date. With just five weeks to prepare, they had to move quickly. But another complication arose. Since late May, Ed had been experiencing stomach cramps that occasionally made him double over. In late June, he visited Dr. H. Z. Lund, who ran a test that showed an elevated white blood cell count. Ed was working full time as janitor at the U. Three weeks from his wedding, he quit his job and checked into the LDS Hospital. The next morning he "had two hypodermics. . . . Dr. Lund removed my appendix about 8:30 A.M. It was fastened to my pelvis bone. I came out of the ether . . . Hermana there."[34] Ed was very pleased with his response to the ether, with the almost complete lack of pain he felt after the operation, and with the absence of any postoperative stomach distress. His diary expresses the same type of pride he had about his body while a missionary. Eleven days later, still hunched over, he left the hospital and limped to the Forsberg's car, exhausted by the short walk. Now he had nine days to recover at home before the marriage.

Two days later, on the sunny morning of her fiancé's birthday, Hermana marveled at the beauty of life and captured her feelings and thoughts about her "dearest boy of mine."

> Six in the Morning
> Home
> Aug. 9, 1927
>
> Dear,
>
> I shall never forget the day you were operated on. All morning I had been fighting back the tears but when I came and saw you looking so still and lifeless I couldn't hold out a minute longer. The realization of all that you meant to me and of how empty life would be without you simply overcame all powers of control.

But all the fears and worries of that morning and the long sleep-less night preceding it were compensated for when you opened your eyes and said "Oh, is that you sweetheart?" And Ed, I shall always remember how you lay there in a semi-conscious condition forgetful of yourself telling me that you loved me.

Isn't it strange that at times when we feel most deeply and should therefore be most expressive we are dumb! The thought keeps coming, "If I could only express my feelings about you!"

Ever since that June 20th [1926] you have been unconsciously shaping my life. The knowledge that you loved me has helped me to be bigger and better in every way.

One week today and I shall be your bride!

Hermana[35]

Just twelve hours after Hermana started her letter, Ed's neighbor-hood and mission friends, formerly the "Woman Hater's Club," threw a stag dinner party to celebrate his twenty-fourth birthday and his upcoming wedding. The party was held at his house, but Ed spent most of the evening sitting down. Among the boisterous guests were Jim Armstrong and Bob Smith, who had recently returned from their missions, and Ed's former missionary companions Andries de Bruyn, Ezra Taylor, Albert Venema, Hilbertus Noorda, and Ed Young. Other returned-missionary friends from the Netherlands and Great Britain also attended, making more than the accustomed jokes about the upcoming marriage and Ed's physical condition for the honeymoon.

The next day, Ed paid fourteen dollars to rent B. Cecil Gates's cabin in Brighton, Utah, for a two-week honeymoon. Ed, like most young men of his day, did not have access to a personal or family car to drive long distances. Bucolic Brighton, nestled in the Wasatch Mountains that he and Hermana had grown to love, was close and lovely. They had been there the previous summer. The day after paying for the cabin reservation, he also paid two dollars and fifty cents for the marriage license, meticulously noting all these expenses in his diary. On Tuesday morning, August 16, 1927, the Lyon and Forsberg families and a few close friends assembled in the Salt Lake Temple. Joseph Christenson, a friend of the Forsberg family, performed the marriage ceremony with David R. Lyon and Gustave W. Forsberg as witnesses (illus. 4-7).[36] Two bright, successful, popular young people with university degrees were now joined for eternity. The future was filled with promise.

Approximately sixty-five people came to the Forsberg home that evening for an informal reception of family and close friends. The house

Illus. 4-7. Ed and Hermana's marriage certificate.

was decorated with zinnias and golden glows, and Hermana's younger brothers had strung colored lanterns from the house to the trees. A small band played popular romantic tunes. It was a scene of shining beauty on a soft summer night. "But most beautiful of all was my wife," wrote a happy Ed. "She had a beautiful blue dress trimmed around the neck and front and sides with exquisite lace—really beautiful combinations, with her pretty golden hair and light hose. She had a bunch of one dozen Bride's Roses."[37] Hermana chose to forgo the expense of a formal but impractical wedding dress and instead wore an airy, light blue, flapper-style shift that she would be able to wear on other occasions. Ed had to sit down during much of the three hours that the guests stayed; his recent operation provided an opportune excuse to sit out the dancing.

Hermana later recalled that after the wedding reception, her new mother-in-law, Mary Lyon, told her that she was now responsible for Ed. Half in jest, she charged Hermana with reminding Ed "to bathe, comb his hair, and [to have Hermana] approve his clothes before he left the

Illus. 4-8. Ed and Hermana at Brighton, Utah, on their honeymoon in 1927.

house."[38] Mary indicated that Hermana's new husband didn't pay attention to the details of his own clothing and lacked color coordination skills.

With the wedding ceremony and reception completed, the honeymoon began (illus. 4-8). Hermana's brother and sister, twins Allyn and Ada, and Ada's boyfriend Clifford Webb, drove the handsome couple the twenty miles up Big Cottonwood Canyon to the Gates's cabin. A huge bouquet of purple and white mountain columbine, picked earlier in the day, greeted them in the cabin.

The cabin was freezing when they arrived at 1:40 A.M. Ed was plain tuckered out and still sore from the appendix operation, and Hermana was exhausted from the taxing day, but the joy of the flowers at this special moment provided a lifelong memory—from this moment on, columbine became "their" flower. For fourteen long days, they lounged in the scent of the pines and took daily walks through woods, meadows, and acres of wildflowers, sweet-smelling mountain bluebells, pinkish-red Indian paintbrush, and secretive and romantic columbine.[39]

Notes

1. T. Edgar Lyon, "Oral History," bound typescript, 78, T. Edgar Lyon Collection, Church Archives, Family and Church History Department, The Church of Jesus Christ of Latter-day Saints, Salt Lake City (hereafter cited as Church Archives). Unless otherwise noted, all citations for T. Edgar Lyon materials are located in the Lyon collection.

2. T. Edgar Lyon, Diary, February 28, 1926, Church Archives.

3. T. Edgar Lyon, Mission Diary, no date or page number, Church Archives.

4. T. Edgar Lyon, Diary, March 28, 1926.

5. T. Edgar Lyon, "Oral History," 78–79.

6. T. Edgar Lyon, Diary, March 28, 1926.

7. "A History of Laura Hermana Forsberg by Her Son, Joseph Lynn Lyon," 1991, typescript, 16–20, L. Tom Perry Special Collections, Harold B. Lee Library, Brigham Young University, Provo, Utah; copy in author's possession.

8. "History of Laura Hermana Forsberg by Her Son," 19.

9. T. Edgar Lyon, Diary, June 20, 1926.

10. Hermana Forsberg, Diary, July 1926, Church Archives.

11. T. Edgar Lyon, Diary, July 10, 1926. Only a portion of the original Dutch is reproduced in the text.

12. T. Edgar Lyon, Diary, July 25, 1926.

13. Forsberg, Diary, July 1926.

14. James Armstrong to T. Edgar Lyon, September 11, 1926, Church Archives.

15. "A History of Laura Hermana Forsberg by Her Son," 16–20.

16. T. Edgar Lyon, "Oral History," 40.

17. T. Edgar Lyon, Diary, April 14, 1926.

18. T. Edgar Lyon, "Oral History," 41.

19. Forsberg, Diary, January 8, 1927.

20. T. Edgar Lyon, Diary, February 14–18, 1927.

21. Forsberg, Diary, July 28, 1926.

22. Lyon, Diary, May 19, 1927.

23. Lyon, Diary, May 20, 1927.

24. Hermana made no diary entries during this uproar.

25. T. Edgar Lyon, "Oral History," 39–41.

26. T. Edgar Lyon "Oral History," 39.

27. T. Edgar Lyon, "Oral History," 39.

28. University of Utah graduation program, spring 1927, Church Archives.

29. T. Edgar Lyon, Diary, June 7, 1927.

30. Ensign Ward Sunday School Conference program, December 26, 1926, Church Archives.

31. T. Edgar Lyon, Diary, January 19, 1927.

32. George F. Richards (1861–1950) had been an Apostle since 1906 and president of the Salt Lake Temple since 1921.

33. T. Edgar Lyon, "Oral History," 243–49.

34. T. Edgar Lyon, Diary, July 28, 1927.

35. Hermana Forsberg to T. Edgar Lyon, August 9, 1927, Church Archives.

36. T. Edgar Lyon, Diary, August 11–16, 1927.

37. T. Edgar Lyon, Diary, August 16, 1927.

38. "A History of Laura Hermana Forsberg by Her Son," 20.

39. T. Edgar Lyon, Diary, August 17–30, 1927.

5

"A Teacher of Boys and Girls," 1927–31

During their romantic and restful fourteen-day honeymoon, both Ed and Hermana took the time to compose letters of thanks to their parents. Ed wrote four long pages. He thanked his mother and father for their financial support, especially during his mission and travels in Europe, for "the good, strong body which [they] gave [him] as a heritage," for educational opportunities, for the gospel, and for the example of their lives. He then advanced the idea of a life-long personal goal: "I have an ideal in life— to live a clean life [and] deal honestly with my fellowmen and my God."[1] He felt deeply indebted to his parents and was stirred by the need to somehow return their generosity. He concluded that "the only way that I can repay you . . . is to pass on the heritage to another generation; and take my place in the world as a teacher of boys and girls."

He and Hermana would soon be leaving their beloved Utah to teach boys and girls in distant and windy Rigby, Idaho. That spring he had signed a teaching contract when a recruiter from the upper Snake River Valley had visited the University of Utah seeking a history and social science teacher for Rigby High School. The salary for the nine-month school year, 1927–28, would be $1,350. The newlyweds borrowed some "start-up" money from Ed's parents, paid $8.48 each for train tickets to Rigby, and on the first day of September 1927, reluctantly boarded the north-bound train for the nine-hour ride. Both had lived away from home before, Hermana while teaching in Sigurd, Utah, and Ed while serving a mission in the Netherlands. However, both had a deep love for Utah and its people, especially their families, and for the mountains and canyons there. The departure was particularly difficult because they knew no one in Idaho, even though it was close to Ed's youthful summer stomping ground of Jackson Hole.

New Teacher

Upon their arrival in Rigby, the school superintendent met the anxious couple at the station and drove them to their new apartment. By letter they had arranged to occupy the back part of an old home, paying fifteen dollars a month for rent. Hermana found it dirty, drafty, and in short, depressing. Cooking was done on an already antique coal stove; Ed would chop the wood for Hermana and Mrs. Kites, the homeowner. There was no indoor plumbing. The outhouse was fifteen or twenty steps to the rear, and water for cooking had to be carried from the pump. The cracked, green linoleum in the two rooms—one bedroom and a hastily arranged kitchen—was cold and smelled musty, and the flowered wallpaper had peeled at the corners. A telephone was not even a consideration, nor could they afford a radio. This was a step back, both in time and luxuries, for the two who had come from relatively well-to-do families in modern Salt Lake City. But it was cheap, just 10 percent of Ed's monthly salary, and it was now home for the teacher and his bride.[2]

Courtesy Church Archives

Illus. 5-1. William Edwin Berrett, Ed Lyon's life-long friend, taught seminary in Rigby, Idaho, in 1927–28.

Previously, Ed had taken an examination for teaching certification in Idaho. He had received a 96 on Idaho State Government and Law and a 97 on the High School Course of Study, sufficiently high grades to warrant a five-year certification. So on Monday, September 5, Lyon, nine other teachers, and the superintendent checked in for the first day of classes at Rigby High School. Included among the new teachers that fall was the seminary instructor, William Edwin Berrett (illus. 5-1).[3] Berrett was employed by the General Church Board of Education but hired by the Rigby Stake board of education.[4] He and his wife Eleanor had come to Rigby just a few days earlier, and they had also been able to rent a couple of rooms from "a widow lady within a block from the school."[5] Since all but a very few of the high school students were members of the Church, and because participating students received seminary grades on their regular report cards, the seminary teacher was an integral part of the educational process. He was included in all faculty meetings and school activities.

Lyon threw himself into the full activity of preparing, teaching, and grading. He taught all the history and social science courses at the high school as well as a debate course. In his classes, he often discussed the role of religion in society, which further linked him to Berrett and the seminary. Lyon taught his classes with youthful enthusiasm for the subject matter and the students. His letters and diary make little comment on the daily chores of teaching, yet his few brief notations and letters to his parents demonstrate that he was happy and enjoyed working with the students and the academic material. Berrett recalled that Lyon was a very popular teacher but a little shy and not as outgoing as some of the young teachers.[6]

Besides the routine teaching activities, Lyon also involved himself in many extracurricular endeavors related to the school. He served as adviser to the *Rodeo,* the school yearbook, and saw it through publication in May 1928. One of his senior students signed Lyon's 1928 yearbook, "I will always remember you as the best teacher I ever had. I enjoyed Debating and Sociology. You teach in a way that appeals to me. I will always remember the instruction. Thank you. Weldon Hess."[7] Lyon also functioned as adviser to the sophomore class and as assistant to the basketball coach by timing games, taking tickets, and encouraging the team. When the "beet-topping and potato-picking" two-week holiday came along in October he joined right in, supervising and assisting his own students in this back-bending task.

Church work absorbed many weeknights and Sundays. Just two weeks after their arrival, both Ed and Hermana accepted calls as teachers in the Sunday School. Hermana also responded to an opportunity to teach the twelve- to fourteen-year-old Beehive girls in the Mutual Improvement Association, where she again had a chance to use her drama experience and creative talents. Ed was sufficiently popular as a teacher and speaker that he soon received invitations to most of the surrounding wards. His stories and pictures of the Holy Land fascinated many of the potato and beet farmers who had only read of these sacred places. These talks and fireside chats gave Lyon and his new bride an exposure rarely accorded to those so young—stake authorities became aware of his unique memory, his love of history, and his ability to stir an audience with a well-told story. Ed was barely twenty-four years old, Hermana just twenty-one, but they were filling Church roles that in the 1920s were often reserved for older adults.

Hermana, however, was not completely happy. She felt isolated with no phone or radio and little communication with neighbors. The tiny apartment was confining, young married friends were almost nonexistent in the community of older adults, and the Church in Idaho seemed different from her experiences in Salt Lake City. She was far away from home, alone during much of the day while her husband taught and worked on school activities, and she desperately missed friends from her Salt Lake ward and schools. Almost the only exceptions to her boring days were the infrequent visits of Lyon's older brother Kyle and his wife, June. Kyle was now a teaching principal in distant Parker, Idaho, and the families occasionally got together in Rigby. One other exception occurred when one of Hermana's girlfriends from the Ensign Ward, Frances Grant Bennett, daughter of President Heber J. Grant, and her husband, Wallace Bennett (later a United States senator from Utah), visited the area and shared a dinner with the Lyons.

As a result of their shared newcomer status, the Lyons and Berretts quickly developed a friendship. Lyon and his wife had no car and hence were limited in their sphere of activities. Berrett and his wife, Eleanor, owned a black Model-T Ford, a one-seater, and the two couples often went on picnics or drove around the valley, pressed together with Hermana sitting on her husband's lap. Lyon and Berrett also took hunting and fishing trips together. The Berretts were the Lyons' closest friends, and they shared a quiet Thanksgiving dinner in 1927. Berrett recalled that "Hermana was [perhaps] too refined for the community."[8] She and Ed had refused to join the local Rook Club and hence had not opened that avenue of friendship, perhaps fostering the image that they were "above" this deeply-rooted tradition of the long-time residents. Hermana and Ed did find friendship with other newcomers, a young medical doctor named Ray West and his wife, who had the young couple over for dinner a few times.

As early as October 1927, just two months after their marriage, Hermana suspected that she was pregnant. Ed's October 22 diary entry in Dutch mentioned *Kindje—Het beste* (a child—the greatest), yet they shared this suspicion with no one, possibly worrying about miscarriage. Hermana was sick during the early part of the pregnancy and in her loneliness yearned for the spiritual support of her sister Ada or her mother-in-law. Ed was solicitous to Hermana's whims and wishes, but she was still unhappy; the displacement from Salt Lake City was difficult. "My wife didn't like the country. Windy and intense cold, and that wind blows all the time," Ed remembered.[9] In preparation for the Christmas season, Hermana left Rigby in mid-December 1927 on a train bound for Salt Lake City. Ed continued teaching and correcting papers and exams until December 23, when he joined his wife and their extended family members for a joyous Christmas homecoming. In Salt Lake City, Hermana consulted Dr. Joe Jack, the husband of her close cousin, and he pronounced her healthily pregnant.

The couple returned to Idaho after New Year's Day, in the Berrett's car, with much less enthusiasm than in September. Their dedication to

Church callings was still apparent and appreciated by the Rigby Ward, as well as by stake officials in the area, but the terrible cold and incessant winter wind caused them to look toward Utah for future work. In early spring, Ed applied with several districts in Utah, "and to my amazement got a contract from the Jordan District to become principal at Highland Boy," a combined rural elementary and junior high school at Bingham Canyon near Salt Lake City.[10] Ed would serve as principal but also teach seventh and eighth grades at a nine-month salary of $1,690. This would be a $340 increase, a twenty-five percent jump in one year. And, just as important, the expecting couple would be near their families and friends. They were elated.

Seminary Man

Early in April 1928, on the day that Lyon intended to sign and mail his contract to the Jordan District in Salt Lake City, John W. Hart (illus. 5-2), the burly and powerful president of the Rigby Stake, came to the high school and insisted that he see Lyon. The secretary refused to get Lyon out of class but promised to give him a message to see President Hart as soon as possible. On the way home for lunch, Lyon timidly stopped at the stake office. A visit to President Hart's office was not taken lightly. Hart was a businessman, banker, and industrialist who controlled many financial activities in southern Idaho. He had served as a member of the Republican National Committee, a representative in the Idaho legislature, and for a month even functioned as acting governor of the state.[11] He was vitally interested in the education of the youth of his stake and was not accustomed to negative responses to his requests. In the office, Lyon nervously took a seat. Hart asked:

"What are you going to do next year?" I said, "Go down and teach in Jordan School District." "Why are you going down there?" I said, "Oh, we want to get back near our people." And he said, "Paying you more money?" I said, "Yes, a good deal more." And he said, "That doesn't matter. We want you to stay here and take over the seminary out at Midway [Idaho]." I nearly fell off my rocker.[12]

Ed had many hesitations. He did not know much about the seminary system, but his biggest concern was Hermana and her feelings. He was also concerned about his professional future—he wanted to advance at least to a principalship and perhaps beyond. "I'm not interested," Lyon responded. "Don't you like it [here]?" asked Hart. Lyon explained that they liked the people but not the place and that from what he knew,

Courtesy Church Archives

Illus. 5-2. As chairman of the Rigby Stake Board of Education, John W. Hart often hired new seminary teachers like Ed Lyon.

seminary teaching promised little advancement. Hart was determined not to let them leave:

> "No, this isn't a blind alley. You can do good." I said "Well, I guess I could do that elsewhere [too]. My wife won't ever accept it anyway. And I've committed myself." "You've signed your contract?" he said; "If you have I'll go down and break it for you." He was a rough guy. And I said, "No." He said "I'll tell you what to do. You go home and think about it and pray about it. . . . Come over and give me the answer on the way to school in the morning. I'll be here in the office by eight o'clock."

So I went home [at noon] and told Hermana and she burst into crying and didn't want [me to accept]. We prayed about it that night. We got up in the morning and the first thing she said to me [was] "Let's stay."[13]

Ed was flabbergasted at this acceptance, but very early in their courtship and marriage he had learned to listen to his wife—her reactions and intuition had already proven to be an accurate direction for his life. If she were happy with the offer, they would stay in Idaho.

In making an offer to Lyon, John W. Hart was acting somewhat precipitously. As chairman of the Rigby Stake board of education, he had some control over curriculum and day-to-day seminary policy but no authority to offer contracts or hire new teachers. Nevertheless, he made the offer. Early the next day he took the train to Salt Lake City to attend general conference and visited with Joseph F. Merrill (illus. 5-3), Commissioner of Education for the Church. Lyon had taken freshman physics from Merrill in 1922 at the University of Utah, and the Commissioner still recalled the eager student. That afternoon Hart sent a telegram to Lyon: "Merrill and I agree you're the man for Midway."[14] The starting salary would be $1,800, even more than Lyon was offered by the Jordan District. In the early stages of the seminary system in the 1920s, the Church was willing to pay higher salaries than public schools in an attempt to entice good teachers and encourage them to make a full-time career of seminary teaching rather than use it as a jumping point to more lucrative work.[15] Lyon was grateful for the $450 increase, a thirty-three percent improvement over the previous year at Rigby High School.[16]

Hart's offer did not come from nowhere; some preliminary work had been done at Church headquarters. On March 10, 1928, the Church's Department of Education had requested a personal letter of recommendation for Lyon from Willard Smith. On letterhead from Zion's Savings, Smith had responded:

Courtesy Church Archives

Illus. 5-3. Joseph F. Merrill, Commissioner of Church Education when Ed Lyon began teaching seminary in Idaho in 1928.

> I wish I could say as many good things of all my acquaintances as I can honestly say of this young man. He is one of the most ideal boys of the present day. There is exemplified in him to the tenth degree, every one of the characteristics referred to in your letter. He stands out strongly in every particular one. If he does excel in any special one, it is in his spirituality, which includes a good powerful influence with boys and girls of the age mentioned, seconded closely with a thorough knowledge of the Gospel, and an entertaining way of presenting its truths. I am sure you need have no hesitancy regarding his ability and personality; and his untiring willing, helpful and dependable service. It is with the greatest pleasure of my life, that I highly recommend this young man, and bespeak for him your earnest consideration. Yours truly, Willard Smith.[17]

This letter confirmed President Hart's impressions of Lyon's abilities—he would be a great seminary teacher.

The simple and abrupt interview with a dynamic stake president set the course for the rest of Lyon's professional life. For the next forty-five years, with the exception of a three-and-a-half year return to the Netherlands, Lyon would be directly associated with Church education. It would provide him self-identification; a salary with which to raise a family; most of his adult friends; an outlet for creativity and publication; recognition; and most of all, association with bright, young students. Lyon would truly "pass on the heritage to another generation" by becoming a "teacher of boys and girls," helping them become thinking men and women.

The Church's seminary system, involving one hour a day released time for religious instruction, was still relatively new. It had begun in 1912 at Granite High School in Salt Lake County, as an outgrowth of the earlier once-a-week "religion class" for elementary students in which Lyon had participated in the 1910s and 1920s.[18] The Granite Stake presidency had recommended instituting such a program at the nearby public high school, and Church leaders accepted the plan. As the program caught on, many stakes adopted it, enthusiastically recruited teachers, and began constructing buildings. At least five thousand students enrolled in seminary in 1922, and by 1928 approximately nineteen thousand students studied in seventy-eight seminaries.[19] In 1919 the first seminary in Idaho was organized in Montpelier, not far from the Utah border. In 1920, President Hart formed the Rigby Stake board of education and, after some pushing, started a seminary program at the high school. Sugar City adopted the seminary system in 1924, Midway in 1926, and Rexburg in 1927. Hart and his fast-moving business ways were largely responsible for this rapid growth. Local boards paid only about 12 percent of the total costs of the program, but Hart exercised more than 12 percent of the power.[20] Lyon would be coming in "on the ground floor" of the new program, with plenty of opportunity for growth and challenge.

Lyon finished the year at Rigby High School in May 1927, hearing speeches from and hosting Commissioner Merrill, Elder Orson F. Whitney, and former Brigham Young University (BYU) President George Brimhall at the seminary graduation. Once again the forceful hand of John Hart was at work—he had arranged these very high-powered speakers for both the high school and seminary graduation ceremonies in his area.

With the promised $450 increase in salary for the next year, the Lyons felt richly blessed and rewarded. They splurged by buying a used bedroom set and a kitchen table from a local doctor who was moving. They packed up their old and new belongings, stored them in the rented home they would occupy the next year in nearby Lewisville, and boarded the train for Salt Lake City.

Family Man

Both Ed and Hermana recognized that Ed would need more education if he were to progress in the Church Educational System, so he enrolled in history and archaeology classes at the University of Utah's summer school. Instead of staying in the large Lyon family home on E Street, they rented a small home on the southwest corner of 4th Avenue and B Street, giving Hermana privacy during her pregnancy. They frequently visited David and Mary Lyon, and these opportunities allowed Hermana to bond with her new mother-in-law. To pay for the rented house and the forthcoming baby, Ed took a part-time job at the University of Utah cleaning rooms and buildings as he had previously done. Hermana was now in her eighth month of pregnancy, very large and very uncomfortable; she was just five feet three inches tall, and the large baby caused a continuous backache and made walking more like waddling. Nevertheless, she and Ed took frequent walks up City Creek Canyon in the sunny afternoon and evening hours, grateful for the chance to return to the hills of home. The last long walk was on Saturday, July 7, 1928, and it had a specific purpose—to encourage onset of labor.

During the next day it became clear that Hermana was about to deliver. She checked into LDS Hospital at 10:00 P.M. Dr. Jack arrived at midnight. The labor was fairly short and at 1:50 A.M., on July 9, she delivered a twenty-inch, seven-pound baby boy. There was little question about the name—he would be David (illus. 5-4), honoring Ed's father as well as his faithful oldest brother. They also christened him with the Swedish name of Waldemar, in honor of Hermana's father. Hermana remained in the hospital for ten days of forced bed rest; however, she complained of feeling weaker upon leaving the hospital than upon entering. Her lengthy stay increased her suspicion of many conventional medical practices. She boldly bucked the wisdom of the day by insisting that she exclusively breast-feed her baby. The nurses were primarily concerned that the child receive exactly four ounces of milk at each feeding and weighed him, albeit on scales that often inaccurately measured the wiggly infant, to assure that he received the precise amount.[21] They suggested supplementing with bottle feeding; Hermana would hear no such argument. She struggled without much encouragement and eventually raised a healthy child with her breast milk. She was happily relieved when she could leave the hospital and take the baby to their rented home in the Ensign Ward.

With a new baby came new needs; it would now be harder for them to get around without a vehicle. Reluctantly, the young couple began shopping for a used car. On August 14, 1928, they purchased an inexpensive green 1925 Essex. Though the purchase was within the limits of Ed's generously increased salary, they still had to borrow most of the money from his father until Ed started teaching in the fall. A few days later, Ed

Illus. 5-4. Ed Lyon with son David in Idaho, winter 1928.

bade a melancholy goodbye to parents and Hermana and drove to Pocatello, Idaho, where he spent the night in the car to save money. The next morning he drove to their home in Lewisville. Hermana came a few days later on the train, with baby "Davey" in her arms (illus. 5-5). When John Hart had called Ed to teach seminary, he had also advised him to "buy a house, start a family, and vote the Republican ticket."[22] The purchase of the house would have to wait, but the family was already begun, and, at least in these early years of marriage, Ed often voted for Republican candidates.

Classes began. Lyon was one of two seminary teachers at Midway, cooperating with principal Merrill Clayson.[23] Lyon taught seminary classes for three full years in Midway, thus experiencing each of the three courses of study: Old Testament history, New Testament history, and Church history. This unified Church approach emphasized the historicity of the scriptures as well as their spiritual and moral aspects. Noticeably absent from the suggested curriculum was any direct study of the Book of Mormon; since its historical and geographical background was not well documented in the 1920s, it didn't find place in the curriculum. In 1930, Lyon did obtain some slides of ruins in Central and South America and once again achieved popularity as he showed them to large audiences of interested Saints. The historical approach to the scriptures suited Lyon well, and he frequently used examples from his postmission tour through Egypt and Palestine.

The motivation of the seminary program was that "religion [was] vital to character training, and no textbook [had] yet appeared to replace the Old Testament as a source of inspiration to that end."[24] Similar statements could be made for the study of the New Testament and Church history. A major extracurricular activity program was also an integral part of seminary, and it included the following:

1. Presentation of programs and worship services in all wards
2. Community projects to aid the needy
3. Production of dramas and pageants in the community
4. "Class projects of educational and religious nature"
5. Group worship services in the classroom
6. "Trips to places of historical and cultural interest"
7. Trips to temples to do baptisms for the dead
8. Recreation in the form of hikes, home parties, swimming, dances, etc.[25]

Again, Lyon was pleased to be able to associate with his young charges during these extracurricular events, trying always to develop leaders by letting the students chart the direction and plan the specific activities. Guidance and counseling was a further expectation of seminary teachers, a task he found delightful and necessary as he counseled the youth through personal problems with parents, siblings, and the gospel. Seminary teaching permitted him to work with the values and morals of his students, creating a closeness and sense of personal service that he had not experienced as strongly during the previous year at Rigby High School.

Illus. 5-5. Hermana, David, and Ed Lyon in 1929.

Midway High School, with its adjacent seminary building, was so named because it was half-way between Lewisville and Menan. It also attracted students from small districts in Grant, Bybee, and other nearby towns, none of which had seminaries. Concerned parents bussed or sent their children to

Midway to take advantage of released-time religion classes. The high school quickly grew larger than intended, and in 1928 the principal needed an additional part-time teacher. He contacted the stake president to see if Lyon, who was teaching only four seminary classes, could offer an extra class or two each year. Hart agreed, and so Lyon received a supplementary salary of $450 a year.[26] He taught American history, civics, and sociology to many of the same students from his seminary classes. The added income, coupled with his $450 salary increase over Rigby High School, meant that he was now earning $900 more than the previous year. Again he and Hermana felt extremely blessed and even well-off. Ed recalled that on this increase he "paid [his] tithing and banked the remainder." He quickly paid his father for the car loan and tuition at the University of Utah and saved the rest for future educational purposes. He knew he would get a master's degree, perhaps even a Ph.D., but in what field? This decision remained unclear for several years.

During late fall 1928, Hermana's younger brother, nineteen-year-old Allyn Lorentz Forsberg, died very suddenly of bacterial meningitis—the same disease that had killed Ed's brother in 1907. Hermana was devastated and immediately took Davey on the train to Salt Lake City to attend the funeral; her husband stayed in Idaho to fill his teaching duties. Ever since the prolonged death of her mother in 1914, Hermana had lived with a deep fear of death, and she now took the tragic loss of her brother very painfully. Years later she recounted that "she was so upset by it [that] she lost her milk, and had to wean David. . . . It taught her the power of emotions on the physical body."[27] For all her life, she struggled with the metaphysical problem of death, with the "why" of it. She concluded that Allyn's death, and indeed most deaths, had little or nothing to do with personal worthiness but were just part of the plan of life, part of a random universe. She always bristled at the supposedly comforting statement that "his mission was completed" or that "he was needed on the other side more than here." Hermana's father, Gustave, who also took the death very hard, finally came to conclusions similar to those of his daughter. He had lost his first wife and now one of their offspring; the grieving was long and draining. Throughout her ten-day absence, Ed wrote to Hermana regularly, expressing and confessing his deep love to comfort and assure her. She returned to Idaho to spend their first Christmas away from Salt Lake City.

During this year, Ed and Hermana established a firm friendship with Melvin and Clarissa Esplin Luke. Melvin was a farmer who lived near Rigby and also served as a member of the stake board of education, which oversaw some of Ed's seminary activities. The friendship eased Hermana's return to Idaho and helped the Lyon family through the Christmas season. The Lukes also had young children; twins Floyd and Lloyd, ages six, endeared themselves to the Lyons and later became playmates with David. Despite twenty years' difference in age, the Lyons and Lukes became fast friends, continuing their relationship throughout the remainder of their lives.

Continued Education

During summer 1928, Lyon had enrolled in classes at the University of Utah, working toward a master's degree in history; this set a pattern that would continue for many years. Church Education leaders felt the need to enhance the background of seminary and institute teachers, as well as the many instructors at BYU who taught religious education. The logical place for this academic "tune up" was BYU in Provo, Utah. Five- or six-week sessions were conducted each summer beginning in 1927. The office of the Church Commissioner of Education encouraged all seminary instructors to attend, but no compensation was provided. Lyon participated in the 1929 session and, contrary to his initial expectations, felt an exhilaration and excitement that he had not previously experienced in any religious education. Commissioner Merrill had asked Sidney B. Sperry to structure the seminar.[28] He was a popular teacher in the seminary system who had recently returned to BYU with a master's degree from the Divinity School at the University of Chicago. Sperry had studied with some of the greatest Old and New Testament scholars in the world, and he ignited a fire in the seminary system with the new, critical approaches of close textual analysis, archaeological investigation, and historical exegesis. Sperry's knowledge of Hebrew and the history of the Old Testament also "converted [Commissioner Merrill] to the idea that we ought to have more education at the University of Chicago," observed one participant.[29] The classes at BYU, inspired by methodology learned at Chicago, were a revelation to Lyon and many other teachers in the system as they understood a wealth of material in the scriptures that they had previously never imagined.

Though hoping to complete higher degrees, Lyon still had to teach and make a living. He returned to Idaho each year, trying to incorporate the new skills he had learned in Provo. This was an exciting time to be in Church education. Among several innovative programs and methods, seminary teacher George S. Tanner developed an evaluative test to try to determine how much seminary students were assimilating. The elaborate test measured knowledge acquired in all three seminary subjects. Tanner was released from teaching for a year, 1929–30, to visit all seminaries and administer his evaluative exam. Tanner and four trained students from Sugar City administered the test in Midway on January 31, 1930. Lyon's students scored exceptionally well: "I felt good [about the exam] and when the reports came out my kids rated highest of anybody in any seminary in the [whole] church." The highest achiever in Lyon's class was a Greek Orthodox boy, an orphan who had come to live with a Latter-day Saint family.[30] The class celebrated their success with a "peanut bust," an old-fashioned party with lots of peanuts.

Though Ed and Hermana were still away from their families in Salt Lake City, home life was a source of satisfaction and pleasure. Davey was almost two and was showing signs of rapid development, especially in his speaking abilities. Hermana was pregnant again, expecting in June. On March 1, 1930, Hermana acceded to her father's wishes and went to Salt Lake City to "baby sit" her younger siblings while her parents went to a business convention and vacation in New York. She took Davey with her. Ed missed them sorely, writing her at least once every day for the twenty-three days she was away; on three occasions he wrote twice a day. In one letter, Ed penned:

> Oh for a night at home, and to have you here with me to love. Today I was talking to [fellow teacher] Rosengreen and he said that he had never fallen in love. I told him that he didn't know he was born yet if he hadn't. . . . I really feel that life was hollow, empty and shallow before you came into my life and took my heart away from me and put yours in its place. I love you dear, and I wish I could be with you tonight. Please come home as soon as you can.[31]

> I love and adore you so much . . . and I'm part of you and I'm not all here when you are away. I'm discontented, restless, and dissatisfied with everything. I'm falling in love with you all over again—and this beautiful Spring weather makes it worse than ever.[32]

Hermana wrote back but not with the same regularity, desperate longing, or poetic flavor. She filled her letters with more of the everyday details of taking care of Davey and her siblings. Life at her old home was a return to earlier times: "The meadow lark's song reminds me of the time you gave me my diamond. I remember how they sang that following Sunday morning."[33] And an affirmation of joy at being in Utah came to the fore: "I do love to walk down Main Street and see the throngs of people and occasionally a friend. I like the noise and bustle and—well just about everything about it. Wonder if I'll ever feel that there's another place on earth I'd rather make my home?"[34] In the same letter she added that she wanted "more of you and more little angels in the years to come." She was obviously deeply in love too but was somewhat cautious and reserved. She asked her husband about how the finances for February worked out. He told her that they spent a total of $124.65: $27.27 for groceries, $10.29 for coal, $13.20 to license their Essex, and so on, but then went on to swear eternal love for her.[35] By the end of March they were joyously back together.

Lyon kept extremely busy, speaking in Sacrament meetings and at funerals, notably that of Don Walker, one of the pioneers of the area. This honor further indicated the esteem Lyon was receiving. On April 6, 1930, he organized and spoke at a special Sunday School centennial commemoration of the founding of The Church of Jesus Christ of Latter-day Saints. He even sang in a double male quartet in a Church meeting. In May 1930, Lyon was called as a home missionary, having earlier been ordained a Seventy by B. H. Roberts (on May 19, 1929), while Roberts visited Idaho. Ed and Hermana were often in the home of President John Hart, visiting with General Authorities and other dignitaries. The Lyon family prospered in other ways, and in May 1930 they splurged and purchased a brand new Wardway Gyrator washing machine, paying $69.50. Despite the comparatively elevated price, the machine would save Hermana's hands and nerves.

By the end of the school year, the Lyons were eager to get back to Utah—Hermana was in her last month of pregnancy, and Ed anticipated the BYU summer school, especially the prospect of sitting in classes with professor Edgar J. Goodspeed from the University of Chicago. The Church Educational System had decided to cement ties with the University of Chicago, particularly its Divinity School, by bringing Professor Goodspeed to conduct one of the religious education classes in Provo during summer 1930. Sidney B. Sperry had sold Elder Joseph F. Merrill on the idea, and Merrill, in turn, had convinced President Heber J. Grant of the value of bringing such a scholar to BYU. Goodspeed had already published a score of books, including his highly respected translation of the New Testament from the original languages. Goodspeed's ability with ancient languages deeply impressed Lyon, once again making him aware of his own linguistic inadequacies. During the 1930 summer session, Lyon not only thrilled at Goodspeed's classes, but he also resolved to master French. In a letter to Hermana in Salt Lake City, he confessed:

> Dearest Lover Girl: I am going to try to learn French this year if I don't learn anything else. However, my one-track mind is too slow to grasp DeJong's French. I have been up by the stadium for two hours this afternoon, trying to talk French and practicing the exercises we had today, out loud. I feel rather discouraged, and sometimes wonder if I have the mental ability to go on higher in education, or if it is just mental laziness. I'm afraid that I don't know much and can't ever learn enough to reach the goal which you have set for me. . . . I'm so lonesome for you, my Dear. I've counted the days until Friday about a dozen times. I'll be glad to see you and the little boy.[36]

The letter not only informs of his struggle with French, reminiscent of the difficulty he had with Dutch, but indicates that Hermana continued to push him to get advanced degrees. Indeed, one of Ed's sons believes that she was the prime mover behind Ed's drive for a Ph.D.[37]

The summers of 1929 and 1930 were life-changing educational moments for Lyon as well as his students. From Sperry, Lyon realized that there was a new and exciting realm of biblical scholarship. He began to understand that education was not just listening to professors, reading their standard texts, and then reproducing canonized information on tests as he had done as an undergraduate. Rather, education and learning could be exciting, even thrilling, involving the use of original sources and ancient languages. Lyon learned that investigation of standard texts must be creative, using modern techniques and innovative approaches. In Goodspeed, Lyon observed a true scholar, a fifty-eight-year-old man who for thirty-five years had been an articulate scholar, a doer, a translator, an original thinker. Goodspeed stimulated his students' minds, causing them to think in previously unimagined ways, to see the Bible and other scriptures as a text open to the same type of criticism as Shakespeare's plays.[38]

Goodspeed so ignited Lyon and other Church educators that Elder Merrill, with President Heber J. Grant's approval, invited Goodspeed to speak in the Salt Lake Tabernacle in one of the regular Sunday fireside sessions. This was a heady time for many in the Church, a time when General Authorities—B. H. Roberts, James E. Talmage, John A. Widtsoe, and Joseph F. Merrill particularly—were reaching out, embracing serious secular scholarship and applying it to the study of Latter-day Saint theology and history. Goodspeed exemplified this approach, using what was then called "higher criticism." Some at BYU, especially the older faculty, were skeptical, even critical. On the other hand, according to Lyon, "The younger men were eating it up. We were hungry for something of this type. [Goodspeed] made the New Testament live."[39] Goodspeed's innovative criticism consisted of "a background of the culture and the politics and the religious movements of the time without destroying the idea of divinity or inspiration."[40] This all-inclusive system appealed to Lyon because it combined several of the disciplines he had studied at the University of Utah—archaeology, political science, and history. It drew equally important ties to his postmission trip through Egypt and Palestine, where he had witnessed archaeological digs and visited museums. The openness of Goodspeed's approach led to some conflicts among Latter-day Saint professors and administrators. Scholars from the University of Chicago quit coming to BYU after 1933 "because of economic restrictions and criticism pertaining to the concepts they taught."[41] Whatever the institutional complaints or constraints, Goodspeed animated Lyon and set the direction for the remainder of his academic life.

Notes

1. T. Edgar Lyon to parents, August 18, 1927, T. Edgar Lyon Collection, Church Archives, Family and Church History Department, The Church of Jesus Christ of Latter-day Saints, Salt Lake City (hereafter cited as Church Archives). Unless otherwise noted, all citations for T. Edgar Lyon materials are located in the Lyon collection.

2. T. Edgar Lyon, Diary, September 1–October 4, 1927, Church Archives.

3. Lyon and Ed Berrett had known each other since 1924 at the University of Utah. Their professional paths crossed many times as they both worked in Church educational activities most of their lives.

4. In a letter to the presidency of the St. George (Utah) Stake, dated June 8, 1888, Wilford Woodruff, as chairman of the Church Board of Education, informed them that

> it was decided that a Board of Education, consisting of not less than five and not to exceed more than eight in number, should be selected in each Stake to take charge of and promote the interests of education in the Stake . . . . We feel that the time has arrived when the proper education of our children should be taken in hand by us as a people. Religious training is practically excluded from the District Schools. The perusal of books that we value as divine records is forbidden. (James R. Clark, *Messages of the First Presidency* [Salt Lake City: Bookcraft, 1966], 3:167–68)

As a result of this and similar instruction, the Rigby Stake maintained a small board; stake president John Hart served as its chairman.

5. William E. Berrett, "My Story" [Autobiography], typescript, 38, L. Tom Perry Special Collections, Harold B. Lee Library, Brigham Young University, Provo, Utah (hereafter cited as Perry Special Collections).

6. William E. Berrett, interview by author and Trent Lyon, Provo, Utah, June 30, 1992.

7. Notation found in T. Edgar Lyon's copy of *Rodeo* (the Rigby High School yearbook published in May 1928), Church Archives.

8. Berrett, interview.

9. T. Edgar Lyon, "Oral History," 80.

10. T. Edgar Lyon, "Oral History," 80.

11. Hart's straightforward, pushy manner, and especially his mixing Church and Idaho state politics, was frequently criticized by the non-Mormon press. See "A Tabernacle Candidacy," *The Christian Statesman* 50, no. 2 (February 1916): 81–82.

12. T. Edgar Lyon, "Oral History," 81.

13. T. Edgar Lyon, "Oral History," 81–82.

14. Years later Lyon recalled a conversation with Elder Merrill over this initial hiring. "That man Hart . . . is a pretty tough customer to deal with," said Merrill. "We have orders [that] we're not to let them [tell us who to hire]. But Hart recommended you [Lyon]. And he said 'Well, tell me where you've got a better man.' And I couldn't because I hadn't been looking for one." T. Edgar Lyon, "Oral History," 82.

15. T. Edgar Lyon, "Oral History," 82.

16. The Church took pride in paying higher salaries to its seminary teachers. In 1928 the average annual salary for all teachers in the Utah public schools was $1,680; seminary teachers in the same year averaged $2,040, about 20 percent higher. This favorable gap was maintained for many years. Milton Lynn Bennion, *Mormonism and Education* (Salt Lake City: Department of Education of The Church of Jesus Christ of Latter-day Saints, 1939), 223.

17. Willard R. Smith to Department of Education of The Church of Jesus Christ of Latter-day Saints, March 12, 1928, Church Archives.

18. Bennion, *Mormonism and Education*, 203–4.

19. Bennion, *Mormonism and Education,* 206–10; Richard O. Cowan, *The Church in the Twentieth Century* (Salt Lake City: Bookcraft, 1985), 111.

20. Bennion, *Mormonism and Education,* 206–10; Cowan, *Church in the Twentieth Century,* 111.

21. Joseph Lynn Lyon, "A History of Laura Hermana Forsberg," 1991, 25–26, Perry Special Collections, copy in author's possession.

22. Joseph Lynn Lyon, "History of Laura Hermana Forsberg," 25.

23. Merrill Clayson was born in Utah County and after education in Provo and at BYU began his career in Church education as principal of the seminary in St. Johns, Arizona, in 1925. He then accepted an assignment in Idaho, where he and Lyon cooperated in teaching and administration. Clayson later moved back to Utah, on assignment, and taught seminary in Provo and later at East and Granite High Schools in Salt Lake City. He retired in May 1965, after having guided the Granite Seminary for many years. In total he spent more than forty years in the Church's seminary system. Besides this seminary work, he completed graduate studies at Berkeley and at the University of Utah. Similar to Lyon, he was called from the seminary system to serve as mission president; he directed the Southern States

Mission from 1937 to 1940. "Ex-Seminary Leader Dies at 71," *Deseret News,* December 15, 1970, B9.

24. Bennion, *Mormonism and Education,* 214.

25. Bennion, *Mormonism and Education,* 215–17.

26. T. Edgar Lyon, "Oral History," 83–84.

27. Joseph Lynn Lyon, "History of Laura Hermana Forsberg," 27.

28. Sperry, eight years older than Lyon, continued his doctoral studies at the University of Chicago, receiving a Ph.D. degree in 1931 in Old Testament languages and literature. He became a respected mentor for Lyon.

29. Russel B. Swensen, interview by Mark K. Allen, September 13, 1978, Perry Special Collections, 10.

30. T. Edgar Lyon, "Oral History," 86.

31. T. Edgar Lyon to Hermana Lyon, March 10, 1930, Church Archives.

32. T. Edgar Lyon to Hermana Lyon, March 11, 1930, Church Archives.

33. Hermana Lyon to T. Edgar Lyon, March 9, 1930, Church Archives.

34. Hermana Lyon to T. Edgar Lyon, March 19, 1930, Church Archives.

35. T. Edgar Lyon to Hermana Lyon, March 23, 1930, Church Archives.

36. T. Edgar Lyon to Hermana Lyon, June 10, 1930, Church Archives.

37. Joseph Lynn Lyon, "History of Laura Hermana Forsberg," 31.

38. As a very young graduate student at the University of Chicago, Goodspeed took advantage of the Greek and Aramaic he had learned as a teenager and began collecting, deciphering, translating, and publishing Greek papyri. He spent two years in Europe, traveling from museum to museum, from digs in Egypt to archaeological sites in Palestine, from the cluttered offices of the Vatican to the ordered offices of the most stimulating German scholars. J. H. Cobb and L. B. Jennings, *A Biography and Bibliography of Edgar J. Goodspeed* (Chicago: University of Chicago Press, 1948), 1–3. He had been teaching at the University of Chicago since 1902 and had already authored thirty-one books and more than forty articles when Lyon met him in 1930. He had translated the entire New Testament from original languages. *The Bible: An American Translation,* J. M. Powis Smith, ed., Edgar J. Goodspeed, trans. (Chicago: University of Chicago Press), 1931.

> He always had several academic projects underway and involved his brightest students as collaborators. He lamented the general ignorance of scriptural study throughout the world. His classes were masterpieces of developing scholarship:

> His method was sheer genius. His classes were utterly informal. He would bring some half dozen books to which he planned to refer, and a manila envelope containing his notes. Some of these notes, the student could see, were written on pieces of old University calendars; they were of varying size, clipped to the area needed for the note. Of course they were constantly brought up to date. They stimulated his thought, and immediately he would launch into a spontaneous conversation so full of interest as to fascinate his students. Informal though the sessions were, the end of the Quarter always found the subject fully and thoroughly covered.

Whatever the subject matter—textual criticism, the canon, one or another aspect of patristic literature, or the synoptic problem—students were stimulated to work at the question involved, and every aspect of it was illuminated from items of Mr. Goodspeed's own experience. No finer example of scholarship could be set than was made alive every day in his classes. (Donald W. Riddle, "Edgar J. Goodspeed," *University of Chicago Magazine*, March 1962, 31)

Goodspeed proposed that

to mediate this new knowledge, this New Testament, to the Christian and to the educated public—this is the great task in which we must take our share. One of the tragedies of the hour is the ignorance of the New Testament on the part of otherwise educated people. This would not matter so much if they would let it alone, but that is just what they will not do. Essayists, journalists, educators, reformers, and reactionaries—all insist upon dealing with the New Testament. If one seeks to correct them, one simply does not know where to begin. (James I. Cook, *Edgar Johnson Goodspeed: Articulate Scholar* [Chico, Calif.: Scholars Press, 1981], xiii.)

39. T. Edgar Lyon, "Oral History," 93.
40. T. Edgar Lyon, "Oral History," 91.
41. Ernest L. Wilkinson and W. Cleon Skousen, *Brigham Young University: A School of Destiny* (Provo, Utah: Brigham Young University Press, 1976), 300.

6

The "Fire" of Chicago, 1931–33

Among the eighty or ninety Church seminary teachers who attended Goodspeed's two classes in 1930—the formation and content of the New Testament—three young seminary teachers immediately caught the flame of serious textual criticism. George S. Tanner, Russel B. Swensen (illus. 6-1), and Daryl Chase (illus. 6-2) felt so inspired that they talked to Commissioner Joseph F. Merrill and received a type of call to study in Chicago. The Church would grant a yearlong leave of absence from seminary and a stipend to pay expenses at the University of Chicago to help these Church educators complete advanced degrees. Commissioner Merrill viewed the probable results as very positive for the Church and its education system, and he arranged for them to receive half their seminary pay during the leave. Merrill was taking a major risk; despite a general healthy respect for higher learning in Church culture, some fears existed that too much secular learning might lead away from the truths of the restored gospel. After all, the seminary and institute programs had been established largely to counter what some Church leaders were calling the pernicious and negative influences of the world.

Understanding the BYU–University of Chicago Connection

Similar to the missionaries sent to learn art in Paris during the late 1880s, Tanner, Swensen, and Chase were called to go to Chicago and assimilate as much knowledge as possible.[1] The men were all cautioned that "re-employment in the Church school system would depend upon [their] faith and continued loyalty."[2] They would all go to the Divinity School, not to study to become ministers, as the school's name might imply, but to better understand and teach the scriptures. The three "education missionaries" departed in summer 1930. Each completed a master's degree in 1931, writing theses that linked the Church's history and doctrine to the Chicago concept of higher criticism.[3] Lyon was envious. He made up his mind that he would follow them the next year, and he sent for a catalog.

Before Ed could think about graduate work at Chicago, however, he had to take care of the moment. He was attending classes in Provo while Hermana awaited the birth of their second child in Salt Lake City.

Meanwhile, their 1925 Essex automobile was dying, so Ed traded in the old car and purchased a used 1928 Chevrolet coach for $425. He usually left the "new" car in Salt Lake City with Hermana and rode the train or hitched a ride with a fellow student to Provo. There he bunked in a tiny basement room in a boarding house and returned each Friday to be with his wife. Once again, he loyally wrote every day, encouraging her with loving words through the final weeks of her pregnancy. On June 18, 1930, he had a dream—which he called one of his worst nightmares—that Hermana had given birth to a ten-pound baby girl but had *not* notified him.[4]

Photo Archives, Perry Special Collections, Harold B. Lee Library, BYU

Illus. 6-1. Russel Swensen attended the University of Chicago with Ed Lyon in 1932.

Eager to know of every change in his wife's condition, he nervously continued in classes. Professor Rufus B. von Kleinsmid lectured on the Old Testament; a Dr. Sears, recruited by Sperry from Stanford, conducted sessions on language and the Bible. Henry Neuman, another invited professor, engaged the teachers on religion and social issues, causing serious discussion and debate. Lyon records that the "seminary teachers met at 1:30 P.M. for a meeting—battling as usual."[5] A few days later, "Dr. Merrill [came] down to set the seminary teachers right about their place at school and what [courses] they were to take [while at BYU summer school]."[6] Apparently some of the seminary teachers objected to the heavy load of course work and readings.

The learning thrilled Lyon, though he began to doubt his own effectiveness as a teacher. From the library in the Heber J. Grant Building he wrote to his wife:

> Beloved Sweetheart Mother: . . . . In fact, at times I wonder if I was ever made to be a teacher. I don't seem to have the ability to get the sympathetic understanding of the students and I don't draw near to them or touch their heart. A seminary teacher should do this more than anyone else. Bro. Wilson said: "Merely teaching or learning *facts* will fail to develop a spirit of worship in the hearts of young people." That drove home hard—facts, facts, facts. I believe that

Courtesy Daryl Chase Photograph Collection, Special Collections & Archives, Utah State University

Illus. 6-2. Daryl Chase *(center)* and others in front of the Salt Lake City seminary building, 1933.

that is all I know or have ever cared for. He said, "The purpose of our Seminaries this year must be to make religious education *religious,* not merely intellectual. We must get out of the field of the intellect, the head, and the facts, and get down to the heart." I think that I shall turn the Seminary teaching over to you, my Dear, as I don't seem to be made right, when it comes to that type of thing.[7]

Lyon felt the conflict between Goodspeed's academic approach and the expectation that he focus on building spiritual testimonies. Once somewhat proud of his ability to memorize and recall facts and details, he now felt condemned by it. He would have to find his own resolution, a combination of faith-filled history with factual analysis of important and accurate detail.

At 11:00 P.M. on June 19, Hermana wrote a long letter to her self-doubting husband. He had also expressed worries that he would not be in Salt Lake City when the baby was born. She told him not to worry yet, noting that she had only experienced a few minor pains. She never mailed the letter. Within forty-five minutes she checked into LDS Hospital. Dr. Jack came quickly, and at 2:49 A.M. on June 20 she delivered a seven-pound three-ounce baby boy (not the ten-pound girl of Lyon's dream). The parents named the baby John Forsberg Lyon, honoring both sides of the family. "John" honored Hermana's grandfather as well as Ed's grandfather and an older brother who had died in 1907; "Forsberg" preserved Hermana's maiden name.

Ed came quickly from Provo, bringing gladiolas. Hermana's sister Ada, her stepmother, and her mother-in-law took care of Davey during the long days of hospital convalescence. Again, Hermana insisted on breast-feeding and achieved her goal, this time with more ease. At the end of fourteen days, Ed paid the eighty-nine-dollar hospital bill and took his wife to their apartment. Later, back in Provo after the birth, he wrote: "Dearest Girl and Mother: . . . . I'm so proud of *you* and *our children*—it certainly sounds wonderful to hear the plural of that word! . . . I've been wishing all day that it was Thursday or Friday, so I could see you soon. I'll work hard and the time will soon pass. I suppose your days are longer than mine, however."[8] The new baby was easier to care for than Davey and at first wanted to sleep all the time. But after a few days Hermana informed her husband that the little babe had become a "ravenous feeder and [now] wants to eat all the time."[9]

In fall 1930, the four Lyons returned to Idaho to begin Ed's third year of seminary teaching. Hermana was by now tolerating, even enjoying Idaho. Ed was happy teaching seminary and extra classes at the high school. Hermana continued working with the young women in MIA. Ed accepted a call from President Hart to serve as stake Sunday School superintendent and also continued as a home missionary in the predominantly Latter-day Saint area, baptizing one young woman from his high school class. The year was normally eventful as Ed and Hermana filled their days and nights with child care (illus 6-3), Church service, teaching, and speaking. The summer classes at BYU had given Lyon new and exciting approaches to the scriptures, and he shared his ideas as he bounced around the speaker circuit in the Snake River Valley. But his ambitions were centered in Chicago, a mystical Mecca of learning. He and Hermana might have chosen to live in a nicer house or purchase a more reliable car, but instead they banked every extra penny for graduate school. The year passed quickly.

Lyon was counting on the same financial arrangement that Tanner, Chase, and Swensen had received to study in Chicago—half salary for a year. However, the United States, by early 1931, was in the midst of the worst economic depression in its history, and the Church was feeling a tremendous pinch that resulted in tighter budgets and the elimination of some programs. In a series of letters to Commissioner Merrill, Lyon reiterated his hopes and reminded the Apostle of the verbal promises that had been made in Provo in 1930. But Merrill simply answered that there would not be any more money to pay for seminary teachers to study for advanced degrees, citing the flak he had taken from certain brethren and noting that "the income of the Church has dropped off so greatly, that our financial outlook is very gloomy."[10] Even the summer training courses at BYU were to be reduced. Commissioner Merrill did guarantee Lyon a job after a year at Chicago but could offer no money for expenses during 1931–32.

Illus. 6-3. Hermana with John *(left)* and David *(right)* in 1932.

For a short time, Lyon and his wife considered canceling the Chicago experience, but they quickly decided they needed to go as they had planned. The money they had saved would help, and the Divinity School at Chicago came through with a scholarship that covered all tuition except for fifteen dollars per quarter. Other money would have to come from Lyon's father; during the course of the school year they would borrow twelve hundred dollars from David Lyon.

Entering the Dragon's Den at the University of Chicago

After the school year ended in Idaho, the Lyons packed up, drove to Salt Lake City to spend a few summer days with their parents, and then departed for Chicago. The Forsbergs accompanied the four Lyons as they drove up Parley's Canyon east of Salt Lake City, and at the summit they bade "good-bye and [they] came back and we headed off into the dragon's den all alone."[11] But it really wasn't such an unknown and fearsome place—Lyon had traveled the route by train in 1923. While returning from

Photo Archives, Perry Special Collections, Harold B. Lee Library, BYU

Illus. 6-4. Sidney B. Sperry recieved his Ph.D. at the University of Chicago.

his mission in 1926, he had toured the campus of the University of Chicago and been impressed by its mystique. He and his family now traversed U.S. Highway 30, following in reverse the route of early Mormon pioneers.

Upon arrival in Chicago in August 1932, Lyon immediately contacted Sidney B. Sperry (illus. 6-4), who was nearly finished with his Ph.D. at the Divinity School. Daryl Chase and Russel Swensen had also stayed to continue their studies, and a Latter-day Saint graduate from Utah State University, Carl J. Furr, arrived at this time. George Tanner was leaving, however, to fill an appointment as the director of the institute of religion at the University of Idaho. The Lyons took the Tanner family's spacious six-room apartment, the entire second floor of a "missionary dorm" originally designated for married couples who had served or were preparing to serve missions. It cost them $42.50 a month, a huge increase from their Idaho costs and particularly painful in Depression days. The apartment was right next to the university hospital, and little David loved the sirens and ambulances. From the Tanners, the Lyons purchased their first radio (for $22.50); Hermana now had news and entertainment right in her comfortable home. And in their first letter to Ed's parents, they pleaded for a year's supply of Figco, a coffee substitute popular in Utah and Idaho but not available in Chicago.[12] At home in their large apartment, Hermana often invited Chase and Swensen for dinner. Carl Furr, although married, had left his young wife and family in Utah, so he, too, frequently appeared at the dinner table.

Lyon was still not quite sure what to pursue as his major area of academic emphasis. Letters to Merrill indicate that he was tempted by American or biblical archaeology, but Merrill had previously counseled him not to pursue this area, since BYU already had an archaeologist, and one was enough in the Church at this time.[13] He also considered educational administration; his brother Kyle was completing Ph.D. work at

Berkeley and wrote Ed that there surely was a future for a well-prepared administrator. The anguish over exactly which area to pursue at Chicago lasted for several weeks during the first quarter of school. Finally, in the late summer, it became obvious. Lyon would stick with the same emphasis as his undergraduate work: history, especially American religious history. This proved to be an excellent choice because the Divinity School at the University of Chicago boasted history as one of its strongest suits. This choice also kept Lyon out of direct confrontation with biblical criticism, which eventually overwhelmed several of his collegiate companions.

First established as the Baptist Union Theological Seminary in the mid-1800s, the Divinity School (created in 1890) had become one of the most highly regarded places in the United States to study religion, history, and theology. Shailer Mathews, dean of the school when Lyon arrived, wrote that "the Divinity School of the University of Chicago (illus. 6-5) has no interest in producing dilettantes. It seeks to train its students for spiritual leadership. The religious leader whom the Divinity School seeks to produce is one trained in a sense of reality, in efficiency, and in contagious faith."[14] He affirmed that the school was in the business of preparing pastors, professors of theology, leaders in religious education, missionaries, and even "women for religious work."[15] These goals represented a sincere desire to mix faith with intellect and harmonize them in serious scholarship. Some criticized the school, suggesting that

Illus. 6-5. The Divinity School (Swift Hall) at the University of Chicago, 1938.

a few godless professors were bent on destroying the religious faith of all students who crossed its doorway, but the sincere and open statement of Dean Mathews contravenes that claim.

The school had a tense academic atmosphere, and Lyon felt keenly out of place among so many graduate students from major Eastern universities, intimidated by their academic and linguistic preparation:

> We [Latter-day Saint students] went back there as a group of ignoramuses because none of us knew Greek or Latin . . . . We were not Hebrew scholars and we didn't know Aramaic . . . and Syriac and things of that sort . . . . We'd get in a

Courtesy Special Collections, Univeristy of Chicago Library

Illus. 6-6. Edgar J. Goodspeed, professor at the Divinity School at the University of Chicago.

class and they'd start talking about a lot of literature in the Christian field that we were just ignorant of, knew nothing about. We kept our mouths shut. But at the same time we learned.[16]

Learning for these young men meant reaching, stretching, reading extra background material, pushing the limits of their knowledge, and attempting to grapple with never-before-imagined problems relating to the scriptures. Lyon audited classes in anthropology and American history to broaden his perspective, and he loved what he learned.

Lyon sat in classes taught by some of the world's greatest professors of religion, history, and theology. Dean Mathews, the "evangelist" of the school, carried the fire of sociohistorical methodology as *the* approach to scholarship. He had published more than twenty major books by the year Lyon arrived. Lyon registered for classes from Goodspeed (illus. 6-6) and continued to be amazed by his masterful lectures. Lyon's thesis adviser was William W. Sweet, a professor of Christian history. John T. McNeill, considered by some to be the best medieval historian in the world, linked European and Christian history in innovative ways. Shirley Jackson Case taught survey courses in the New Testament and was similarly regarded as a leading world authority in his field. J. M. P. Smith taught Old Testament based on his myriad books and original research in Palestine.[17]

Despite the fame of the teachers, Lyon had some serious doubts about their methodology and, more specifically, about the obvious lack of faith among these professors of religion:

> Down in their hearts they are all either . . . infidels or agnostics . . . . I fail to see how a young man can come here to school, and then go out after graduation as a minister of a church, and still preach what we call Christianity. The U. of Chicago is noted as being the most liberal (and that means Modernism) schoool in America. All religion is taught as product of social growth and development, and anything supernatural is looked upon as merely a betrayal of one's own ignorance and primitive mind. They make no attempt to harmonize Science and the Bible—they merely throw the Bible away, and teach scientific "truths" as the only thing to follow. I have taken a course called "Systematic Theology" this summer. It consisted of a brief discussion of the God of the Old Testament, who was merely a sign of the fear of the Hebrews, how He grew into the <u>Gods</u> of the New Testament, and then Dean Mathews informed us that he only existed in the minds of the believers. After that the study of theology has consisted of Physics, Psychology, Sociology and Psychiatry. I have been trying to find out what type of God the Christian world accepts, but I can not understand it, and I doubt if any of these professors can, yet they even open classes with prayer at times, and talk about going to God with our troubles. Of course, they merely feel sorry for us, when they hear that we are so ignorant and primitive that we still believe in a personal God. Their God, here at this University, is "the cosmic force of the Universe", "the personality producing force of the cosmos," the "in all and all" and a few more phrases just as unintelligible and meaningless. I readily see why the modern preachers talk about psychology, sociology, astronomy, prison reform, etc., in their churches on Sunday—that is all there is left to talk about after they have finished robbing Jesus of His Divinity, and miracles, and resurrection. In fact, around the Divinity School, the professors are always talking of "the Social Gospel." I am glad that I do not have to accept such rot, and that I do not have to study [it]. I miss most of it in the Church History Dept. where I am doing most of my work. The more I see and hear of it, the more it makes me appreciate the simple truths and teachings of . . . "Mormonism", even though we are called primitive. I am able to see so many places in the lectures each day that seem to me to be so obviously clear and simple for us to accept, yet these "learned men" pass right over them and can not see anything but their own view. I think that they are just as narrow-minded in their interpretations as they claim that we are in ours.[18]

This letter, from twenty-eight-year-old Lyon, criticizes the structure and approaches taken by many eminent scholars of religion. Yet there is irony in the fact that only a very liberal divinity school would even entertain the idea of admitting Latter-day Saint students, who did not fit the traditional Christian mold and certainly were not preparing to become professional clergy "for the ministry." Lyons' view that such preachers had to turn to the "social gospel" because the spiritual aspects had been lopped off or explained away by psychology or sociology is still held by many. Lyon's studies in the department of religious history, however, spared him from much of this "modernist" approach.

Lyon also worried, and probably with some justification, about the many Latter-day Saint students at the University of Chicago who, attempting to appear "modern," were too easily abandoning their founding faith:

> We have several of them [LDS students] here on the campus who think that they are outgrowing our little narrow-mindedness about our doctrines, and try to go with the world by attempting to take all of the supernatural elements out of our religion. . . . I suppose that I am too old fashioned to accept their way of thinking, but I fail to see how we can ever discard these views that have been the building force of the Church. Brother Sperry, who receives his Doctor of Philosophy degree here next Friday, and I are the two "Orthodox Mormons" around here, and many of the others laugh at us, for our simple trusting faith. . . .
>
> I am really worried what the outcome of the next thirty years will mean to the church. Even many of the BYU professors are going over to this view, and teaching things that are far more radical than those taught by Peterson and Chamberlain at the time they were dismissed from that institution.[19]

He was also concerned about his fellow Latter-day Saint classmates and how the Church would be able to reconcile contemporary discoveries and critical methods with its revelatory and spiritual base.

In the midst of these dilemmas, a telegram arrived from Salt Lake City in October 1931. Hermana's father had been called to preside over the Swedish Mission. He had served there thirty years earlier and would now return with his wife and three youngest children, Ada, Frances, and John. The Forsbergs were not able to sell their house as they desired but had to rent it. Ed noted the obvious "sacrifice that our Church calls upon its members to make when they are asked to leave home and business and go on a mission. . . . It is one of the strongest proofs of the strength of the

Gospel."[20] The Forsbergs' sacrifices would continue: by the time he returned to Utah in 1934, Gustave's electrical contracting business was more than six thousand dollars in debt.[21]

Creating a Thesis

Lyon could not ponder too long on the family or contemporary Church; he had to get on with his thesis. He wanted to write on Mormons and Freemasonry, but after futile attempts to get information from the Masonic archives in Chicago, he next approached his thesis adviser with the idea of "writing on Orson Pratt. 'Well, what was he?' [asked Sweet]. And I said, 'Well, he was the first theologian the Mormons had.' 'Well [said Sweet] how much did he know about theology?' And I said . . . 'He was exploring like the rest. He wasn't a trained man, but he read widely.'"[22] Pratt had often been in the home of Lyon's grandmother Carrington, and stories about his great mind abounded. The Lyon family had revered and praised him.

With Sweet's support and suggestions, Lyon decided to write a biography of Orson Pratt, explicating his theology and interpretations on religion and plural marriage and examining his myriad publications. The task was daunting:

> I hope that I can write a life of him that will do justice and credit to him, and at the same time be acceptable to the University as a piece of scientific investigation and research. I know now, this early in the beginning, that I shall have to rob him of some of his reputation as a scientist, as he plunged into the future and made theories, based on the so-called scientific facts of his day. These have since been proved to be wrong, and changed again, so that the modern scientific world will no longer accept his views in many respects. However, I know that he deserves a great deal of credit for his pioneering, and his fearless courage to move ahead and his efforts to increase the sum of human knowledge. For all this he should be given credit. His doctrinal treatments are going to prove ticklish things for me, as I must handle them for an atheistic, scientific world. But I am going to do all that I can to do him justice.[23]

Lyon applied much of the rigorous methodology from his course work and by the end of spring term 1932 had completed a 127-page thesis, "Orson Pratt—Early Mormon Leader." Lyon's thesis was the first major study on Pratt done in the Church. Although not widely available, it stood for more than fifty years as the basis for further study of Pratt and his theology.[24]

The thesis caused Lyon to come to grips with some problems and misconceptions in Church history, a pattern he would pursue the rest of his academic life. "I cannot refrain from endeavoring to explode some of the untrue stories which are commonly met with in [contemporary Church] books," Lyon wrote.[25] In the same letter, Lyon talked of Orson Pratt's supposed apostasy as well as problems between Joseph Smith and Orson's wife. Then he explained that he had been reading the six-volume *Comprehensive History of the Church* by B. H. Roberts. Ed confided his astonishment to his father that Roberts

> was allowed to publish some of the things which he has. I imagine he must have had a struggle to get some of it in print. For example, his exposé of the poor judgment used by the Saints in Missouri which caused their persecutions; his criticism of the Nauvoo City Council for destroying the Nauvoo Expositor, which he says was absolutely illegal and they should have known better. I think that some of the Prophet's indiscretions happened when he was not acting as a prophet, as he said "A prophet is not always a prophet, but only when acting as such."
>
> . . . But I think that it is far better to make a bold admission of facts and truth, and do it now, than wait until it is forced down our throats at a later date when it will be more embarassing to us. I am convinced that we must face the future with a little broader view than we have done in the past (I mean certain people in the Church), or we are going to lose our young people and have no power to hold them. Personally, Hermana and I say that you (Father and Mother) are the broadest people we have ever known. It is a pity that the other Latter-day Saints cannot develop more of it.

Lyon also reported that he had "gathered ten or twenty times as much material about Orson Pratt's missionary work and labors than I have been able to put in the thesis." He looked forward to returning to Salt Lake City, "where I can have more access to the Church Historian's Office with its records, I hope to be able to make a fuller and more complete study of [Pratt's] life and then get someone who has literary talent [to] write up his biography in an interesting manner." Through his research, Lyon developed a deep appreciation for Pratt, believing him to have been "an intellectual genius, and had he lived in a large city and not been primarily an ecclesiastical worker, he would probably have made a real contribution to the knowledge of the world."[26]

In Salt Lake City, Ed's father hand-copied materials from the Church Archives and sent them to Chicago to help with Ed's thesis. Later his father read and critiqued drafts of each chapter; the thesis truly was a father-son cooperative venture. Then once the thesis was written and approved, to save the forty-dollar preparation fee, Hermana typed the entire work on a black Remington portable typewriter, a machine she used for the rest of her life. With the thesis finally completed, Ed received a master's degree at the impressive and colorful June 1932 commencement, ten months after his matriculation (illus. 6-7).

Evaluating the Chicago Experience

The time in Chicago yielded more than a degree for Lyon. Both Hermana and Ed were very involved and active in the University Branch of the Northern States Mission. Ed and Hermana taught Sunday School classes. They loved the gothic Latter-day Saint chapel with its impressive pipe organ, so different from more practical Church buildings in Utah and Idaho. However, far from her Salt Lake City support system, Hermana faced some personal problems. One of Hermana's sons explained it this way:

Mother talked about the struggles she went through with her own testimony during this time. It was not the intense intellectual atmosphere that caused this struggle, but her own feelings of inferiority instilled in her [she felt] by her stepmother. Mother said that she and Dad talked for long hours night after night about her feelings. She finally came to realize that she had to try to forgive her stepmother. Once she had made that decision, she was able to come to a much stronger testimony of the Church. This is the only time I ever heard Mother talk about this struggle. She did not elaborate, but I suspect that her stepmother was so tied up with her feelings about the Church that she could not easily separate the two.[27]

Illus. 6-7. Ed Lyon in academic robes after receiving his master's degree at the University of Chicago in 1932.

Hermana came out stronger as a result of facing this long-fermenting conflict within herself.

Ed also emerged a stronger teacher, a better scholar, and a more spiritually committed[28] Latter-day Saint than before. Some Church leaders were skeptical, even critical, of this "experiment in Chicago," but for several of the seminary teachers who participated, the effect was life-changing and long-lasting, for better or worse. A handful of well-prepared, disparate, dynamic teachers returned to the West ready to serve and inspire, challenge and stimulate students in the Church. Just as the 1888–91 art missionaries had a dual role—that of painting the inside of the Salt Lake Temple *and* stimulating the entire artistic community of Utah[29]—so too did the Chicago-trained seminary and institute teachers advance their own academic skills and then influence at least two generations of Latter-day Saint students, encouraging them to study seriously and to attend top graduate schools outside Utah. In all, eleven seminary and institute men earned advanced degrees at Chicago during the early 1930s.[30]

Although their exposure to the academic world was relatively brief, these participants looked back on these experiences nostalgically. In the early 1970s, George Tanner evaluated "the four quarters I spent at the University of Chicago [as] easily the highlight of my intellectual life," where he learned that "non-Mormon scholars were honest, sincere and interested in our welfare."[31] In a 1970 letter to Russel Swensen, Lyon evaluated the beneficial results of the Chicago training for the entire Church:

> It appears to me that the securing of graduate degrees . . . represents a landmark in an educational outreach which the Church had never known before, and which has profoundly influenced the teaching in the seminaries and institutes since that day. The importation to the B.Y.U. summer school for the teachers of religion of Doctors Goodspeed, Graham, McNeill, and Bower . . . is reflected in the lessons and textbooks written for use in the Church schools and auxiliaries since that time. It was a time of an intellectual and spiritual awakening which was the entering wedge that put the Church educational system in contact with the ongoing mainstream of Christian scriptural and historical research. This outlook has aided in the metamorphosis of the L.D.S. Church from a sectionally oriented to a worldwide Church in less than forty years.[32]

So positive was their personal experience at Chicago that Ed and Hermana decided that Ed should continue with Ph.D. studies at the Divinity School. He began doctoral studies during summer 1932, taking more classes in Christian history and biblical exegesis but could not afford to stay another year in Chicago. He was already deeply in debt to his father and would have to return that fall to teaching in the West.

During his studies at Chicago, Lyon maintained correspondence with Commissioner Merrill. Lyon wanted assurance that despite the Depression, he would have a teaching job in the Church's educational system when he wanted one. Ariel Ballif had taken his place at the Midway seminary and was well liked, especially for his musical talents. Lyon did not want to displace Ballif, nor did he or Hermana really want to return to tiny Midway. They angled for a seminary job in Utah, but Merrill explained that this was a period of no expansion in the seminary system. A seminary job would be available for Lyon but likely in Rigby, if Ed Berrett took an unpaid leave.[33]

The Church's declining tithing funds during the Depression closed some career doors for Lyon—but it opened others. During the Depression, the Church began ridding itself of junior colleges in St. George, Cedar City, Ephraim, and Ogden, Utah. Church leaders also tried to persuade the Idaho legislature to accept Ricks College as a public institution. On May 26, 1932, Merrill wrote that Ricks College wanted Lyon. This may have been the doing of Lyon's ecclesiastical mentor John Hart, who also served on the Ricks College board and carried considerable weight with college president Hyrum Manwaring. Merrill informed Lyon that "Ricks wants your master's degree to count in their list which they think will help to get the instruction over to the public."[34] In short, Ricks wanted to use Lyon by touting his academic credentials to show that some faculty had advanced degrees from major universities and to make the college more attractive to the Idaho legislature.

Starting at Ricks College

The decision was difficult. Ricks College represented a step up the academic ladder for the seminary teacher, but its future was clouded by the fact that the Church was trying to sell or give it to the state of Idaho. If Lyon accepted the position, he might soon find himself working for the state rather than the Church. In the Church's employment, he had found joy in teaching gospel principles along with academic subject matter. And what Lyon really wanted was to take Hermana back to Utah. President Hart assured him that he would prosper at Ricks and that all the Saints in Idaho would fight the decision to sell the small college. Hart and many local Church members argued that Idaho Saints paid as much tithing as members in Utah, and if the Church was going to keep and fund BYU it must also maintain Ricks College.[35] Based on these tentative assurances, Lyon accepted the offer from Ricks for the 1932–33 school year. He groused considerably over a sixty-dollar discrepancy in his first salary offer, which was eventually restored (to total $1,980). But at least he did not have to take a 10 percent salary reduction, as the Church had mandated for all seminary teachers that year.[36] The fact that he would haggle with an Apostle over sixty dollars in the midst of a terrible economic depression indicates that he felt a considerable amount of confidence in his position and new master's degree as well as pressure to begin paying off his college debts.

Elder Merrill had warned Lyon that "at Ricks . . . you will be asked to teach some subjects for which, I think, you are not very well prepared."[37] Lyon had already taught history, sociology, and seminary in Idaho schools, but at Ricks he became *the* professor of political science. At the University of Utah, he had studied basic political science, which merited him a minor, but his recent studies were quite removed from the political scene. Lyon felt ill-prepared to teach the subject; nevertheless, he began reading intensely during summer 1932. There were only twenty-three faculty members at Ricks in 1932, and so Lyon also had the chance to teach some religious education. In this area he again enjoyed particular success: "I had 112 in my lecture, and [then] on Thursday . . . in spite of the 47 below weather, I had 139 present. President Manwaring felt a little jealous, I fear, as the people left his department and came to mine. . . . I feel that I made better speeches than I have ever given before."[38] He was gaining great personal confidence in teaching religious education.

The next weekend, returning to his old Sunday habit of speaking somewhere in the Snake River Valley, Ed delivered a sacrament meeting talk. In a letter to Ed's parents, Hermana observed that

> He spoke last Sunday night in the 4th Ward here and gave the finest talk I've ever heard him give. He talked on "Conditions in the Religious World at the Time of Joseph Smith." You'd have been so proud of him if you could have heard him. . . . He has such a fine spirit with him too which is better than any of the other gifts. Everyone was impressed greatly with his talk—even the youngsters were interested.[39]

Hermana often perceived Ed's strengths and abilities more acutely than he did. She realized that he was now becoming a sought-after speaker, able to engage and hold an audience not with charismatic voice or flashy rhetorical style, but with accurate anecdotes, original insights into Church history, and honest spirituality (illus. 6-8). According to information from his datebooks, during the five years he and Hermana spent in Idaho Ed delivered at least 260 talks, mostly in sacrament services.

Lyon's year of teaching at Ricks was successful, but it was clouded by the Church's desire to get the state of Idaho to take the junior college. In January 1933, many Saints from the upper Snake River Valley attended the state legislature in Boise to oppose the transfer of Ricks to the state. The proposal for transfer failed by only a few votes. "So the Church decided to continue [Ricks for] another year or two and then try to get the [Idaho] legislature to take it again. They [also] decided to cut the faculty from twenty-three to ten" according to Lyon.[40] The local leaders had won the battle to keep the college, but more than half the faculty would have to seek other work, right at the most difficult point in the Depression. Manwaring and Merrill wanted Lyon to stay because he was one of only four professors who had a master's degree. But this meant that a local man with a B.A. from BYU who had lived in Rexburg for twenty years would lose his job. "Hermana and I said, 'It just isn't fair.' So I said to Dr. Merrill, 'I would never feel right about forcing that man out of this place where he's made his life. Can you find me a job in the seminary?'"[41]

After more haggling, some misunderstanding, and numerous letters, Elder Merrill promised Lyon a job in Ogden, Utah, at Weber High School, if he would first go to Rigby for one more year. The salary would be only $1770, a $210 decrease, due to the reduced revenues of the Church. The Church simply did not have funds: during March 1933, the Ricks faculty had received only half their monthly salary; the other half was to be paid at a later date. In his datebook, Lyon recorded that on March 3, 1933, a fifteen-day moratorium on all banking business in Idaho began, coterminous with President Roosevelt's bank holidays. In Salt Lake City, Lyon's father lost nearly two thousand dollars in a

Illus. 6-8. Ed Lyon, c. 1933.

bank failure. In this climate, Lyon willingly agreed to the contract and sought assurances that he would get back to Utah in fall 1934.

Before going to Rigby, the Lyons enjoyed an eventful summer. In June 1933, they stored their meager furniture at Ricks College and drove to Salt Lake City. Ed and Hermana hiked a bit in the foothills, usually bringing five-year-old David and three-year-old John with them. After a few days of deserved vacation, Ed left in the old Chevrolet for Berkeley, California. He still intended to complete his Ph.D. at the University of Chicago, but since he had received a master's degree there, the school required him to attend another major university before completing his doctorate in their program. Ed chose the University of California–Berkeley not only for its excellent reputation, but also because his older brother Kyle was completing his Ph.D. there and spoke highly of the academic atmosphere. After finding an apartment in California, Ed sent for his wife and children.

Though Hermana was pregnant again and experiencing her worst morning sickness thus far, she trundled the two boys and herself to the train station and on to Berkeley. The cool California summer was a relief after the previous two summers in muggy Chicago. Ed enjoyed classes in frontier history from Frederick Paxson and in English history from a visiting professor from Oxford.[42] So severe was Hermana's sickness, however, that she had to spend several weeks in bed. The ward Relief Society sisters regularly brought meals and tended the two young boys. At the end of the summer, the family returned to Salt Lake City for two weeks, enjoying more hikes in the mountains with Ed's sixty-five-year-old father. Hermana visited Dr. Jack, who informed her that she was expecting twins to be born in February or March. This provided some explanation for the unusually severe sickness she was experiencing.

The six years since graduation from the University of Utah had been intense. Lyon had attended four different universities—University of Utah, Brigham Young University, University of Chicago, and Berkeley— as a graduate student, received a master's degree, and completed nearly half of his doctorate course work. He had left public school teaching, favoring the rewards of seminary, but had recently found the joys of teaching college students at Ricks. He had gained great confidence in his abilities to speak and teach and to compete with other graduate students at two of the best universities in the country.

The Lyon family returned to Idaho on Saturday, September 2. They arrived in Rigby at 5:00 P.M. and began to unpack. At 6:00 P.M. the bulky shadow of President John Hart fell across the door. "What the hell have you been doing?" he said to Lyon. "After that opening remark, I said

'Well, what do you mean?' He said, 'Well, one of us is in trouble and it ain't me. Have you been teaching heresy?'"[43] He handed Lyon a telegram from President Heber J. Grant requesting a meeting with Lyon and Hart the next morning in Rexburg. Lyon wondered if his academic formation in Chicago and Berkeley had seriously damaged his future. Was his orthodoxy being questioned? Sleep was scarce that night.

Notes

1. For a detailed description and analysis of this program, see Russel B. Swensen, "Mormons at the University of Chicago Divinity School: A Personal Reminiscence," *Dialogue: A Journal of Mormon Thought* 7 (summer 1972): 37–47. Swensen affirms that the faith Church leaders placed in the experience was duly rewarded—each of the men remained active in the Church and all made major contributions to the Church's institute and seminary system, even if they did not stay with the system all their lives.

2. Swensen, "Mormons at the University of Chicago," 40.

3. Chase completed a master's thesis on Sidney Rigdon, Tanner on "The Religious Environment in which Mormonism Arose," and Swensen on the "Influence of the New Testament on Latter-day Saint Eschatology." Swensen, "Mormons at the University of Chicago," 43.

4. T. Edgar Lyon to Hermana Lyon, June 18, 1930, T. Edgar Lyon Collection, Church Archives, Family and Church History Department, The Church of Jesus Christ of Latter-day Saints, Salt Lake City (hereafter cited as Church Archives). Unless otherwise noted, all citations for T. Edgar Lyon materials are located in the Lyon collection.

5. T. Edgar Lyon, Diary, June 12, 1930, Church Archives.

6. T. Edgar Lyon to Hermana Lyon, June 17, 1930, Church Archives.

7. T. Edgar Lyon to Hermana Lyon, June 24, 1930, Church Archives.

8. T. Edgar Lyon to Hermana Lyon, June 23, 1930, Church Archives.

9. Hermana Lyon to T. Edgar Lyon, June 24, 1930, Church Archives.

10. Joseph F. Merrill to T. Edgar Lyon, January 31, 1931, Church Archives.

11. T. Edgar Lyon, "Oral History," bound typescript, 95, Church Archives.

12. T. Edgar Lyon to parents, August 17, 1931, Church Archives.

13. Joseph F. Merrill to T. Edgar Lyon, January 31, 1931.

14. Charles H. Arnold *Near the Edge of Battle* (Chicago: Divinity School Association, 1966), 17.

15. Arnold, *Near the Edge of Battle*, 18.

16. T. Edgar Lyon, "Oral History," 94.

17. T. Edgar Lyon, "Oral History," 92–101.

18. T. Edgar Lyon to parents, August 21, 1931, Church Archives.

19. T. Edgar Lyon to parents, August 21, 1931.

20. T. Edgar Lyon to father, November 2, 1931, Church Archives.

21. T. Edgar Lyon, "Oral History," 105.

22. T. Edgar Lyon, "Oral History," 96.

23. T. Edgar Lyon to parents, August 21, 1931. Once again, Lyon's selection of this topic was based on some personal acquaintance—Orson Pratt's son often came to the David Lyon home:

> During my younger years Orson Pratt's son, Milson, and his daughter, Mrs. Alvin Beesley, both lived in the ward where my father was Bishop. Milson was a widower, and Mother often had him come to dinner on Sundays. (T. Edgar Lyon to Duane E. Jeffery, September 22, 1972, Church Archives)

24. In 1985 the University of Utah Press published Breck England's *The Life and Thought of Orson Pratt,* a 359-page biography that gives considerably more detail and insight on the life of this early leader.

25. T. Edgar Lyon to father, April 18, 1932, Church Archives.

26. T. Edgar Lyon to father, April 18, 1932.

27. Joseph Lynn Lyon, "A History of Laura Hermana Forsberg," 1991, p. 32, L. Tom Perry Special Collections, Harold B. Lee Library, Brigham Young University, Provo, Utah.

28. T. Edgar Lyon, "Oral History," 100–101. In later years Lyon recalled the reaction of some General Authorities:

> I remember George F. Richards came to attend a conference of the mission in Chicago. . . . He was very anti-education in the talks he gave in the conference and afterward in similar fashion very anti-information. . . . He knew me a little bit because I was in the [prayer] circle, and when he was in town he of course presided over it.
>
> Well, I went to the morning session and then I went up across the town to the other one up to Logan Square and attended the afternoon session. At the afternoon session I went up and told him I'd enjoyed very much the talk he'd given there. He didn't have a university audience now; he had dental students, and mostly that wasn't much of a problem. I can remember him saying, "Well now, Brother Lyon, it's all right to get an education but don't lose your testimony, and don't read the books they tell you to read." See he was fearful of me, but I told him that I hoped I could understand. I think there was fear on their part more than there was in some of us . . . Joseph F. Merrill was positive toward it. Very definitely . . . John A. Widtsoe? He was non-committal. (T. Edgar Lyon, "Oral History," 100–101)

29. Several articles and one book examine this art "mission." One evaluation notes: "The results of the Paris training were many. They [the participants] became the nucleus of Utah's art circle for years to come. They spread their influence through teaching, the organizing of various arts organizations, and actively exhibiting their work." Brigham Young University Museum of Art display, 1995. See also

Linda Jones Gibbs, *Harvesting the Light: The Paris Art Mission and Beginnings of Utah Impressionism* (Salt Lake City: The Church of Jesus Christ of Latter-day Saints, 1987).

30. The participants were Anthony S. Cannon, Daryl Chase, Carl J. Furr, Therald N. Jensen, Vernon Larson, Wesley P. Lloyd, T. Edgar Lyon, Heber C. Snell, Sidney B. Sperry, Russel B. Swensen, and George S. Tanner.

31. Cited in Swensen, "Mormons at the University of Chicago," 46–47.

32. Cited in Swensen, "Mormons at the University of Chicago," 47.

33. Joseph F. Merrill to T. Edgar Lyon, March 14, 1932, Church Archives.

34. Joseph F. Merrill to T. Edgar Lyon, May 26, 1932, Church Archives.

35. In a letter to his parents, Lyon reported a meeting in Rexburg:

> Apostle McKay was here on Friday, and 1966 people came to hear him. President Hart was here and the people had a really stormy session, concerning the closing of Ricks College. The attitude was almost one of defiance, with a threat to secede from the Church and use the tithing paid by Idahoans in Idaho, and not for the BYU. I feel, however, that these local people are barking up the wrong tree. The stake presidents did not mince words, either, when they criticized Dr. Merrill. Hermana was afraid that Br. McKay would go through the ceiling while Pres. Hart was talking about Dr. Merrill. (T. Edgar Lyon to parents, February 15, 1933, Church Archives)

36. Joseph F. Merrill to T. Edgar Lyon, March 14, 1932, Church Archives.

37. Joseph F. Merrill to T. Edgar Lyon, May 26, 1932.

38. T. Edgar Lyon to parents, February 15, 1933, Church Archives.

39. Hermana Lyon to David Ross Lyon family, February 15, 1933, Church Archives.

40. T. Edgar Lyon, "Oral History," 102.

41. T. Edgar Lyon, "Oral History," 103.

42. T. Edgar Lyon, "Oral History," 103–4.

43. T. Edgar Lyon, "Oral History," 104.

7

President Lyon, 1933–37

On Sunday morning, September 3, 1933, Hermana was not feeling well and stayed in Rigby with the two boys. Ed picked up President Hart and drove the fifteen miles to a conference in the neighboring Rexburg Stake. Seventy-six-year-old Church President Heber J. Grant (illus. 7-1) was the visiting authority and had arranged special seating for Lyon and Hart; upon arriving they were ushered to chairs near the stand. Both fidgeted nervously through the morning session, and when it finally concluded, Hart walked over to talk with President Grant. Lyon anxiously watched the lengthy conversation. Hart returned to his seat and said, "I told you it was you [who was in trouble]. Go up there and face the fire."[1]

Unique Call

Ed had known President Grant in Salt Lake City, had passed the sacrament to him, had visited his home as a block teacher, had worked with his grandson in the ward scout troop, and had gone to LDSU with two of his granddaughters. Yet none of this made him any less apprehensive as he approached the president of the Church.

> He [Grant] was sitting down, and he said, "—Sit down, Brother Lyon." And I sat down by the side of him. The first question he asked was, "Are you in debt" I said, "Yes." He said, "How much?" I said, "About $1,200." He said, "What right has a man your age being in debt? There are only two reasons to have any excuse for being in debt and one of them is to buy a home and the other is to establish a business or a profession." I said, "Well, this is a debt from establishing a profession." "What do you mean?" I said, "I was away at school at Chicago a year before last and I haven't paid off my debts yet." "Oh, that's a different thing. Who do you owe it to?" I said, "My father." He said, "He can wait." He was very brusque. Then he said, "We've selected you to go preside over the Netherlands Mission." Well, if he had said, "We're going to send you to Timbuctu," I'd have been no more surprised.[2]

Ed's twenty-seven-year-old wife was pregnant and sick; he himself had just turned thirty years old, and he had been home from his first mission for

only seven years. He felt very
insecure about his language
and leadership abilities, and
besides, he had not even
unpacked his bags after a
summer of intense study in
California. President Grant
did not ask whether Ed
would accept the call but
merely inquired, "How soon
can you be ready to go?"[3]
President Grant explained
that the current mission
president's wife had cancer
and that she had already
returned to the United
States. Ed did not hesitate or
doubt but quickly accepted
the call. Then, quite suddenly, he realized that he had
not discussed the call with
his wife. He tried to phone
her, but the party line was
busy. Anxiously he sat

Courtesy Church Archives

Illus. 7-1. Church President Heber J. Grant
called Ed Lyon to be the Netherlands mission
president in 1933.

through the afternoon session of the stake conference, pondering his
future in Europe but most concerned about his more immediate conversation with Hermana in Rigby.

When Ed finally got to the house, Hermana immediately inquired
about the interview with the president of the Church. He teased her,
stringing out the suspense, telling her that now she did not need to worry
about giving birth to the twins in Idaho. He knew that she dreaded the
prospect, preferring that Dr. Jack in Salt Lake City assist in the delivery.
One of her sons records, "When he finally told her [about the mission
call], she immediately wanted to know if he had told President Grant
'yes'. When he said he had, Mother demanded to know why she had not
been consulted. Dad explained that you simply do not say 'no' to the
President of the Church."[4] Hermana began to cry, and five-year-old
David and three-year-old John joined the chorus of tears. But they would
go to the Netherlands because they were called to do so by a respected
authority. Hermana never doubted the call—she only worried. She knew

that three or four years away from extended family in a strange land with a difficult language and unfamiliar customs would be as hard for her, or more so, than for her husband.

Ed pondered the reason for his call. Why him, at such a young age? "It wasn't because of me. It's because I had a job that I could return to," he later speculated.[5] He felt that President Grant, ever the businessman, had anguished over the financial losses that mission calls had occasioned for many Church members during the Depression. Ed's own father-in-law, serving in Sweden, had already lost thousands of dollars. It was safe for the Church to call seminary and institute teachers because it could assure them a continuation of their teaching jobs upon their return.[6] Further, President Grant knew and respected Ed's parents. In a letter to his father, Ed explained:

> Yesterday when Pres. Grant asked me to accept the call and I said I would, I told him that I felt weak and incapable of doing it. He said "You can do it, because you are David R. Lyon's son. He could do it, and would do it, and you must try to be as good a man as your father." I was proud to hear him say it, because it was more than true. He also spoke very highly of Brother Forsberg.[7]

Ed's acquaintance with Church leaders paved the way for his new calling. This explanation, however, overlooks the spiritual basis for a major Church calling. In 1933, fourteen new mission presidents were called, representing almost a 50 percent turnover that Depression year, to staff some of the thirty-one missions of the Church. Ed was among the small group, obviously selected for his spirituality and his successes as a teacher of youth as well as other reasons.

The call to serve created many concerns, and the most worrisome was Hermana's pregnancy. They phoned Dr. Jack, who advised that there would be little danger—if the transatlantic voyage took place within the next six weeks. So the family began planning a rapid departure. Scores of other details arose. The month of September was a blur of business for the young couple. Hermana and the children had to have passports; Ed's had to be renewed. He also had to secure insurance for his wife and children, since the Church insured him but not his dependents. A new teacher had to be assigned to teach the two hundred students in the Rigby seminary. Ed taught for the first two weeks until R. Welling Roskelley arrived to replace him. On September 18, they boxed up what few things they had not yet packed or sold and returned to Salt Lake City.

The very next day, seeking advice and support, Ed visited with his former mission president Charles Hyde. Here he "learned of the big problems ahead in Holland," though he records no specific details.[8] Harold Reynolds, secretary to the Missionary Committee, provided a few hours of instruction on duties of mission presidents—the only training or preparation provided by Church headquarters. Both Hermana and Ed received a father's blessing from Patriarch David Lyon. Hermana was obviously anxious about the journey and its effects on her pregnancy; the blessing calmed her. A hastily arranged farewell (illus. 7-2) took place in the Ensign Ward where $26.85 was collected to help pay family travel expenses.[9] The Church paid the presidents' train and boat expenses, but each family had to pick up the tab for wife and children.

On Friday, September 29, 1933, President Grant set Ed apart, promising a greater command of the foreign language as well as the ability to solve problems from petty squabbles to major conflicts. Anthony W. Ivins (illus. 7-3), First Counselor in the First Presidency, set Hermana apart as "Mission Mother," which included being president and "consulting supervisor" of the Relief Society, the Primary, and the Young Women's Mutual Improvement Association for the mission. These apostolic blessings were reassuring, but still the Lyons felt insecure:

> We both feel that the responsibility of the call is almost more than we can bear. We are both so young, and I never was a good Dutch speaker, so I feel that we are going to have a serious time of it in trying to succeed Pres. [Frank I.] Kooyman. He is such a gifted Dutch speaker and writer that it will be difficult to even approach the standards which he has set.[10]

Illus. 7-2. Farewell program for the Lyon family.

Courtesy Church Archives

Illus. 7-3. Anthony W. Ivins (c. 1933) set Hermana apart for her mission to the Netherlands.

Despite their understandable uneasiness, Ed and Hermana continued hectic preparations, and as the time to leave drew near, things started to fall into place. The passports arrived on time, friends hosted farewell parties, and the family was able to store their much-traveled furniture at the large home of Ed's parents. Exhausted after finishing such extensive preparations in just four weeks, the Lyons finally climbed aboard the Los Angeles Ltd. on October 2, 1933, again going "back east." They had arranged to stop and sightsee in three cities—Chicago; Washington, D.C.; and New York. In Chicago, after a hot, dusty train ride, they stayed with friends and visited the "Century of Progress" World's Fair, which had opened in May. The Lyons were among the fair's thirty-nine million visitors. They took special interest in the Church's large historical and doctrinal displays, tastefully designed by Avard Fairbanks.[11] Missionaries, under the direction of mission president George S. Romney, manned the display's replica of the Salt Lake Tabernacle. The Lyons were impressed by this approach to missionary work.[12] After three days in Chicago, they boarded a clean, air-cooled Pullman car for Washington, D.C., where they again visited friends and saw the sights.

The four Lyons boarded the SS *Manhattan* on October 11, in tourist class. Ed wrote home, "We have a lovely cabin, with an outside porthole . . . and the cabin is in the middle of the ship, where the motion . . . is least noticeable."[13] These features were important, especially for Hermana, whose difficult pregnancy still caused her some nausea. One evening the sea was so rough that John rolled out of bed; luckily, his father caught him in midair. As the ship neared Plymouth, England, seven days later, Ed reported that despite rolling seas, "we have all escaped seasickness as Father promised Hermana when we left Salt Lake."[14] They had been blessed with good health, calm stomachs, and safe arrival in England.

In March 1933, the European Mission was in a state of transition. Church leaders had moved the mission headquarters from Liverpool to London, a logical transfer since residence in London allowed the president easier access to Europe.[15] After six years of service, Elder John A. Widtsoe (illus. 7-4) and his wife had received their release and were preparing to return to Utah. Joseph F. Merrill, Ed's former teacher and administrative head in the seminary system, had just recently arrived to replace Widtsoe as president over the eleven missions of the European Mission.[16] The Lyons arrived at the mission home in the midst of the change. During several hours of instruction, mainly from Elder Merrill but also from Elder Widtsoe, the Lyons learned some of their specific duties. Widtsoe had reversed a decades-old Church policy by insisting that local members be given leadership experience in Church branches. He had observed the leadership vacuum caused by World War I, and sensing future conflict, mandated that local leaders be called, first as counselors to American missionaries, and then as branch presidents.[17] Lyon fully agreed.

The next evening, Elder Merrill and his wife hosted a dinner for the Widtsoes and the Lyons. During the meal, Elder Widtsoe admonished, "Now Brother Lyon, there are several things that you need to remember. The first one is, God loves the Dutchmen just as much as he loves the Americans. Remember. . . . There's going to be a war before too many years. It's inevitable."[18] He also urged Lyon to continue the work begun by the outgoing president Frank I. Kooyman (illus. 7-5) of properly preparing local leaders. This gave Lyon a plan, a firm goal to work toward. At the same meal, Widtsoe cautioned against taking the approach to religion that Lyon had learned at Chicago: "What you learned back there was probably all good, but you're just to forget all that now. It has no application in the mission field at all."[19] Lyon, on the other hand, felt that his scholarly experience definitely would be an asset to his missionary work. Merrill sided with Lyon; after all, Merrill had initiated the program of sending seminary teachers to the Divinity School. During the dinner, Hermana and Ed were surprised to

Courtesy Church Archives

Illus. 7-4. John A. Widtsoe was released as the European Mission president in 1933; the Lyons visited with him breifly on their way to the Netherlands.

learn that, due to health reasons and financial blows to his business in Utah, Hermana's father would be released as mission president in Sweden as soon as a replacement could be found.

Hermana was delighted to be in London, the theater capital of the world, but she had no free time to attend a play. After just two short nights in London's lovely National Hotel, the Lyons crossed the rough North Sea in six hours, during which time David and John both vomited frequently. Hermana felt nauseated but remained relatively well; Ed's iron stomach hardly knew the boat was rocking. President Kooyman and six missionaries met the Lyons and accompanied them by train to the mission home and office at Crooswijkschesingel 166 in Rotterdam.[20]

Courtesy Church Archives

Illus. 7-5. Frank I. Kooyman as a young missionary. Kooyman served as president of the Netherlands Mission from 1929 to 1933.

Home Away from Home

Lyon was the youngest president to preside over the Netherlands Mission since its establishment in 1861, with the exception of a short period when Sylvester Q. Cannon as a young missionary also served as a temporary president.[21] He knew that this would mean additional pressure, especially from members who might recall him as the inexperienced, struggling missionary of just a few years earlier.

During Lyon's first mission, from 1923 through 1925, the mission had averaged approximately 66 missionaries and 209 baptisms per year. When Lyon returned as mission president in 1933, there were only 25 missionaries and 30 baptisms. The number of missionaries had decreased by slightly more than half, but baptisms were down to one-seventh of the earlier average. Membership had also fallen during the past ten years: in 1923 there had been 2,965 members in the Netherlands, but there were only 2,542 in 1933.[22] Some had been excommunicated but many others had immigrated to the United States, and the reduced number of baptisms simply did not replace those who were cut off or who emigrated. The worldwide Depression eventually slowed emigration from the Netherlands—not a single member left the country in 1933, and only four left the next year. By 1936 the number of emigrants grew to 129, almost double the number of baptisms that year.[23] In short, the mission that Lyon had known in the mid-1920s was now limping along at a much reduced pace. Perhaps this was what former president Charles Hyde had in mind when he tried to prepare Lyon for "the big problems ahead in Holland."

The statistics cited above, not available to Lyon when he first arrived, do not correspond with his initial positive evaluation of the mission. Just three days after his arrival, for instance, Lyon wrote to his parents, informing them that

> President Kooyman ... has made [the Netherlands Mission] one of the most progressive missions in the entire Church. It will be utterly impossible for us to ever begin to approach the standards set by him, due to his wonderful gift as a translator and speaker. There is much discontent, but that is to be expected, when generation-old policies are changed and reversed.[24]

Again, Lyon felt inadequate when he compared his language abilities with those of his predecessor. Within a few weeks he would harbor very different feelings about the mission as he became better acquainted with its problems and lack of progress.

Lyon was in a bind. Although he admired Kooyman very much and had praised him to many people, as he learned more about the state of the mission, he found that the financial records were in disarray, the missionaries were not working hard, and the members felt very discouraged.[25] Furthermore, President Kooyman[26] was involved in a major translation project (*The Beehive Handbook*) and simply did not want to turn over control of the mission to Lyon. Kooyman had moved to an upstairs room in the mission home, giving the main floor to the Lyons, but he relinquished no control of mission affairs. During a month of waiting, Lyon felt superfluous, wondering why he and his wife had rushed so rapidly to get to the Netherlands. In letters to his parents as well as to President Merrill, Lyon is surprisingly critical. Lyon now judged his predecessor to be "very inefficient, [he] procrastinates everything except his literary work, and sometimes opens himself for severe criticism."[27]

To President Merrill he complained that Kooyman had delayed more than a week simply finding the book of instruction for mission presidents, that he would not transfer the bank account to Lyon even though

Kooyman was not properly monitoring the money, and that Kooyman had not given him a firm date on which to take over the mission. Elder Merrill sympathized but quite firmly reminded Lyon that Kooyman's release would take effect "when he cares to accept it" and that "Pres. Kooyman is still the president of the mission until he accepts his release. You are president-elect, but without authority to function as president until this time comes."[28] A few days later, Elder Merrill encouraged Lyon by noting, "You have a man's job on your hands. But, of course, you are a man—an educated man, too. . . . I guess [you] will have to [just] get in and dig."[29]

The Lyons bided their time for a month before officially assuming duties. During that stressful time, Hermana made contact with the mission doctor, a Dr. Hertzeberger, who recommended an obstetrician for her. This specialist informed her that the diagnosis of her Utah doctor was absolutely incorrect and that she was not expecting twins, just a single birth. She was perplexed but accepted his opinion. During the month of waiting, Hermana assumed many of the duties relating to the Relief Society, Young Women's MIA, and Primary. President Kooyman's wife had been in Utah for a full year, and these mission organizations had been neglected. The Dutch language was an expected problem for Hermana, but she jumped in with enthusiasm, using the mission maid as her sounding board. A year later, many Saints said her pronunciation was more accurate than her husband's. Ed struggled to achieve fluency after being away from the sound of Dutch for seven years. While he impatiently awaited the official transfer of control, he and Kooyman visited and interviewed all twenty-six missionaries in the four mission districts. Kooyman's extended stay actually proved a blessing to Lyon—by the time he inherited the reins of presidency he had traveled to every branch, talked with each elder at least twice, and was able to assess the problems he would face. A month after the Lyons arrived in the Netherlands, Kooyman turned over the mission to Lyon—but not officially. The formal documents were lost in scattered piles of papers on the former president's desk.[30]

Mission Planning

The unexpected month of preparation allowed Lyon to begin his presidency with a firm plan. He would

1. Continue to implement Elder Widtsoe and Elder Merrill's plans to call and develop local leaders.

Courtesy Church Archives

Illus. 7-6. Ed and Hermana meet with mission board members of the Primary, Sunday School, MIA, and priesthood quorums, c. 1935.

2. Bring order to mission finances.

3. Reduce the monthly amount of money the Elders spent.

4. Clarify the legal status of Church properties.

5. Improve the comportment of elders.[31]

This personal plan called for him to go out and work with every set of missionaries. His day usually began at 5:30 A.M. He would hurriedly swallow a small breakfast and then catch a train heading for one of the branches, where he would often find the elders still in bed. After they got up, he would study with them, instruct them in their duties, and then go out tracting. Many elders had developed a fatalistic attitude: "The psychology of the missionaries when I arrived was 'The end of the world is coming right now and we haven't time to do much. All the blood of Israel has been gathered.' With that attitude you don't get anywhere."[32] He worked long hours, including meeting with local Church leaders (illus. 7-6), often not arriving home until 11:30 at night. Mission morale and compliance with Church standards increased markedly under his leadership. Lyon could also boast that the Netherlands Mission enjoyed the second highest rate of converts per missionary in the European area during his presidency.[33]

Almost immediately after Lyon assumed mission duties, a crisis arose. In the United States, President Franklin D. Roosevelt effected a "managed currency" policy, took the country off the gold standard, and hoped to relieve the debt by causing minor inflation.[34] The U.S. dollar immediately lost 40 percent of its value compared to the Dutch guilder. Rooms, food, and clothing cost as much as ever in the Netherlands, but the money sent from home resulted in 40 percent fewer guilders. This devaluation created a hardship for many Latter-day Saint families already strapped by the Depression; to keep their sons in the mission field they would now need to send more money. Again Lyon took to the road. He held meetings with "all the missionaries and with a blackboard just [showed] them what the problem was they were facing. They could get into cheaper living quarters [for example]."[35]

As a result of this personalized training for every missionary, expenses dropped from approximately thirty-five dollars per month to twenty-eight—this in spite of the major devaluation of the dollar. Under Lyon's frugal management, the Netherlands Mission became the least expensive in Europe during the Depression.[36] Lyon recalled that, as a result, some parents in the United States actually requested that their sons be sent to the Netherlands. The number of missionaries increased from an all-time low of nineteen to forty-five at one point.[37] Just before Christmas 1933, six elders arrived, calling themselves the "New Deal" group, an indication that the decimated missionary force was on the upswing.

Further contact with home came in December 1933, when the mission history casually notes that "Brother and Sister Lowell Bennion, of Salt Lake City, visited mission headquarters on their way [home]." Hermana had known Merle Colton (Bennion) in Utah, and the two young women now renewed their acquaintance. Ed was deeply impressed with the brilliant twenty-five-year-old Lowell, who had completed a mission in Germany (1928–31) and then remained in Europe, carrying out graduate studies in Germany and Vienna and completing a Ph.D. in 1933 at the University of Strasbourg. This was the first acquaintance of what would become a life-long friendship between Ed and Lowell.

The small mission home was comfortable but not luxurious, yet the boys could not play outside safely due to cold weather and lack of space. "We have been trying to find something for the kiddies to do. . . . We have recently heard of a Montessori school near here [and] shall do our best to get them placed in it."[38] After the new year, the two boys entered the Montessori/Froebel school, where they established a few friendships and found relief from their cramped home quarters. Just three of the small rooms in the mission home were heated with gas, so each night was chilly. Furthermore, all four Lyons experienced the mysterious "missionary itch" that Ed had known on his first mission.

Birth of Twins

As Hermana gained weight and appeared close to delivery, Ed stayed close to home, visiting missionaries near Rotterdam so he could assist her. Hermana was huge, and she was having difficulty getting around. Three days after Hermana celebrated her twenty-eighth birthday, Ed took her in a taxi to Eudokia hospital. At exactly 11:00 P.M. Dr. Hertzeberger delivered a boy weighing five pounds, ten ounces. But soon the surprised doctor, who had been so confident that there was only one fetus, realized that there was still another baby to deliver. He panicked and began screaming at the nurses to prepare another set of instruments. After a few minutes of frenzy, an eight pound, four-ounce boy was born—the largest child Hermana ever bore. The total weight of the two was nearly fourteen pounds, and diminutive Hermana lost forty pounds in the process of delivering the two children. She hemorrhaged and was so sick that she stayed in the delivery room all night. But the next morning, she "was the marvel of the hospital, and had a steady stream of hospital personnel coming to see this thin American woman who had produced these twins."[39]

If the doctor was not sufficiently prepared for the delivery of twins, neither were the Lyons prepared for the Dutch law that required registry and naming of newborns within twenty-four hours. They found out about this requirement just minutes before the fifty-guilder fine and mandatory naming by the State were to take effect. After a hasty conversation, they decided to name the oldest baby James Karl Lyon and the chubby one Allyn Laurence, to honor Hermana's deceased brother who was also a twin. Soon Hermana changed her mind, desiring that the names be switched. But it was too late—Ed was already in a taxi and on his way to the registry.[40]

The weeks that followed were tiring and trying. Hermana was intractably determined to nurse both babies, an approach discouraged by the hospital staff. She developed painful abscesses in both breasts, likely due to the incessant demands of two hungry little mouths. No antibiotics were available in 1934, so she could only hot pack the breasts. She suffered chills, high fever, and lethargy but continued to nurse. Just a few weeks after the births (illus. 7-7), David and John contracted a severe case of measles, a potentially fatal disease. Soon both babies were also seriously infected, and in Allyn Laurence (called "Larry" and later "Laurie"), the disease turned into pneumonia. The doctor ordered a nurse to stay with the family. Baby Larry often coughed until he became limp and turned blue from lack of oxygen. Hermana despaired for his life, recalling that Lowell and Merle Bennion had sent a baby girl back to the United States in a coffin. "As [Hermana] was holding [Larry] after a particularly bad coughing spell . . . and praying for comfort, she heard a voice tell her that [he] would be all right."[41] Larry did indeed recover, but Hermana's fear of death, now for one of her own sons, had again surfaced.[42]

Ed wrote, "I had to get out of bed every few minutes throughout the nights" to bring water to feverish children. He also "was up much in the night" when John had terrible earaches after the measles.[43] Hermana was nursing nearly six hours a day, the nurse caught influenza, and Ed had to fire the cook during the turmoil of serious sickness. All of this he confided in letters to his parents, observing that "this letter probably sounds like a note from a terrible pessimist, but it is merely a chronicle of a lot of hard luck. I hope the next letter will be more newsy and optimistic."[44] He did little missionary work during this time, devoting himself instead to his wife and children.

Lyon and his wife often viewed this period, the six weeks after the birth of the twins, as the most trying time of their lives. Though sickness lingered, no long lasting effects remained. In reality the mission brought Ed and Hermana closer. He learned to appreciate her active, organized mind as well as her dedication to the gospel. She admired his energy and diligent work ethic. Despite the difficulties of mission life, they later told their sons of the joys they felt in working together. Ed remembered Hermana with small kindnesses on special days, as in a made-up check from the "Bank of Love" (illus. 7-8).

Illus. 7-7. Hermana holds Laurie while Ed holds Jamie. David *(left)* and John *(right)* are in front, c. 1934.

President with Problems

As family health improved, Lyon resumed his hectic schedule as president. A typical day now was filled with visits to missionaries, resolution of legal matters, unexpected visits of members to the mission home, and daily letter-writing. Pages from his 1934 datebook indicate the activities of two "typical" days. On April 3, he wrote ten letters (most to members or missionaries in the Netherlands); edited a proof for the *Ster* (the Church's magazine in Dutch); helped set up a missionary display; took an elder and his own son David to the dentist; visited with at least two irate Church members; and helped Hermana with the newborn twins. On December 3, he typed fourteen letters, wrote part of two lessons for a Sunday School manual in Dutch, went by train to nearby Dordrect to counsel with a member, and indexed and edited the *Ster*. At 10:50 P.M. a young sister who had run away from an abusive home rang the bell to the mission home and asked for a listening ear. Lyon put her up in a nearby hotel around midnight. Then he returned home and climbed in bed after 1:00 A.M.; he was up five hours later to begin the next hectic day.

During the forty-five months Lyon served in the Netherlands, he wrote nearly nine thousand letters, or almost two hundred a month. Lyon's diaries and datebooks mainly contain unannotated records of day-to-day details. His letters, however, flesh out his feelings:

> I had quite an experience here two weeks ago. A supposed ideally-married young couple—he is second counselor in the local branch presidency in Rotterdam, and both are looked upon as being about perfect—had a family quarrel, due to too much mother-in-law and sister influence, and after a hectic scene of anger and excitement, separated and went to their respective homes. Knowing what it would do to the peace of the branch as soon as it became known, I tried to bring about a meeting of the two. . . . Arrangements were made for them to embark on the

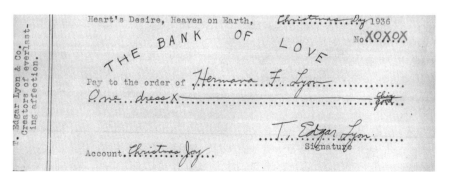

Illus. 7-8. A creative gift from Ed to Hermana for Christmas 1936.

matrimonial boat again, and as far as I have heard, everything is going along smoothly again. But such jobs, are too big for me. They need an older man here for these things. Then again, perhaps, I may not be orthodox or old-fashioned enough in many views about family life, to fit in with these Holland places. I at least like to see a woman get a square deal in the bargain, and that is something they do not get over here.[45]

Hermana praised her husband's ability to resolve problems. After Ed had spent countless hours with the couple from Rotterdam, she observed, "It's a blessing that Ed has a disposition such as he does, or he would be a nervous wreck with a few more months of listening to troubles."[46] Later, she noted that "Ed straightened out a terrible mess in the Hague last Sunday. Anybody with less patience would have excommunicated half the branch, but he restored peace between the two factions."[47] And Ed valued Hermana's wise insights. On many occasions he counseled with her, seeking advice on how to handle an enraged husband, a nonworking elder, a critical article in a local newspaper, or even a conflict with the European Mission. The two truly functioned as a team during their years in Europe.

Part of their cooperative efforts dealt with the creation of programs and manuals for each organization—the priesthood, Sunday School, Primary, Relief Society, and the Young Men and Young Women. Some of the local Saints assisted, but Lyon and his wife had the heavy responsibility to see that each auxiliary had a manual. No translations of official manuals came from Salt Lake City or London, so the Lyons had to translate from English to Dutch. In 1935 no manuals came at all, so the Lyons wrote their own, gaining experience for when they would both be called to write manuals for the entire Church.

Despite considerable advice from Elders Widtsoe and Merrill, Lyon felt very much alone in the work, isolated from other mission presidents and unable to see a unified direction for the European missions.[48] In spite of Lyon's earlier efforts in late 1933, there were still many elders who made life difficult for themselves, their companions, and the mission president. Lyon anguished, "I have had about all that I could handle lately—with unconverted missionaries and missionaries chasing girls, quarreling Saints, and attempting to pay off [church] debts."[49] These problems continued during much of the first year. Lyon had entered with a firm plan to create success in the mission and had put in long hours writing letters and working with every pair of missionaries. He had weathered the initial pressures of the Depression. His youthful enthusiasm had

Illus. 7-9. Hermana with sons Laurie *(left)* and Jamie *(right)*, c. 1935.

carried him through the first few months, but it did not make him immune to feelings of discouragement and isolation.

Amid the frustrations, Hermana was a positive strength. In a Mother's Day letter to her mother-in-law, she explained: "I don't know when I've been happier than I am now. I'm able to nurse my two darlings and they're growing wonderfully and then too the spirit of this missionary work is a wonderful thing."[50] For almost four months, Hermana had been confined inside the mission home, but the first Sunday in June, she took the twins out—Laurie for the first time—to the Rotterdam Branch, where Ed gave each a name and a blessing (illus. 7-9).

The family was prosperous and happy. By the end of the first full year in the Netherlands, life was looking more positive than during the gray summer. The Lyons had passed the personal crises of the birth of twins and the serious sicknesses of the spring. They had weathered the frequent conflicts among Church members, the long counseling sessions with quarreling parties, and the ever-present pressures of a few missionaries who were not doing their jobs. Hermana lamented her husband's frequent absences but recognized the need. "I'm not complaining," she wrote. "This [mission] is a wonderful experience and I wouldn't miss it for the world. We both feel that we've reawakened spiritually."[51]

European Mission Presidents Gather

President Joseph F. Merrill and his wife visited the Netherlands at least once a year for special conferences. They also sponsored a larger gathering of European mission presidents to foster unity, provide mutual stimulation, and discuss the problems of members and missionaries. In summer 1935, the Lyons attended their first conference of European mission presidents in nearby Liege, Belgium. Following summers found the group gathered in Berlin (1936) and Paris (1937). These lengthy annual meetings became a much anticipated spiritual highlight for Ed and Hermana. When Lyon first arrived in late 1933, the European Mission area consisted of eleven missions, as indicated below:

European Missions and Their Presidents—October 1933

Mission	President	Age	Other
(European Mission)	Joseph F. Merrill	65	Educator
British	James H. Douglas	—	
Czech-Slovak	Arthur Gaeth	—	
Danish	Alma L. Peterson	55	SLC, business
French	Daniel J. Lang	62	SLC, ZCMI
German-Austrian	Oliver H. Budge		
Netherlands	T. Edgar Lyon	30	ID, seminary teacher
Norwegian	Milton H. Knudson	52	Utah, Idaho
Palestine-Syrian (Armenian)	Badwagan Pinanian	42	Born in Turkey
South African	Don M. Dalton		
Swedish	Gustave W. Forsberg	74	Born in Sweden; SLC
Swiss German	Francis Salzner	—	

In May 1937 when Lyon attended his last conference (illus. 7-10), he was still the youngest of the European mission presidents, but in 1936 and 1937 he was the longest-serving president and hence was listened to and sought out for advice. In June 1937 the European mission presidents were[52]

Mission	President
European Mission	Richard R. Lyman
British	Hugh B. Brown
Czecho-Slovak	Wallace F. Toronto
Danish	Mark Garff
French	Octave F. Ursenbach
German Austrian	Thomas E. McKay
Netherlands	T. Edgar Lyon
Norwegian	A. Richard Peterson
Palestinian-Syrian	Joseph Jacobs
South African	LeGrand P. Backman
Swedish	Gustave O. Larson
Swiss Austrian	Philemon M. Kelly

Lyon called the three conferences he and his wife attended "great experiences . . . there were sessions morning, afternoon, and quite often in the evening, sometimes departmental with the women together talking about auxiliaries."[53] The presidents discussed common problems and worked to find solutions.

In the exhausting, fourteen-day (June 19–July 2, 1935) Liege meeting, several presidents raised a concern about Church publications. Besides the official magazines in various languages, each mission had been receiving translations of talks by General Authorities. These publications carried advertisements for products that were available only in Utah. Lyon and his wife raised their voices against such provincialism and commercialism, whereupon Elder Merrill appointed Ed to head a committee to make recommendations. Hermana sat on the committee, and her strong voice assisted in drafting a policy, approved by Merrill and then forwarded to the First Presidency, that no more miscellaneous published translations emanate from Salt Lake City to the European missions.[54]

The 1936 meeting in Berlin focused on problems relating to American missionaries and European girls and methods the presidents had used to curb the dancing and dating that were too prevalent in most missions. After hearing many "horror stories," Lyon concluded that the Netherlands had relatively minor problems compared to other missions.[55]

This conference took place from June 10 to 15, two months before the Berlin Olympics. Hitler was on everyone's minds. Lyon had been in

Courtesy Church Archives

Illus. 7-10. European mission presidents' conference in Paris, 1937. Hermana and Ed Lyon sit with Wallace and Martha Toronto on the front row. Amy and Richard Lyman (European Mission president), in the middle on the second row, meet with presidents from Norway, Demark, Germany, Sweden, Britian, France, and Czechoslovakia.

Berlin a year earlier and had observed the reverence many held for the German leader. In one Latter-day Saint meeting hall, he "saw on one side of the wall a large portrait of Joseph Smith and on the other, one of Hitler."[56] He then heard a sermon by the branch president about these two great prophets, one of the nineteenth and the other of the twentieth century. Lyon was impressed that German schools were teaching chastity and that he saw so few people smoking, a stark contrast to pervasive public smoking in the Netherlands.[57] But he also observed the beating of an old Jewish woman by brown-shirted guards and cruelty to a tiny Jewish girl in an ice cream store by the secret police.[58] Ed and Hermana actually saw Hitler and heard him give a brief talk:

> Hitler came out on the balcony and stood up there and had all of his Elite Guard down there goose-stepping and the clatter of their hobnails on those paving stones was a din. People gathered and the street was filled. We got in there just before it started and got up fairly close to the fence and we could see. Then the ambassador [from Argentina] got out of the car and Hitler came out of the door dressed in a pair of striped trousers and a cutaway coat. I never before realized how small he was. He was smaller than all the men around him. He was not large. The ambassador got out of the car and they shook hands and he ushered him into the chancellory. So we had a chance to see the people yell and scream "Heil Hitler" there that afternoon.[59]

Hermana had a perceptively negative reaction to Hitler. In her tenacious pursuit of knowledge she had read *Mein Kampf* and knew of Hitler's aggressive ambitions. She recalled Hitler as "the most persuasive speaker she had heard,"[60] a fact that further increased her mistrust of him. Ed's 1936 letters are somewhat positive about what Hitler was achieving in Germany but mistrustful of his expansionist ideas. "Everywhere one sees militarism and drill training. . . . They are preparing for something, but no one knows what it is. Many people are preparing to see a general European conflagration in the fall."[61]

While in Berlin, Ed and Hermana decided to visit Sweden and see Hermana's father and stepmother (illus. 7-11). The hired woman in the mission home would take care of the four boys, so on June 17, 1936, they sailed for Sweden. The trip was almost a second honeymoon, a delightful week in the country of Hermana's ancestry. They toured Stockholm and traveled to Horndal, the birthplace of Hermana's father, where they met with previously unknown aunts, uncles, and cousins. A few days later they took a night ferry to the romantic island of Gotland. They continued on to Denmark and saw the Midsummer's Day festival before they finally returned to the Netherlands on June 26.

Mission Motivation

Following their sight-seeing, the Lyons hurried back to the Netherlands to prepare for a missionwide conference. In 1936, Elder Richard R. Lyman (illus. 7-12) had replaced Elder Merrill as the European Mission president. Elder and Sister Lyman now took the train from Paris to Rotterdam for their first Netherlands conference. The Lyons showed off their MIA organizations and youth activities (dance, drama, sports, pageants). The conference also included "Relief Society Handiwork (re-made clothes and quilts exclusively) and . . . Primary and Genealogical works." The Lymans and Lyons spoke to an audience of 567 in a large rented hall. The three-day conference concluded with two dramatic productions, written and directed by Hermana with the assistance of William Mulder, a creative missionary of Dutch descent with obvious writing talent.[62]

Lyon wrote that at the end of the gala affair, "We placed the Y.M. [Young Men's] M.I.A. in the hands of a local presidency . . . so that the local board will now have to run the affair to suit the people."[63] Lyon was proud of this achievement—he felt that he had followed the admonitions of President Grant and Elder Merrill by turning over most of the branch and district presidencies to the local Saints by 1937. President Lyman, however, did not approve of the policy. "He sent out orders [in late 1936] that everybody locally should be released and [American] missionaries put back. This is when I [Lyon] had a conflict with him and opposed him."[64] Lyman wanted all branch reports in English to avoid translation problems and also to be able to communicate directly with each branch leader. But Lyon

Illus. 7-11. Gustave and Zina Forsberg while on their mission in Sweden, 1934.

reasoned, "I was not going to insult the good [Dutch] people that I had known [and called] and that my predecessor had trained for the positions. . . . So, I just ignored [Elder Lyman's order] and went ahead."[65] This act put Lyon in direct conflict with an Apostle, but he held firm, insisting that he was following orders from the president of the Church. The conflict worried Lyon and exposed him to disagreement among General Authorities, but it illustrated the need for each individual to make prayerful decisions.[66]

In spite of this conflict, Lyon loved his work as mission president. It allowed him to be somewhat creative and to continue his historical interests. William Mulder recalled that "what stands out . . . is President Lyon's giving

Courtesy Church Archives

Illus. 7-12. As incoming European Mission president, Richard R. Lyman visited the Lyons in Rotterdam in 1936.

his headquarters' staff an hour a week, as I remember it, in the morning, a course in Church history. . . . A gifted teacher, animated, informal, ranging from the jocular to the profound, he must have enjoyed these sessions himself."[67] Mulder, who continued academic studies and became a prominent scholar and professor at the University of Utah, pondered, "I think it not unlikely that my own scholarly interests were stimulated by what I regarded as his [Lyon's] open, searching approach to church history. He was rooted in faith but understood the utility of skepticism as a tool for inquiry."[68]

In early 1936, Lyon realized that Church missionaries had been in the Netherlands for seventy-five years and therefore a jubilee celebration was in order. The first missionaries had arrived in the country on August 5, 1861, just months after the beginning of the U.S. Civil War; two months later they baptized three people in Friesland.[69] Employing research methods he would use throughout his life, Lyon consulted all Church records in Rotterdam, journeyed to the northern villages of Friesland, consulted local records and police registers, and then went out searching through the villages and dikes for the local history of the Church.

In his explorations, Lyon ran into three old farmers and struck up a conversation. They had been young boys in 1861 but could still remember the baptism ceremony, the names of the converts, and the place—a flax cleaning pond—where the first baptisms occurred. They willingly showed Lyon the spot. Church records confirmed the farmers' recollections. Lyon wrote up a descriptive narrative of his discoveries, which appeared in the *Improvement Era*.[70] This interesting account is Lyon's first published article dealing with Church history. It exudes the excitement of historical discovery and the characteristic storytelling technique of Lyon's teaching.

To celebrate the jubilee event, artist Jacob Bosklopper designed a monument (illus. 7-13), and in November (exactly seventy-five years after the baptisms), Lyon dedicated the brick and concrete structure. William Mulder penned a detailed article about the event for the *Deseret News*.[71] Hermana wrote a pageant to commemorate the diamond jubilee. President Joseph F. Merrill came from London to speak and attend the dramatic pageant (illus. 7-14). Hermana had created a series of historic tableaus depicting the baptisms, further conversions, and emigrating Saints. Closing scenes portrayed the significance of the Church in the Netherlands. Scores of people of other faiths came to watch the pageant, and Lyon and his missionaries hailed it as a new tool in missionary work. The Church Section of the *Deseret News* printed a lengthy story and prominently displayed Lyon's picture. Hermana enjoyed the chance for an aesthetic expression of her deep gospel feelings. She wrote and supervised several other short plays and pageants during her final year and a half in the Netherlands; they were usually presented at branch and district conferences.

As mission president, Lyon experienced great joy from pronouncing a "Church blessing" on seventeen marriages.[72] He also participated in excommunicating sixteen members. Another task of the mission president was countering anti-Mormon articles and books that appeared in the Dutch press. The "Historical Records and Minutes" of the Netherlands Mission mentions eleven negative articles and one book that Lyon tried to counter and correct. On one occasion, he and two Dutch-born elders visited Reverend F. Tollenaar and spent more than two hours explaining the errors in a series of anti-Mormon articles he was publishing. According to the "Records and Minutes," Tollenaar "admitted . . . that he had published untruths, although it had been unintentional."[73] Whenever he could, Lyon confronted authors who attacked the Church.

Illus. 7-13. Ed Lyon and others at the monument dedication in November 1936 celebrating the seventy-fifth anniversary of the first baptisms in the Netherlands.

Mission Evaluation

Among the accomplishments of the Lyons must be noted the construction of the Overmaas Branch chapel in south Rotterdam. This was the first Church-built chapel in the Netherlands, and it resulted from Lyon's efforts. After months of legal paperwork, ground was broken on July 13, 1937, the day that the Lyons departed for Utah.[74] A further accomplishment was Lyon's work toward gaining official recognition for the Church in the country. Early in his mission, Lyon wrote to the Presiding Bishopric that "many members feel that if they must remain here in this land, that our church should seek a legal standing to increase its prestige."[75] Lyon felt that with official recognition, the foreign missionaries would have less hassle with local police and the Church would better be able to contradict libelous news stories. Lyon prepared the legal papers and made application with the Department of Justice in conjunction with the Church's seventy-five-year celebration. In spite of very favorable reaction from officials, and a thorough study of the Church by the government at that time, recognition was not granted until 1955.[76]

Lyon also introduced the use of the slide projector to assist missionary work. From his earlier experience teaching seminary, he found slide lectures

Illus. 7-14. Hermana and Ed Lyon *(seated, center)* with Elder and Sister Joseph F. Merrill *(seated, left)* pose with several Dutch missionaries, c. 1934. Elder Merrill was the European Mission president at the time and had come to visit the Netherlands.

to be an effective teaching tool. He modeled the procedure for the missionaries and then sent them out to give lectures and lessons on Central American archaeology and the Book of Mormon, temples and temple building, and, his favorite, Church history, including a lecture he entitled "Down Pioneer Trails." Lyon was looking for creative ways to increase the numbers and draw prospective members from diverse social classes, but he often had to struggle with a negative attitude among the missionaries.

The mission still used the same tracts that Ed had known ten years earlier, and he yearned for a more systematic and sound pedagogical method. He and Hermana experimented but never implemented a unified plan. He often gave elders of Dutch descent a week off to contact and teach their relatives, affirming that this was not lost time because it usually resulted in investigators and even some converts.

As mission president, Lyon was loving but firm, and he expected long, dedicated hours from each missionary. A few rebelled, but the majority responded well. Most truly loved him. One missionary reflected years later that Lyon had been the most influential teacher of his entire life. "I, for one, sat all day long without tiring, listening and making notes of everything he taught. . . . His teachings changed my life and gave me the testimony I needed to call others to repentance and teach them the value of the gospel."[77]

Hermana bragged about her husband to his parents, noting that President Joseph F. Merrill had written: "I want to congratulate you on the very excellent work which you are doing. . . . You and two others [are] mission presidents par excellence." Hermana took this as very sincere praise because Elder Merrill was usually very reserved.[78] The members likewise loved President Lyon. One family even named their son Thomas Edgar.

The letter of release from Elder Richard R. Lyman praised specific aspects of Lyon's leadership style:

> Fortunate indeed is the community where you are to labor. Most fortunate are those young folks who are to have the pleasure of enjoying the scholarship and inspiration with which you are so richly endowed.
>
> And they are no less fortunate to have the opportunity of coming in contact with your talented wife. She is an outstanding credit to the remarkable Forsberg family."[79]

Franklin Murdock, who followed Lyon as mission president, praised Lyon's administrative skills: "We realize more and more what a lot of hard work you folks did and sometimes I wonder how you carried the load so long and remembered so many details and still seemed to accomplish so much. I'm wishing I had your patience."[80]

Perhaps the most insightful evaluation comes from William Mulder:

> It seemed to me that [T. Edgar Lyon] was a model of diplomacy, humanness, and also firmness. . . . He set an example of ceaseless energy that was just amazing. . . . He had this sense of being on his toes in every situation, just alert, snappy actions.[81]
>
> President Lyon was constantly in the field, visiting his missionaries, keeping in touch with local problems, and actively participating in [all] branch, district, and mission conferences.[82]
>
> I would emphasize his intelligence, his energy, his openness, and frankness. Because he could see quickly into pretense and foolishness, some may have found him sharp. I admired such penetration and honesty.[83]

When President Heber J. Grant set Lyon and his wife apart in 1933, he "promised us that we would all return home in safety."[84] But the anguishing question for the Lyons was *when* they would return home. Then in April 1937, they learned unofficially that Murdock, Lyon's former mission friend and often-seasick traveling companion, would replace him.

Illus. 7-15. Ed, David, Laurie, John, Jamie, and Hermana, 1937.

Lyon then wrote to Dr. Franklin L. West, commissioner of education for the Church, reminding him of promises made by Joseph F. Merrill regarding future seminary teaching after the mission. Lyon expressed the hope that "something can be arranged for us in a civilized place."[85] By "civilized place" Ed meant Utah, near Salt Lake City. He wanted to be close to family members and to walk in the warm mountain sunshine, away from "the land of frogs and rain." West offered Lyon five choices: teaching seminary in Salt Lake City, Montpelier, or Idaho Falls; teaching at the institute at Snow College in Ephraim, Utah; or teaching at the college in Flagstaff, Arizona (now Northern Arizona University). Ed opted for any of the seminary jobs in Salt Lake City.[86]

The Lyon family (illus. 7-15) packed their few treasures into three large trunks, sadly said goodbye to three hundred members, missionaries, and friends at the dock in Rotterdam, and sailed for England on July 13, 1937. After two days in London, they boarded the SS *Washington* for a rocking, lurching, and foggy nine days to New York City. When they arrived in New York, Hermana's Aunt Eva and Uncle Haaken Haglund greeted them and congratulated them on Ed's important new assignment as director of the Salt Lake Institute of Religion at the University of Utah. The Lyons were shocked at the news.

Notes

1. T. Edgar Lyon, "Oral History," bound typescript, 105, T. Edgar Lyon Collection, Church Archives, Family and Church History Department, The Church of Jesus Christ of Latter-day Saints, Salt Lake City (hereafter cited as Church Archives). Unless otherwise noted, all citations for T. Edgar Lyon materials are located in the Lyon collection.

2. T. Edgar Lyon, "Oral History," 105.

3. T. Edgar Lyon, "Oral History," 105.

4. Joseph Lynn Lyon, "A History of Laura Hermana Forsberg," 1991, 37, L. Tom Perry Special Collections, Harold B. Lee Library, Brigham Young University, Provo, Utah (hereafter cited as Perry Special Collections).

5. T. Edgar Lyon, "Oral History," 105.

6. My research does not fully confirm Lyon's observation that he was called because he was a seminary teacher. Only one other mission president in Europe in late 1933, Roy A. Welker, had been a seminary teacher; the great majority were businessmen, usually from Salt Lake City. Many worked for the Church after their mission presidency or took jobs at ZCMI (Daniel J. Lang), *Deseret News* (Hugo D. E. Peterson, Elias S. Woodruff and James M. Kirkham), Zions Bank, or other Church-affiliated businesses. President Grant was deeply concerned about the economic status of returning mission presidents and how they would survive the Depression.

7. T. Edgar Lyon to David Ross Lyon, September 4, 1933, Church Archives.

8. T. Edgar Lyon, Diary, September 19, 1933, Church Archives.

9. T. Edgar Lyon, Diary, September 27, 1933.

10. T. Edgar Lyon to David Ross Lyon, September 4, 1933.

11. Gerald Joseph Peterson, "History of Mormon Exhibits in World Expositions" (master's thesis, Brigham Young University, 1974), 39–49.

12. Peterson, "History of Mormon Exhibits," 41. This exhibition was one of the Church's most ambitious public relations activities to date. For the first time, missionaries openly discussed the temple and its ordinances for the dead. Marden E. Broadbent, "The Mormon Exhibit at the Century of Progress Exposition at Chicago," *Improvement Era* 37 (October 1934): 579–81, 608–9, as cited in Peterson, "History of Mormon Exhibits," 43. The history of the Church and its experiences in Nauvoo, Illinois, became a focal point to explain the "Mormon Epic." The general theme of the entire exposition was a "Century of Progress," and the Church tied into this topic by featuring displays and statues dealing with eternal progress. Peterson, "History of Mormon Exhibits," 46. The Northern States Mission published a special pamphlet on the Church's exhibit. Elder Joseph F. Merrill justified the Church's expenditures and public involvement by pointing out that the exhibits had created "a better understanding by the people [of the world] of the principles and objectives of the Church." Joseph F. Merrill, "Tabernacle Choir at Chicago Fair," *Millennial Star* 94 (September 6, 1934): 568–69, as cited in Peterson, "History of Mormon Exhibits," 49.

13. T. Edgar Lyon to parents, October 14, 1933, Church Archives.

14. T. Edgar Lyon to parents, October 17, 1933, Church Archives.

15. Journal History of the Church, September 23, 1931; March 13, 1933, Church Archives, microfilm copy in Harold B. Lee Library, Brigham Young University, Provo, Utah.

16. On February 2, 1933, in preparation for the change of the office from Liverpool to London, an editorial in the *Millennial Star* explained the function of having a European Mission office when the same administrative structure did not exist for other mission areas of the Church. The editorial affirmed its necessary functions as:

1. Coordinating financial, proselyting and membership activities

2. Coordinating magazines (the *Star*) in six different languages

3. Handling problems with elders, including their postmission travel

4. Securing constructive publicity

5. Rapidly communicating Church items that could not wait for written response from the First Presidency.

A small staff of seven people, including Elder Widtsoe and his wife, conducted the operation. (*Millennial Star* 95 [February 2, 1933]: 72–73)

17. Lyon observed in his "Oral History" that when Widtsoe briefly returned to Salt Lake City in 1930, President Grant had told him that the Church would be facing very difficult times in Europe and that Widtsoe should "put [his] effort in training the local people" (121–23). Widtsoe wrote editorials and articles on the subject in the *Millennial Star* and had them translated into all European languages. He preached this idea at each conference of mission presidents, created Sunday School lessons on the topic of local autonomy, wrote a pamphlet entitled *District Supervision,* and in many other ways tried to prepare the European missions for full local leadership. Editorials in the *Millennial Star* from January 29, 1931 ("Offices, Officers and Members"), October 20, 1932 ("The Missionary and the Branch"), and January 26, 1933 ("Progress in Mission Organization") emphasize the need for the missionaries to step back from branch callings and train the local brethren: "It is according to the activating spirit of the Gospel that the members should manage the affairs of the branches, under the general Church organization" ("The Missionary and the Branch").

18. Lyon, "Oral History," 123.

19. Lyon, "Oral History," 101.

20. "Netherlands Mission History," October 20, 1933, Church Archives.

21. At a party in Salt Lake City honoring the Lyons hosted by President Grant's daughter, Dessie Grant Boyle, in September 1933, President Grant came and sat down by Lyon. He asked,

"By the way, Brother Lyon, how old are you?" I said, "I just turned thirty in August." He said, "Oh, that's good. I'm glad to hear it. You know I've been criticized for calling you on a mission when you're so young and inexperienced. I'll tell the Twelve when we meet on Thursday that they don't have any reason to criticize me at all. I was a stake president when I was twenty-four and an apostle when I was twenty-six. You're a mission president at thirty. That's getting along in years." (Lyon, "Oral History," 122)

22. Keith C. Warner, "History of the Netherlands Mission of The Church of Jesus Christ of Latter-day Saints, 1861–1966" (master's thesis, Brigham Young University, 1967), 155.

23. Warner, "History of the Netherlands Mission," 155.

24. T. Edgar Lyon to parents, October 23, 1933, Church Archives.

25. T. Edgar Lyon to parents, November 6, 1933, Church Archives.

26. Frank Iemke Kooyman was born in Holland, November 12, 1880, the sixth of nine children. He joined the Church in 1899 (baptized by Elder Alonzo A. Hinckley). In 1905, after serving a three-year mission in the Netherlands, he emigrated to Utah. He was called as mission president in 1929 and served four years. He demonstrated great zeal in defending the Church, often answering numerous misrepresentations that appeared in the Dutch press. He assisted with the retranslation of the Book of Mormon, the Doctrine and Covenants, and the Pearl of Great Price as well as the translation of the temple ceremony in Dutch. His excellent bilingual skills allowed him to translate many articles and manuals for the Church. Even after his release as mission president he continued writing articles for the *Ster* (*Frank I. Kooyman: As He Was Known*, Florence K. Pickering, comp., 1981, Americana Collection, Perry Special Collections).

27. T. Edgar Lyon to parents, November 6, 1933, Church Archives.

28. Joseph F. Merrill to T. Edgar Lyon, November 4, 1933, Church Archives.

29. Joseph F. Merrill to T. Edgar Lyon, November 15, 1933, Church Archives.

30. T. Edgar Lyon, Diary, October 28 to November 24, 1933.

31. T. Edgar Lyon to parents, November 24, 1933, Church Archives.

32. T. Edgar Lyon, "Oral History," 131.

33. Warner, "History of the Netherlands Mission," 151.

34. Thomas A. Bailey and David M. Kennedy, *The American Pageant*, 9th ed. (Lexington, Massachusetts: Heath, 1991), 789–90.

35. T. Edgar Lyon, "Oral History," 109.

36. Warner, "History of the Netherlands Mission," 151.

37. T. Edgar Lyon, "Oral History," 109.

38. T. Edgar Lyon to parents, December 26, 1933, Church Archives.

39. Joseph Lynn Lyon, "History of Laura Hermana Forsberg," 39.

40. Joseph Lynn Lyon, "History of Laura Hermana Forsberg," 39.

41. Joseph Lynn Lyon, "History of Laura Hermana Forsberg," 40.

42. It was likely this experience, the birth of twins and all the ensuing sickness, that caused such fright and nightmares for Hermana. Years later she would sometimes come to breakfast, saying that she'd just had a terrible dream—she had dreamed that she was back in the Netherlands.

I think this episode alone may explain why Mother never had a desire to return to the Netherlands, even for a brief visit. Mother did retain a sense of humor about some of her experiences and often told the story of the woman reporting the obvious. She [Hermana] could only nurse one baby at a time, so she would have to ignore the cries of the other until she was finished nursing the first. One day while she was doing this, John and

David had gotten into a fight, and she was powerless to intervene because of the nursing baby. While listening to this cacophony the doorbell rang. She finally answered the door and was confronted by a woman who [casually] told her that her baby was crying. (Joseph Lynn Lyon, "History of Laura Hermana Forsberg," 41)

43. T. Edgar Lyon to parents, March 21, 1934, Church Archives.

44. T. Edgar Lyon to parents, March 21, 1934.

45. T. Edgar Lyon to parents, February 8, 1934, Church Archives.

46. Hermana Forsberg Lyon to the David R. Lyon family, January 21, 1934, Church Archives.

47. Hermana Forsberg Lyon to the David R. Lyon family, May 31, 1934, Church Archives.

48. The Lyons also received a visit from Louisa Y. Robison, Relief Society general president. "Netherlands Mission History," July 30, 1934, Church Archives.

49. T. Edgar Lyon to parents, June 1, 1934, Church Archives.

50. Hermana Forsberg Lyon to Mary C. Lyon, May 14, 1934, Church Archives.

51. Hermana Forsberg Lyon to the David R. Lyon family, January 8, 1935, Church Archives.

52. Information for these two charts was taken from Lyon's personal letters and diaries, as well as the *Directory of General Authorities and Officers* (Salt Lake City: The Church of Jesus Christ of Latter-day Saints, 1996).

53. T. Edgar Lyon, "Oral History," 108.

54. T. Edgar Lyon, "Oral History," 109–10.

55. T. Edgar Lyon, "Oral History," 136.

56. T. Edgar Lyon, "Oral History," 127.

57. T. Edgar Lyon to parents, June 15, 1936, Church Archives.

58. Lyon recalls,

In the summer of 1935, when I went over to get a projector, I saw two of these brown shirt guys kick an old woman down the street and jump on her, her head bleeding right in the street, and walked off and left her. Their only complaint was that she was a Jew. They left her there and nobody dared move a hand to touch her until they were out of sight. They hurried and picked her up and somebody called an ambulance and they took her away. But it was right there on a busy street in the town they just jumped on this old Jewish woman. I don't know what happened before but I would guess she was in her seventies or something like that. She was very, very old I thought. So we saw some of the violence even that early. (T. Edgar Lyon, "Oral History," 128)

59. T. Edgar Lyon, "Oral History," 125–26.

60. Joseph Lynn Lyon, "History of Laura Hermana Forsberg," 43.

61. T. Edgar Lyon to parents, June 15, 1936.

62. T. Edgar Lyon to parents, June 11, 1937, Church Archives.

63. T. Edgar Lyon to parents, June 11, 1937.

64. T. Edgar Lyon, "Oral History," 124.

65. T. Edgar Lyon, "Oral History," 124.

66. A broader account of this conflict appears in Lyon, "Oral History," 124–30. Lyon asserted that the Dutch branches survived much better during World War II because they had experienced leaders when the Americans were forced to leave. Hermana Lyon felt that Elder Lyman did not have the spirit of his apostolic calling in this matter, and she was not surprised in October 1943 when Lyman was excommunicated. Ed's relationship with Apostle Lyman was generally quite cordial: "His [Lyman's] visit here made a wonderful impression on the members. He is a very appealing speaker, humorous, has a good voice, and is so friendly and kind." Lyon recalled that Elder Merrill had not mixed with the members as had Elder Lyman, and his speeches were rather formal. T. Edgar Lyon to parents, March 2, 1937, Church Archives.

67. William Mulder, written responses to questions from John Duffy, December 13, 1983, copy in author's possession.

68. Mulder, written responses.

69. Keith C. Warner, "Historical Review of Christianity in the Netherlands," 9–11, Perry Special Collections.

70. T. Edgar Lyon, "Landmarks in the Netherlands Mission, 1861–1936," *Improvement Era* 39 (September 1936): 546–47, 573.

71. William Mulder, "A Monument in the Netherlands," *Church News,* published by *Deseret News,* December 12, 1936, 1.

72. "Netherlands Mission History," Church Archives. Since all Hollanders had to be married by civil authorities, Church leaders took up the practice of holding a ceremony in the meetinghouse after the marriage in which a branch or mission president gave counsel to the couple. Then the leader pronounced a "Church blessing" on the marriage.

73. Netherlands Mission, "Historical Records and Minutes," July 29, 1935, Church Archives.

74. Netherlands Mission, "Historical Records and Minutes," July 13, 1937.

75. Warner, "History of the Netherlands Mission," 158.

76. Warner, "History of the Netherlands Mission," 93–95.

77. Neil W. Kooyman, "My Most Influential Teacher," *Church News,* December 2, 1978, 2.

78. Hermana Forsberg Lyon to the David R. Lyon family, September 16, 1935, Church Archives.

79. Richard R. Lyman to T. Edgar Lyon, July 24, 1925, Church Archives.

80. Franklin L. Murdock to T. Edgar Lyon, September 8, 1937, Church Archives.

81. William Mulder, interview by Ted and Trent Lyon, Salt Lake City, June 25, 1992.

82. Mulder, written responses.

83. Mulder, written responses.

84. Hermana Forsberg Lyon to the David R. Lyon family, February 28, 1936, Church Archives.

85. T. Edgar Lyon to parents, June 11, 1937.

86. T. Edgar Lyon to parents, June 19, 1937, Church Archives.

8

Institute: "A Different Point of View," 1937–45

The Lyons arrived in Utah on July 29, 1937. While Salt Lake City was home, there was no house to return to, only some battered furniture and debt—no savings, no car, and no home ward. After ten years of marriage, the Lyons were poor in material possessions but flush with experience. They had spent five years teaching in Idaho, two summers at BYU, one year studying in Chicago, one summer at Berkeley, and nearly four years serving in the Netherlands. Finally the time had come to settle down. Ed's parents had sold their spacious home on the Avenues in early 1937 and moved to an apartment. The loss of the home he had come back to for thirty-four years created an emptiness for Ed as well as his wife. Upon arrival from Europe, the six Lyons spent three weeks with Hermana's parents before renting a home near the university. The previous renters of the house had been their old friends Lowell and Merle Bennion.

After returning from Europe in late 1933 with his Ph.D. in hand, Lowell Bennion (illus. 8-1) struggled through Depression joblessness for a few months but soon landed government work as an education adviser to the Civilian Conservation Corps. A few months later, John A. Widtsoe, a member of the Quorum of the Twelve and Commissioner of Education, offered Bennion an opportunity to head the Church's institute of religion at the University of Idaho. When Bennion expressed his reluctance to move to Idaho, Widtsoe complied by offering a more tempting position: perhaps Bennion would found a new institute at the University of Utah.[1] Bennion eagerly accepted and in January 1935 made personal visits to students and faculty, creating the climate for this religious and academic endeavor. After two and a half years, he had developed a dynamic program serving at least 173 college students.[2] Bennion also involved most of his students in Lambda Delta Sigma, the social fraternity he founded in 1936. His successes led the newly appointed Commissioner of Education Franklin L. West to reassign Bennion to Tucson for two years to open another new institute at the University of Arizona.[3]

Illus. 8-1. Lowell Bennion directed the Salt Lake Institute of Religion for nearly three decades.

Home in Salt Lake City

The Bennions' reassignment created a job for Lyon and left a frame home for rent for thirty-two dollars a month. The Lyon family moved in at 20 South 1200 East on August 16, 1937, their tenth wedding anniversary. Lyon's contract with the Church gave him twenty-four hundred dollars for the 1937–38 school year, a fairly decent sum in economically depressed Utah. His duties included writing manuals and materials for the Church and the institute program. He would not teach during the summer quarters because he expected to continue his Ph.D. studies in Chicago. Bennion oriented Lyon to the institute, which was housed in a single room on the first floor of the stately university ward chapel, across the street from the campus that Lyon knew so well from his undergraduate days. Lyon and Bennion enjoyed three weeks of talk and transition, planning out courses and strategies for the institute.[4] They quickly recognized that they would be a compatible team.

Before his classes began, Ed and his family worked on their home, painting, organizing, and gardening. The family also bought a two-year-old tan Ford Sedan De Luxe for $490, a necessary luxury for Ed because of his need to travel between the university, the Church Office Building, and home.[5]

Just four days after the Lyons moved into their rented house, Ed's seventy-three-year-old father suffered a brain hemorrhage and became incapacitated for more than a month. This shocked and demoralized the slender, elderly man, who was still fit enough to climb mountain trails and regularly swim at the Deseret Gym. The illness weighed heavily on Ed as well. For three weeks he spent every night in his parents' apartment, helping his father when he had to arise in the dark. This reflected a pattern in his life: Lyon was usually the nighttime caregiver, not only for his aging father but for his own children as well.[6] In this solicitous way, he tried to help Hermana enjoy a full night's sleep. His ability to get by on just five or six hours of sleep, even if it was interrupted by duty, had been evident since his years as a missionary. However, he occasionally took catnaps during the day when the previous night had been particularly trying.

A second effect of his father's illness was that Ed assumed the duty of keeping the books for the Magazine Printing Company. His father had handled all the financial matters of the company for fifty years but was now unable to continue; Ed willingly stepped in. Without any formal training in accounting, he learned the skills for the task. Ed had already been an inveterate record-keeper—a counter of things—for many years. He found the tax, billing, and purchase records in good order but a few months behind schedule. He spent five or six hours every Saturday at "the shop," still located at 62 South Richards Street (the area now occupied by the Crossroads Plaza Mall). The meticulous bookkeeping work required occasional evenings as well. For this moonlighting, Ed paid himself a dollar an hour; in 1937 he supplemented his institute income with $99.25 from the Magazine Printing Company, and he earned $187.15 in 1938.[7] Ed's father recovered from the stroke, but Ed continued to work as bookkeeper until 1965, often finding the job a good source of extra cash to provide a special Christmas for his wife and children.

Other activities expanded an already busy schedule. Ed accepted a position as a Sunday School teacher and Hermana was asked to serve in the Young Women's program. Then in 1940, Ed was called to the new Emigration Stake high council and ordained a high priest by Elder Albert E. Bowen.[8] Up to this point, even during his service as a mission president, he had been a Seventy in the Church.

Sought-After Speaker

Upon their initial return to Salt Lake City, the Lyons presented talks in the Ensign Ward. From that time on, Ed became an increasingly sought-after speaker around the Salt Lake Valley. During 1937 he kept a fairly extensive diary (as well as his usual brief datebook), which indicates that nearly every week he spoke in a sacrament meeting, Sunday School class, or special-occasion meeting like firesides. In the October 1937 general conference, President Grant called him from the audience to speak briefly. Hermana sometimes joined Ed at the speaker's podium.

Once in a while they would take along the children, dressed in native Dutch costumes with baggy trousers, and the family would sing a song or two from the Netherlands. This pattern of speaking in Church meetings continued throughout his life and increased to as many as three or four talks a week during the 1950s and 1960s. Lyon noted each speaking engagement in his datebook and recorded his exact mileage to use as an income tax deduction for volunteer driving. This record reveals that from 1937 to 1978 he delivered at least forty-seven hundred formal talks in firesides, sacrament meetings, Sunday School and priesthood classes, and special study groups!

Besides these voluntary speaking engagements, Church officials asked Ed to deliver Sunday evening speeches over KSL radio. These were part of the station's regular Sunday programming, which often featured General Authorities and other prominent speakers. Church members were not accustomed to such a youthful returned mission president. Nonetheless, the program took positive advantage of Lyon's energy and novel ideas. These broadcast speeches opened an even wider audience to his influence, and T. Edgar Lyon soon became known throughout Utah. Even so, his insecurity rattled his nerves as he contemplated the radio microphone. While preparing for the first talk, eleven days in advance, he confessed, "I wrote a rough draft of the radio speech—it is punk!"[9] The topic was the sacrament of the Lord's Supper. Other radio talks delivered between 1937 and 1939 addressed the themes of temples, the concept of a prophet, and tithing.

In fall 1948, again by invitation, he presented a series of twelve speeches on KSL centered around the theme of contributions of modern scriptures to religious living. Lyon formulated the challenging, sometimes philosophical, topics himself. The *Church News* often commented on or reprinted his speeches; many were later modified and published in the *Children's Friend,* the *Relief Society Magazine,* or the *Instructor.* All were reprinted by the Church and distributed in pamphlet form. In a short time, Lyon became an extremely popular speaker and writer. All this exposure was good for his institute teaching too—his name became familiar to would-be students and their parents.

Dynamic Teacher

Lowell Bennion had set the pattern for dynamic classes during the previous two years at the institute. Lyon wanted to follow the pattern, but he was not comfortable teaching the same innovative courses Bennion had offered.[10] To Bennion's popular classes dealing with interpretation and analysis of the Latter-day Saint experience, Lyon added courses on Christian history, the Doctrine and Covenants, and missionary preparation. Lyon's first institute classes began on the last Tuesday of September 1937. He taught an extremely heavy load: six different courses during fall quarter, with multiple sections of several of these courses, yielding a total of fourteen classes. One hundred thirty-nine students enrolled in institute classes during fall quarter.[11]

The next fall he again taught six subjects:

1. Mormonism: An Interpretation and a Way of Life (7 sections)

2. History and Religion of Early Christianity (2 sections)

3. Missionary Training (2 sections)

4. Seminar in Religion and Modern Thought (2 sections)

5. Doctrine and Covenants (2 sections)

6. History of the [LDS] Church (1 section)

Lyon was in the classroom for twenty-four hours each week, meeting the 296 students enrolled in sixteen sections during fall quarter 1938.[12] The enrollment had more than doubled since the previous fall. While the popularity was pleasurable, the work load was taxing. As the only teacher, Lyon spent extra hours at home preparing for the diverse classes.

Up until this time, the Church Educational System had allowed each teacher to create and prepare his own classes according to his own spiritual and academic preparation. There was no set curriculum, no standardized course outlines. During the period that Lyon was the sole institute teacher at the University of Utah, the Church Board of Education effected plans to establish a more uniform curriculum for the many institutes that had been founded during the Depression at universities in California, Wyoming, Arizona, and Idaho and at most of the colleges in Utah.[13] Stimulating and innovative course outlines were developed under the direction of Church Commissioner of Education Franklin L. West and Vernon Larson, West's assistant for curriculum development, with major input from institute teachers.

Over a period of four years, in summer workshops and retreats at West's cabin in Logan Canyon, the institute teachers came up with twelve course titles and were assigned to create outlines for each:

1. The Nature and Mission of the Church (created by Lowell Bennion)

2. The Restoration of the Gospel (Lowell Bennion)

3. Courtship and Marriage (Lowell Bennion)

4. Joseph Smith and the Restoration (T. Edgar Lyon)

5. Marriage and Family Life (Lowell Bennion)

6. Doctrine and Covenants and the Pearl of Great Price (T. Edgar Lyon)

7. Book of Mormon (Roy Welker)

8. Old Testament: Message of the Prophets (Sidney B. Sperry)

9. Old Testament: The Writings (Sidney B. Sperry)

10. Mormons on the American Frontier (Milton R. Hunter)

11. Christianity through the Centuries (Daryl Chase)

12. The Literature of the New Testament (Russell Swenson)[14]

Most of the writers had studied at the University of Chicago, an indication of its effect on Church education at the time.

Lyon was aided in his efforts to follow Bennion's example by the many characteristics the two teachers shared: energy and willingness to work long hours, an ability to harmonize gospel and secular learning, a fun-loving nature, and a desire to be part of the students' total life experiences. Like Bennion, Lyon spent much time counseling with students. A student, Grant Anderson, came to the university from Garland, Utah, as a bewildered freshman with an interest in music. Lyon called tabernacle organist Frank Asper and arranged for Anderson to use the complex pipe organ in the university ward chapel for practice. Ed Hart, a university student from rural Idaho who held a track scholarship, found that "religion could be deep; it touches all phases of life; things like faith, repentance, and so on, are not dry as dust—they operate in one's life—it became a living religion [under Lyon and Bennion]." Hart remembered Bennion as a marvelous Socratic questioner and Lyon as more organized and adept at lecturing. Hart attributed much of his intellectual success, including the honor of being named a Rhodes Scholar, to the learning approaches he found at the institute.[15]

Lyon did more than just teach institute classes. In fact, his social life centered on the Salt Lake institute and Lambda Delta Sigma (illus. 8-2). His first students recall him as "warm, congenial, considerate."[16] Leah Yates Hart, who served as the institute's secretary from 1937 to 1941, vividly recalls a Lambda Delta dance at the Hotel Newhouse in 1939 with the theme "A Night in Heaven." The salon and orchestra were draped in white; giant haloes hung suspended above the dancing couples. Lyon stood at the door dressed as St. Peter, joking and kidding with the "angels" as they presented credentials for admission. Other students remember "just having such a good time" with hay rides, sleigh rides, scavenger hunts, canyon parties, and dances at the Old Mill. They also enjoyed singing at the home of President Heber J. Grant and putting on sacrament meeting programs around the valley, which were planned and supervised by Lyon and Bennion.

After the close of the first year (1937–38) at the institute, Lyon again went by train to Chicago to continue work on his Ph.D. Not only was he lonely there, but the trip represented a difficult financial sacrifice. He paid for tuition, apartment rental, and travel expenses while still maintaining his home in Salt Lake City. Once a day he wrote to Hermana, letters filled with information about his activities but also replete with feelings of nostalgia and love. He confessed that he had become academically rusty and that school was very difficult for him after an absence of six years: "After floundering about all week, I've come to the conclusion that it will be necessary for me to organize, to systematize my supposed knowledge."[17] He took courses in religion and history from the University of Chicago's finest teachers—Edgar J. Goodspeed, John T. McNeill, Ernest Chave, William C. Bower, S. J. Case—completed a reading exam in German, and passed his "intermediate exams," a confirmation that he was doing well and was halfway done with his Ph.D. program.[18]

Changes in the System

In spite of the exhilarating success that Lyon was having with the institute program, not all his superiors were pleased. The open policies of commissioners Joseph F. Merrill, John A. Widtsoe, and especially Franklin L. West were coming under fire from some Church officials. At a seminar for Church educators in Aspen Grove in August 1938, Commissioner West gathered most of the nearly ninety men who were teaching in the institutes and seminaries for a first-ever training session, which lasted eight weeks. West planned well and showcased the pedagogical work of some of the best teachers in the system.[19] However, the "stimulating and progressive agenda exploded on the last day when J. Reuben Clark Jr, First Counselor in the LDS First Presidency, denounced Church educators who were teaching 'philosophies of the world.'"[20] According to President

Courtesy Church Archives

Illus. 8-2. Ed Lyon *(right)* at a Lambda Delta Sigma activity.

Clark, institute and seminary instructors should teach only two basic concepts: "That Jesus Christ is the Son of God" and that the "Father and Son actually and in truth and very deed appeared to the Prophet Joseph in a vision."[21] President Clark continued: "The teaching of a system of ethics to the students is not a sufficient reason for running our seminaries and institutes. The great public school system teaches ethics."[22] He bore down hard on those who used "the things of the natural world . . . [to try to] explain the things of the spiritual world."[23]

Finally, in an obvious allusion to teachers trained with Church approval and support at the University of Chicago, President Clark referred to those "who have gone to other places for special training. . . . I refrain from mentioning well-known and, I believe, well-recognized instances of this sort of thing. I do not wish to wound any feelings."[24] The speech did wound some and, according to Milton Lynn Bennion, West's vigorous assistant, "had a crushing effect on our [recruitment] efforts and [creative] program" and caused many promising young religious scholars to chart a different course for their lives. President Clark's poetic "call to repentance," however, was "received gratefully by believing students and teachers," and it has provided a road map for much future Church education; its influence is still visible in the early twenty-first century.[25]

Lyon was in Chicago at the time the talk was given, but when he returned a few days later, he heard the echoes and sensed the implications. Lyon was surprised; he did not consider himself a negative, testimony-challenging teacher, and his students had responded very positively during his first two years of teaching. Two days after his return, Lyon tersely noted, "Went to Church Office—called on [Presiding] Bishop Le Grand Richards—given an admonition about my negative teaching."[26] In part, Bishop Richards's admonition might have resulted from a misunder-standing about what Lyon was teaching or from misgivings by some authorities about the Church Educational System at a university level in general, but it may also have arisen from reports about Lyon's teaching style and his academic preparation in Chicago, which had resulted "in many students returning as merely cultural Mormons."[27]

Especially when dealing with Church history, Lyon went beyond history as a testimony-building tool. He wanted students to learn and deal with complete, accurate information. Lyon was unshakable in his own testimony, which he bore repeatedly inside and outside the classroom. At the same time, he believed that a testimony comprised of accurate facts coupled with the witness of the Spirit (and he saw no contradiction between them) grounded students more securely in the gospel. He believed that testimonies based on incomplete, inaccurate, or glorified accounts sometimes left students ill equipped to meet the challenges of the secular learning they experienced each day in their college classes.

Lyon spent most of September 1938 "at [the] Church Office . . . working with Vernon Larson, Dr. West and Bennion on a new institute course of study on 'Mormonism,' to take the place of the one written by Lowell B[ennion] and [Daryl] Chase which [two General Authorities] condemned."[28] The discord and conflict that was growing in the Church Educational System called into question Lyon's academic future. A member of the Quorum of the Twelve, Joseph F. Merrill, had mentored him and encouraged him to study history at the University of Chicago and to go on for a Ph.D. Another member of the Twelve, John A. Widtsoe, had approved of his master's thesis on Orson Pratt and even wanted to publish it. But other authorities were highly critical of what they considered to be an academic, nonspiritual approach to history and scripture, and Lyon appears to have been categorized as one who followed this approach. He questioned the worth of the enormous sacrifice of time away from family to pursue a doctorate, but Hermana, ever confident of her husband's abilities, fortified him. And Bennion's example, earning a Ph.D. at a youthful age, pressured him. Lyon decided to pursue the degree.

He did not go to Chicago in summer 1939, however, for on May 13, 1939, Hermana delivered their second set of twin boys. Ed devoted every spare moment to helping her. Once again Hermana, despite her slight build, had delivered babies totaling fourteen pounds. They were born late Saturday evening, just an hour before Mother's Day. After the traditional flowers were presented to the mothers in the university ward the next morning, Ed accepted a large spray of gladiolas and was accused of stealing the show. Ed and Hermana named the first twin Thomas Edgar Lyon Jr. and the second Joseph Lynn Lyon. The Lyons had waited until the birth of their last sons to bestow the father's name. Now the rented house on Twelfth East was crowded with boisterous boys, noise, and loving excitement—six children was a very large family in the Depression era. To find a roomier home, the family began searching in the East Mill Creek and Holladay areas of the Salt Lake Valley (illus. 9-2).

As promised by Commissioner West, Lowell Bennion returned from Arizona to assume the directorship of the institute in fall 1939. Enrollment had grown steadily during the two years of Lyon's administration, from 173 students enrolled in spring 1937 to 298 in spring 1939.[29] Lyon and Bennion were pleased with the numbers and the quality of the students. The new administrative situation, however, could have been awkward. Lyon, who had been director for two years, was expected to step down and return the directorship to Bennion. Bennion worried about the transition, but Lyon accepted his new role gracefully and willingly. "The fact that Ed did so in such style was always a marvel to me; it speaks to his character," Bennion recalled.[30] Lyon was five years older than Bennion, but "it didn't bother him a bit to be the associate director to a younger man."[31] There were now two dynamic, challenging teachers to instruct the four hundred students attracted to the institute that year (1939–40). The two teachers became a team, a vibrant intellectual and spiritual duo that would complement each other for the next twenty-three years. The names Bennion and Lyon became synonymous with the Salt Lake institute at the University of Utah (illus. 8-3). In 1939, Marion D. Hanks, a former student body president at West High School in Salt Lake City, was attracted to the small institute by the "mystique of Lowell Bennion and T. Edgar Lyon." Years later as their colleague, Hanks (illus. 8-4) recalled, "I can't think there were ever two men more respectful and compatibly engaged" than Bennion and Lyon.[32] They wrote together, solved problems together, shared the responsibility of counseling students, and socialized together with their wives. Both purchased homes and small farms in East Mill Creek—Lyon in 1941 and Bennion in 1943.

Farewell to Chicago

Before moving to a new house, Lyon spent another summer of study in Chicago. The 1940 student body of the Divinity School had expanded due to the return of many Protestant missionaries from warring Europe. Lyon enjoyed their perspectives on Greece, Turkey, Egypt, and other countries he had visited, but he did not enjoy Chicago as much as in previous years. He was desperately lonely during the twelve weeks, and the city was burdensome. "The more I see of big cities the more I am convinced that Joseph Smith was right in his condemnation of cities of more than 20,000 people," he wrote to Hermana.[33] The big city did keep Lyon busy, however. He was frequently invited to lecture or preach in Latter-day Saint wards, and he even delivered a sermon on Latter-day Saint history in the Woodlawn Presbyterian Church.[34]

Lyon struck up a friendship with classmate Reverend Lawrence J. Taylor, a Methodist minister from Addison, Michigan, who invited Lyon to visit his congregation in Michigan and preach a sermon on Mormonism. The escape from Chicago to the tranquillity of a small town lifted Lyon's spirits. He spent Friday night in the old parsonage. The next morning he observed the sagging porch, and with permission from the skeptical Taylor, Lyon, in a single day, constructed a rock and brick foundation, replaced a fallen pillar, and repaired the broken steps and deck. He wrote, "Taylor was astonished that I could do that kind of work."[35] Lyon loved the physical exertion and the chance to use tools and ingenuity. The next morning he preached an hour-long sermon that he titled "Mormonism: A Practical Religious Way of Living." At the conclusion of the service, Reverend Taylor boasted of Lyon's own practicality in using hammer and saw, trowel and mortar.[36]

While in Chicago, Lyon saw his religious faith in a new perspective, much of it positive. A few years later, Elder Richard R. Lyman heard Lyon relate his Chicago experiences and asked for a written record of the incidents. Lyon responded with a positive account. He noted that one day eminent historian John T. McNeill had stated that "there was more religious vitality manifested in LDS communities, and a closer application of the principles of Christianity to life situations than among any group with whom he had come in contact." Another famous professor, William C. Bowers, had observed that "if the LDS people can maintain their standards

Illus. 8-3. First Salt Lake Institute of Religion building, c. 1946.

and ideals, they need not worry about anything stopping their growth because they are bound to become the dominant Church of the earth, for, to paraphrase the Savior, 'The birth rate shall inherit the earth.'"[37] In the same letter, Lyon reported other enthusiastic evaluations of the Church, especially of its youth programs.

Though Lyon was obviously proud of these evaluations, he was also aware of unresolved problems. The question of blacks and their status in the Church plagued him and his professors at Chicago. Lowell Bennion and many students at the University of Utah were also struggling with the problem. Lyon began clipping articles on the topic and wrote a twenty-one-page paper entitled "The Attitude of the Mormon Church toward Slavery and the Negro."[38] His paper did not resolve all his concerns, but the research allowed him to examine the historical and social implications of the doctrine.

Another problem in Church history similarly occupied Ed's thoughts. In summer 1938, Hermana had written him about a newly arrived Dutch convert who had been lured into a polygamous marriage when she came to Utah. Hermana then waxed angry over the Church's former practice of plural marriage. After venting her emotions, she concluded, "I really like *you* quite well but sometimes I hate all other men (except of course my father and your father and a few others). I think most [men] are snakes. Am I justified?"[39] Lyon expressed his deepest feelings to his wife about plural marriage:

Courtesy Church Archives

I cannot understand. I have tried to see it and to justify the principle, even if not the practice, but have never been converted. . . . I argued for hours with Father when I was younger about it. . . . It seems to me that life and eternal life mean more

Illus. 8-4. Marion D. Hanks taught at the Salt Lake institute during the 1950s and early 1960s.

than just begetting children. It should mean harmonization of developing personalities and *mutual* regard and understanding.[40]

Several times in Chicago, Lyon was asked to defend or explain this practice in the Church's history, but he could not fully harmonize it with his tender feelings for Hermana—marital love was too unique to be shared, he often said.[41]

Lyon's course work in Chicago was rigorous. Over two summers, 1938 and 1940, he enrolled in fifteen classes.[42] World-renowned historians William W. Sweet and John T. McNeill agreed to direct his program and his dissertation; by the end of 1940, he was only two summers away from completing his degree. However, the University of Chicago set a five-year time limit, after which courses could not count for graduation. Lyon's work in summer school 1932, following his master's degree, had already been declared invalid in 1938. Sadly for him and Hermana, World War II and family urgencies would terminate his dream of earning a Ph.D. from the University of Chicago.

Studying at the Divinity School had meant considerable family sacrifice for the Lyons. Though scholarships helped pay Ed's tuition, they did not compensate for missing his son John's baptism in July 1938 or David's ordination as a deacon two years later. Summer 1940 was a particularly difficult time to leave Salt Lake City. In June, Ed's father had died from a heart attack at age seventy-five while visiting his daughter in California. He had been Ed's beacon and example. Ed wrote to Hermana, "In spite of Father's lack of education in school, he was an exceedingly well-educated man. . . . I took him to BYU [in 1930] . . . and he talked to professors and ministers of the Gospel from the East [Goodspeed, for example], and never used an incorrect word or made a grammatical error."[43] Ed felt a strong spiritual tie to his father: "I have done a great deal of thinking about Father since I left home [for Chicago] . . . his passing has given me the most profound conviction of immortality I have ever had. . . . We'll know him again."[44]

When Ed was away from home, he wrote not only to Hermana but to their children as well. He anticipated David's and John's birthdays and wrote about incidents that would be memorable to them. To David he described a fellow student with no arms who took off his shoe and sock, stuck a pencil between his toes, and began taking notes in class; to John he wrote of a young boy he had met who had lost all his hair due to an infection. When David turned ten years old, Ed wrote to Hermana, "The days of their [his sons'] first creations have been sacraments to me, partaken of with you and God. How happy I am that you are my wife and the mother of those . . . good boys."[45] To Hermana he also wrote: "You are charming, Beloved. I still think that you are the most beautiful girl I have ever seen."[46]

Once he returned home, Ed planned activities with the family. Hiking was an important and frequent activity—in City Creek Canyon, to Snell's Mine, up Twin Peaks or Mt. Timpanogos. Ed's diaries mention taking the children to the state fair, Liberty Park, and the zoo. Ed took the older boys to evening functions of Lambda Delta Sigma in the canyons or on service activities. Some of this activity was done to give Hermana a needed break. The family took a four-day outing to Zion, the Grand Canyon, and Bryce Canyon over Labor Day weekend in 1938. During most of his time at home, Ed was deeply dedicated to his wife. He helped her with cleaning; canning Utah peaches, apricots, pears, and grapes; washing dishes and clothes; and planting and caring for flowers. Occasionally he took her to movies. Despite her busyness with the six boys, Hermana reciprocated by hosting many students and participating in Lambda Delta functions.[47]

Life was hectic in the Lyon's crowded home on Twelfth East. Hermana described the time after the birth of her second set of twins as the "tired years."[48] To cope with all the work, she called on her unmarried sister

Ada for assistance. Jans van Dongen, a sister of a missionary the Lyons had presided over in the Netherlands, also regularly baby sat, cleaned, and worked in the home. All the Lyons called her by the affectionate "Tante (aunt) Jans." Sickness plagued the children. John was often ill. Once after a streptococcal infection, he developed rheumatic fever and spent several months in bed.[49] Doctors removed Jamie's and Laurie's tonsils in 1939.[50] Hermana herself suffered from a goiter; in 1940 she agreed to an operation to remove part of her thyroid gland. The operation was successful, but it upset her, and she experienced considerable fatigue for years after. Health problems, fatigue, and lack of sufficient money to buy a home weighed on Hermana. On one occasion, six-year-old Laurie "found Mother crying. . . . When he asked her why she was crying she told him [it was because] they were poor."[51]

The Move to Rural East Mill Creek

Living near the university and not far from the center of town was convenient for the Lyons but not satisfying. They had been renting ever since their marriage in 1927; it was time to buy a house. They had an ideal in mind—with six boys they sought a rural setting, space for a garden and fruit trees, and a place for animals. They desired a small farm that would sustain their family and teach their boys to work. Money was certainly a problem, though, and such a move would break from Lyon and Forsberg family traditions. Both sets of parents had always lived near the center of town for business, cultural, and social purposes. It was an act of faith to leave the city for rural life.

The family saved and searched for two years after the second set of twins was born, finally finding a dark-brick bungalow at 3087 South 2300 East in the rural East Mill Creek area. Hermana had once "vowed to never live in a bungalow,"[52] but this small home came with an acre and a half of property, partially covered with mature fruit trees and with open space for a garden and barn (illus. 8-5). The land had originally belonged to the descendants of East Mill Creek's first settler, John Neff. After a difficult title clearance, the eight Lyons moved in on March 31, 1941.[53] This became the family home, the only home the Lyons would ever own. The old house needed considerable repair, but Ed and his two oldest boys were willing and sufficiently skilled to do the work. A monstrous coal furnace in the basement heated the house, and a coal-fired "monkey stove" heated the water. The three bedrooms upstairs provided sleeping for six, but John and David had to create a bedroom in the unfinished and partially dirt-floored basement. The house cost $4,250, and by paying a little more each month, the Lyons acquired the full title after just twelve years.[54]

The added space in the home as well as the huge backyard afforded Hermana a bit more tranquillity than their rented home had. Neither Ed nor his wife had much experience in farming, but Hermana organized the home and yard work, and Ed saw to it that the boys worked with him. He and Lowell Bennion had often discussed the need to teach boys to work, and this setting was ideal for such a program. The land came with 7.7 shares of irrigation water, so every eight days during the summer, Ed and his boys took water from the ditch and watered fruit trees and vegetables.[55] They learned to prune the apple and peach trees. They planted cherry trees, plum trees, and more peach trees. They harvested apricots, strawberries, raspberries, and grapes. Hermana once remarked that "some years [we] had [canned] 1000 bottles of preserves."[56]

Ed and Hermana bought a cow and taught their boys how to milk it. From a former student, they received a worn-out range horse named Nig, which the boys rode through the sparse neighborhood and beyond, to nearby Mt. Grandeur and Mt. Olympus. Feeding skittish chickens and smelly pigs was part of the boys' routine. Rabbits, cats, and a gigantic St. Bernard dog (another gift) rounded out the rural life. Hermana prepared

Illus. 8-5.   Lynn, Teddy, Jamie, Laurie, Ed, David, and John in their backyard, East Millcreek, 1945.

daily lists of chores for each boy—weeding, cutting lawns, more weeding, feeding animals, milking, continued weeding, hauling prunings to the "upper yard" for burning, and helping their father in a variety of chores. This was part of the ideal Ed and Hermana had dreamed of.

In 1941 no city bus service reached East Mill Creek, so Lyon drove to the institute. He extolled the rural life to the point that Lowell and Merle Bennion followed the Lyons two years later, purchasing four acres and a run-down house just two miles southeast of the Lyon home. Ed was instrumental in finding the property for his teaching mate,[57] and the two often rode to school together after the Bennions moved. Though both families had now comfortably settled down, the advent of World War II made drastic changes in everyone's life. Jobs became plentiful. Both Ed and Lowell secured extra work. Bennion labored part-time in the Tooele copper smelter.[58] With six children, Lyon easily received a deferment from military service, so during summer 1942 he worked as a carpenter, building tract homes in the old clay pits east of Highland Drive. This work limited his writing and extracurricular activities with Lambda Delta Sigma but added construction work to his collection of practical skills. During the summers of 1943, 1944, and 1945, Utah Power and Light employed Lyon to repair and maintain the old wooden pipeline in Mill Creek Canyon. He loved this outdoor work, sometimes walking the five-mile length of the snakelike pipeline with his sons.[59]

Gas rationing during the war curtailed driving and family vacations, as well as some institute activities. Women's chapters of Lambda Delta Sigma increased in numbers, but the shortage of men led to fewer dances. Total attendance at institute classes remained relatively constant during the war years (illus. 8-6), meaning that the number of female students increased markedly while the men were away. The earlier criticisms of the institutes died down. Commissioner West ably defended his teachers to Church leaders. Furthermore, Bennion and Lyon were teaching students from prominent Latter-day Saint families who generally received positive reports from their children. All this created an enjoyable teaching environment. The two young teachers were also reaching the less well-known, the lonely, and the out-of-towners who were seeking a stimulating religious and academic experience.

The Salt Lake institute was no longer a single room where 173 students came to hear one teacher as in 1937. The program had continually grown, and the facilities had expanded along with it. Soon after Bennion's return from Arizona in 1939 and after delicate negotiation with leaders of the university ward, the facilities were enlarged. The institute teachers moved

Illus. 8-6. Ed Lyon and Lowell Bennion standing outside the first institute building near the University of Utah, c. 1945.

upstairs, knocked out a partition, and created a large classroom. Lyon and Bennion received small, remodeled offices and found room to establish a library and a lounge for socializing, making the institute a warm and comfortable place for teaching, counseling, and developing friendships. Although Lyon might not have been socially adept earlier in his life, he had come to recognize the necessity of such activities for college students.

The Salt Lake institute was now filling the social, intellectual, and spiritual needs of students and was serving as an effective supplement to the secular teachings these young Latter-day Saints received in their University of Utah classes. Ed Hart considered the students who attended the institute to be "above average in intellectuality. . . . There was an intellectual awakening [in the late 1930s and 1940s] and many drifted away [from the Church]." Lyon and Bennion helped to harmonize academic learning with spiritual truths and kept many close to the Church. Recalling these early years, Lyon said:

> I hardly go anywhere that I don't meet people who used to be students who are active in the Church today. . . . Many of them will say to me, "Frankly now, if it hadn't been for the Institute, I'd have been out of the Church. I came at a time when I was doubting . . . and you and Lowell . . . gave us something, you know, a different point of view."[60]

Yet it was more than just a different point of view. Students sensed Ed's and Lowell's commitment to the precepts they were teaching. Their teachers' dedication and conviction produced personal, intellectual, and spiritual growth in an entire generation of Latter-day Saint students.

Notes

1. Mary Lythgoe Bradford, *Lowell L. Bennion: Teacher, Counselor, Humanitarian* (Salt Lake City: Dialogue Foundation, 1995), 55–56.

2. T. Edgar Lyon, "Notes," n.d., files of the Salt Lake Institute, University of Utah.

3. Bradford, *Lowell L. Bennion,* 55–56.

4. T. Edgar Lyon, Diary, August 18–September 6, 1937, T. Edgar Lyon Collection, Church Archives, Family and Church History Department, The Church of Jesus Christ of Latter-day Saints, Salt Lake City (hereafter cited as Church Archives). Unless otherwise noted, all citations for T. Edgar Lyon materials are located in the Lyon collection.

5. Ed recorded every penny spent on the vehicle. During the four and a half months of car ownership in 1937, he purchased 147 gallons of gasoline, usually in quantities of five or ten gallons at a time, at twenty-four cents a gallon. The car used one and a half quarts of oil, at thirty cents a quart. T. Edgar Lyon, datebook, end pages of 1937, Church Archives. In 1938, Ed drove the car 5,182 miles. T. Edgar Lyon, datebook, end pages of 1938, Church Archives.

6. As a young child, I often experienced terrifying nightmares. Responding to my screams, Dad always rushed to my room, calming me, assuring me that the dream was now over and that he would stay until I got back to sleep; he often fell asleep until morning, lying beside me on the narrow bunk bed.

7. Lyon carefully noted the hours he worked each Saturday. Totals for each year appear on the final pages of the diary or datebook.

8. T. Edgar Lyon, "Line of Ordination of T. Edgar Lyon," in author's possession.

9. T. Edgar Lyon, Diary, October 20, 1937.

10. Bradford, *Lowell L. Bennion,* 63–84. Bradford's book presents an excellent analysis of Bennion's founding and early teaching at the institute. Bennion taught courses that grew from his own academic and spiritual preparation: The Position of Mormonism in the Religious Thought of Western Civilization; Religion and the Rise of Our Modern Economic Order; Comparative Religions, Mormonism: An Interpretation and a Way of Life; and Religion and Modern Thought. He later added classes in courtship and marriage, marriage and family life, the Book of Mormon, and the Old and New Testaments.

11. Institute Records, Salt Lake Institute of Religion, Salt Lake City, September 29, 1937.

12. Institute Records, September 30, October 28, 1938.

13. William E. Berrett, *A Miracle in Weekday Religious Education: A History of the Church Education System* (Salt Lake City: Salt Lake Printing Center, 1988), 64.

14. T. Edgar Lyon, "Oral History," bound typescript, 142, 143, Church Archives. Lyon savored these creative, hard-working experiences, recalling the stimulus they gave to Church education:

> Dr. West was a great outdoors man. He had a cabin up Logan canyon. So he would take us up there for ten days in the summertime and hire an old fellow he knew in Logan as a cook. . . . We would pay our own portion of the total cost. . . . We had to help with the dishes and clean up, each taking turns.
>
> But there was a period of time in the morning, about three hours, when we worked hard. We would read what we had produced during the last year and criticize it. A lot of brainstorming went on. We would have lunch and then we would have an afternoon session. Then we would have about an hour and a half off where we would go a little ways up the road and play softball. We would hike up to the big old juniper tree up in there somewhere. Sometimes we would go fishing along the river. Then in the evening we would stay outside and if the mosquitoes were too bad we would go inside and have a fire in the fireplace. We talked until two and then were up at six o' clock the next morning. Those were strenuous days. But we had a lot of fun and we did that brainstorming for a couple or three summers. Some of these new courses, like family and married life, came out of the expansion of the original twelve courses. (T. Edgar Lyon, "Oral History," 142, 143)

Further evaluation of Dr. Franklin L. West and his creative administration (1935–53) appears in Berrett, *A Miracle in Weekday Religious Education.*

15. Edward L. Hart, interview by author, Provo, Utah, January 23, 1996.

16. Leah Yates Hart, interview by author, Provo, Utah, January 23, 1996.

17. T. Edgar Lyon to Hermana F. Lyon, June 24, 1938, Church Archives.

18. T. Edgar Lyon to Hermana F. Lyon, June 24, 27; August 2, 4, 1938, Church Archives.

19. Milton Lynn Bennion, *Recollections of a School Man: The Autobiography of M. Lynn Bennion* (Salt Lake City: Western Epics, 1987), 104.

20. Bradford, *Lowell L. Bennion,* 77–78.

21. J. Reuben Clark, "The Charted Course of the Church in Education," appendix in Boyd K. Packer, *Teach Ye Diligently* (Salt Lake City: Deseret Book, 1975), 308–9.

22. Clark, "The Charted Course of the Church in Education," 314.

23. Clark, "The Charted Course of the Church in Education," 312.

24. Clark, "The Charted Course of the Church in Education," 316.

25. Bennion, *Recollections of a School Man,* 108. See also Noel B. Reynolds, "The Coming Forth of the Book of Mormon in the Twentieth Century," *BYU Studies,* 38, no. 2 (1999): 6–47; and J. Reuben Clark Jr., "The Charted Course of the Church in Education," in *Educating Zion,* ed. John W. Welch and Don E. Norton (Provo: BYU Studies, 1996), 13–27.

26. T. Edgar Lyon, Diary, September 6, 1938.

27. Reynolds, "Coming Forth" 22–26.

28. T. Edgar Lyon, Diary, September 8, 1940.

29. Institute Records, 1937–39.

30. Lowell L. Bennion, interview by Ted and Cheryl Lyon, Salt Lake City, January 18, 1989.

31. Lowell L. Bennion, "Oral History," 103.

32. Marian D. Hanks, interview by Ted and Trent Lyon, Salt Lake City, August 4, 1992.

33. T. Edgar Lyon to Hermana F. Lyon, June 22, 1940, Church Archives.

34. T. Edgar Lyon to Hermana F. Lyon, July 14, 1940, Church Archives.

35. T. Edgar Lyon to Hermana F. Lyon, August 13, 1940, Church Archives.

36. Lyon often told the story of this close friendship with Taylor and how the reverend was so enamored with the Church's concept of "marriage for eternity" that he too began using this terminology each time he performed a marriage in his church. He confessed to Lyon that this made him very popular with young people, who came from great distances to be married for "all time and eternity." For many years, Taylor and Lyon traded letters discussing their summers in Chicago.

37. T. Edgar Lyon to Richard R. Lyman, March 28, 1952, Church Archives.

38. His paper is now located in the T. Edgar Lyon Collection, Church Archives.

39. Hermana F. Lyon to T. Edgar Lyon, August 12, 1938, Church Archives.

40. T. Edgar Lyon to Hermana F. Lyon, August 15, 1938, Church Archives.

41. T. Edgar Lyon to Hermana F. Lyon, June 20–August 15, 1940, Church Archives.

42. The fifteen exciting courses Lyon took during these two years were
   1. Rise of Christianity
   2. Luther and the Rise of Protestantism
   3. The Church in the Age of Big Business
   4. Systematic Theology
   5. Reformation in England
   6. Christianity in Its Jewish Environment
   7. Beginning of Old Testament Literature and History
   8. Puritanism and Nonconformists
   9. Administration of Student Personnel
   10. The Church on the Early Frontier
   11. Slavery Controversy and the American Church
   12. Moral Ends of Education
   13. Christian Unions and Cooperation
   14. Advocates of Church Reform
   15. Systematic Theology (T. Edgar Lyon Collection, Church Archives)

43. T. Edgar Lyon to Hermana Forsberg Lyon, August 13, 1940, Church Archives.

44. T. Edgar Lyon to Hermana Forsberg Lyon, June 22, 1940, Church Archives.

45. T. Edgar Lyon to Hermana Forsberg Lyon, July 9, 1938, Church Archives.

46. T. Edgar Lyon to Hermana Forsberg Lyon, August 21, 1938, Church Archives.

47. Bradford, *Lowell L. Bennion,* 70.

48. Joseph Lynn Lyon, "A History of Laura Hermana Forsberg," 1991, 52, L. Tom Perry Special Collections, Harold B. Lee Library, Brigham Young University, Provo, Utah.

49. Joseph Lynn Lyon, "History of Laura Hermana Forsberg," 52.

50. T. Edgar Lyon, Diary, August 31, 1939.

51. Joseph Lynn Lyon, "History of Laura Hermana Forsberg," 52.

52. Joseph Lynn Lyon, "History of Laura Hermana Forsberg," 52.

53. T. Edgar Lyon, Diary, March 31, 1941.

54. T. Edgar Lyon's personal house file, in author's possession.

55. Since early pioneer days in the West, streams of water had been diverted to irrigate farmlands. First the bishops and later an appointed "watermaster" allotted the water according to the size of land owned by each shareholder. Each share of water meant a certain amount of time each farmer would have as his turn to use the ditch.

56. Joseph Lynn Lyon, "History of Laura Hermana Forsberg," 55.

57. Bradford, *Lowell L. Bennion,* 94.

58. Bradford, *Lowell L. Bennion,* 97.

59. He often took us children with him as he checked the pipeline for leaks caused by rock slides, Boy Scouts' hatchets, or wood rot. The most memorable section was the area known as "Rattlesnake Gulch," where Dad often caught a live snake and put it in a gunny sack to show the Boy Scouts at the nearby Tracy Wigwam.

60. T. Edgar Lyon, "Oral History," 165.

9

A Golden Era, 1946–62

The fifteen years following World War II were a golden era for Lyon in his personal life and in his career as a gospel scholar and teacher in the Salt Lake Institute of Religion. Lowell Bennion's biographer calls the decade of the 1950s the "Heyday of the Institute," though the splendor actually extended a little longer in both directions.[1] From the time the flood of returning servicemen hit the University of Utah campus in 1946 until Lowell Bennion left in 1962, Lyon and Bennion created for their eager learners what hosts of former students remember as a remarkable time in their lives. Lyon and Bennion also achieved widespread recognition and appreciation as gospel scholars, teachers, and leaders in Church education. They published scores of books, manuals, and articles on historical and spiritual topics. They achieved respect, even begrudging admiration, on the University of Utah campus. They planned and oversaw the construction of a new institute building at 274 University Street. They put into use the revised, improved institute curriculum. The number of students who participated in classes rose from a wartime low of 324 in 1944–45 to 2,229 in 1961–62.[2] Lyon and Bennion touched the lives of thousands of young men and women in a powerful way.[3]

Dynamic Duo

The impact of Lyon and Bennion is best understood through the recollections of their bright University of Utah students. These students came to the Salt Lake institute to seek answers to gospel questions, to reconcile secular learning with religious belief, and to participate in recreational and service activities with other Latter-day Saints. One such student, according to Lyon, "met his wife in Brother Bennion's courtship and marriage class and did his courting in my Doctrine and Covenants class."[4] From his later perspective as a General Authority in the Church, that student remembered: "We really learned in [Lyon's] classes; his classes were like a fatherly chat—intimate. That's where I really learned the gospel." The student, Thomas S. Monson (illus. 9-1), was not alone in his assessment of Lyon's influence on his knowledge of the gospel.[5]

Courtesy Church Archives

Illus. 9-1. Thomas S. Monson (c. 1940s) attended classes at the Salt Lake institute taught by Ed Lyon and others.

James B. Mayfield, professor of political science at the University of Utah, remembered, "I was a returned missionary, but I only learned to study scriptures in [Lyon's] Doctrine and Covenants class—it was amazing."[6] Another recalled that Stanford Cazier and Douglas D. Alder, later presidents of Utah State University and Dixie College respectively, both said that Ed Lyon, Lowell Bennion, and George Boyd had profoundly influenced their devotion to the Church.[7]

Bill and Erlyne Gould met and married as a result of an institute class. The two later expressed their gratitude to Lyon:

We'll never forget your untiring patient counsel and valuable advice. You meant so much in helping me, inexperienced, naive, and knowledgeless, to have a firm conviction of the rightness of truth and the need for an understanding of all things. Though some of the academic teachings [at the U of U] may become dimmer and hazier in our box of stacked college notes . . . we live the Gospel every day.[8]

Gloria Schaffer Melendez, a student of the era, stated that "I needed the Institute; I was living away from home and had no anchor. I was studying anthropology and reading a lot of things that attacked my faith, a lot of them. I would have lost my testimony had it not been for the 'Tute.'"[9] She appreciated the humble attitude, the idea that "we students and instructors may not have all the answers, but we'll explore together," which she found in Bennion and Lyon and which was so different from her U of U professors.[10] Ruth Fetzer Carr and many others confessed that they "practically lived at the Institute." It was a fun place, a place to meet casually and make friends in a stimulating spiritual environment. Describing the significance of the institute's programs, Carr affirmed, "Our devotion to the Church [really] grew. The teachers impacted our desire to learn. They provided us with an insatiable appetite to learn, especially T. Edgar Lyon, because he knew so much."[11]

Lyon and Bennion were unusually effective in engineering positive experiences for their students. Erma Darley later wrote: "Bro. Lyon, many thanks goes to you for helping me 'find myself.' I don't believe you really know how lost I was there at the U, but I grew, blossomed, and got a little confidence."[12] Erma and Carma Darley's parents wrote Lyon that "for Carma her year as an Inter-Chapter Officer was the highlight of her college career. She seemed to live Lambda Delta Sigma. . . . It was to you she wished to come whenever she had problems." Another daughter, Lucille, "would select Institute classes she wanted and then build the rest of her [university] courses around them."[13] Another student of that period, Bobbie Jo Worthen, wrote: "What a wonderful feeling to have fifty 'sisters' at once as I did in Psi [chapter of Lambda Delta Sigma]."[14] And after visiting one of his daughter's activities, U of U history professor David Miller ventured that "he'd never seen such a happy bunch of kids . . . together as there were that night."[15]

The students of the 1940s and '50s "had little money for recreation, so they created their own, something we've [now] lost sight of," Lyon said in 1975.[16] He often talked of the loss of creativity among his university students in later years when students would hire a caterer instead of cooking their own food for a party or go to a movie rather than talk and interact. During the earlier years, Lyon chaperoned the "conjoints," went roller-skating with the students, organized campuswide songfests, and helped plan "no-date parties," "work parties," and events jokingly referred to as "polygamy parties." During the war, he insisted that young women could still date if they were willing to share the scarce males. Four or five women and one man would go on a picnic or a service project to a widow's home. "Then I reminded them that in polygamy days the Mormons had made an adaptation of the square dance, so a man could dance with two wives at the same time . . . [so the students also] started having polygamy dances. . . . [Those were] exciting, creative years."[17]

It was not uncommon for Lyon to be at the institute every night of the week. He later calculated that he often spent seventy to eighty hours a week at work and praised Hermana for her major role in raising their sons during his frequent absences. He viewed his job as a calling, and he never complained of the evenings and weekends spent chaperoning socials. During the late 1940s, all institute classes—with as many as fourteen hundred students enrolled each year—were taught exclusively by Bennion and Lyon. They each spent up to twenty-two hours a week in the classroom. Each also maintained an open-door policy so that students would feel welcome to drop in during the day; personal counseling and mentoring were a vital part of their work. On evenings and Saturdays, Lyon and Bennion often spoke at meetings and participated in social events. On Sundays during the 1940s and early 1950s, before university wards and stakes were created, Lyon taught a special Sunday School class for university students at the institute—a forerunner of the later student wards. With Bennion and Lyon, the students planned Sunday "devotionals," short services combining scripture-reading, music, and a short talk or two. No announcements or business were allowed. Either Lyon or Bennion was always present. The "Tute," with its students and programs, absorbed much of Lyon's life—and he loved it.

After long planning and working closely with Church architect Edward O. Anderson (illus. 9-2), Bennion, Lyon, and their students came up with a design for a new institute building (illus. 9-3). The building's approval was the direct result of Lyon and Bennion's success in attracting students. Construction was completed by late 1949, and with the help of scores of students, Lyon and Bennion moved in on December 31. Franklin L. West dedicated the new building early on the morning of January 1, 1950, and he called it "his finest monument" as commissioner of Church education.[18] Bennion occupied the main floor office area; Lyon was downstairs. As one student remembers, Lyon's office "was at the bottom of the steps, going down to the lunch room, or recreation room. Well, his door was always open . . . and . . . you were welcome in his office all of the time."[19]

Though excited by his association with thousands of stimulating students, Lyon's long and close relationship with his friend and coworker Lowell L. Bennion proved to be even more exhilarating. They worked and taught together almost daily from 1939 to 1962. Lyon respected Bennion's intellect, his dedication, and his true Christian character, stating that he "took

Courtesy Church Archives

Illus. 9-2. Church architect Edward O. Anderson examines blue prints for the new Salt Lake Institute of Religion building, late 1940s.

Illus. 9-3. The new Salt Lake Institute of Religion building, 1950s.

seriously . . . that if you don't respect the widows and the orphans and so forth, it isn't real religion."[20] The pair planned institute activities around the concept of service. According to Ed, "Lowell had an expression that if the day ever came when Lambda Delta Sigma degenerated into a punch and cookie fellowship, it ought to be abolished."[21] Under Bennion's administration, the Salt Lake institute never held a faculty Christmas party, but rather sponsored work parties, where students pitched in to make and repair toys for the needy. Lyon observed that Bennion was "a master at having [university] kids discover what he's thinking they ought to do. And not in a selfish way, not in a manipulating way, but [to] lead them."[22]

Bennion later reflected that he and Lyon "got along beautifully. Not a single harsh or angry word or feeling passed between us in twenty-three years of close association. I think we loved each other—and still do—even as Jonathan and David of Biblical times."[23] In a 1990 interview, Bennion confided that he could only recall one incident when "I got upset at [Ed]. We had to return to the institute for an evening activity or something. I drove down to pick him up but your mother informed me that he'd be a few minutes because he was reading a bedtime story to [Ted] and Lynn. I waited and fumed. . . . But now I think I was wrong."[24]

Bennion was impressed by Lyon's skills in "practical things like plumbing and electrical matters" as well as his record-keeping abilities.[25] Bennion recalled, "The one thing that surprised me was that [Ed] didn't seem to have much of an aesthetic side. . . . [Hermana] used to have to drag him to plays and musicals at the university."[26] Bennion, deeply in love with Beethoven and most classical music,[27] attempted to infuse his colleague with the same aesthetic appreciation. Lyon attended the Utah Symphony but often dozed, and he usually was interested most in learning about a work's historical setting and the life of its composer. When he read a novel, he wanted to know if the events were accurately portrayed.

Writer, Scholar, Speaker

During these stimulating years at the institute, Lyon also became a Church scholar. His students considered him highly learned, but he felt a need to write and publish to demonstrate his scholarship to himself and his peers. No outside pressure seems to have been exerted by his superiors—it was all internal. In 1936, Lyon had tasted the satisfaction of publishing the results of his research when the *Improvement Era*[28] published his article about the location of the first baptisms in the Netherlands. During the same year, the *Millennial Star*[29] featured Lyon's "A Blessing and Its Fulfilment [*sic*]," a four-page story recounting Lyon's experience with the gift of tongues in 1923. Both of these were first-person narratives, brief moments of contemporary history, but Lyon had not yet found his voice in writing.

His studies, talks, and classes provided the subject matter for entrance into critical writing. By invitation from a former colleague at Chicago, Lyon composed a short article on "Recreation and the Mormon Church," which was published in 1939 in the journal *Character and Citizenship*. In 1943 he explained the origins and traditions surrounding Christ, Christmas, and Santa Claus for the *Improvement Era*. Yet it was not until the postwar years at the Salt Lake institute that he really hit his stride. Between 1946 and 1962, he wrote and published four major books or manuals, researched and produced a 274-page doctoral dissertation, published two volumes of his radio talks, penned thirty-five articles (mainly in Church publications), and offered his critical evaluation in scores of book reviews.[30]

Most of what he wrote during this prolific period were articles and books commissioned by Church leaders or auxiliaries for immediate use. All but a few of the articles appeared in the *Instructor* magazine or the

Improvement Era. He wrote books to be used as manuals for institute classes, for the M-Men and Gleaners in the Mutual Improvement Association, for Church seminary classes, and for use in Melchizedek Priesthood quorums.

Lyon's articles dealt with the life of Orson Pratt, the Apostasy, an explanation of the Articles of Faith, and "Hearsay or History," to name a few topics. There were not as many outlets for serious scholarly publishing in the 1940s and 1950s as there are in the twenty-first century, and Lyon lacked the time or the academic confidence to submit articles to major scholarly journals. However, two articles from this period were published in the *Utah Historical Quarterly*. Lyon generally geared his books and short articles to a general, popular Latter-day Saints audience, and he became well known among a large readership for his knowledge and insights into Church history. With few exceptions, his articles and texts published during this period grew from the research he did in preparation for his teaching.

Lyon wanted to address his audience from a position of faith and conviction, but his writing was also influenced by his education at Chicago. The editorial process his books underwent reflects a productive tension between spiritual and intellectual approaches to the gospel. It also demonstrates Lyon's gospel conviction and his willingness to accommodate requests from Church leaders.

In the early 1940s, Commissioner Franklin L. West invited Lyon to write an introductory manual to the Doctrine and Covenants and the Pearl of Great Price, the first real historical and doctrinal commentary on this modern scripture. Lowell Bennion had already published three books or manuals—*What about Religion* (1934), *Youth and Its Religion* (1939), and *The Religion of the Latter-Day Saints* (1939),[31] and Lyon felt some pressure to get his ideas in print. He worked on the Doctrine and Covenants book from 1942 to 1944, principally in the summertime and late evenings. By 1945 the manuscript had circulated among institute teachers, but before being printed it had to pass through the Church Publication Committee, consisting of Elders Harold B. Lee and Marion G. Romney and chaired by Elder Joseph Fielding Smith. Franklin West submitted Lyon's one and only typewritten version.

After many months of waiting and multiple inquiries about the Doctrine and Covenants book, Vernon Larson, West's assistant, informed Lyon, "The thing's [manuscript's] disappeared and nobody knows where it is." Lyon was devastated: "I didn't [even] have any finished copy of it. I just had my rough copy that I typed from."[32] West told him to "do it over again." He did so without complaining and resubmitted it after eight hectic months. Finally, in 1947, Lyon received forty-two "suggestions and criticisms" from the committee.[33] Lyon recalls, "Later on I heard that they'd taken the first manuscript to President J. Reuben Clark, and he said, 'It smacks too much of higher criticism. Don't use it.'"[34]

Many of the committee's criticisms grew from different perspectives on the Doctrine and Covenants. As a trained historian, Lyon attempted to place each revelation in its historical setting and examine the events in Joseph Smith's life that prompted each of his inquiries to the Lord. Lyon wanted to explain how human interaction played a role in Joseph Smith's receipt of divine revelation. Since Lyon's early boyhood, Joseph had been a warm, real-life, inquiring human being. Lyon's scholarship reflected those early feelings. In some instances the committee did not approve of this approach, feeling that it de-emphasized God's hand in Joseph Smith's life. The Publications Committee wanted to emphasize divine presence whenever possible. "The objection," Lyon recalled years later, "had been that [the committee] thought that the book ought to be designed to build spirituality, and I was trying to be too intellectual."[35] The committee did not reject the book, but requested "the return of this manuscript for final checking of these *corrections* before the book goes to press."[36]

Lyon was willing. He followed many of the suggestions and changed the problematic words, but he left unchanged a number of others. The 235-page *Introduction to the Doctrine and Covenants and the Pearl of Great Price* was eventually accepted and published by the Church Department of Education in early 1948; it became a standard text for all institutes during the late 1940s and 1950s.

Before this assignment had been successfully completed, a second manual was published: *We Believe* appeared in 1947. It was also commissioned and was designed for use by M-Men and Gleaners, the college-aged students he understood so well. The book consisted of twenty-one lessons dealing with the Church's well-known thirteen Articles of Faith and topics such as belief in a literal resurrection, missionary service, and the Word of Wisdom. Lyon drew heavily on his experiences at the University of Chicago and in the Netherlands, relating stories of the gospel as it came in conflict with other beliefs and value systems. Each lesson contained a story or two, often so transparent that Lyon's life experiences shone through. One story recounted the experience of a young Latter-day Saint student at a "large eastern university" who took a Methodist minister to a sacrament meeting. This was assuredly Lyon's friend, the Reverend Lawrence J. Taylor.[37] *We Believe* was translated into German, French, Swedish, Finnish, Danish, Spanish, and Portuguese.[38] It became very popular as an MIA manual and was circulated worldwide; when Lyon's sons served missions, their last name was frequently recognized by young people in many countries as a result of the manual.[39]

During the extremely busy year of 1947, Lyon also authored a series of twelve articles on the life and contributions of Orson Pratt for the *Instructor* magazine that had been solicited by the editor, Wendell J. Ashton. Lyon reworked some sections of his master's thesis to create each of the four-page articles. Most of the articles underwent editing designed to present a more faith-promoting history, sometimes ignoring or eliminating historical information about human weaknesses. Lyon felt upset by such editing, but he was not a fighter over such matters. He accepted the changes rather than insist on his original version.

In the late 1950s, the General Priesthood Committee assigned Lyon to condense a long unfinished manuscript on the Apostasy for use in priesthood quorums throughout the Church.[40] Lyon had been recognized as an authority on the Church's concept of the Apostasy since the mid-1940s. The manuscript had been written by James L. Barker, who had hoped his extensive study of the Apostasy would be the definitive text for the Church until death cut short his plans. Lyon soon began working on the two-thousand-page manuscript but found it almost impossible to condense in a meaningful way without rewriting most of it. He also began writing an accompanying teachers' supplement.

During summer 1959, the committee concluded that the Barker book was too complex to use as a manual, even in condensed form. The committee decided to have Lyon write a separate manual for the priesthood quorums and to use the book that grew from Barker's manuscript as a supplement to it. Unfortunately, it was not until the September 1959 committee meeting that Lyon learned of the change in plans and was told that the material in his teachers' supplement was not long enough or sufficiently detailed to stand alone. He had to write a separate manual in a few short weeks so it could be published the next year.

The manual needed to be printed before January 1, 1960, which meant the manuscript had to be in the printer's hands by November 1, 1959. With less than two months to work, Lyon was quickly relieved of all his teaching duties at the institute for the fall quarter. He retreated to his favorite writing place—the family's now-unused ping-pong table in their basement, with a large fluorescent light overhead and plenty of space to spread out books and notes. Using an old portable typewriter and working twelve to fourteen hours a day on the project, he completed the thirty-five chapters of the manual by the November 1 deadline. When a son asked him how he managed it, he responded that he just used the notes from classes he had taught. After Lyon spent intense hours reading galleys and page proofs, the manual, quite academic as well as spiritual and historical in nature, appeared under the title *Apostasy to Restoration.*

Throughout the Church the manual aroused real excitement for historical understanding and analysis. A former student wrote that the "book has been so thrilling to me that I have vowed to express this to you. I don't know when I've found a book so full of information to be so easy and enjoyable to me."[41] In 1960, "Lyon" became at least a priesthood quorum word, if not a household word, in the Church. He had no contract for the work, so when he received a $2,000 check for the manual and another $1,500 for the Barker revision, he was more than delightfully surprised.[42] These two checks totaled half of his salary that year.

His publications, speeches on KSL, and the growing body of admiring former students intensified the demand for Lyon to speak in public. From 1945 to 1962, he spoke in at least twenty-one high school baccalaureate services. In 1957 he was the featured speaker at his own sons' baccalaureate services from Olympus High School, and he found it the most difficult place of all—"one is not a prophet in his own country," Lyon wrote of the occasion.[43] He spoke at hundreds of missionary farewells as his former freshman and sophomore students prepared to serve. Lyon usually spoke from notes, briefly outlining the basic facts of his subject. Otherwise he relied on inspiration and his phenomenal memory. Frequently he dozed peacefully on the stand until just before his name was announced.

Lyon also responded to many invitations from universities or assignments from the Church to present ideas at events variously known as "Spiritual Exploration Week," "Religious Emphasis Week," or "Religion in Life Series" held on university campuses throughout the western United States. Lyon journeyed to Idaho, Arizona, Nevada, and California to participate with ministers, priests, and leaders of other faiths.[44] These broad spiritual exploration experiences were common in the 1950s and allowed Lyon close, regular contact with other religious leaders. He developed an ecumenical outlook uncommon to most Church members of the period.

For many, Lyon also became an authority to whom many turned with questions on doctrinal and historical issues. His files from these years are

Illus. 9-4. BYU vice president Ed Berrett helped administer Church education programs. He was also a member of Ed Lyon's stake presidency in the 1940s.

filled with letters from hundreds of Church members, often his former students, asking him to clarify a troublesome matter. Some were upset by a certain talk or lesson or by their own historical research. Lyon thoughtfully took time to respond to each letter, giving his observations on problems such as whether all plants and animals have souls, whether mortals existed before Adam, and when the Spirit enters the body. Lyon also offered clarifications on statements by early Church leaders like Joseph Smith and Sidney Rigdon.[45]

During this golden era, Lyon held several regular Church callings. Each Sunday he went to the institute, where he served as an unofficial branch president for hundreds of students at the ward bishop's request. From 1945 to 1949 he served on the high council of the newly created East Mill Creek Stake, working closely for a short time with his old friend Ed Berrett (illus. 9-4) and later with Gordon B. Hinckley, both members of the stake presidency.[46]

Lyon was released from the high council in 1949 and called to work as a volunteer guide on Temple Square, where he served until 1964. As early as 1941 and until 1962, he also served as an unpaid instructor in the Salt Lake Mission Home, teaching thousands of new missionaries about the Apostasy, the Restoration, and the Doctrine and Covenants. He volunteered as a guide and host for the Church's foreign visitor program (1946–58) and then offered his guide services to Salt Lake City officials who were hosting visitors who wanted a personal, human experience in the city. Later, he assisted the Utah Foreign Visitors hosting committees (1958–72). During the mid-1950s, Commissioner of Education Ernest L. Wilkinson often assigned Lyon and Bennion to speak at stake conferences as visiting "educational authorities" to promote university education among young Latter-day Saints.[47]

Home Front

Ed kept active at home, too, and enjoyed excellent relationships with his wife, his children, and his neighbors. In 1946, when the end of the war made gasoline available once again, the Lyons took their first-ever family vacation. Crowding eight people and their luggage into their 1935 Ford V-8, they toured Yellowstone Park. Ed also squeezed in visits to his mother and sister Janette in Long Beach, California, in 1947, 1950, and 1953. In the early 1950s, Janette, who continued to write to her older brother as "Teddy Boy," offered to pay Ed and Hermana's way to Hawaii to surprise their son John as he returned from the Samoan mission. Ed wrote to her, "I am a rather unemotional person that is not easily moved to tears, but your letter melted my heart, as it did that of Hermana, and we could hardly believe that anyone could make such a stupendous offer to us."[48] He also told her that they could not accept her generosity. Janette's insistence changed his mind, and in June 1953, Ed and Hermana flew to the islands at her expense, finding the next seven days to be the most relaxing of their hectic lives. Ed thanked his sister with specific details:

> We were so completely relaxed. . . . For a period of four days, at one stretch, I never even thought of what was happening in Salt Lake, the Institute, my classes, our boys, or what I would normally be doing in the garden. . . .
>
> At night, on the beach, and on the boat and plane, I actually read a detective story, and the novel, *Return to Paradise*. Such loafing I haven't done in years! Perhaps never in my life have I felt so utterly lazy.[49]

More than the long-distance family vacations, Ed's sons remember the annual three- or four-day backpacking trips in Mill Creek Canyon, east of Salt Lake City. With old surplus army backpacks and even older blankets from home, Ed guided and cajoled his children and numerous neighborhood friends up Porter's Fork to a sagging miner's cabin at Baker's Spring or to shallow Dog Lake. His sons and their friends, beginning at age seven or eight, eagerly anticipated these pleasant summer days and nights. They all slept under the stars because no one owned tents. Ed taught the boys to gather flowers and dry grass to make relatively soft, warm beds. Outdoor skills he had developed years earlier in Jackson Hole came in handy when he helped the boys make a large log raft to pole across the lake. On another occasion, he created a makeshift table so he could sit in comfort while eating his whole wheat pancakes.

On his first camping trip to the Baker's Spring cabin, Ed forgot the frying pan. Never at a loss, he found a rusty shovel left over from mining days in the region. He hammered the shovel out with a rock, scoured it with sand from the spring, and turned it into a serviceable frying pan. On another trip, he noticed an abandoned wheelbarrow in a mine. He retrieved it and wheeled it all the way down Porter's Fork to his car. His resourcefulness impressed his sons, who glimpsed in him some of the pioneer spirit of his ancestors.

One son later recalled: "I was always impressed with how heavy Dad's pack was [on those trips]; I couldn't even lift it, and this assured me that my father was some type of superman, certainly much stronger (and tougher) than our friends' fathers."[50] As the boys grew older, their love for camping continued, and they would often heft their own heavy packs for a week or two in the Uinta or Wind River primitive areas. For Father's Day 1960, Hermana proudly penned a note to her husband: "No boys ever had a better [father]. . . . You've worked with them and taught them the importance of work; you've guided them, and loved them, and played with them. You've given them an ideal of hard work, integrity, love, patience, to work toward in being fathers themselves."[51]

In their rural surroundings, the Lyon children outgrew most of the childhood diseases that had plagued them in the Netherlands and in central Salt Lake City. Ed and Hermana were very trusting parents, allowing their children to roam the neighborhood and even the mountains. Like their father, the boys all experienced their growth spurts at early ages, which helped them forge a youthful independence. As the boys grew, though, they seemed to trade illness for accidents.

One snowy night in January 1947, seven-year-old Teddy and a friend were gathering discarded Christmas trees for a large bonfire. In the heavy storm, a teenage driver struck the two boys in a hit-and-run accident. The friend, Rex Dahlberg, was cut and bruised but able to wander to his home, dazed. Teddy, however, lay unconscious and alone on the snowy road, at risk of being run over by other vehicles. At home, Teddy's failure to return in the blinding snow worried Hermana. Ed went out searching and found their unconscious son two blocks away. The boy had serious cuts on his face, broken bones, and multiple skull fractures. An ambulance took him to the hospital, limp and unresponsive. Lynn Lyon recalled, "I do not remember much about the next few hours except realizing that I might not have a twin brother [any more]. I also recall that Mother did not handle such events well. Hysteria would be the best description of her reaction."[52] Hermana's anguish and fear of death again surfaced.

Teddy remained unconscious for ten days; the family and doctors feared he would never fully recover. Lynn wrote, "During this time Mother insisted that she or Dad had to [always] be with him. She took the days and Dad took the nights. He would teach his classes and then go to the hospital and spend the nights sleeping [in a chair] next to Ted's bed."[53] Teddy eventually regained consciousness and recovered after weeks in the hospital and a long recuperation at home.

A further upset occurred in March 1950. With parental license for independence, tall (6'6"), adventuresome, and accident-prone John, then nineteen years old, had taken up mountain climbing and cave exploring. He and sixteen-year-old Jamie had recently discovered what for a number of years thereafter was listed as the deepest cave in the United States, a near-vertical fissure plunging almost two thousand feet into the Wasatch Fault in Neff's Canyon. John and two friends climbed down into the "Great Pit," a 180-foot vertical drop, and began to explore. Others friends waited above to pull the tired climbers back up once they emerged from their explorations. When John and his group failed to come up at the appointed time, the two friends at the top climbed out of the cave and called the Salt Lake County sheriff.

A small rescue operation was underway by the time Ed and two of his younger sons arrived at the trailhead expecting to meet John. Instead they found police cars and panic. Ed and the boys trudged through deep snow to the cave's narrow entrance. Jamie, who had been in the cave several times with John, volunteered to go in with another climber, who did not know the cave. Ed had a double concern—John's welfare and Hermana's state of mind. The rescue was successful. The three missing young men had returned only a few minutes late to the bottom of the Great Pit, but when they found that their friends above had left, they were too exhausted to climb out hand over hand. They waited for sixteen hours until Jamie and his companion pulled them up, after which they climbed to the entrance. Lynn reports, "John related that when he and Dad were walking down Neff's Canyon to the car after the rescue, Dad's only comment to him was, 'John, you've upset your mother very much.' That was the worst rebuke Dad could administer."[54]

Hermana's Roles

Other, more permanent, losses occurred during this period. Seven men in the house and only one woman seemed lopsided; Hermana and Ed wanted a daughter. Hermana suffered at least two miscarriages during the 1940s,[55] and Lyon indicated to his sons that at least one of the fetuses was a female. As the mother of only boys, Hermana either wrote or modified a poem that described her feelings:

"God Sent Me Boys"

God sent me boys; no girls to help me sew
And make sweet cookies, don't you know.
But boys so full of life and fun
Still bubbling o'er when day is done.
No girls to help me with the beds;
When tired—no cool hand on my head;
But boys to follow a guiding hand
And preach the gospel in a foreign land.
No daughter here in frilly lace
No trace of powder on smooth face
But if God wills in years to come,
My six sons will bring me some.[56]

Hermana was the constant support at home for Ed and her beloved boys (illus. 9-5). Though she experienced periods of anxiety and distress when her children were threatened, she was otherwise a tower of strength and spirituality.

On April 25, 1944, the Primary General Presidency, "with the approval of the first Presidency," called Hermana to serve on the Primary General Board of the Church.[57] For the next twenty-one years she met with the board weekly, wrote lessons almost daily, talked and brainstormed on the phone incessantly, and traveled fearfully to "Primary Conventions" throughout the United States. The calling brought her a new kind of spiritual and social stimulation; she now had regular contact with many intelligent, dedicated, hard-thinking women. They hammered out concepts, critiqued each others' ideas, and wrote manuals and programs for the Primary of the entire Church. She approached her tasks with dedication, energy, and a significant time commitment.

Unlike the Melchizedek Priesthood manuals, Primary manuals were generally written by committees, and no names appeared on the published work.[58] Hermana wrote hundreds of lessons, totaling at least four or five complete lesson manuals, during her years on the board. She pounded out most of them on the old Remington on which she had typed Ed's thesis. The weight of her contribution may never be known because of the anonymity of the writing, but at the time she was released (to accept another writing assignment), one tribute summarized her dedication:

Illus. 9-5. Ed and Hermana, with grandchildren Kathy and Michael, in the driveway of their house in East Millcreek, c. 1960.

> You helped prepare material for summer Primary. You helped name the Pilot groups and helped to write their lesson books. You have been the Primary strength to the missions—struggling in behalf of mixed age groups. You've chairmanned many committees—worked diligently at conventions, April conference and [many] special assignments. You have truly taken the special gifts that God has endowed you with and used them not for self praise but to glorify Him.[59]

At Hermana's Primary farewell gathering, a vocalist sang "Hermana the Lioness" to the music of "The Wind Is a Lion" from Crawford Gates's *Promised Valley.*

Her experience writing lessons and creating special programs in the Netherlands helped Hermana and the board as they faced the challenges of the expanding Church. Hermana fearlessly preached the need to get rid of Wasatch Front–thinking and to write lessons and create programs that would apply to small groups and even home primaries in the diverse areas of the Church. Anchored in her mission experiences, she perceived the needs of a worldwide Church long before many of her contemporaries.

Her work on the board also brought her in regular contact with many General Authorities. She was more positive about these men than she had been in 1938 when she angrily wrote to her husband about plural marriage and men in general, but she would not tolerate pettiness, shallow thinking, or inconsistency—in either men or women. Hermana demanded excellence and broad understanding. She was critical of narrow-minded people, of materialism, and of those who sheltered themselves too much. She wanted substance instead of spectacle and show. She knew and respected Elder Gordon B. Hinckley, first as he served in the presidency of the East Mill Creek Stake, and later as he oversaw the Primary and other general Church programs. She often spoke of his incredible efficiency as supervisor over the Primary. Elder Harold B. Lee also served as adviser to the Primary, and Hermana spent many hours explaining new programs and soliciting his support and guidance. Elder Lee became a family friend, setting apart many of the boys for their missions and performing their marriage ceremonies.

Hermana's son Lynn has distinct memories of her service on the board. He remembers that "Thursday night was always 'do it yourself' dinner night." The Board held its meetings from 4:00 to 7:00 P.M. on Thursdays, but Hermana often stayed later in smaller committee meetings, or simply discussing and wrestling with ideas. She frequently came home from these meetings "announcing that she had a terrible [migraine] headache and [was] going straight to bed. Some of the board meetings must have been intense, and there was undoubtedly some controversy," wrote Lynn.[60]

Hermana also accepted frequent assignments to participate in Primary Conventions, a type of outreach in which two or three women from the board would travel to outlying areas of the Church to instruct local Primary leaders. These conventions typically lasted several days. Hermana lectured and modeled Primary skills in San Francisco in 1948, throughout southern Utah in 1950, in the Pacific northwest in 1954, in New Orleans in 1956, and around the Chicago area in 1959. During these absences, Ed took over as mother. Meals became simpler, and his sons discovered one of their father's weaknesses. He loved bakery goods, especially cinnamon-raisin sweet rolls, which often appeared as desserts when Hermana was away.

Hermana's sons recall that her life during this period seemed to center around the telephone:

My mother must have spent about ¼ to ⅓ of her later adult life talking on the telephone to her close friends and family. That's pretty amazing considering all the writing she did for Church committees and the like as well as raising six very active and often challenging sons. She was a remarkable woman in a variety of ways. She is also the one who got me hooked on reading Agatha Christie and the one who taught me to ask a lot of questions about things, just as she did. But she loved her telephone. I know. I was often practicing the piano or composing music in the next room while she carried on long and detailed conversations, which she often shared with me.[61]

As Laurie indicates, his mother was a question-asker: Why are things this way? How could they be better? What has to be done to improve this lesson? Her questions often challenged and sometimes upset those with whom she worked.

To help satisfy her quest for answers and information, Hermana returned to the University of Utah in 1957, hoping to complete her bachelor's degree. Though she never actually finished the degree, over the next four years she took many classes in literature, education, geology, and psychology.[62] In winter quarter 1958, she and five of her six sons all attended the University of Utah together.

Hermana was an inveterate list-maker. Not only did she create a list of daily chores for her sons during the summer, she also made frequent lists for herself. Often after an event, she pondered and evaluated how it could be improved the next time. One Christmas afternoon she apparently sat down with the intent of improving future celebrations and listed eight ways to improve her preparations for the coming year, including "give books," and "cook ahead of time."[63]

Her neighbors and friends held her in great respect. Bill Mulder, a missionary who had served with the Lyons in the Netherlands, and his wife, Gwyneth, moved into the home next door to the Lyons in East Mill Creek. He recalled Hermana's great creativity and observed that despite being the "soul of patience . . . she now and then became exasperated." In summary, however, Mulder esteemed her to be "the most saint-like person I have ever known."[64]

Family Dispersal

The 1950s could be called the "decade of dispersal" for the Lyon children. All of the Lyons' six sons commenced some form of military service during the decade. Five of the six boys left on missions, and four were married during the 1950s. In July 1954 alone, Ed and Hermana sent two sons on missions and one to the military. They accepted the dispersal as a necessary part of a family that had learned values of independence, planning, and missionary service.

The Lyon Sons

Son	Mission	Military	Marriage	Education
David	Illinois Peoria Mission (Nauvoo) Dec 1996–May 1998	ROTC National Guard 1947–1949 Reserve 1949–1957	August 1950 Lois Taylor, Deceased '82; Margene Barker Sept. 1984, Md. by Spencer W. Kimball	BS-U of U-1951
John	Samoa Oct 1950–May 1953 Samoa Oct 1995–Sept 1997	Active Duty, 1954–1956	September 1957 Carole Elsmore, Md. by Adam S. Bennion	BA-U of U-1958, MA-BYU-1985
Jamie	Germany July 1954–Dec 1956	ROTC; Active Duty, July 1963–Nov 1966	December 1959 Dorothy Burton, Md. by Harold B. Lee	BA-U of U-1958, MA-U of -U-1959, Ph.D.-Harvard U-1963
Laurie	Netherlands July 1954–Dec 1956 Chile Osorno Feb 1999–Dec 1999	ROTC; Active Duty July 1962–July 1964	March 1958 Donna Reeder, Md. by Hugh B. Brown	BA-U of U-1958, MA-U of U-1960, Ph.D.-Eastman-1956
Ted	Argentina June 1959–Nov 1961 Chile Osorno July 1996–June 1999	Reserve 1956–1963 Active Duty, Jun 1957–Dec 1957	June 1962 Cheryl Larsen, Md. by Harold B. Lee	BA-U of U-1963, Ph.D.-UCLA-1967
Lynn	New Zealand June 1959–May 1961	Reserve 1956–1963, Active Duty, Jun 1957–Dec 1957	July 1964 Juneil Fetzer, Md. by Harold B. Lee	BS-U of U-1964, MD-U of U-1967, MPH-Harvard-U-1969

For many years, Hermana had worried about her unmarried sister Ada. At age thirty-eight, Ada met and married Fred Fielding, a World War II veteran who had lost his right leg in the war. The only child from this marriage, Ellen, was born premature, and while in the incubator, the fragile baby received too much oxygen, which caused permanent blindness. Then, in June 1950, Ada died suddenly in her sleep, leaving little Ellen motherless. Hermana cared for the blind baby for several months until Fred remarried. Hermana and Ed kept in close contact with Ellen the rest of their lives.[65]

Ed's mother, Mary Cairns Lyon, passed away quietly in Long Beach, California, on September 23, 1948, at age eighty-two. Ed's sister Janette had been caring for Mary for many years, and the death was not unexpected.

Services were held at the Ensign Ward in Salt Lake City, where Mary's husband, David, had served as bishop, and she was buried in the family plot.

Hermana's father, Gustave Forsberg, suffered for many years with Parkinson's Disease. After a fall and two broken bones in 1957, he came to live with Ed and Hermana for five months. They cared for him through another operation, which was intended to relieve the tremor caused by the disease, but he died a few days later on November 4, 1957, at age seventy-eight. Lynn Lyon recalled that after Gustave's "death [Hermana] walked in the hall . . . in deep distress [but] had the feeling that he was beside her."[66] Hermana's stepmother, Zina Widdison Forsberg, developed cancer of the stomach and died in 1960. Hermana, as the only daughter, spent considerable time caring for this woman who had been unable to show her much affection as a child.

Midway through the 1950s, an unexpected tragedy hit the family. While the Lyons sat in sacrament meeting on March 25, 1956, in the Rosecrest Ward, they heard distant sirens but paid little heed until an usher quietly tapped Ed on the shoulder. There had been an accident—would he come out in the foyer? Lyon's oldest grandchild, three-year-old Davey, had been hit by a car. Death came instantly. Lois T. Lyon, the child's mother, had witnessed the accident but had been unable to prevent it. She and her husband, David, were devastated. Hermana and Ed shared their grief at the loss of what Ed called a "ray of sunshine . . . it is going to be a gap that will not be filled. We could tell you stories by the hour of his cute antics."[67] Hermana wrote that "David said to me 'I've never known what people meant when they said <my heart is broken> but now I know.' He's like Dad in that he doesn't cry [but feels deeply]."[68] Hermana was concerned about Lois, who was eight months pregnant and whose grief, she felt, was "so deep and terrible that there are no words to describe it."[69]

Hermana also endured her first bout with cancer during the decade. In May 1958, at age fifty-two, Hermana underwent a hysterectomy, with panicky feelings that "she would die during surgery and never see her sons again."[70] She came through well, but the recovery was turbulent and prolonged. The boys took turns with her in the hospital, but, Lynn records,

> Dad stayed with her constantly. . . . This episode brought to me the deep bond of love that existed between my parents. . . . Seeing Dad's concern over Mother told me that, while he loved his sons, we were peripheral to his love for his wife.
>
> I also saw Dad's love illustrated in another way. After this surgery Mother developed severe hot flashes. She was miserable,

one minute sweating, and chilly the next. Despite the finances that were his ever present worry, [he had] the house air conditioned [for her]. . . . This act spoke volumes about his devotion to her.[71]

Hermana recovered after the operation, but from that time until her death in 1980, she lived in constant dread of cancer.

Though Hermana's physical health was fragile and threatened during this period, Ed remained strong and fit. He worked in the garden, pruned the orchard, and irrigated the large garden and fruit trees. He milked the cow, cleaned out the barn, and fed the chickens when the boys left for missions or military service. He hiked and camped with his sons each summer. He repaired plumbing, put in a sprinkling system, and built extra shelves and cupboards. He did not engage in any routine exercise program—the normal activities of rural East Mill Creek life kept him in sufficiently good physical condition.

The Institute

Despite occasional discouragement, family accidents, deaths, and children striking off on foreign missions, military assignments, marriage, and advanced schooling, Lyon continued his hectic pace at the institute. There, his time was filled with letter-writing, class preparation, teaching, speech-giving, accounting and bookkeeping, counseling, reading, writing, and attending frequent Lambda Delta Sigma activities. And the students came in ever larger numbers. The year 1950 was the last in which Bennion and Lyon were the only teachers at the institute; that year about fourteen hundred students heard their lectures and participated in their classes— too many students for two teachers to handle.[72] In 1950, Marion D. ("Duff") Hanks, a young attorney and popular early-morning seminary teacher, began teaching part time at the institute. Because of his charismatic personality, his energy for life and learning, his innovative Book of Mormon classes, and his emphasis that God loves all mankind equally, Hanks quickly acquired a devoted following. In the early 1950s, George T. Boyd was transferred from the University of California–Berkeley to the Salt Lake institute. Boyd was a thinker who "gave no quarter to those who liked their philosophy diluted."[73] He never achieved the same high enrollment in his classes as Bennion and Lyon, but like Hanks, Boyd enjoyed a fine reputation among some of the students at the university. A few years later, Wendell O. Rich, W. Richard Nelson, Wallace F. Toronto, Alfred S. Nielsen, Pearson H. Corbett, and Albert Payne also accepted assignments to join the staff. Enrollment expanded to 2,200 students by 1962.[74] In the 1950s and early 1960s, the institute was likely the largest social gathering place for University of Utah students (illus. 9-6).

From nearly every side came praise and more work. Commissioner West thanked Lyon for his writing, for his organizational skills, and for excellent planning. From Brigham Young University, Sid Sperry insisted that Lyon again come and teach summer courses.[75] Elder John A. Widtsoe congratulated Lyon on his radio talks—"they sound well indeed. . . . Yours is a work well done."[76] The Relief Society kept asking him to write lessons.[77] Presidents Clark and McKay often granted him permission to perform marriages for his former students who were not marrying in the temple.[78] He spoke in numerous Church-wide MIA June Conference sessions. Church Educational System leaders organized a training session for early morning seminary teachers and asked Lyon to instruct the course. Administrator Dale Tingey wrote that "in talking with some of the fellows from Salt Lake they thought your summer session was the best thing thus far for . . . teachers."[79] After Lyon delivered a major speech at BYU, historian Gustive Larson offered highest congratulations; Lyon's talk had been "like coming upon a flowering spring after the disappointments of numerous dry water holes. . . . What a responsibility rests on us to teach Church history on a factual basis."[80] Positive feedback came at every turn.

In 1957 the editor of the *Instructor* magazine asked Ed to write an article on the topic of accuracy in Church history. In response he created a short article, "Is It Hearsay or History?"[81] He began by stating that he had returned home very discouraged from a number of recent priesthood and Sunday School classes, but not because the teachers were poorly prepared. Why was he discouraged? "Because each lesson was based on erroneous foundations and developed by false accusations, having more error than truth in it."[82] Lyon offered guidelines for serious scholarship and truth-filled teaching. He encouraged every teacher to ask these questions of all material: "Is [it] reliable? Does it stand the test of [being] reasonable [to] human experience? Is it in harmony with the teachings of Christ and the Gospel as a whole? Is it historically sound?"[83] Some of these concepts came from his training at the University of Chicago; some derived from his testimony of the restored Church; others came from trying to help students "unlearn" popular errors or unfounded assumptions in Church history.

In this article, Lyon indicated that he had been "jotting down, under the heading 'Myths of Mormonism,'" ideas that he had heard that would

Illus. 9-6. Salt Lake institute graduation in 1957. Pictured are Lyon and Bennion *(seated)* with President McKay and Marion D. Hanks *(standing)*.

not stand up under critical scrutiny. One excerpt from this extensive file, which deals just with Nauvoo and the 1847 westward trek, lists:

> Nauvoo—teachers and body guards
> non-Mormons—tunnels
> ice on river
> # babies born first night
> 25,000 people in Nauvoo
> 25,000 driven out of Missouri
> 5,000 in Nauvoo Legion
> Pioneers didn't know where they were going
> Plural Marriage—carefully controlled—2,000 limited
> Mormon Battalion—to destroy the Church—James Little
> flag on Ensign Peak
> 1 tree in S.L. Valley (Clayton's Diary)
> No granite west of Denver—miracle for temple[84]

Throughout his career, Lyon was troubled by inaccuracies, even small ones. He abhorred inaccuracy in the name of testimony-building, or emotionalism that distorted or misrepresented truth. He stated that "anything that is taught that must be 'unlearned' at a later period . . . should not have been taught in the first place . . . [because it] often leads to a loss of faith."[85] In this article as well as in his classes, Lyon was attempting to strengthen faith by establishing it on a truthful, factual basis.

So passionate was Lyon about a truthful presentation of LDS history that he was fearless in correcting misinformation, whether it came from inside or outside the Church. In 1950 he confidently criticized his now-retired major professor at the University of Chicago, William W. Sweet, regarding Sweet's treatment of the Book of Mormon in his book *The American Churches: An Interpretation*. After correcting him on many specific points, Lyon boldly wrote, "In view of these facts it appears to me that you have again been guilty of following a preconceived idea of relying upon information that someone has conveyed to you without adequate research."[86] He then continued for another paragraph, thanking Sweet for his excellent classes, and noting that it was Sweet who had taught him this thoroughness. Sweet responded with a grateful letter explaining the sources of the errors.[87]

United States Senator Wallace Bennett, a friend of the Lyon family, came under Ed's fire for historical mistakes in his book *Why I Am a Mormon*. Bennett wrote back thanking him for "calling my attention to some sloppy scholarship," and promising to make corrections in a second edition.[88]

Lyon even wrote to novelist Irving Wallace telling him that "in general you have written a very interesting account . . . in your recent book *The Twenty-Seventh Wife*." Lyon acknowledged that the book was written for "the purchasing public," which might excuse some inaccuracy; but then he filled two full pages with Wallace's errors of fact and of interpretation.[89] For example, to counter Wallace's sensationalist claim that Brigham Young neglected and mistreated his wives, Lyon noted that "records kept by the storekeeper of the disbursements indicate that if Brigham Young sinned against his family it was through overindulgence rather than stinginess."[90] Lyon then suggested that Wallace consult original sources before writing another book on the Mormons.

He wrote to the Presiding Bishopric suggesting that some type of name markers be placed in front of LDS chapels as "a wonderful opportunity for publicity and good public relations."[91] Church officials soon put up such signs.

To Elder A. Theodore Tuttle of the First Council of the Seventy, Lyon wrote suggesting correction of a missionary proselyting book used in the Norwegian mission that was filled with factual errors, fallacies of interpretation, and historical distortions.[92]

On the other hand, when praise was warranted, he gave it freely. He thoughtfully congratulated President J. Reuben Clark Jr. for the book *On the Way to Immortality and Eternal Life* and then observed that "many of the books now appearing by LDS authors and compilers will in time, I think, become 'corn in the mill' of anti-Mormon writers to be used against us as some material of a half century ago is being used today."[93] Clark's book would not fall in that category, he assured him.

During these years, from 1946–62, Ed Lyon truly experienced a golden age. He had become an established, publishing scholar; a widely recognized speaker; a willing answerer of gospel questions; a dedicated Church worker; a successful father with a happy wife and committed sons. He had nearly completed his long-expected Ph.D., was financially stable, and settled on his small farm in East Mill Creek. But he felt that the major accomplishment of the period was the deep testimony of truth fostered in the hearts of his students. Lyon, Bennion, and Albert Payne taught at least 20,000 students during these years; Ed had seen at least half of them in his own classes.

The difficult times before World War II gave way to a great time, a golden era spanning fifteen years. Speaking of this era, former colleague Dale LeCheminant observed, "Some thought [Lyon] was an iconoclast, but he wasn't. I think his intention was to get people off dead-center, to get them thinking."[94] Yet Lyon's, and Bennion's, questions and insistence on accuracy were not merely theoretical—as teachers, they were on the firing line, meeting with questioning students every day, students who wanted answers that would harmonize academic learning and gospel truths. Lyon was a teacher, a master teacher, one who could pose the questions that would bring about thinking and the building of testimonies in his students.

Notes

1. Mary Lythgoe Bradford, *Lowell L. Bennion: Teacher, Counselor, Humanitarian* (Salt Lake City, Utah: Dialogue Foundation, 1995), 105–25.

2. A. Gary Anderson, "A Historical Survey of the Full-Time Institutes of Religion" (Ph.D. diss., Brigham Young University, 1968), 147.

3. Bradford, *Lowell L. Bennion,* 108.

4. T. Edgar Lyon, "'Will Ye Also Go Away?'—'Lord, to Whom Shall We Go?'" (Salt Lake Institute Devotional, March 14, 1975), 9.

5. Thomas S. Monson, telephone interview by author, April 9, 1996. Quoted with permission.

6. James B. Mayfield, interview by author, Salt Lake City, December 10, 1994.

7. Kenneth W. Godfrey, interview by author, Logan, Utah, July 10, 1992. George Boyd was a newly assigned teacher to the institute in the 1950s who had a background in philosophy.

8. Erlyne Gould to T. Edgar Lyon, July 31, 1962, T. Edgar Lyon Collection, Church Archives, Family and Church History Department, The Church of Jesus Christ of Latter-day Saints, Salt Lake City (hereafter cited as Church Archives). Unless otherwise noted, all citations for T. Edgar Lyon materials are located in the Lyon collection.

9. Gloria Schaffer Melendez, interview by author, Provo, Utah, March 28, 1996.

10. Melendez, interview.

11. Ruth Fetzer Carr, interview by Melinda Silver, Salt Lake City, September 2, 1993.

12. Erma Darley to T. Edgar Lyon, September 14, 1953, Church Archives.

13. Arch and Lavern Darley to T. Edgar Lyon, July 29, 1962, Church Archives.

14. Bobbie Jo Worthen to T. Edgar Lyon, August 2, 1962, Church Archives.

15. Cited in T. Edgar Lyon, "Oral History," bound typescript, 175, Church Archives.

16. T. Edgar Lyon, "'Will Ye Also Go Away?'" 7.

17. T. Edgar Lyon, "'Will Ye Also Go Away?'" 7.

18. Bradford, *Lowell L. Bennion,* 100.

19. Carr, interview.

20. T. Edgar Lyon, "Oral History," 175.

21. T. Edgar Lyon, "Oral History," 176.

22. T. Edgar Lyon, "Oral History," 176.

23. Lowell L. Bennion, "Memories," approx. 1975, holograph, 47, copy in author's possession.

24. Lowell L. Bennion, interview by Ted and Cheryl Lyon, Salt Lake City, January 18, 1989.

25. Bennion, "Memories," 47.

26. Bennion, interview.

27. Bradford, *Lowell L. Bennion,* 38.

28. T. Edgar Lyon, "Landmarks in the Netherlands Mission, 1861–1936," *Improvement Era* 39 (September 1936): 546, 573.

29. T. Edgar Lyon, "A Blessing and Its Fulfilment [*sic*]," *Millennial Star* 98 (1936): 613–15, 620–21.

30. A list of Lyon's published books and articles appears in appendix E. The ordering is chronological.

31. Bradford, *Lowell L. Bennion,* 357–58.

32. T. Edgar Lyon, "Oral History," 200.

33. Joseph fielding Smith and others to Franklin L. West, August 4, 1947, Church Archives.

34. T. Edgar Lyon, "Oral History," 201.

35. T. Edgar Lyon, "Oral History," 201.

36. Joseph Fielding Smith to Franklin L. West, August 12, 1947, Church Archives.

37. According to the story, after the impressive service, the minister observed:

> Tonight, for the first time I have seen something that I thought was impossible. I saw a church led by non-professional leadership that was equal to much of what I have observed among my Methodist colleagues. Furthermore, the congregation appeared to me to be more alert and above the average in intelligence of the Methodist groups I have served. I don't understand how you can do it. (T. Edgar Lyon, *We Believe* [Salt Lake City: General Boards of the Mutual Improvement Association, 1947], 219–20.)

38. Theo A. Mebius to T. Edgar Lyon, April 27, 1961, Church Archives.

39. When I served a mission in Argentina in 1959, *Nosotros Creemos* (We Believe) was still being used in MIA classes. Not all new Church manuals originating in English were translated into Spanish, so Church leaders simply recycled those that existed in their language.

40. This practice disappeared in the 1960s when the Church, primarily through its Correlation Committee, adopted a policy of group-written lessons, with no names or authors ever mentioned.

41. Ron Eliason to T. Edgar Lyon, October 9, 1960, Church Archives.

42. Information found in the T. Edgar Lyon collection, Church Archives.

43. T. Edgar Lyon to Janette L. Halton, January 29, 1952, Church Archives.

44. T. Edgar Lyon, Diaries and Notebooks, 1944–59, Church Archives.

45. T. Edgar Lyon, Diaries, 1946–54.

46. T. Edgar Lyon, "Oral History," 195.

47. Ernest L. Wilkinson to T. Edgar Lyon, May 31, 1954, Church Archives.

48. T. Edgar Lyon to Janette L. Halton, November 20, 1952, Church Archives.

49. T. Edgar Lyon to Janette L. Halton, June 7, 1953, Church Archives.

50. Ted Lyon, "Dad the Camper," Perry Special Collections.

51. Hermana F. Lyon to T. Edgar Lyon, June 16, 1960, Church Archives.

52. Joseph Lynn Lyon, "A History of Laura Hermana Forsberg," 1991, 68–69, L. Tom Perry Special Collections, Harold B. Lee Library, Brigham Young University, Provo, Utah.

53. Joseph Lynn Lyon, "History of Laura Hermana Forsberg," 68–69.

54. Joseph Lynn Lyon, "History of Laura Hermana Forsberg," 71. For more detail, see John F. Lyon's published account of this cave experience in "Rescues in Neff's Canyon Cave," *N[ational] S[peliological] S[ociety] News,* May 1989, 110–11.

55. T. Edgar Lyon, Diary, August 24, 1946.

56. Poem by Hermana F. Lyon, from the T. Edgar Lyon collection, Church Archives.

57. First Presidency to Hermana F. Lyon, April 25, 1944, Church Archives.

58. The technique of lesson writing by committee served Hermana and her associates well. When she later (1964) accepted a call to write family home evening manuals, she and a coworker from the Primary General Board, Arta Hale, modeled and adopted this plan for the new manuals.

59. Information found in the T. Edgar Lyon collection, Church Archives.

60. Joseph Lynn Lyon, "History of Laura Hermana Forsberg," 78.

61. A. Laurence Lyon to brothers, March 5, 1995, in author's possession.

62. T. Edgar Lyon Collection, Church Archives.

63. Hermana Forsberg Lyon, Diary, December 26, 1948, Church Archives.

64. William Mulder, interview by Ted and Trent Lyon, Salt Lake City, June 25, 1992.

65. Hermana Forsberg Lyon, Diary, June 1950.

66. Joseph Lynn Lyon, "History of Laura Hermana Forsberg," 107.

67. T. Edgar Lyon to Jamie Lyon, March 25, 1956, in author's possession.

68. Hermana Lyon to Jamie Lyon, March 28, 1956, in author's possession.

69. Hermana Lyon to Jamie Lyon, March 28, 1956.

70. Joseph Lynn Lyon, "History of Laura Hermana Forsberg," 109.

71. Joseph Lynn Lyon, "History of Laura Hermana Forsberg," 109.

72. Anderson, *A Historical Survey of the Full-time Institutes of Religion,* 147.

73. Bradford, *Lowell L. Bennion,* 107.

74. Anderson, *A Historical Survey of the Full-time Institutes of Religion,* 147.

75. Sidney Sperry to T. Edgar Lyon, February 2, 1948, Church Archives.

76. John A. Widstoe to T. Edgar Lyon, October 20, 1948, Church Archives.

77. Various letters in box the T. Edgar Lyon collection, Church Archives.

78. The T. Edgar Lyon collection, Church Archives.

79. Dale Tingey to T. Edgar Lyon, September 19, 1954, Church Archives.

80. Gustive Larson to T. Edgar Lyon, November 6, 1960, Church Archives.

81. T. Edgar Lyon, "Is It Hearsay or History?" *Instructor* 66 (April 1957): 116, 122.

82. Lyon, "Is it Hearsay or History?" 116.

83. Lyon, "Is it Hearsay or History?" 116.

84. The T. Edgar Lyon collection, Church Archives.

85. Lyon, "Is it Hearsay or History?" 122. Lyon's file on "Myths of Mormonism."

Another document, an outline of a talk or lesson for seminary and institute teachers, prepared in summer 1956, discusses the "Task of the Historian." Lyon notes that the historian's work is to "determine the truth" and "tell the truth," and that despite sounding simple, it is not easy (box 35, fd. 17), Church Archives.

86. T. Edgar Lyon to William W. Sweet, October 26, 1950, Church Archives.

87. William W. Sweet to T. Edgar Lyon, box 14, fd. 30, Church Archives.

88. Wallace F. Bennett to T. Edgar Lyon, April 29, 1958, box 15, fd. 11, Church Archives.

89. T. Edgar Lyon to Irving Wallace, June 28, 1961, Church Archives.

90. T. Edgar Lyon to Irving Wallace, June 28, 1961, Church Archives.

91. T. Edgar Lyon to LDS Presidency Bishopric, Church Archives.

92. T. Edgar Lyon to Theodore A. Tuttle, June 14, 1960, Church Archives.

93. T. Edgar Lyon to J. Reuben Clark, May 12, 1949, Church Archives.

94. Dale LeCheminant, interview by author, July 9, 1992, Salt Lake City, Utah.

10

Master Teacher, 1937–75

While Lyon and Bennion were both master teachers, drawing more students than could sometimes fit into their classrooms, the contrast in their teaching styles could hardly have been greater. Bennion conducted his classes in a Socratic method by creating questions and then exploring them in depth. He might ask, "What is the purpose of life?" and invite students to struggle with the answer. When a student gave the standard reply, "To be tested," Bennion would respond kindly, "General Motors tests the cars they build. Is that why they build them?"[1] Venturing deep into the realm of feeling and challenging unexamined beliefs, he led students beyond pat answers and into spiritual thought and sincere conviction.

Lyon, by contrast, seldom displayed deep emotion, though it underlay much of what he taught. His orientation was more practical—not only because he was primarily a historian, but also because he rarely displayed personal emotions in public. He used history as a means of challenging his students to think more deeply about the practical, day-to-day problems that underlay their faith.

Insightful Teaching

In discussing how the pioneers crossed the plains, Lyon might ask a class of city-dwelling students to think about how they would move pigs, or geese, or chickens almost 1,300 miles. Most had never thought of the daily challenges of pioneers; history often describes them only in terms of virtues such as sacrifice, dedication, and testimony. "How do you herd pigs, really now?" he would query. "Have you ever tried it?" Or he might ask why Brigham Young chose oxen instead of horses or mules to move wagons westward. Then he would describe the differences between the animals—oxen could survive on poor grass without the need for supplemental grain, and oxen ate much less in comparison to the weight they could pull. "Better gas mileage," he would beam, "better fuel economy." Lyon would describe the hundreds of apparently temporal decisions that often brought about spiritual ends, an exercise that implicitly or explicitly raised the interconnection for his students between spiritual and temporal decisions made by Church leaders ever since. "The testimony is in the details," he would affirm.

In a course on the history of Christianity, Lyon would talk of Bernard of Clairvaux and how he came to a struggling monastery in France, redefined its mission by helping church members grow better crops to ward off starvation, and developed new types of wheat and fruits to raise in northern Europe's short growing season. Then Lyon would tell of other monks who found the stone floor in the chapel wet from Bernard's tears after he had prayed for what was sometimes several hours. Or quoting a line or two from Francis of Assisi's great hymn "All Creatures of Our God and King," Lyon would make the priest a vivid example of devotion to Christ that grew out of his deep reverence for all living things, including animals.[2]

In courses on Mormon history, he might tell the story of Edson Whipple, a carpenter who left Nauvoo with finished oak planks stowed on top of the running gear (wheels and axles) of his wagon, which meant considerable extra weight and slower travel. Lyon asked students to think why Whipple might have made this sacrifice. After he had listened respectfully to several possible answers, he told them that the correct answer was to build coffins. This surprised some students, but Lyon explained that Brigham Young had promised that the Church would take anyone who wanted to get to Zion, including the elderly and sick, and that some would inevitably die along the way. What kind of burial were they to receive? A shallow grave that wolves and coyotes could dig up? Absolutely not! Brigham wanted them to be buried deep, in a good coffin if possible, and the graves were to be marked. Then Lyon would ask students to think about what this meant for the traveling Saints: delayed arrival, increased risk of winter storms, and expended energy to build coffins and dig graves. Lyon then made the spiritual connection between the way people treated their dead—with respect and sure of a real resurrection—and its meaning for their professed faith. The lessons drawn from a simple, unvarnished story about a carpenter who left Nauvoo could teach Lyon's students more about faith, devotion, and sacrifice than dozens of formal sermons.

Lyon would round out his classes by introducing humorous stories from Church history. Describing the settlement of Utah, he emphasized how Brigham Young wanted to build a society worthy to receive the Savior and that he expected settlers to get out of their log homes and build more permanent structures as soon as possible. Brigham also wanted them to make improvements in streets and public buildings. On a visit to the town of Goshen one year, Brigham delivered his message on community improvement. Returning the next year and seeing that the members had made no progress (they believed the Second Coming of Christ was at hand and they should not bother with such efforts), President Young proposed that the town be renamed "We Won't" because the residents had made it clear that "we won't build brick homes, we won't plant trees, we won't improve the irrigation systems, etc." At 3 A.M. the next day, several residents hitched up their wagons, drove to the nearby mountains, dug up two live pine trees, hauled them into town, and replanted them on either side of the road that President Young would take out of town that day. Then they strung a banner between the trees proclaiming, "*We Will*, Brother Brigham!" Though humorous, this vivid story taught multiple lessons, including following the counsel of a prophet, sacrificing, and not neglecting the practical in the name of the spiritual.

Lyon's command of Church history sometimes left his listeners in awe. One former student remembered that "he had more facts in his head than any person I have ever known,"[3] but Lyon was far more than a lecturer who merely transmitted facts. Fred Buchanan, a former student, recalls that "he was not simply a dispenser of information—he helped students probe beneath the facts to determine what they all meant. He took time in and out of class to raise questions, promote discussion, and above all to get students thinking critically and creatively about Church history and the implications for the religious life." Buchanan also recalls Lyon's "infectious enthusiasm for history, the twinkle in his eye when he got students involved in thinking about difficult historical issues, and his ability to communicate the human dimension of . . . divine events."[4]

Ronald K. Esplin, another former student who later became director of the Joseph Fielding Smith Institute for Latter-day Saint History at BYU, made other observations about Lyon's teaching: "His detailed knowledge was not that of an antiquarian. He analyzed, integrated, interpreted, and shared his knowledge in a way that made it comprehensible and come alive for the rest of us. He made his students feel that he knew the people of whom he spoke."[5]

Command of Details

When teaching about the Saints' departure from Nauvoo, Lyon insisted that his students recognize the detailed planning that followed the spiritually confirmed decision to leave. He would tell them: "On September 30, 1845, the Brethren were already preparing for the move

west. And what preparations they were!" Then he might write on the
board, "3,285 LDS families in and around Nauvoo: 1,505 wagons available at that time, and another 1,892 additional ones under construction—
a total of 3,397 to move the 3,285 families." He explained that Heber C.
Kimball had surveyed the wagons and found that many were simply farm
wagons and were too fragile and run-down to make the long journey.
"You wouldn't start a trip to New York from Salt Lake in a 30-year-old
jalopy would you?"

According to Lyon, Church leaders wisely and with great foresight
stressed that tire rims must be at least two inches wide and that the front
wheel had to be three feet high, and the rear, four, so as not to bog down
in the inevitable mud of the prairie. "How are your tires; will they make
it to New York?" Then he praised the leaders for their detailed planning,
which he considered to be a confirmation of their inspired calling. He
further taught of Church leaders' foresight in adding another ninety
wagons to haul mill stones, mill irons, construction tools, looms, books,
scientific apparatus, Church and Nauvoo City records, and so on. To
complete the journey successfully, Church leaders calculated that they
would need 53,635 head of livestock, and Lyon emphasized that they must
be healthy and truly *live stock*. He broke down this prodigious number
into specifics:

> 14,000 oxen, mules, or horses (4 animals for each wagon)
>
> 3,500 extra draft animals (for the likely case of accidents, disease,
> or death)
>
> 6,570 milk cows (for milk and cheese along the way)
>
> 6,570 beef cattle
>
> 3,285 saddle horses (for herd and guard duty, also for the hunters)
>
> 9,855 hogs (3 per family)
>
> 9,855 sheep
>
> Total: 53,635 livestock animals[6]

"Dogs and cats were optional," Lyon would explain with a smile. "Now,
where would they get all these animals and wagons?" he urged. His
students quickly understood the magnitude of the enterprise, an
endeavor that seemed to involve moving the whole city of Nauvoo to the
Great Basin.

The details continued. When should they leave? How important
was it to plan when to leave? When would they be ready with all these
animals and wagons? "Every home in Nauvoo became a workshop, right

in the front room—making wheels, harnesses, yokes, and more." The Saints could leave only when they were ready and only after the "grass grows and the water flows" on the prairie. Lyon had learned this couplet from his grandmother and other "Old Nauvooers" residing in Salt Lake City. He had later asked experienced farmers in the rural Midwest to tell him when the ice in streams usually melts or has reduced in size to be sufficiently safe to cross ("water flows") and when the grass is high enough for the oxen, horses, and sheep to eat properly ("grass grows"). They informed him this was usually in the first week of May. After Lyon explained this, his class began to understand the panic of the forced departure in February 1846: the Saints were not prepared, the grass was not growing, the water was not flowing. Students had the background to understand the subsequent suffering in winter storms without enough food, animals, or fully finished wagons. Students gained a vivid picture of the Saints' struggles in their old farm wagons—their "jalopies."

Lyon would then ask, "How many of you have ever seen oxen?" To the few who responded positively, he questioned, "Did you examine them closely? What's the difference between their mouth and that of a horse?" Usually he got no response to this question. He would explain that, unlike horses, oxen have teeth on only one jaw and hence cannot bite off the grass as horses do. Instead, they wrap their tongues around the grass and pull. If the prairie soil is too wet, the oxen pull the grass up by the roots and get not only the grass but a mouthful of dirt in the roots as well. The dirt, which they cannot digest, makes them sick and unable to pull a wagon. Hence the pioneers needed to wait until at least the first week in May to exit Nauvoo, until the prairie was sufficiently dry. The question "What, then, were the consequences of their early departure?" would often spark a meaningful class discussion.

Lyon might read aloud excerpts from early diaries, noting, for example, the details of a snowball fight as the pioneer company reached South Pass in Wyoming. These stories humanized history as students imagined the Brethren tossing and ducking snow balls, or shouting in joyous merriment. "You see, they were young men in 1847, not the bearded, dark-suited faces we see in the photos of the 1870s and 1880s," explained Lyon.

Turning to the roles of pioneer women, Lyon would ask his students about pioneer fashions (illus. 10-1). They usually repeated the time-worn answers of homespun and coarse wool in grays and blacks. "Yes," answered Lyon, "but a strange thing happened. After the railroad came, Brigham Young and the Relief Society sisters would get pictures and drawings of the latest European and East Coast fashions, and within

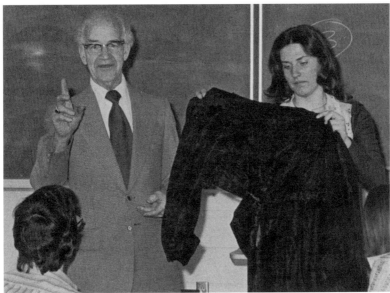

Courtesy Church Archives

Illus. 10-1. Ed Lyon in the classroom with a student displaying a pioneer dress.

three or four weeks similar type dresses and hats would appear in ZCMI. Brigham Young wanted the women to be happy in Zion."

The Storyteller

Lyon's gift as a vivid storyteller made history "come alive" for his students. He was able to interweave scriptures with historical events as only a master teacher can. In his Doctrine and Covenants courses, for example, he would explore the mundane daily circumstances and the practical doctrinal questions that often inspired Joseph Smith to seek divine revelation. While he seldom used printed visual aids and only sometimes showed historical artifacts to his classes, his stories created such powerful, mental images that former students could still repeat them years later. Like many good teachers, Lyon realized that visual images created in the mind were as powerful as photos.

A simple story about the term "hitch-hiking" made the entry of the advance party of pioneers and their exploration of the Salt Lake Valley memorable for Lyon's students. "Hitch-hiking," he would say, "that's a strange term, isn't it? What does it mean; have you ever thought about it?" The question generally elicited blank stares but set minds churning to try to fit it into context. "Well, Orson Pratt and Erastus Snow were designated to get to the Valley of the Great Salt Lake before the main pioneer company. But they only had one horse between them. So now can you see the origin of the term?" Still no response, but the students were interested. "The two of them would start off together, Erastus walking and Orson on the horse. Pratt would ride on quickly, for a mile or two, tie up the horse—*hitch* it—and begin walking. Erastus would follow along—*hiking*—until he came to the rested horse, unhitch it, ride rapidly, passing Orson, and continuing on ahead of him for a couple of miles. . . . Then, what do you suppose he would do?" Several hands would now go up. "Yes," said Lyon,

> "hitch and hike" on. The concept had been known and used for many years, much before the pioneers of course. So you see, when you "thumb" to get a ride to school, you're not really hitch-hiking. But this was how Orson Pratt and Erastus Snow were able to explore a large section of the Salt Lake Valley before Brigham Young and others in the main party arrived. The information gained "hitch-hiking" allowed the main company to begin immediately to lay out the city and plant crops the day they arrived in the valley.

A former student, Truman G. Madsen, who became a professor of philosophy at BYU, explained the depth of Lyon's knowledge: "In his class we used to play a game—we'd just give him any date in Church history, say 4 January 1841, and he'd be able to tell us something that happened that day. . . . Since the death of Joseph Smith no other man has taken so much knowledge of Church history to the grave."[7] Madsen "took every class that T. Edgar and Lowell offered—most of them twice, because [Lyon] was constantly preparing by everything he read; and he seemed to remember it all."[8] Lyon often brought notes to class but rarely used them. Rather, "the class came from his head." When he dealt with sensitive and difficult issues, "he did it with candor; and he was always sweet-spirited."[9]

A colleague at the institute, Kenneth Godfrey, remembers Lyon as a true teacher: "He was not an entertainer. He had so much information stored up he did not hide that fact. . . . He was the best of his time. . . . We used to say that Ed Lyon has probably forgotten more Church history that anyone else knew at the time."[10]

Despite his daunting knowledge of Church history, Lyon did not intimidate students. His cheerful demeanor, excellent listening skills, and open-door policy drew students to him to discuss personal or doctrinal problems. Many wondered how he did any work or preparation for teaching during the day because he seemed to always be with his students. Still undue reverence for his vast knowledge did not blind students to his idiosyncrasies. Though he got by on relatively little sleep at night, he sometimes cat-napped during the day. This did not go unnoticed; one day Lyon found a bit of doggerel that one of his students had slipped under his door:

> Brother Lyon watches us
> As if we're all his sheep
> But we sometimes find our shepherd
> Has fallen fast asleep!
>
> He's like the force of nature
> He's full of "give and take."
> He'll do good deeds forever
> If he can only stay awake![11]

Another imaginative student, Ron Crosby, drew a caricature poking fun at the bald heads of Lyon, Bennion, and Boyd (illus. 10-2). It showed only the top of each bald head protruding above a screen (they were in a faculty meeting) but in a way that made each of the three immediately recognizable. The fact that students could joke about their instructors' lack of hair reflects the rapport and appreciation that they felt toward these master teachers.

Many former students recall that Ed had a certain "twinkle"— a fun-loving smile, a sense of humor, an ability to chuckle and even laugh out loud at himself, at others, and at foibles in history or life (illus. 10-3). This part of his personality often came out when Ed unveiled an inconsistency in a current situation or an incongruity in a historical moment. His students relished this effervescent twinkle. Juanita Hanson O'Brien remembered one of her classes where Ed jokingly, but somewhat seriously, said, "'The greatest testimony of the truthfulness of the Church is that the inexperience of the [young] missionaries hasn't ruined it.' Then he would laugh and tell stories about missionaries and their innocent mistakes. . . . He always seemed to have a twinkle in his eye."[12]

One day while eating lunch from a wrinkled brown sack in his office, Lyon was interrupted by a troubled graduate student, Fred Buchanan. In agitated terms, Buchanan explained a serious dilemma resulting from his recent research into Church history and a visit to the temple. He anguished over how to reconcile history and testimony and pleaded for some kind of easy explanation. Lyon listened patiently, leaned back in his green swivel chair, and put his hands behind his head. Buchanan waited,

Illus. 10-2. A comical sketch of the three Salt Lake institute instructors.

--. Ron Crosby
Courtesy Ron Crosby

and then Lyon "looked at [him] in mock horror, [and] smiled that huge T. Edgar Lyon smile." After what seemed like too long a pause, Lyon said, "What've you been doing, Fred? Thinking?!"[13] Buchanan smiled, they discussed his concerns in detail, and he left satisfied an hour later. He and thousands of other intelligent, inquisitive University of Utah students came to the Salt Lake institute to seek and find answers and to reconcile secular learning with religious belief. Lyon did not have an easy answer for Buchanan, but he always had time to faithfully explore the historical and religious background and lead students toward the gospel of Jesus Christ.

In 1970 a friend wrote Lyon requesting his views on teaching techniques. Lyon replied that forty-two years of teaching had shown him (1) that there had to be "freedom in exchange of ideas"; (2) that the "instructor [must be] close enough to on-going student life" to understand the students' problems; (3) that the teacher must be very approachable; and (4) that "both teacher and student [should] have an awareness that neither can expect the other to accept dogmatic statements."[14] In countless cases, these techniques paid off as Lyon and his students found common ground for both testimony and discussion. One former student, Macoy A. McMurray, appreciated Lyon's style and wrote: "With the approach of Thanksgiving, I am prompted to express my appreciation to you as one of the great teachers in my life."[15]

The very qualities, however, that made Lyon an engaging teacher and sought-after speaker also contributed to some of the problems that persisted during the golden era. He and Bennion did not discuss these difficulties with their students, yet some of the same teaching methods that urged students to think deeply, to question, to explore on their own, to go to original sources, to tackle large moral problems, and to ask the big questions also created some conflicts, especially among administrators in the developing Church Educational System.

Illus. 10-3. Ed Lyon, 1961.

Notes

1. Information on Bennion's teaching style comes from class notes taken by the author in 1958 and 1959.

2. Information on Lyon's teaching style and the examples here cited have been condensed from notes taken in several of his classes at the Salt Lake institute from 1955 to 1962; notes in possession of A. Laurence Lyon, James K. Lyon, and the author.

3. Ruth Fetzer Carr, interview by Melinda Silver, Salt Lake City, September 2, 1993.

4. Frederick S. Buchanan, interview by author, Salt Lake City, June 14, 1991.

5. Ronald K. Esplin, interview by author, Provo, Utah, August 28, 1995.

6. T. Edgar Lyon to Mark E. Peterson, August 8, 1969, copy in author's possession.

7. Truman G. Madsen, interview by author, Provo, Utah, May 14, 1996.

8. Madsen, interview.

9. Madsen, interview.

10. Kenneth W. Godfrey, interview by Trent Lyon, Logan, Utah, July 10, 1992.

11. Anonymous poem, in author's possession.

12. Juanita Hansen O'Brien, telephone interview by Melinda Silver, September 3, 1993.

13. Fred S. Buchanan, "I Remember Brother Lyon," three-page memoir, undated, in author's possession.

14. T. Edgar Lyon to Joe Morton, August 8, 1970, Church Archives.

15. Macoy A. McMurray to T. Edgar Lyon, November 23, 1974, Church Archives.

11

Change of Direction, 1962

In 1951 newly sustained Church President David O. McKay named Ernest L. Wilkinson president of Brigham Young University. Two years later, Wilkinson and the Church education board of trustees "unified" the entire Church Educational System under his control,[1] precipitating the retirement of Commissioner Franklin West (illus. 11-1). The sixty-seven-year-old West had passed normal retirement age but remained vigorous and creative and had expected to continue for many more years, so West did not view his departure as a retirement but as a firing.[2] There were those who were suspicious of West's open, dynamic spirit and of anyone closely associated with his administration because in their view he represented an aggressive, liberal mindset within the Church Educational System.[3] In these nervous days of McCarthysim, the Korean War, and the beginning of the Cold War, many in the nation were unsettled by those who seemed unorthodox or unconventional. In this climate, West's closest allies and admirers, Lyon and Bennion, felt saddened by the departure of this innovative leader. Lyon chaired the committee for West's retirement banquet, putting in a heartfelt effort for his dear friend. He personally solicited his colleagues for donations, which he used to buy a very modern luxury, a television set for the departing commissioner. Bennion spoke at the banquet, thanking West for his free and open discussions. So after 1953, the Church's educational programs were centered in Provo rather than Salt Lake City.

Wilkinson appointed Lyon's old teaching, hunting, and fishing friend Ed Berrett as vice-administrator for seminaries and institutes.[4] Despite their past friendship, some tensions developed between Berrett and Lyon, including a concern about the relatively low graduation rate from the Salt Lake Institute of Religion, which became an issue in 1954.[5] Bennion and Wilkinson also clashed on other points, and Bennion made his feelings known on new policies that bothered him. Wilkinson proposed to the Church Board of Education that Bennion be transferred to the religion department at BYU, but no change took place.[6] The reasons for the suggested transfer were not recorded, but Bennion did not view this proposal as a reward or a promotion.

In August 1954, Berrett and Wilkinson brought all seminary and institute teachers to BYU for three weeks of training and spiritual instruction. According to Bennion's biographer, there is little doubt that part of the purpose was a "campaign against the Salt Lake Institute."[7] Bennion, Lyon, and their new colleague George Boyd attended all the sessions, where they were instructed by General Authorities J. Reuben Clark, Joseph Fielding Smith, Adam S. Bennion, and others. During the last week, two controversial issues predominated—first, the position of blacks in the Church, and second, the question of evolution. The latter topic arose from discussions over Elder Joseph Fielding Smith's recently published *Man, His Origin and Destiny*, which was being considered for mandatory use as a textbook in Church institutes. In one session, Lowell Bennion openly questioned Elder Smith's position on both topics. Many other teachers empathized with Bennion's position, but they generally kept quiet during the vigorous and heated discussion.[8] Though he did not say much in the sessions, Lyon was deeply upset by the BYU conference. At first Lyon felt that Bennion may have been too outspoken in defending his position against Church authorities, but he soon changed his view. A few days later, Lyon typed a note of gratitude and admiration for his colleague:

> It wasn't until you raised your question on Thursday about the problem of a [black LDS] boy who needs to be treated as a Christian that anyone sounded a sweet note . . . your words fell like manna from heaven on a starving people. . . . A Y man sitting back of me . . . said to me in a low voice as you finished, "What a thrill it must be to work with a man of love, vision, wisdom, and insight, as well as great faith. You are to be envied." . . . You said everything that I had thought, but said it ten time[s] more pointedly and in a nicer spirit than I could have. . . . Others there felt the same way, but none had courage to speak out as you did.[9]

The dust that was stirred up in Provo in 1954 took a long time to settle; perhaps it never fully calmed down. A few days after the conference, Bennion and Lyon were asked to visit with Elders Joseph Fielding Smith and Mark E. Peterson "about the age of the earth and [origins] of man."[10] The meeting lasted nearly two hours as Smith attempted "to convince us that his position was right. He didn't succeed."[11] Still feeling wounded by this unsettled conflict, Bennion and Lyon sought a direct audience with President David O. McKay. A week later, at Bennion's request, Bennion,

Lyon, Boyd, and seminary coordinator Joy Dunyon met with the Church President, who demonstrated respect for Elder Smith's views "but stated that he himself felt that the earth is very old and that evolutionary ideas have much to commend them." In emphatic terms, President McKay reminded them that *Man, His Origin and Destiny* had not been officially approved or authorized and "did not represent the position of the Church."[12] In a letter to his missionary son Jamie, Lyon wrote that during the hour-long meeting President McKay stated that "you brethren are doing a good work [at the institute]. Go on teaching the Gospel of Jesus Christ as you have

Courtesy Church Archives

Illus. 11-1. Franklin West, commissioner of Church education for eighteen formative years.

been and pay no attention to these foolish ideas that some people are trying to make appear to be the word of the Lord."[13] The teachers felt quite satisfied with the discussion and returned to the institute. They soon learned, however, that Wilkinson was very annoyed that they had bypassed his authority by going directly to the Church President.[14] A short time later, Dunyon was replaced and Bennion, Lyon, and Boyd appeared on Wilkinson's "list of teachers who have critical attitudes."[15] However, no further direct conflict occurred at this time, and both enrollment and graduation rates at the Salt Lake institute continued to increase rapidly.

Dr. Lyon

The institute programs kept attracting bright students through the 1950s and into the '60s. The year 1962 was pivotal in Ed's life. At least five major incidents occurred, events of both elation and sadness. Ed, at age fifty-eight, finally completed his Ph.D.; he wrote a book review that caused an uproar and set him at odds with certain authorities; the Bennion-Lyon team broke up after twenty-three successful and happy years; the Lyon family built a mountain cabin; and Ed directed his first tour to the Holy Land.

Lyon's plans for his advanced academic degrees had not gone as he had hoped. Immediately after completing his master's degree in spring 1932, he had begun his Ph.D. studies with two summer terms at the University of Chicago. During the next summer, he had taken classes at the University of California–Berkeley, filling a requirement that he have graduate experience at another major university. He had intended to complete his Ph.D. in 1937 or 1938 by regularly enrolling in Chicago summer classes, but his call as mission president had dramatically changed those plans. After four years in the Netherlands, Lyon had returned to Chicago for the 1938 and 1940 summer sessions, but Chicago's five-year statute of limitations on course work that could be applied to the Ph.D. had already invalidated the work done in 1932. After two 1940 summer sessions, Lyon had judged that he was nearly halfway through with classes. However, the pressures of extensive Church service, manuals to write, a large family to maintain, and the outbreak of World War II had effectively ended the possibility, due to the difficulties of travel to the Midwest and the reduced offerings at that institution. The dream of a Ph.D. from the University of Chicago was never realized because Ed devoted himself to the Salt Lake institute and his family.

In the early 1950s, Lyon visited with professors from the History Department at the University of Utah to explore the feasibility of obtaining a Ph.D. there. He had achieved some status and reputation as a historian by that time, but there appeared to have been doubts from some of the history and philosophy professors about his ability to do objective historical research. Nevertheless he was admitted in 1952. A departmental committee accepted several of his courses from Chicago and Berkeley, but they required ten more classes. In addition they required the completion of foreign-language reading exams in French and German. So, along with his heavy teaching load, Lyon jumped into re-learning French, his nemesis since the 1920s. During spring quarter 1954, he passed examinations in that language and in German a few months later.[16] He registered for day classes in history and philosophy, courses taken during hurried breaks from his institute teaching, and found real academic stimulation in classes from Leland Creer, Emil Lucki, and W. Harold Dalgliesh.

By 1958 he had completed all his course work and was ready to take written exams in history, his major, as well as philosophy, his minor. The questions for the philosophy examination included: "Explain the case for religious liberalism as opposed to fundamentalism," and "Examine the problem of evil in theistic philosophy." These broad questions taxed his thinking and writing skills for a total of sixteen hours over three days. The dissertation he had hoped to complete in the same year received little attention while he helped care for Hermana's father for five months and then Hermana herself during the slow recovery from her surgery.[17] History professor Leland H. Creer suggested to Lyon that a study of evangelical missionary work in Utah might prove insightful as a dissertation topic. In his usual meticulous fashion, Lyon began reading and taking notes, eventually creating the title "Evangelical Protestant Missionary Activities in Mormon Dominated Areas: 1865–1900."

Lyon researched primary sources while establishing contacts with ministers and historians of other faiths in Utah. His 274-page dissertation documents the efforts of six traditional Protestant churches to convert Mormons in post–Civil War Utah to a more traditional Christianity. Lyon explains how Mormons were often viewed as non-Christian, citing the 1897 pamphlet "Ten Reasons Why Christians Cannot Fellowship the Mormon Church." To these ten, Lyon adds eight more reasons gleaned from numerous evangelical tracts of the period.[18] In his studies, Lyon discovered that at first the traditional Protestant churches had relatively little success in direct conversion, so most of them established schools instead, filling a need that neither Latter-day Saint schools nor public education adequately covered. The intent of the schools was to enroll children at an early age and thus convert them to "true Christian" religions.[19] The dissertation combines topics in religious history with education, a perfect match for Lyon's preparation and experience following his undergraduate schooling days.

After Lyon submitted what he hoped would be the final draft, Professors W. Harold Dalgliesh and Emil Lucki "pointed out many omissions which I had overlooked because the subject appeared so clear to me that I had failed to explain the problem . . . to the satisfaction of those not familiar with the 'Mormon Country' of the intermountain West."[20] Lyon made additional revisions. He had intended to graduate in summer 1961 but missed the deadline. After other revisions, his dissertation was fully accepted and copyrighted in June 1962. He later added a final chapter, reporting that in 1890, seventy-seven non–Latter-day Saint Church schools enrolled 3,487 students in Utah. He found that these mission schools provided at least "some schooling to an estimated 50,000 or more children . . . the majority of whom were from families of Mormon background."[21] On May 26, 1962, Lyon spent two tense hours with Professors Creer, Dalgliesh, Lucki, Miller, Latimer, Attiya, Reed, and Rogers in a final oral examination. This exceptionally large Ph.D. committee passed him with praise. Exactly thirty years after beginning Ph.D. work in Chicago, he could finally take the title of doctor.

The Ph.D. was granted at the university commencement on June 11, 1962. Lyon wrote of the event,

> I received the degree officially, which the students long since conferred on me by usage. When my name was called and I stopped to get the doctor's hood placed on me, the students in the gathering started to applaud. Of course, I have taught and worked with more students on the campus than anyone else getting a degree, and so had more personal friends among them. As a matter of fact, I was embarrassed that I got more applause than even the governor of the state or the president of University of Michigan, both of whom were given honorary doctorates. Conceited, eh?[22]

He felt much more embarrassed than conceited. Hermana, proud to finally witness her husband's long-awaited degree, noted that a local television station reported that "by all odds the most popular graduate was T. Edgar Lyon." Then Hermana observed, "I'm glad President [Ernest L.] Wilkinson was there to hear it."[23]

For the moment, at least, the Lyons did not have time to worry about Wilkinson. Less than twelve hours after the graduation ceremony, their son Ted married Cheryl Larsen. The wedding reception was a drain on Hermana, who coordinated the food and made most of the refreshments for nearly six hundred well-wishers. Ed loaned the family car to the newlyweds, and he and Hermana drove home in Ted's decorated 1954 Ford, dragging tin cans and a "Just Married" sign placed by friends who assumed that Ted would be using his own vehicle.

Two days later, Lyon was in Provo for the national meetings of Lambda Delta Sigma; he had served as its president for a year and kept its financial records for sixteen. Now he sensed major changes coming to the organization. President Wilkinson, concerned that Lambda Delta Sigma activities were not contributing to testimonies, had initiated an investigation of the organization a few months earlier.[24] During the same busy month, Lyon delivered lectures and conducted seminars at the annual MIA June Conference in Salt Lake City.[25] To make matters even more complex, Lyon was in the midst of a random audit by the Internal Revenue Service. But there were other, more serious, problems.

At least part of Hermana's reference to Wilkinson following Ed's graduation had its roots in a series of events that had begun quite innocuously several months earlier. Without his being aware of it, Lyon's passion for accurate history, and his belief that distortion of the Mormon heritage did more damage than good, had led him into a serious controversy.

The Review

In late 1961, University of Utah president A. Ray Olpin instructed his assistant Neal Maxwell to find a professor to review a new book by Richard Vetterli, a recent graduate of the U. Maxwell coordinated with Paul Cracroft, editor of the alumni magazine, and asked Lyon to write the review. Ed later explained, "The idea was that it would be a great book and do credit to one of the former students of the 'U.'"[26]

Shortly afterward, on a Saturday while Lyon was working on the Magazine Printing Company's finances, Vetterli came to the office's front desk inquiring for him. Delivering the book personally, the twenty-five-year-old author handed Lyon a copy of *Mormonism, Americanism, and Politics* and informed him that the recently published book was "basically my master's thesis" written at the University of California–Los Angeles (UCLA). Vetterli inscribed the book: "To T. Edgar Lyon in deep appreciation and in great admiration."[27] Lyon generally was not involved in politics and did not know the author but later noted that Vetterli had apparently sat in on "some of our [institute] classes . . . and he wanted me to write a review of [the book] for the *Utah Alumnus* magazine."[28]

Lyon found the title of Vetterli's 735-page book intriguing, and after the rush of the Christmas holiday, Lyon began reading. He recalled his reaction to the book: "I hadn't read ten pages before I was aware of the fact that the thing was full of all kinds of errors."[29] With his usual eye for historical accuracy and in his normal teaching mode, he underlined and wrote in the margins, highlighting more than a hundred places where he saw problems with one-sided interpretation or incomplete historical research. Vetterli, naturally hoping for a favorable review, had asked Lyon to meet a short deadline. Lyon completed the work on schedule and sent it to Vetterli on February 2, 1962, inviting him to call if he could defend the many errors that Lyon had found.[30] The writer, who was not in Utah at the time, did not call back, so Lyon "called him one night. We talked for nearly three quarters of an hour at my expense."[31] Lyon tried to pin him down on historical inaccuracies, distortions, and specific details but received only vague and incomplete answers.[32]

Frustrated by the writer, but with full confidence in his facts and views, Lyon sent the review to Paul Cracroft, who published it in the February 1962 *Utah Alumnus.* Lyon's three-page review began with a fair summary of the book's contents. While *Mormonism, Americanism, and Politics* dealt mainly with politics and the constitution, Lyon's review went on to highlight what he believed to be the book's major flaws: errors of historical fact, one-sided presentation, failure to evaluate, conjectures and speculations, bias, lack of depth, romanticizing, and paradoxes. Lyon called attention to a sociological paradox implicit in the book's claim that "Mormons living their religion cannot be socialists or communists" while at the same time Mormon missionaries were "expanding the Church in socialist countries" and "members of socialist nations (Britain, New Zealand, Samoa, etc.) are being placed in positions of Church leadership."[33] It was primarily this small portion of the review that would end up fueling a controversy lasting several months. In spite of this paradox and the other problems, Lyon concluded the review by observing that "Mr. Vetterli has produced an intriguing book, if one is interested in speculating about political theory."[34]

More polished than other alumni publications of the era, the sixteen to thirty-two page *Utah Alumnus* enjoyed a large circulation; more than eight thousand copies were printed and distributed to graduates of the University of Utah. Among these alumni were prominent men and women in high Church positions.[35] The magazine had a history of publishing book reviews only occasionally, which may have made Lyon's review seem somewhat anomalous, throwing some readers off balance.

This particular issue of the *Utah Alumnus* became widely read and ignited an immediate furor. Cracroft remembers that calls and letters poured into his office, most applauding Lyon. Sales of the *Mormonism, Americanism, and Politics*—with its glossy red, white, and blue cover—skyrocketed. And Vetterli demanded "equal space" in the alumni magazine for a rebuttal, claiming character assassination,[36] even though Lyon's initial review had only attacked the accurateness of the book and not its author. Cracroft did not agree with Vetterli's insinuations, but he agreed to publish the author's rebuttal. Vetterli's response appeared in the April *Utah Alumnus* magazine, which escalated the conflict by adding the editorial title "Politics and the Mormons: Round Two" and included a sketch of two men engaged in a sword fight.

Vetterli added fuel to the fire by rewording parts of Lyon's critique. Among other things, Vetterli especially took issue with the paradox that Lyon had highlighted. Vetterli represented Lyon as saying "that the book is wrong in asserting that Mormonism and the socialist-communist *philosophy* are incompatible since people in socialist countries are being converted to Mormonism," and claimed that "the quotes Mr. Lyon takes issue with in this instance came directly from some of the General Authorities of the Church."[37]

This misreading of Lyon is at least understandable in light of the politically charged moment of the 1960s and perhaps because of rhetoric coming from certain Church leaders. Some readers might have associated Lyon's critique of the book in general and his paradox in particular with the kind of undermining of American solidarity that Elder Ezra Taft Benson had spoken of clearly in April 1962 general conference when he said,

> We must protect this American base from the brainwashing, increasingly administered to our youth in many educational institutions across the land, by some misinformed instructors and some wolves in sheep's clothing. . . . "The danger that threatens us is an internal danger. It lies in our hearts and minds and not in the hands of Khrushchev. It is our own ignorance . . . that threatens us."[38]

Whether intentional or not, the battle lines were drawn; Vetterli made it look as if Ed were at odds with the Brethren, but such was not the case. Ed had recently written a manual that had been used by the Melchizedek Priesthood of the entire Church, he still spoke regularly at stake conferences, and he enjoyed the confidence of President McKay.

The publication of Vetterli's rebuttal fanned the flames of controversy even more. Mormon scholars rallied around Lyon. Gustive Larson, professor of history at BYU, wrote, "congratulations on a devastating analysis of this eighth literary wonder of the west . . . [and] the masterful job you have done."[39] Former student and respected scholar Truman Madsen applauded Lyon for his review.[40] From the University of Chicago Law School, Dallin Oaks wrote that "a friend recently showed me a copy of your review of the Vetterli book. It was delightful. Do you have a reprint I might have?"[41] Utah State University history professor George Ellsworth wrote a review of the same book and to Lyon's list of eight problems added many more. Ellsworth compared the original master's thesis with the book, observing that the thesis in book form "is now used for the political purposes of ultra-conservatives. . . . In so doing, thesis findings are in many cases directly reversed, and . . . have been substituted [with] generalities, half-truth, and propaganda—and without changing the footnote citations! It is difficult for me to believe that Mr. Vetterli is responsible for all of these changes."[42] He then charged that "the thesis appendixes were cribbed, complete with notes, from the Master's thesis of Richard D. Poll" and noted that other sections of the thesis may have also been plagiarized.[43]

Richard Poll, then a well-established scholar in the history department at BYU, was irritated when he learned that his own graphics and notes had been lifted and used by young Vetterli without attribution. Poll wrote the chairman of the Political Science Department at UCLA, pointing out that the thesis "relied heavily on my own M.A. thesis . . . and [the author] then lacked the integrity to cite the work either in footnote or bibliography."[44]

The *Improvement Era* requested that Leonard J. Arrington, the well-respected economic historian at Utah State University, review the book. He wrote a thorough and very critical analysis and sent it to the Church magazine. However, it never appeared in print. In his personal papers, Lyon recorded that "the Era editors were afraid to publish it."[45] Lyon now found himself embroiled in a controversy much larger than he could have imagined when the young author first requested that he write a simple book review.

Although *Mormonism, Americanism, and Politics* had its followers and received a positive notice in a local Mormon newspaper, *California Intermountain News,* written by well-known ultraconservative DeVar Lillywhite, the academic community almost unanimously dismissed it. In his review, Ellsworth wrote, "The claims made for the book by the red, white and blue jacket and the Introduction prove to be extravagant. . . . Future historians of our age will find its chief value as a work worthy of study as a product symptomatic of our time."[46] "Our time" referred to the 1960s, tensions with Russia, the Cuban missile crisis, and the attempt by some to link the Church with the political right and the John Birch Society. Author Cleon Skousen had published *The Naked Communist* attacking Communism in 1958, and some General Authorities were espousing the book's tenets.

Lyon was aware of these strong feelings; he expressed concern to his family about a stake president friend from the socialist Netherlands who attended general conference in Salt Lake City and found some of the talks more political than spiritual. The man anguished over how to harmonize what he was hearing from the pulpit with the seemingly innocuous and smoothly functioning socialized system of the Netherlands. Confused and discouraged, he confessed that he didn't know what to report to his members when he returned home. Lyon had heard the same talks in general conference and in frequent firesides that praised the United States and decried the evils of Communism and Socialism. Lyon himself struggled to harmonize this ultranationalism with the broader view of a worldwide Church.

Many Latter-day Saint students and long-time members worried about the unbalanced attempt by some to politicize the Church, and they complained directly to General Authorities. President Hugh B. Brown responded to one of these concerned students:

> Many of us have been trying to counter [the extreme right-wing activities] and I think at last have succeeded in removing some of the agitators which have justified the assumption that their line is, as you say "the official Church line on politics". . . . Perhaps an official statement will be published shortly but of this I am not yet quite sure.[47]

Lyon was caught in an ideological battle with several ultraconservative Church members who began labeling him as a liberal and falsely claiming he was in trouble with the Church. At the request of the *Utah Alumnus,* he responded to Vetterli's rebuttal, once again stating that "no historian has a right to make his prejudices paramount to the facts that he should record."[48] Lyon's correspondence indicates that he had invited and wanted to sit down and discuss the historical problems in the book with the writer, but the writer would not meet him. Perhaps in frustration, Lyon's response took aim at Vetterli personally and at what Lyon saw as misrepresentations and distortions. His reaction is especially understandable given the nation's volatile cultural atmosphere and the rising rhetorical posture of those espousing extremely conservative tenants.

Illus. 11-2. Ernest L. Wilkinson, oversaw education in the Church from 1953 to 1965.

The controversy swirled from April to July 1962. Commissioner of Education Ernest L. Wilkinson (illus. 11-2) read the review and "was quite chagrined that [Lyon] should not support Vetterli's interpretation. He hadn't read the book . . . but thought [Lyon] made an unwarranted attack because it went against his basic ideas of conservative Republicanism." Upholding a conservative agenda, Wilkinson would run for the United States Senate just two years later. Years later Lyon still vividly remembered how he had been accused of being an "atheist, a communist, and everything else" during this time for his honest but critical review of young Vetterli's book.[49]

Wilkinson charged Lyon with being disloyal to the Church and upsetting members' testimonies. Wilkinson's vice-administrator, Ed Berrett, informed Lyon that it was President David O. McKay who had been most offended by the February book review and that Lyon must write a letter of apology to President McKay and send a carbon copy to Wilkinson.[50] Lyon drafted the letter and sent it to Berrett for his advice. Berrett penned in several suggested changes and returned it to Lyon. On June 7, 1962, four days before he would receive his Ph.D. diploma, Lyon received Berrett's changes, revised the letter, and sent it to President McKay. In the letter, Lyon explained why and how he had written the review and defended himself by describing the scholarly support he had received since the publication. As a scholar with a firm and proven testimony, he was apologizing for what he was sure was an honest historical review. In the letter, he wrote, "I . . . apologize for what was printed that was disturbing to Latter-day Saints, *and that seemed to indicate a lack of loyalty on my part.*"[51] These italicized words of this sentence are Berrett's additions to the rough draft. Lyon concluded:

> Let me assure you that I have not lost my testimony, have not become disloyal to the Church, and have no intention of doing so. I bear testimony daily to my belief in the divinity of Christ, His atonement, and resurrection; to the divinity of Joseph Smith's calling and work; and the continuity of his work in the Church today. I sincerely apologize and ask your forgiveness, promising that I shall not again be guilty of such indiscretion.
>
> Sincerely your brother,
>
> T. Edgar Lyon[52]

No response to this letter exists in Lyon's files; this is surprising, since he was such a meticulous keeper of letters and documents. Besides Berrett's claim that President McKay was upset, staff historians at Church Archives could find no record of any negative reaction from him to Lyon's review.[53] The tortuous process of the apology is also surprising, since President McKay knew both Lyon and Bennion and highly respected their work at the institute. In 1958, McKay personally drove his black Cadillac to the Salt Lake institute to visit and to request that Bennion speak in "the priesthood session of the upcoming general conference."[54] Elder Marion D. Hanks affirmed that to his knowledge Lyon's book review did not disturb President McKay or destroy Lyon's relationship with the Church President. When asked whether Lyon's loyalty had ever been an issue in Church councils, Elder Hanks again responded with assurance, "Never! Not on one occasion. . . . President McKay of course would not have been a party to that."[55] Ed Berrett, when interviewed about the matter in 1992, could not recall the letter of apology or even why it had been requested.[56]

In a 1993 interview, Richard Vetterli recalled the reason he had asked Lyon to write the review: "He [Lyon] had a great reputation as a scholar and I needed his endorsement." Vetterli had hoped that the review would foster book sales, which it probably did. Vetterli confirmed that he was surprised at the anger that developed after the exchanges in the *Utah Alumnus* and admitted that because it was his "first book; [he] was under an incredible pressure, and [he] needed Lyon's critique."[57] The entire controversy had long-range consequences.

Turmoil at the 'Tute

While all this was going on, the unexpected and major changes at the Salt Lake Institute of Religion were more important than Lyon's personal troubles. Lyon had planned to continue teaching the students and working in the program he loved until age sixty-five. In the turmoil surrounding the book review and its rebuttal and the busyness of duplicating and submitting final copies of his dissertation, Lyon's old friend Ed Berrett had arranged for a meeting at the Salt Lake institute on May 29, 1962. Berrett came early, stepped into Lyon's office, and, almost too casually, inquired whether Lyon had considered teaching at BYU. He appealed to Lyon's scholarly desires, stating that he would have more time and support for research in BYU's Church History Department.[58] Berrett also indicated that Bennion would be invited to join the BYU faculty, perhaps trying to appeal to Lyon and Bennion's long-standing friendship. "I told [Berrett] that I was not interested in moving but if they forced me to, I'd probably have to accept it," Lyon wrote.[59] Berrett couched the move as a promotion; Lyon wrote that "neither of us [Bennion nor Lyon] wants to be 'promoted'—we'd rather remain here."[60]

A few minutes after the conversation in his office, Lyon, Bennion, Berrett, institute supervisor Dale Tingey (illus. 11-3), and a young faculty

Courtesy Church Archives

Illus. 11-3. Dale Tingey supervised institutes during the 1960s.

member who had been recently assigned by Commissioner Wilkinson to the Salt Lake institute met together. The new teacher had made several serious accusations against Lyon and Bennion to a General Authority, and word of the charge of "teaching false doctrine" had filtered to Lyon, Bennion, and Berrett.[61] Lyon and Bennion were fully vindicated by the end of the meeting but sensed that major problems still needed to be resolved.[62] After the formal meeting, Berrett talked to Bennion alone, first offering—and then insisting—that he leave the institute and join the faculty at BYU, where he "could make a greater contribution to the church [than] you could in this place."[63]

If this were not yet agreeable, Bennion could take a leave of absence for a year, write manuals, and then go to the "Y." Bennion and Lyon sensed that they were no longer wanted at the Salt Lake institute.[64]

Ed left town with his family to celebrate the Memorial Day weekend in the mountains, but he slept little and celebrated even less. Neither he nor his colleague had actually been "fired" from the institute, but they were to be transferred within the Church Educational System to allow them to make a "greater contribution." Reacting without deliberating or talking to Hermana, Lyon gave the suggestion no quarter. Perhaps he was uncomfortable about working even more directly under the surveillance of BYU president Ernest Wilkinson, or perhaps he did not want to leave his home and neighborhood. Whatever the reason, transfers within the Church Educational System were not as common in those days as they would later become, and the vague "promotion" was sufficiently transparent to cause Ed and Hermana to begin contemplating a future outside the institute and the Church Educational System. Ed had already taught several BYU summer sessions.[65] He enjoyed association with and respected many members of the BYU faculty, frequently corresponding with Sidney Sperry, Richard Poll, Gustive Larson, Monte Nyman, and others. However, he knew that he simply did not want to move to Provo. Further, he had quarreled with the university's president and had had conflicts with a friend who was a vice-president. Ed was nearly fifty-nine years old and he contemplated leaving teaching altogether to manage his family's Magazine Printing Company,[66] but his heartfelt desire was to continue teaching. With his Ph.D. now completed, the University of Utah might consider him for their history or philosophy departments, but his strongest desire was to continue with what he and Bennion had been doing so successfully: teaching religion, building testimonies, sharing love, and giving service. Ironically, Ed received his Ph.D. the same week his superiors in the Church Educational System talked to him about leaving the institute.

The first two weeks of June 1962 were perhaps the most hectic of Lyon's and Bennion's lives, filled with anguished discussions regarding their futures. Bennion, as director of the institute, was a larger target than Lyon. Despite (and perhaps in part because of) Bennion's close friendship with President McKay and his extreme popularity with students, he had ruffled the feathers of a few key educational and ecclesiastical authorities. Many believed that Bennion's opposition to Elder Joseph Fielding Smith's *Man: His Origin and Destiny* in 1954 continued to upset some powerful people in the Church.[67] Within a week of Berrett's first "invitation" to come to BYU, the First Presidency and Quorum of the Twelve met as the Board of Trustees of BYU and head of the Church Educational System. "Lowell Bennion" was the last item on their long agenda.[68] At the meeting, the Board approved the popular and successful Joe J. Christensen, then director of the institute of religion at the University of Idaho, to become director of the Salt Lake institute, starting in the fall. The Executive Committee of the Board of Trustees then carried out "a full discussion of certain problems relative to the services of both Lowell and Ed."[69] No final decisions were reached.

Reasons for Conflict

Lyon tried to understand the "why" of this nebulous and life-shattering transfer. In his datebook, letters to family members, and miscellaneous papers, he jotted down various possible reasons. From these sources, as well as Bennion's "Memories" and Wilkinson's summary of complaints to President McKay, the following items emerge:

1. Stagnant enrollment at the Salt Lake institute.

2. Advancing age of Bennion and Lyon.

3. Instructors' teachings too "liberal."

4. The aforementioned charge of "teaching false doctrine."

5. Administrative problems.
   a. Low scholastic requirements to graduate from Salt
      Lake institute.
   b. No campus recognition for certain courses that could
      be transferred.

To members of the board of trustees, the biggest problems were what
they considered to be low enrollment and lack of growth. Evaluation by
statistical analysis was becoming a crucial measuring stick of success in
Church education. Official enrollment figures for the year 1961–62 show
a total of 2,229 students in institute classes, an increase of one hundred
students from the previous year but a 6 percent drop (from 31 percent to
25 percent) in the number of students in institute classes when compared
to the increased number of Latter-day Saint students on campus. With
the exception of the 1960–61 school year, this percentage, roughly 25
percent, had remained relatively stable since 1954.[70] Church Educational
System administrators viewed this as stagnation and lack of progress
when compared to other programs in the dynamic, rapidly expanding
system. They blamed Bennion for not recruiting more students. Church
Educational System administrators did not measure teaching impact,
testimony-building, or Church activity among current or former students
in the Salt Lake institute—these were either impossible to measure or too
difficult to gauge objectively over a short time period.[71]

Lyon defended himself and Bennion by determining precisely how
many students were in which classes during the 1961–62 school year. He
realized that he and Bennion had taught 68 percent of the students. This
dominant statistic reflects both part of the problem and some of Lyon's
strength, but he saw it only as a factor in defense of his staying. In a letter
to his sister, he complained that if administrators would just look beyond
total numbers "they would see that Lowell and I are each teaching more
than two thirds of the total enrollment, and the other five and a half
teachers are teaching less than a third of the enrollment combined."[72]
The same letter expresses Lyon's opinion that many of the new teachers
that Berrett and Wilkinson assigned to the institute were simply not "up
to standard." Lyon based this subjective evaluation on the fact that courses
taught by him and Bennion were always crowded, even in the largest
classrooms, with students often standing in the halls to hear; the other
instructors rarely drew a full class.

Lyon also addressed the matter of age. "They [BYU administrators]
think we are too old, apparently, and that younger men will attract the

students," Lyon wrote.[73] In June 1962, Lyon was fifty-eight, and Bennion, fifty-three. Lyon and Bennion were energetic and in good health, and they regularly participated with students in all activities including dancing, hiking, and strenuous service work. Lyon thought numerical age should not have entered into the question. Nevertheless, they were viewed by Wilkinson and Berrett as representing in several ways an older generation in Church education.

Lyon and Bennion's teachings may have been considered too liberal, challenging, and unsupportive for some authorities. In a letter to President McKay, Wilkinson cited Bennion's "unorthodox position on the 'Negro question' and the missionary program."[74] Bennion and Lyon often publicly argued in favor of reexamining these Church practices and teachings, which at that time denied the priesthood to blacks of African descent.[75] (This had been an issue with Lyon since the 1930s.) Both Lyon and Bennion also became concerned as they heard reports from returning missionaries in their classes that many youth and children were being rushed into baptism to swell statistical reports. Certain so-called "baseball baptisms" bothered these returned missionaries, who believed that the practice put missionaries under undue pressure to baptize without really teaching and converting. Lyon discussed this practice in his classes, but he never intended to demean missionary service or destroy testimonies. These same concerns were shared by many General Authorities, who later enacted major changes to this proselyting method.

Wilkinson criticized the way that Bennion and Lyon had administered programs, believing that they should have worked harder at getting the university to offer credit for institute classes in courtship and marriage, Christian history, and Old and New Testament. He was displeased that grades were not usually given in institute classes and that records were not always kept:

> This year I want a procedure whereby I will know more of what is going on in the institutes and seminaries. . . . I was chagrined that not until the crisis arose regarding Lowell Bennion and T. Edgar Lyon, did I know that Bennion had practically refused to keep rolls and had practically no methods of grading his students. Had I known that, I am sure I would have resolved the matter much earlier.[76]

In typical fashion, Bennion sought an audience with the authorities responsible for his requested "transfer." He met with Wilkinson in early July and tried to figure out why he was being pressured to go to BYU or leave the system. Bennion wrote of that meeting, "It was intimated that I might be too liberal, not energetic enough in seeking college credit [for institute classes], lacking in administrative ability."[77] By mid-July, Lyon reported that "Lowell Bennion has severed relations with the Institute—we learn now that it was Wilkinson . . . who was the prime mover in getting Lowell out."[78] The Bennion and Lyon era at the Salt Lake institute had come to an end.

Bennion's talents as a teacher and peacemaker easily won him work "across the street," at the University of Utah. Because Bennion was particularly adept at harmonizing diverse entities and ideas, or at least creating a meaningful coexistence, University President A. Ray Olpin hired him as Associate Dean of Students with a part-time teaching appointment in the sociology department. Jerry Johnston, writing in the *Deseret News,* paraphrased Kipling's "If" ("And walk with kings nor lose the common touch") when he characterized Bennion as one who was "a touchstone for apostles, apostates and those in between. He was a human Switzerland, a place where anyone and everyone could go for sanctuary and to hold peace talks."[79] Referring to his "dismissal," Bennion assumed a philosophical stance: "I don't believe in being defeated twice, once by circumstance and once by myself."[80]

Lyon's situation was more difficult. He did not have a job waiting "across the street" or the same degree of recognition as Bennion. He applied to the history department at the University of Utah, but no slot was immediately available. On June 18, Ed Berrett, realizing the firestorm that Bennion's compelled resignation had unleashed, came to Salt Lake City and pleaded with Lyon: "Will you please stay at the Institute?"[81] This was a major departure from the transfer that had been offered three weeks earlier. Lyon sought advice from professors and friends at BYU and the University of Utah. The Church Educational System issued a contract for the coming year, but Lyon did not sign it at that time. On a separate page in his diary, Lyon collected his thoughts about returning to the institute:

—34 years of faithful service

—Repentance

—No chance for a hearing—weak excuse

—"If you keep the Institute job, I'll lose respect for you completely" 6/18/62

—Why so late?

—Another position.[82]

It is not clear who made the statement about "losing respect."[83] Whatever the source, it must have cut deeply—at age fifty-eight, Lyon had little hope for another job becoming available immediately. The summer was a period of torment: "disturbed—sleepless nights, troubled days, and generally upset."[84]

The Salt Lake institute students, as well as thousands of former students, were in an uproar as they got bits and pieces of news about Bennion's forced resignation. Lyon and Bennion refused to foment campaigns or foster organized dissent among these disgruntled students. However, more than a hundred letters of support poured in to Lyon from across the country, many from missionaries. All the letters expressed anger at the "firing" and pleaded for information to understand what had transpired. Former students soon began a letter-writing campaign. Graduate student Fred Buchanan was a leader in this activity, encouraging others to write to influential people. In his diary, Buchanan recorded, "Thank God for men like Brother Bennion and Lyon. They *think and have faith*."[85] Winnie Erickson, an institute student from the late 1930s, was not the only letter-writer to use the words "shocked," "amazed," "upset," "angry," "dismayed," and "surprised beyond belief." Former students, whose testimonies, and indeed whole lives, had been shaped by Lyon and Bennion, assumed that the two "giants" would be at the Salt Lake institute forever, or at least long enough to influence their children. One wrote, "I had so hoped that all my eight children . . . would have the privilege of having classes under the fine influence and intellectual approach of these two brilliant men." She called them the most saintly, Christlike men she had ever known and clarified the fact that Lyon and Bennion had not chosen to leave, as official news releases had stated.[86] She sent her letter to hundreds of former Salt Lake institute students, urging them to write to Church leaders or BYU officials.

Lyon saved scores of these letters. Some are angry, vitriolic accusations against unknowing or unfeeling authorities; most express extreme sadness. All bear strong witness of the personal benefits reaped from the "tireless energy" of the "dynamic duo," Bennion and Lyon.[87] Bobbie Jo Worthen found it "difficult to believe that honest, righteous men could disagree with principles that have helped so many of us to find ourselves and to really know and try to live the gospel."[88] Stephanie Smith Hinckley thanked Lyon for the "wonderful influence" and reflected that the first time she ever bore her testimony was in a Lambda Delta Sigma meeting.[89] Erma D. Hill testified that "I am certain that I'd never have gone on to finish college had it not been for you [two] men." She continued, expressing her worry about Lyon's future, "I hope you'll not get away from teaching though. I have never really enjoyed history until I took it from you."[90]

In 1992, Ed Berrett recalled his unpleasant role in the breakup of the Lyon-Bennion team thirty years earlier. He affirmed that he had admired Lyon ever since their student days at the U in the 1920s. Berrett praised Lyon effusively: "No student ever forgot him. I remember more from the class he taught me in 1939 than any other teacher I'd ever had. . . . He could read a book and remember all the details twenty years later."[91] Berrett was deeply hurt by what he had to do. He recalled that "Hermana [had] blamed me for the firing of Lowell; this was not true." When directly queried about his specific role, Berrett replied indirectly, "I think it was the most difficult thing I've ever had to do—when you work in a position like mine you have many bosses—and you don't always agree."[92] He made no further comment, but it was surprising that he used the word "firing," a term that was so vehemently denied in 1962. In a letter to her sons, Hermana passed on secondary information that "a man in the history department at the 'Y' . . . said he had talked to Ed Berrett a few days ago and he said Wilkinson would like to undo the whole mess now, and Ed [Berrett] had said that if they had only listened to him and had Lowell in to talk with him, it would never have happened."[93] It is impossible to know if or how this turn of events could have been averted, but perhaps it could have been.

After months of personal agonizing, pleas by Berrett, and the development of a good rapport with the new director, Joe J. Christensen, Lyon signed a contract, agreeing to accept a year's leave of absence at full pay to write a history of Christianity manual for institute classes. "This is better than going back to the institute," he wrote to his children.[94] When school began he moved from his spacious associate director's office into a tiny cubbyhole room that was also used to prepare the sacrament on Sundays. He wrote that it didn't matter much since "I don't expect to spend much time there anyway."[95] Much of Lyon's spirit, heart, and excitement was gone. As a way to get his foot in the door, Lyon taught one class in American history at the University of Utah during his leave. He was to have been on leave for a full year, but institute enrollment dropped seriously during fall 1962, so Lyon dutifully responded to a request from Berrett to teach winter and spring quarters. To a former student he reported that "I had over 400 [students] in my classes, and this made the statistics, the only part that matters anymore, look good."[96]

Bennion and Lyon continued their friendship for the remainder of Lyon's life, but they never again enjoyed the personal closeness, daily cooperation, exciting spiritual stimulation, and the thrill of teaching together as they once had. At Christmastime 1962, Bennion in his characteristic honesty wrote:

> This is my second attempt to convey my feelings toward you. . . . It is almost like praising myself to praise you—you have become so much a part of my life and thought. When I think of all the things you have done for me both in personal affairs and at the Institute I realize my eternal debt. Thanks, my friend.
>
> You are the best scholar and teacher of history in the Church. . . . Spend the next twenty years leaving a legacy to the generations to come both in their hearts [by teaching] and in print. Pray don't let bookkeeping or the hammer and saw detract from larger goals too much.[97]

Family Cabin

The "hammer and saw" that Bennion mentions refer to a much happier event—the construction of a mountain cabin. For several years Ed, Hermana, and the boys had been talking of jointly buying or building a family cabin. Ed and Hermana had picnicked, hiked, and camped in Utah's mountains since they began courting, and later they were joined by their sons on these outings. They now determined to acquire land cooperatively as a family. In summer 1960, Ed and Hermana "bought an acre of land, with the Bear River forming the west boundary, in a grove of pines and quaking aspen."[98] The pristine land was on the isolated north slope of the Uinta Mountains, eighteen miles north of Mirror Lake and thirty miles south of Evanston, Wyoming. For this idyllic acre, just a few hundred yards outside the national forest, they paid $2,500. Ed and his sons worked weekends during July, August, and early September 1962, building a rock wall foundation. After the foundation and a platform were completed, the already-cut cedar logs arrived. With total family cooperation and the help of friends and neighbors from Salt Lake City, the Lyons assembled the cabin over three long weekends in September and October 1962.

This venture seemed bold and a little out of character for Ed. He had been extremely frugal all his life, and a mountain cabin, to be used merely for recreation, seemed almost frivolous. But work on the cabin unified the family and restored Lyon's wholeness and his sense of self. For Ed, working out the practical details of the cabin, coupled with the hard physical labor of clearing dead falls and beaver-chewed aspen from the land, provided a needed relief from the heavy pressures of making decisions about his future.

Tour Director

Ed did not see the cabin fully completed that fall. While his sons placed the heavy ceiling beams, put on the roof, and nailed down the redwood shingles, Ed left the country, directing a tour. A new phase had opened in Ed's life in 1959, "another one of those flukes that happen," he later observed.[99] When J. Spencer Cornwall, director of the Mormon Tabernacle Choir, fell sick, Lyon was asked to direct a bus tour to the Hill Cumorah. Lyon had never previously had such an assignment, but he quickly gathered his things and left with a full busload. On their way to New York, the group stopped in sleepy Nauvoo, a town Lyon had known since his childhood from the stories told by his grandmother and the Twentieth Ward's "Old Nauvooers." The bus trip was his first visit to the Cumorah pageant as well. "We had a very successful tour, I thought. . . . When we got back . . . I heard Vida Fox Clawson say to [the driver], 'How did you get along?' He said, 'That man knows how to take a tour. He's the best you've ever had.'"[100] Ed repeated the experience with Hermana during summers 1960 and 1961, gaining a reputation as a popular, insightful, and twinkly-eyed director.

Courtesy Church Archives

Illus. 11-4. Frank Murdock, founder of Murdock Travel and Ed's former missionary companion, invited Lyon to lead tours during the 1960s and '70s.

During summer 1962, former traveling companion turned travel agent "Frank Murdock wanted to know if [Lyon] would take a tour to Palestine."[101] The invitation may have come as a result of the publicly known troubles at the institute, but it was more likely that Murdock (illus. 11-4) had heard of Lyon's popularity as a tour leader. A few years earlier, Murdock had written to Lyon that "it's nice to think back over the trip we made in [1925 and] 1926. . . . Someday you and I and Walt [Perkins] will have to go around the world. If we do I want you to keep the money and the diary and I'll go along and carry your luggage.""[102] Now Murdock was willing to pay the bills, too. Ed and Hermana departed Salt Lake City on October 5, 1962, and returned seventeen days later, recharged, renewed, and removed from the summer's turmoil. "Hermana and [Frank's] wife went with us . . . in Egypt and Israel and Beirut, Syria, Athens, Rome" and more.[103] Lyon and Murdock reestablished personal contact with Fareed Imam, their Palestinian guide in 1925, and continued to use his services as Lyon conducted subsequent tours in 1963, 1964, and 1965. Tensions and a short war in 1967 canceled the tours for a few years, but Murdock again sent Lyon to Israel and surrounding countries in 1973, 1974, and 1975. When asked to describe his experiences as tour director Lyon effused,

> I love it. I really like it. I love traveling and I see new things every time. . . . I always get a new understanding and appreciation of people and get closer to them. . . . I could never have been able to afford it if it hadn't been for this. This is easy. . . . It [tour directing] doesn't worry me.[104]

The pivotal year, 1962, ended in ambiguity. Lyon still had a job in the Church Educational System, but he no longer enjoyed a dynamic and daily close association with Lowell Bennion. He had finally received his Ph.D. and could now officially be called "doctor," but he had lost status and participation in the directorship of the Salt Lake institute. He had written a bluntly honest book review and rebuttal that had gained high accolades among historians but had brought the displeasure of some of his superiors, forcing him to write an apology. He was now recognized as an authoritative and exciting director of foreign and domestic tours. Finally, the construction of a family cabin in the refreshing mountains ensured that Lyon would recover from this chaotic year.

Notes

1. How Wilkinson became the "administrator" (changed to "Chancellor" in 1960) of the Church Educational System is not fully known. During his first two years as president of BYU, he had frequent disputes with Commissioner Franklin West. Lowell Bennion's biographer believes that Wilkinson viewed West's scientific background as confirmation of a weak testimony and cites Wilkinson's personal diary that the Church's "Executive Committee is suspicious of anyone associated with Dr. West." Mary Lythgoe Bradford, *Lowell L. Bennion: Teacher, Counselor, Humanitarian* (Salt Lake City, Utah: Dialogue Foundation, 1995), 127. It is clear

that Wilkinson wanted full control over the system, and many Church leaders agreed that this was appropriate; by gaining control he could limit unhelpful or unwanted public criticism of BYU by institute instructors. Lyon, Bennion, and George Boyd had indeed spoken against administrative policies at BYU that were also to be implemented in the institutes. Bennion was particularly critical of the concept of a standardized curriculum in which each institute had to harmonize their classes, testing, and grades with similar courses at BYU.

2. Bradford, *Lowell L. Bennion,* 129.

3. Bradford, *Lowell L. Bennion,* 127. For a more complete discussion of the changes in the Church Educational System in the 1950s, see Bradford, *Lowell L. Bennion,* chap. 7. Bradford's access to the diaries of Ernest Wilkinson provides valuable insights into this matter.

4. William E. Berrett, *A Miracle in Weekday Religious Education: A History of the Church Education System* (Salt Lake City: Salt Lake Printing Center, 1988), xv.

5. Bradford, *Lowell L. Bennion,* 130.

6. Discussed in Bradford, *Lowell L. Bennion,* 130, 154.

7. Bradford, *Lowell L. Bennion,* 131.

8. See Bradford, *Lowell L. Bennion,* 131–36, for a very well-researched discussion of this conference and its conflicts.

9. T. Edgar Lyon to Lowell L. Bennion, August 1954, T. Edgar Lyon Collection, Church Archives, Family and Church History Department, The Church of Jesus Christ of Latter-day Saints, Salt Lake City (hereafter cited as Church Archives). Unless otherwise noted, all citations for T. Edgar Lyon materials are located in the Lyon collection.

10. T. Edgar Lyon, Diary, September 7, 1954, Church Archives.

11. Lowell L. Bennion, "Oral History," bound typescript, 95, Church Archives.

12. Bennion, "Oral History," 96.

13. T. Edgar Lyon to Jamie Lyon, September 19, 1954, in author's possession.

14. Bennion, "Oral History," 96.

15. Bradford, *Lowell L. Bennion,* 131.

16. T. Edgar Lyon to William E. Berrett, May 27, 1958, Church Archives.

17. T. Edgar Lyon to William E. Berrett, May 27, 1958.

18. T. Edgar Lyon, "Evangelical Protestant Missionary Activities in Mormon Dominated Areas: 1865–1900" (Ph.D. diss., University of Utah, 1962), 60–61.

19. T. Edgar Lyon, "Evangelical Protestant Missionary Activities," 67–92.

20. T. Edgar Lyon, "Evangelical Protestant Missionary Activities," iii.

21. T. Edgar Lyon, "Evangelical Protestant Missionary Activities," 250.

22. T. Edgar Lyon to Janette L. Halton, June 23, 1962, Church Archives.

23. Hermana Lyon to Donna and Laurie Lyon, June 17, 1962, T. Edgar Lyon Collection, Church Archives.

24. Bradford, *Lowell L. Bennion,* 187–88.

25. T. Edgar Lyon, Diary, June 16, 1962.

26. T. Edgar Lyon to George Boyd, April 4, 1962, Church Archives. Richard Vetterli, the book's author, had received a certificate in public administration from the University of Utah in early 1961.

27. T. Edgar Lyon, "Oral History," bound typescript, 178, 179, Church Archives.

28. T. Edgar Lyon, "Oral History," 178–79.

29. T. Edgar Lyon, "Oral History," 179.

30. T. Edgar Lyon to Richard Vetterli, February 2, 1962, Church Archives.

31. T. Edgar Lyon, "Oral History," 179.

32. Lyon recalled the following conversation in his "Oral History":

> I said, "Well, Richard, I've come to the conclusion so far that this is not your work. Somebody else has been doing it." He said, "It was my master's thesis." I said, "Well, I'd like to see your master's thesis and see how much has been changed by someone else. In other words you had a ghost writer." He wouldn't answer. I said, "Who was it? Was it here or in California?" He wouldn't answer. And I said, "Well, there's no use going on. Unless you can tell me something that's wrong I'm going to let Paul [Cracroft] have [the review] and go ahead." He said, "You'll regret it if you do it." I said, "Well, tell me what's wrong." He wouldn't do it. (T. Edgar Lyon, "Oral History," 180)

33. T. Edgar Lyon, review of *Mormonism, Americanism, and Politics,* by Richard Vetterli, *Utah Alumnus* (February 1962): 9.

34. T. Edgar Lyon, review of *Mormonism, Americanism, and Politics,* 7–9.

35. Paul Cracroft, telephone interview by author, January 8, 2000.

36. Richard Vetterli to Paul Cracroft, March 9, 1962, T. Edgar Lyon Collection, Church Archives.

37. Richard Vetterli, "Politics and the Mormons: Round Two," *Utah Alumnus* (April 1962) :29. Italics added.

38. Ezra Taft Benson, "The Lord's Base of Operations," *Improvement Era* 65 (June 1962): 456–57.

39. Gustive Larson to T. Edgar Lyon, March 20, 1962, Church Archives.

40. Truman Madsen to T. Edgar Lyon, April 11, 1962, Church Archives.

41. Dallin Oaks to T. Edgar Lyon, August 3, 1962, Church Archives.

42. S. George Ellsworth, "Reviews and Recent Publications," *Utah Historical Quarterly* 30 (summer 1962): 273–74.

43. Ellsworth, "Reviews and Recent Publications," 273.

44. Richard D. Poll to Ivan Hinderaker, March 30, 1962, T. Edgar Lyon Collection. Penned on the bottom of Lyon's carbon copy of this letter are notes indicating that UCLA took action and refused to allow Vetterli to continue further graduate work at that university as he had planned. Vetterli moved on to the University of California–Riverside, where he completed a Ph.D. in 1972.

45. Leonard J. Arrington to T. Edgar Lyon, August 4, 1962, Church Archives.

46. Ellsworth, "Reviews and Recent Publications," 275.

47. Hugh B. Brown to Hyrum L. Coon, March 2, 1962, T. Edgar Lyon Collection. An official statement appeared in the *Deseret News and Telegram,* January 3, 1963, 1. It was signed by the First Presidency (David O. McKay, Henry D. Moyle, and Hugh B. Brown):

The following statement is made to correct the false statements and unwarranted assumptions regarding the position allegedly taken by the leaders of the Church on political questions in general and the John Birch Society in particular. . . .

We deplore the presumption of some politicians, especially officers, co-ordinators and members of the John Birch Society, who undertake to align the Church or its leadership with their partisan views.

48. T. Edgar Lyon, book review rebuttal, *Utah Alumnus*, July–August 1962, 16.

49. T. Edgar Lyon, "Oral History," 184, 181.

50. William E. Berrett, interview by Ted and Trent Lyon, Provo, Utah, June 30, 1992.

51. T. Edgar Lyon to David O. McKay, June 7, 1962, Church Archives. Italics added for emphasis.

52. T. Edgar Lyon to David O. McKay, June 7, 1962.

53. Staff historians carefully searched President McKay's papers and found that Lyon's review was not even mentioned. However, in one 1962 meeting, the topic of Vetterli's book appeared on the agenda. No meeting minutes exist to provide other details. It is conceivable that this item was merely an announcement about the book's publication rather than a discussion of the review.

54. Bradford, *Lowell L. Bennion,* 117–18.

55. Marion D. Hanks, interview by Ted and Trent Lyon, Salt Lake City, August 4, 1992.

56. William E. Berrett, interview by Ted and Trent Lyon, Provo, Utah, June 30, 1992.

57. Richard Vetterli, interview by Melinda Silver, Provo, Utah, February 9, 1993. During the interview, Mr. Vetterli denied that he was ever supported by any General Authority of the Church. "I know that some of them enjoyed reading it, however their support was not sought or received." He also denied that he had ever had a ghost writer. A more detailed version of these two points appears in T. Edgar Lyon, "Oral History," 181.

58. Bradford, *Lowell L. Bennion,* 154.

59. T. Edgar Lyon to Donna and Laurie Lyon, June 17, 1962, in author's possession.

60. T. Edgar Lyon to his siblings, June 1962, L. Tom Perry Special Collections, Harold B. Lee Library, Brigham Young University, Provo, Utah (hereafter cited as Perry Special Collections).

61. Lyon confided to his family and close friends that the new, young faculty member had been sent as a "mole" or spy to discover heterodoxy and report it to Commissioner Wilkinson. No documentation exists to prove this allegation, but it is consistent with similar activities on BYU's campus in that decade.

62. Lowell L. Bennion, "Memories," approx. 1975, holograph, 50, copy in author's possession.

63. Bradford, *Lowell L. Bennion,* 154.

64. Bennion's and Lyon's "departure" is covered in Bradford, *Lowell L. Bennion,* 154–80. Bradford gained access to the diaries of Ernest L. Wilkinson, as well as those of University of Utah president A. Ray Olpin, both of whom had been "bargaining for Bennion's soul" for months. This access allowed her an intimate and insightful entry into the reasons behind Wilkinson's audacious action of removing Bennion as director. As a result of Bradford's exhaustive coverage, I will not repeat the details here. Further, when interviewed by Davis Bitton in 1974 and 1975, Lyon responded to all questions about the Salt Lake institute but then requested that the section on the "dismissal" be sealed until 2004. This was his way of protecting those most directly involved with what he called "a poorly handled misunderstanding."

65. T. Edgar Lyon, "Oral History," 203–8.

66. Joseph Lynn Lyon, "A History of Laura Hermana Forsberg," 1991, p. 129, Perry Special Collections.

67. Joseph Lynn Lyon, "History of Laura Hermana Forsberg," 128.

68. Bradford, *Lowell L. Bennion,* 157.

69. Bradford, *Lowell L. Bennion,* 157.

70. A. Gary Anderson, *A Historical Survey of the Full-Time Institutes of Religion* (Ph.D. diss., Brigham Young University, 1968), 147.

71. Even a cursory examination would have revealed that Lyon, Bennion, Hanks, Boyd, and Albert Payne had achieved great success in retaining many highly intelligent students who underwent serious struggles trying to reconcile faith and academic learning. We have little insight, however, into what they said or did to achieve this. Marion Hanks recalled that "President McKay and others . . . were anxious for our kids [students] getting humbled and faltering in testimony, and wanted bright minds with some credentials [at the Salt Lake institute]." Hanks, interview.

72. T. Edgar Lyon to Janette L. Halton, June 23, 1962, Church Archives.

73. T. Edgar Lyon to Janette L. Halton, June 23, 1962.

74. Bradford, *Lowell L. Bennion,* 165–67.

75. Bradford reports a bold conversation between Bennion and McKay on the subject of the priesthood and the marriage of a couple in which it was thought that the girl had some black ancestors three generations back. Her brother, a blond, blue-eyed student at the U, came to see Lowell. The young man was still active in the Church but had never received the priesthood and sincerely hoped his sister could be married in the temple. In typical fashion, Bennion took the problem right to the office of his friend, President McKay. The story is detailed in *Lowell L. Bennion,* 165–66.

76. Ernest L. Wilkinson to William E. Berrett, July 30, 1962, cited in Bradford, *Lowell L. Bennion,* 169.

77. Bennion, "Memories," 51.

78. T. Edgar Lyon to Janette L. Halton, July 23, 1962.

79. Jerry Johnston, "Lowell L. Bennion," *Deseret News,* March 1, 1996, C-1.

80. Bradford, *Lowell L. Bennion,* 155.

81. T. Edgar Lyon, Diary, June 18, 1962.

82. T. Edgar Lyon, Diary, June 1962.

83. This statement was not from Bennion, who on that date was still undecided about his own future.

84. T. Edgar Lyon to Janette L. Halton, June 23, 1962.

85. Fred S. Buchanan, cited in Bradford, *Lowell L. Bennion,* 170.

86. Winnie Erickson to former students of T. Edgar Lyon, July 1962, in author's possession.

87. Quotations come from several letters written to T. Edgar Lyon from June 1962 through December 1962, Church Archives.

88. Bobbie Jo Worthen to T. Edgar Lyon, August 2, 1962, Church Archives.

89. Stephanie Smith Hinckley to T. Edgar Lyon, July 5, 1962, Church Archives.

90. Erma Darley Hill to T. Edgar Lyon, July 31, 1962, Church Archives.

91. Berrett, interview.

92. Berrett, interview.

93. Hermana Lyon to sons, September 4, 1962, original in possession of A. Laurence Lyon.

94. T. Edgar Lyon to Jamie and Laurie Lyon, July 16 and 22, 1962, original in possession of A. Laurence Lyon.

95. T. Edgar Lyon to Jamie and Laurie Lyon, September 17, 1962.

96. T. Edgar Lyon, as cited in Bradford, *Lowell L. Bennion,* 185.

97. Lowell L. Bennion to T. Edgar Lyon, December 22, 1962, Church Archives.

98. T. Edgar Lyon to his siblings, October 1, 1960, Church Archives.

99. T. Edgar Lyon, "Oral History," 251.

100. T. Edgar Lyon, "Oral History," 252.

101. T. Edgar Lyon, "Oral History," 252.

102. Franklin L. Murdock to T. Edgar Lyon, March 30, 1955, Church Archives.

103. T. Edgar Lyon, "Oral History," 252.

104. T. Edgar Lyon, "Oral History," 253.

12

The Restoration of Nauvoo, 1963–78

The last fifteen years (1963–1978) of Lyon's life were completely absorbed by a stimulating research topic—Nauvoo. The research was not entirely new but the intense focus was. The town and its history consumed each of Lyon's summers from 1964 through 1971, and also provided personal renewal and a bevy of new subjects for speeches, fireside talks, and study groups. In the minds of many, Lyon became "Mr. Nauvoo" (illus. 12-1). When he was first asked to work in Nauvoo, Church Educational System administrator Alma P. Burton judged that "in my opinion there is no one in the Church who is better qualified to undertake this research project than T. Edgar Lyon."[1] While this early judgment may have been flattery, after eight or ten years on the job it was indisputable fact. In a sense, Lyon's work in Nauvoo became like a personal Church service mission, so strong was his dedication to a subject he had felt strongly about since his youth.[2] He was still being paid for his work at the Salt Lake institute, but he freely contributed all his nonteaching time to researching, lecturing, and archaeological digging in and about Nauvoo.

Nauvoo Restoration Inc. was chartered as an Illinois not-for-profit corporation in July 1962. The First Presidency (David O. McKay, Henry D. Moyle, and Hugh B. Brown) authorized and organized the new enterprise "to perpetuate in history the part played by the Mormon Pioneers in the building of the west."[3] The Articles of Incorporation outline the organization's purposes to "acquire, restore, protect, and preserve . . . all or part of the old city of Nauvoo . . . [and] to interpret and dramatize [its] story."[4] The guiding hand behind the corporation was Dr. J. LeRoy Kimball, a Salt Lake cardiologist. Since his days as a medical student in Chicago, he had felt a kinship with the quiet Mississippi River town. In 1954, Kimball acquired the home of his great-grandfather Heber C. Kimball, but "his personal project soon became of Church-wide interest" as LDS tourists flocked to see the town and buildings in which their ancestors had also lived.[5] Kimball was named president and chairman of the Nauvoo Restoration board, which was composed of Salt Lake City residents: Harold P. Fabian, A. Hamer Reiser, and Thorpe B. Isaacson (third

Illus. 12-1. Ed Lyon, 1960s.

counselor in the First Presidency); as well as prominent LDS businessmen David M. Kennedy (illus. 12-2) of Chicago and J. Willard Marriott of Washington, D.C. In 1966, Edwin Kendrew, senior vice president of Colonial Williamsburg in Virginia, was also added to the board.[6] Almost from the beginning the board saw the need to hire a project manager and various specialists. University of Utah history professor David Miller first accepted the job as historian in 1962 but soon found himself too involved on campus and asked to resign. Kimball decided on Lyon as his next choice.[7] On the evening of December 31, 1963, Kimball called Lyon at home and set up an appointment.[8] Early the next morning in Kimball's office, Lyon enthusiastically accepted the position as research historian for Nauvoo Restoration Inc.[9]

Lyon's sixteen-year involvement with the restoration of Nauvoo came at a time when he had lost some of his excitement and enthusiasm at the Salt Lake institute. It allowed him to redirect his energy and pursue his demand for historical authenticity in a creative way. Nauvoo rekindled the excitement Lyon had known during the earlier years of the institute. Although he already had a reduced teaching load that allowed him to write, Church Educational System administrators began cutting his teaching responsibilities even more. Lyon typically spent three days at the Salt Lake institute and two at the Nauvoo Restoration office, but as the demands for more research on the old town grew, he often spent three or four days a week immersed in research.

"Everything Is To Be Done Accurately"

Lyon's excitement for the project complemented the board's desire for authenticity. Kimball stressed the need for painstaking research into old diaries, books, notes, microfilms, letters, pictures, and drawings from

Courtesy David M. Kennedy Center for International Relations, BYU

Illus. 12-2. David M. Kennedy (c. 1980), member of the Nauvoo Restoration board, often met Ed Lyon at the Chicago airport. Kennedy would host Lyon and travel with him to Nauvoo to do research.

all possible sources. "Everything is [to be] done accurately,"[10] he stressed, and this approach appealed to Lyon, who dug in and found "the Nauvoo work [to be] fascinating, but discouraging, as each day indicates how little we [really] know about the true history of the community."[11] Lyon spent three weeks (from April 17 through May 9, 1964) in Nauvoo, crawling into abandoned red-brick homes, squeezing through basement cellar doors, and just walking the quiet streets to get a feel for the town. He recalled that his grandmother Carolyn Holland had lived there as a little girl and that his great-grandfather had died there of malaria in October 1844. Lyon felt like he was almost coming home. He struck up relationships with the local residents who had noticed the pith-helmeted gentleman sauntering around and poking into the oldest buildings in town. Lyon's easy-going nature allowed almost immediate rapport, and he gained their confidence. He asked questions of the locals, who willingly shared old photographs, maps, and newspapers.

Mormons were not the only people interested in Nauvoo. Nauvoo's local historian, Ida Blum, had been writing weekly columns and feature articles in the *Nauvoo Independent* and other area papers since 1930.[12] Lyon read these and became so fascinated with Blum's penchant for detail and her knowledge of the people in town that he dropped in to see her on his 1964 research visit. Lyon's open manner won her favor, and the two cooperated and corresponded for years. Together, they often helped to calm the parochial animosity that developed when Nauvoo Restoration Inc. came into town and began buying property, which inflated local real estate prices. When BYU Librarian Dennis Rowley arranged a ceremony to accept Blum's research work, Lyon read a lengthy tribute to this grand historian in which he called her "Mrs. Nauvoo."[13]

With initial surveys supplied by Lyon and personal insights gained from Ida Blum, LeRoy Kimball began to make plans for restoring some of the remaining houses, rebuilding certain businesses, refurbishing shops and homes with period furniture and tools, and providing guides in 1840s costumes to offer historical insights. They would also build a visitors' center to acquaint tourists with the history of the Mormon settlement. Kimball praised Lyon as "one of the Church's prominent historians" and applauded his uncanny ability to ferret out obscure details and records. "Dr. Lyon, on a search for additional records, went into the attic [of the Hancock County courthouse]," explained Kimball, "and between some ceiling joists . . . found the tax collector's reports from 1846 to 1849."[14] The lure of this primary research hooked Lyon on Nauvoo. He returned to Salt Lake City for a few more weeks of teaching, but on June 7, 1964, he boarded another train bound for Illinois. Ed wrote daily letters to Hermana, who had stayed in Utah to finish some Primary General Board assignments and to work on the new Youth Correlation Committee of the Church.

After the humid summer days of Nauvoo, Lyon returned to Utah in late August. A passenger on the train, Nancy Simmons Andrews, penned a letter of appreciation to Lyon eleven years later. As a member of another religion at that time, Nancy had previously never met a Mormon:

> My mother and I were bound for California on the Zephyr. You were headed back to Salt Lake City. . . . We sat across from you for several hours and were enthralled by your marvelous knowledge of the countryside and, ultimately, by your insights of the Mormon people . . . and I, at least, came away wanting to know more. The 1965 World's Fair gave me an opportunity. Again I met people who had your same enthusiasm and "glow."[15]

She married two years later, moved to Rochester, New York, and on a short drive got lost and "ended up at the Joseph Smith Home in Palmyra." Then, a year later, "two young men plodded through the worst blizzard of the year" to her doorstep. These two missionaries taught the gospel to her family, and they all joined the Church. At the time of her letter, Nancy was the Relief Society president and her husband the branch president; the couple rejoiced in having also brought "two wonderful friends into the Church. . . . In closing I just want to thank you with all my heart for opening the door to what I hope will be my eternal progression and ultimate perfection. . . . Eternally in your debt, Brother and Sister Wm. Andrews."[16] The restoration of Nauvoo would provide the backdrop for thousands of other missionary moments; in fact, this was one of its chief reasons for being.

While in Utah during late summer 1964, Lyon continued work on the family cabin with his children, researched and wrote lesson manuals, and prepared to teach three classes at the institute. But Nauvoo again beckoned, and Joe J. Christensen (illus. 12-3) covered Lyon's classes during part of the fall quarter. From October 7 through November 12, 1964, Lyon and several board members journeyed eastward in search of an example of first-class restoration. Colonial Williamsburg turned out to be the model they had been looking for. After this fact-finding trip, the Nauvoo restoration project began incorporating techniques, and even personnel, previously used in Williamsburg, Virginia. As the group drove back to Utah they had a difficult time containing their enthusiasm for the exciting activities in which they were engaged. Lyon's work schedule shifted to two-thirds time on the Nauvoo restoration project and one-third at the Salt Lake institute.[17]

Courtesy Church Archives

Illus. 12-3. Joe J. Christensen, director of the Salt Lake institute, often substituted for Lyon while he was doing research in Nauvoo.

Lyon spent two or three months of each summer from 1964 through 1971 in Nauvoo, where he actually lived in the old homes of Orson Hyde and other Church leaders to gain a feel for them. Hermana usually accompanied him, carrying box loads of Church writing and editing with her. At the close of 1965, Lyon noted that "it was reported at the annual meeting of NRI that as of that date, NRI has purchased 822.26 acres [in Nauvoo] for $1,538,480.35."[18] Lyon's task was to complete the historical background so an authentic restoration could be carried out.

> My assignments were essentially to find everything I could about the city, the City Council, the families that lived there, their names, places of origin . . . as they tended to bring their architectural forms and house furnishings with them, what they had in their houses, what they did at Nauvoo for their trades, births in the family at Nauvoo, their part in the preparation for the exodus to the West, their trades, occupations, newspapers they published, schools, printing plant, etc., etc. Items of social and cultural life, etc.[19]

From his research, Lyon created individual 5" x 7" cards and at one time calculated that he had between fifteen to twenty thousand such research notes.[20] He also identified an estimated seven thousand of the eleven thousand residents of Nauvoo in 1845, placed them on a city lot, and identified when they arrived, where they came from, and where they went after 1846.

"Walking Encyclopedia"

As news of the initial restoration projects in Nauvoo spread, thousands of tourists began to visit the town. In 1967, Kimball (illus 12-4), as chairman of the Nauvoo Restoration board, optimistically observed that "last year more than 97,000 people registered at our information and exhibition houses, and we expect about 120,000 registrations this year. By 1974 our estimates show that a minimum of 400,000 people per year will visit us."[21] The projections were confidently high: for example, three decades later in 1995 only 161,564 visited Nauvoo. The statistics for 1966 that had been used to make the projection were inaccurate, since they counted people who wrote their names at the information center as well as at each restored house. This distortion of numbers concerned Lyon, who felt that the inflated count would eventually hurt the organization. Whatever the actual numbers, the corporation quickly saw the need to secure summer guides who could help interpret Nauvoo's history for tourists.

Nauvoo Restoration recruited returned missionaries from Brigham Young University and the University of Utah for summer 1965. Lyon provided historical background information to the young guides, usually in early morning classes. He also took hundreds of families on motor tours around the town. Many wrote letters thanking Lyon for the free and inspirational instruction. His correspondence files contain more than one hundred such notes of gratitude. The following from visitor Sharon Droge is typical:

> I went to Nauvoo to get a feeling for the pioneers. . . . But . . . I learned an entirely different lesson. . . . For the first time I am able to feel that the faith, devotion, friendliness of our early members still exists today. And this is mainly due to you Brother Lyon and the marvelous group of people who work with you. I love you and your sweet wife for the warm, sincere friendship you bestowed on me. . . . Brother Lyon you have a gift for working with young people—they need you.[22]

Illus. 12-4. Dr. J. LeRoy Kimball, president and chairman of the Nauvoo Restoration board.

Adults as well as youth responded positively to the town tours. In July 1968, Elder Howard W. Hunter and his two adult sons and their families came to Nauvoo on a rushed visit because the sons needed to gather material for their early-morning seminary classes in the fall. Project manager Byron Ravsten asked Lyon to give them a hurried visit. As they began the tour, the Hunters recognized a stimulating spirit in the town and changed their itinerary to spend an extra day there. On their second evening, Hermana invited them over for a meal of "thick-crusted home-made bread" as well as Nauvoo-grown beets, carrots, fresh blackberries, ham, and fruit salad.[23] They stayed until after midnight, quizzing and examining Lyon on how such a successful city could have been built without any banks or lending institutions, what really caused the mob action against Joseph and Hyrum Smith, and how eleven thousand people could move to the far West. Lyon remembered that "time and again I tried to turn away from their questions. . . . I fear we slaughtered some sacred historical cows that night."[24] He recalled Elder Hunter's praise:

> Of all the historic sites we visited, the tour of Nauvoo was the most exciting. On other sites we saw physical objects and were told a story, but the places seemed to lack the human element. Nauvoo was the only place where people were alive so we could relate to them. We felt their hopes, struggles, frustrations, fears, and above all, their undying testimonies of the prophetic calling of Joseph Smith and Brigham Young, his successor, and their willingness to sacrifice their world[ly] acquisitions and creature comforts to maintain the spiritual values which they had acquired through accepting the covenant of the restored gospel. The real Nauvoo story is more exciting than the myth[s] we have made up about it.[25]

Upon returning to Utah, Elder Hunter wrote to the Nauvoo Restoration office in Salt Lake City. Rowena Miller relayed the Apostle's comments to Kimball in Nauvoo, reporting that Elder Hunter had said, "Lyon is simply tremendous."[26] Lyon had immersed himself so deeply in the diaries and letters from the 1840s that he remembered the names of people, the dates they moved into town, when they built their first house, and even when their children were born. He stored all this information in his memory and called it up for Elder Hunter, Sharon Droge, and thousands of others who wanted to know where and how their ancestors lived. Tourists often referred to Lyon as a "walking encyclopedia."

Most were pleased with Lyon's interpretations; a few were not. Institute teacher Ken Godfrey recalled:

> There were times when Ed was too blunt [on these tours] and Byron [Ravsten] would then have to do some rebuilding of faith. . . . Ed lived in the field of history so long that he was not conscious that some things could shock people that were no longer shocking to him because he had dealt with it. At times maybe he was not sensitive to these good and faithful Church members.[27]

Yet Lyon was fully convinced and deeply committed to the Church's most sacred truths. Nadine Cook insightfully wrote that

> Our trip [to Nauvoo] enriched our testimonies and widened our vision of how carefully the Lord has planned for his kingdom. How blessed we are . . . to have people like you who feed us spiritually and support that spiritual food with knowledge and understanding.[28]

Lyon was practically obsessed with creating a truthful restoration of Nauvoo. In 1966 he wrote an old missionary companion: "I'm trying to find the kind of door locks they used, hinges, window sash, floor coverings, drapes, dishes, etc., and it is like looking for a needle in a hay stack."[29] To Emily Smith Stewart, daughter of former Church president George Albert Smith and granddaughter of Wilford Woodruff, Lyon explained the difficulty of getting the precise mix to match the extant mortar of Woodruff's home.

> They have set up a dozen experiments with bricks and mortar. They took sand from the basement of the home—a logical place for him to have secured sand, as it was mostly sand—and sand from the river, sand [from the] banks on the bluffs, and north of town, and mixed various proportions of lime mortar with the sands. Then they laid up a few bricks with each concoction, and now have them weather[ing] in the sun, sprinkling them, letting them dry, and repeating this procedure, to find a sand-mortar relationship which appears similar to the Woodruff mortar in hardness and appearance.[30]

Lyon continued describing his efforts to "determine the original front elevation of the house, and the nature of his step and walking, and back door area."[31] It all had to be exact.[32]

One of Lyon's early concerns centered around the type of buildings to be restored. The initial thrust of the Nauvoo restoration project had been to restore the old homes. Lyon argued that this would interest women, but most men would lose interest after visiting just one or two houses. Lyon proposed that business sites be restored to show activities that had made Nauvoo so unique. Due to his insistence, the Webb Blacksmith shop, the Browning Gun shop, the offices of the *Times and Seasons* printing complex, and several other shops received priority and were fully restored. Lyon wrote the "house histories" for many of these restored homes and businesses. However, he watched with dismay as the three-story Masonic Hall became the "Cultural Hall," fearing that the term was employed to deny the Church's close involvement with the Masons in Nauvoo.

Detail Man

In 1965, Don and Loretta Enders accepted work as grounds keepers and guides for the project. The relationship between the Enders and Lyons, built on long talks and tasty treats, lasted until Ed's death. Don Enders appreciated Lyon's emphasis on authenticity, and he still remembers Lyon saying, "We've got to do [the restoration] absolutely right. Most of our visitors would not really know the difference but two or three percent would, and they're the ones who'll go home and write articles and reviews in papers or professional journals, and we'll lose credibility."[33]

In 1969 an archaeological crew was digging around the Jonathan Browning home. In the backyard they came across some rotted cloth and rusty nails above the delicate bones of a tiny baby. Called to help interpret the find, Lyon spent days checking diaries, death records, and family histories. He finally determined that these were the remains of baby Emma Eliza Browning, who was born October 10, 1843, and died seventeen days later.[34] Lyon then explained the cultural custom of the time that dead infants were often buried near home so that they would not be far from their mother and family. The carpenter shop of Nauvoo Restoration fashioned a new coffin and the baby's bones were reburied in the same place they were found, this time with a headstone.

Yet another example of his thoroughness occurred while completing the restoration work on the Brigham Young home (illus. 12-5), when Lyon pointed out the unique space-saving features of the "bustle" oven, the only one in Nauvoo. The hearth in the Young home was so narrow that without such an exterior extension, no useful cooking or heating could occur. The restoration team was about to tear it down, considering it a later addition to the house, until Lyon traced its complex origins to earlier use in upstate New York, the area where Brigham Young had grown up. For this and other activities in September 1971, Nauvoo's modern *Times and Seasons* praised Lyon's "unlimited patience and tenacity . . . [in] solving riddles of the past centuries."[35]

To equip the printing shop, Lyon tracked leads across Illinois and Iowa in a quest for an authentic press. In Brockton, Illinois, he discovered a working 1840s "C. Foster and Co." Greek revival ornamental printing press and bought it for $1,000.00.[36] Lyon also became an expert on tools, guns, and machinery of the Nauvoo period. In 1978 he still held the office of research historian, "but [I] don't do much [now], as I have done so much research I am way ahead of the archaeologists, architects and builders."[37] While working on the printing house's restoration, Lyon began thinking about the 1844 destruction of the press, combining historical insight and a strong personal conviction with some common sense.

Lyon had read historian Richard Crabb's *Empire on the Platte* and, through Ida Blum, arranged to meet the author. Crabb had grown up on a farm east of Nauvoo and by the 1960s was a highly respected journalist and prolific historian, residing in Wheaton, Illinois. Crabb later recalled that he came to Nauvoo and met Lyon:

> [Lyon] was planning out the restoration of the printing office. He told me of the destruction of the "Expositor" press, scattering the type, and the subsequent problems this caused for Joseph Smith. Then he said, "Now, if you were trying to immobilize a heavy press, what would be most important to get rid of?" I couldn't answer. Then he said, "well, the type is the easiest thing to disperse. The press is too heavy to carry far, but it can be smashed. But the type can be easily scattered. So where do you think it would be? Type is also heavy so they likely wouldn't have carried it very far." This got him thinking.
>
> He then told me that in a few days the Illinois Department of Transportation was going to be digging down to establish a good road base, and then resurface the road where the "Expositor" was located. He was going to talk to the foreman on the road crew and ask to be present when they dug there.
>
> I was fascinated and asked if I could also be present, but I was skeptical. Excavation day came in early August 1974, and Dr. Lyon was there with a shovel, a screen, and a small crowd of onlookers. It was a storybook experience. Indeed, when they dug down with

their equipment, he found several pieces of type, and he knew exactly what they were [because of his work in a print shop as a young boy]. He got the whole town excited about history that day.[38]

Illus. 12-5. Ed Lyon (c. 1960s) leaning on the bustle oven in the Nauvoo home of Brigham Young.

On a second visit to Nauvoo, historian Richard Crabb and Lyon drove to Hannibal, Missouri, where "Dr. Lyon entertained us constantly by relating little-known stories about Mark Twain's career."[39] Crabb was deeply impressed that Lyon, a Mormon historian from Utah, knew so much about a midwestern humorist. The men and their wives commenced a relationship and close cooperation that lasted until Lyon's death. Crabb stood in awe of this research historian who had "come out of nowhere" and seemed to know more about Nauvoo and Hancock County than any local historian. So deep was his admiration that "during the 1970s [Crabb] went to Salt Lake City at least twice a year to 'sit at the feet' [of] the man who was the greatest authority on the Mormon period in Nauvoo."[40]

While working on the Nauvoo restoration project, Lyon also established positive ties with the churches in town, including the Reorganized Church of Jesus Christ of Latter Day Saints (RLDS, now known as the Community of Christ Church), which owned the Joseph Smith properties. The powerful Nauvoo Restoration Inc. posed a considerable threat to their small but vital holdings, but Lyon kept the relationship as positive as possible. After an open meeting on June 26, 1969, with Nauvoo Restoration representatives and workers from the then RLDS Church, Lyon recorded that an RLDS guide suggested mutual cooperation: "Bro. Muir said to me: 'I hope this will be the beginning of a new era for our Churches. There is no reason why visitors to Nauvoo should get two conflicting interpretations.' I suggested we should be able to unite on a historical basis. He agreed."[41] Lyon's personal files are filled with cordial and respectful letters to and from RLDS historians documenting exchanges of books, records, diaries, and articles. Lyon was among those who helped establish the present goodwill that exists between the two churches. But he also gently pointed out that 90 percent of the people in Nauvoo had gone west with Brigham Young. His studies led him to respectfully refer to the RLDS Church as the LDS Church without Nauvoo, or the pre-Nauvoo Church.

In May 1969, ground was broken for a large "Nauvoo Information Center." Hermana flew in for the service with an "entourage—Secy. of the [U.S.] Treasury [David M.] Kennedy, secy. of HUD, George Romney, Willard Marriot . . . Pres. Hugh B. Brown, Harold B. Lee and wife, Delbert L. Stapley and wife, the presidents of the General Boards of the Relief Society, Primary, etc."[42] The dignitaries flew into Burlington, Iowa, and were escorted to Nauvoo by Iowa and Illinois state police. Press conferences aided the publicity for this significant event in an out-of-the-way town. Lyon counted 1,660 people in attendance.[43]

By 1970, Lyon reported that the Church had acquired ninety percent of the land of old Nauvoo, slightly over one thousand acres. The total number of visitors in that year, however, was only 40,000—far short of the optimistic 400,000 projected for the mid-1970s—and most were Church members.[44] When Lyon asked tour bus directors why many chose not to include Nauvoo on their itinerary when they were already so close, they said they feared being proselyted, were unfamiliar with the restoration project, or didn't consider it "authentic living history."[45]

The town was not fulfilling the ambitious missionary function Kimball had envisioned. The problem was not only lack of visitors—costs were also mounting. The dilemma, according to Don Enders, was simple: "The Church could restore one house in Nauvoo, or pay for five full-time seminary teachers in Central America with the same amount of money."[46]

Conflicts

As early as 1964, after his three visits to Nauvoo that year, Lyon sensed organizational problems. In a letter to William E. Berrett detailing his time allocation between the Salt Lake institute and Nauvoo Restoration Inc., Lyon observed that "the road ahead [for the Nauvoo restoration project] does not look too cheery—some opposition is arising within the Church."[47] Further, historical errors in the furnishings of some restored homes bothered Lyon. His diaries and letters to Hermana in 1967, 1968, and especially 1969, reveal a sadness at the glitzy spin rather than an authentic restoration. To a former student and experienced restoration worker who desired to volunteer time in Nauvoo, Lyon wrote that "the end result [of one house restoration] was a mess—little that was authentic to the period. . . . But I have been dressed down pretty sharply and told to mind my own department—history—and not meddle in other departments."[48] The groundbreaking for the visitors' center in 1969 had bothered him—his foundation work was not even mentioned, and his name did not appear in the program. He was also troubled by what he perceived as a negative tone toward the work of the RLDS Church.[49] The next day, the Nauvoo Restoration executive committee held a meeting from which Lyon was excluded. He recorded that there was "no inquiry or concern for me. Why? How much do I count on the project? An insult!"[50]

Upset at his status—or lack thereof—and the inaccurate house furnishings, Lyon wrote letters to restoration consultants who were also working on the project, namely Pinky Harrington and Edwin Kendrew, seeking their advice. Kimball found out about the communication and was "furious about [his] letter."[51] Early the next morning Lyon turned in his resignation, but Kimball would not accept it. So Lyon "agreed to stay on—but not convinced I can take it."[52] It appeared that Lyon's research and knowledge may have been a threat to those who wanted to hurridly complete the job and to those who wanted to restore the homes with nonperiod, overly elegant furnishings. There was some disagreement among board members because they approached the project with different backgrounds and expectations. In his oral history interviews with Davis Bitton, Lyon discussed his involvement with the Nauvoo restoration project in candid detail, but then requested that Bitton seal that portion until 2004. A more complete account of Lyon's struggles and viewpoints on Nauvoo Restoration Inc. will have to wait until that date.

Despite this disappointment, Lyon's experiences in Nauvoo yielded many positive results. Perhaps one most important outcome is it allowed him to deepen his understanding of Joseph Smith's amazing life and to appreciate his greatness. Lyon gained an intimacy with the prophet of the Restoration that he willingly shared with visitors. Salt Lake institute colleague Dale LeCheminant remembered that Lyon "said one of the most impressive things in a [faculty] testimony meeting once. . . . We could have been around a campfire. He was brief but [stood and] said simply, 'Boys, Joe Smith told the truth'!"[53] Ironically, it may have been the word "Joe"—rather than the more formal "Joseph"—that upset some who knew Lyon. One worker on the restoration project, Don Enders, recalled that to some this term may have "appeared disrespectful but in reality [Lyon] was using it in an intimate, friendly way; he got to know Joseph Smith well enough to call him Joe as many of the Saints did back in those days."[54]

Due to these conflicts and to Hermana's worsening health, Ed spent less time in Nauvoo and less research time on the Nauvoo restoration project while in Utah. Summer 1971 was Lyon's last full summer in Nauvoo. Although he continued to research and frequently gave talks on the subject to large audiences, he rarely visited Nauvoo anymore. Nauvoo provided exciting research and focused his energy until the month he died.

Notes

1. Alma P. Burton to T. Edgar Lyon, January 9, 1964, Church Archives, Family and Church History Department, The Church of Jesus Christ of Latter-day Saints (hereafter cited as Church Archives).

2. Although Church service missions were not officially instituted until later, Lyon's endeavors in Nauvoo mirror the description of such a calling.

3. Henry A. Smith, "Steps Taken to Restore Historic Nauvoo," *Church News* (June 30, 1962): 3, 14.

4. "The Era Asks About Nauvoo Restoration," interview with Dr. J. LeRoy Kimball, *Improvement Era* 70 (July 1967): 12, 14, 16–17.

5. Smith, "Steps Taken to Restore Historic Nauvoo," 3.

6. "Nauvoo Group Names New Board Member," *Church News* (May 7, 1966): 15.

7. William E. Berrett, interview by author and Trent Lyon, June 30, 1992, Provo, Utah. William E. Berrett took credit for Lyon's appointment—"I insisted that Ed be hired as historian," but Lyon never mentioned this. It appears that Berrett was still smarting from having to "fire" his friend and was looking for ways to make amends.

8. T. Edgar Lyon, datebook, December 31, 1963, Church Archives.

9. The restoration of Nauvoo was necessarily a complex and cooperative activity. Dr. Kimball's detailed planning called for a research historian (T. Edgar Lyon); archaeologists (J. C. Harrington, Dale L. Berge); an architect (Steven T. Baird); a construction supervisor (Robert E. Smithson); and a decorator (Christine H. Robinson). J. Byron Ravsten was the project manager. Perhaps the most important team member was Rowena J. Miller, full-time executive secretary, the person Lyon credited with keeping the organization running.

10. "The Era Asks About Nauvoo Restoration," 12, 14.

11. T. Edgar Lyon to William E. Berrett, April 3, 1964, Church Archives.

12. Lynn Larkin, "At 90, Ida Blum Author, Columnist, Historian, Cook, Hostess, . . . Whew!" *Hancock County Journal-Pilot*, September 12, 1979, 4.

13. T. Edgar Lyon, "Tribute to Ida Blum," L. Tom Perry Special Collections, Harold B. Lee Library, Brigham Young University, Provo, Utah (hereafter cited as Perry Special Collections).

14. "The Era Asks About Nauvoo Restoration," 12, 14.

15. Nancy S. Andrews to T. Edgar Lyon, September 16, 1975, Church Archives.

16. Andrews to Lyon, September 16, 1975.

17. T. Edgar Lyon, Datebook memo section, 1965.

18. T. Edgar Lyon, Datebook memo section, 1965.

19. T. Edgar Lyon to David Johnston (*Detroit Free Press*), October 19, 1973, Church Archives.

20. Lyon made this calculation in a January 25, 1978 letter to Leonard Arrington, Church Archives. These twenty thousand notes are in Perry Special Collections.

21. "The Era Asks about Nauvoo Restoration," 12, 14.

22. Sharon L. Droge to T. Edgar Lyon, July 20, 1971, Church Archives.

23. Lyon, Diary, July 22, 1969, Church Archives.

24. Lyon, "Church Historians I Have Known," 14–22.

25. Lyon, "Church Historians I Have Known," 14–22.

26. Rowena Miller to J. LeRoy Kimball, July 28, 1968, T. Edgar Lyon Collection, Church Archives.

27. Ken Godfrey, interview by Trent Lyon, June 7, 1992, Salt Lake City, Utah.

28. Nadine Cook to T. Edgar Lyon, August 4, 1967, Church Archives.

29. T. Edgar Lyon to Leroy T. Ostler, June 30, 1966, Church Archives.

30. T. Edgar Lyon to Emily S. Stewart, July 2, 1966, Church Archives.

31. T. Edgar Lyon to Emily S. Stewart, July 2, 1966.

32. T. Edgar Lyon to Richard H. Jackson, June 15, 1977, Church Archives. Lyon made such precise calculations that years later, in 1977, he wrote BYU geography professor Richard Jackson, congratulating him for an excellent article on Nauvoo in *BYU Studies* but offering a few minor suggestions for the sake of precise accuracy. For example, Lyon wrote, "Nauvoo blocks are not square . . . east and west [they are] 396 feet (24 rods), but north and south they are 363 feet (22) rods," and most "streets were to be 49½ feet wide (3 rods) not 50 feet" as Jackson had stated. Lyon gave other specific details of the original city:

1. Nauvoo's Main Street was eighty-two feet wide to allow for a ship canal through its center.

2. Water Street was sixty-four feet wide. Obviously this and Main Street were intended to be the business streets of the city. The county surveyor and some Mormons who assisted him must have done their surveying on hot and cold days with no consideration of the expansion of the metal chains, or else they were very careless. Many city lots and even streets do not fit the grid. Some streets are not straight, some blocks have more than 2 [extra] feet, others the same amount less, than the deed descriptions indicated.

33. Don Enders, phone interview by author, March 25, 1996.

34. Dale Berge, phone interview by author, March 29, 1996, notes in author's possession.

35. "Brigham Young's Restored Nauvoo Home Open to Public," *Times and Seasons* 7, no. 1 (September 1971): 18.

36. T. Edgar Lyon, Diary, September 1, 1971. His study of nineteenth-century presses coupled with his boyhood printing experiences provided the basis for a close relationship with the seventy-seven-year-old owner of the 1840s press. T. Edgar Lyon to Janette L. Halton, January 29, 1959, in author's possession.

37. T. Edgar Lyon to June H. Spring, January 25, 1978, Church Archives.

38. Richard Crabb, interview with author and Cheryl Lyon, February 13, 1987, Salt Lake City.

39. Richard Crabb, "My Ten Years with Dr. T. Edgar Lyon," May 10, 1996, in author's possession.

40. Richard Crabb to Sister Bateman, October 17, 1987, original in author's possession.

41. Lyon, Diary, June 26, 1969.

42. T. Edgar Lyon to siblings, July 1, 1969, Church Archives.

43. Lyon, Diary, May 24, 1969.

44. James E. Padfield, "Church Moves Ahead on Nauvoo Project," *Church News* (October 3, 1970): 15.

45. Enders, phone interview. The drive for authenticity caused Lyon to write from Nauvoo to Evans Advertising Agency about a presentation at Carthage Jail. He congratulated them on the new slides and pictures that replaced the previous "disgraceful hodge-podge of caricatures, cartoons and poor drawings." But he had taken along two officials from the Illinois State Historical Society, one of whom said, "We realize this is a propaganda Center and to that we cannot object. But can't you make propaganda without resorting to falsehoods?" Lyon continued that "to those who know their history, such errors discount the entire presentation."

46. Enders, phone interview, March 25, 1996.

47. T. Edgar Lyon to William E. Berrett, November 13, 1964, Church Archives.

48. T. Edgar Lyon to Nancy Richards, September 23, 1969, Church Archives.

49. Lyon, Diary, May 25, 1969.

50. Lyon, Diary, May 26, 1969.

51. Lyon, Diary, May 30, 1969.

52. Lyon, Diary, May 31, 1969.

53. Dale LeCheminant, interview with Trent Lyon, July 9, 1992, Salt Lake City.

54. Enders, phone interview, March 25, 1996.

13

"Deep Well-Spring of Vitality," 1963-78

The major personnel changes at the Salt Lake institute in 1962 and Lyon's conflicts with a director of Nauvoo Restoration Inc. did not damage Ed's reputation as a scholar nor alter his hectic pace. During the final years of his life he continued writing, researching, teaching, and lecturing at the same rate he had for decades. He even increased the degree of his traveling, physical labor, and intellectual creativity. His unflagging energy was a constant marvel to many younger friends. "We students used to speculate about the source of that energy. It was not what has been called 'nervous energy'! It came from some deep well-spring of vitality."[1] Colleagues recalled his remarkable physical strength. Even at age seventy-two, "we would go on [institute] retreats and Ed would go and chop wood. . . . He was always a hard worker."[2] University professors marveled at his intellect and memory. "You were both convincing and truly impressive in your handling of the Campbellite-Rigdon-J. Smith problem. Never have I seen such a display of historical knowledge," wrote University of Utah professor J. D. Williams.[3] Until the very last weeks of his life, he continued with "an intelligence and a steady, calming cheer carried forth in a voice always on the verge of laughter."[4]

Still the Writer

After the 1962 imbroglio at the Salt Lake institute died down, Lyon turned his energies to writing study manuals for institute courses. His 1962-63 part-time leave of absence permitted several hours each day to research and prepare a manual for a course on the Doctrine and Covenants and Church history from 1820 to 1844. He had been teaching a similar course for years, so he pulled together many notes, supplemented by much new research, and by mid-1963, he had completed the manual.[5] That summer he attended workshops at BYU, where he was assigned several other writing projects: (1) Church history from 1845 to 1895, (2) the Church in the twentieth century, (3) Christian history to the fifteenth century, (4) Christian history after the fifteenth century, and (5) great figures in Christian history.

Lyon also accepted an assignment to write a New Testament course of study, and in the mid-1960s, he submitted the first twelve chapters for evaluation. Reviewers found the text very readable but commented that "there is nothing in the text to identify it as LDS; it remains an historical approach [only]."[6] Specifically, Lyon was faulted for his objective writing style; the reviewers asked, "Why go along with the [non-LDS] scholars in their rejection of the authorship of certain N.T. books?" Lyon's notes in the margins of this letter indicate that he recognized that indeed he had not included enough Latter-day Saint understanding as a spiritual base to the New Testament.[7]

Lyon next began revising the text for a course on the Church in the twentieth century, collaborating with historian James B. Allen, but duties in Nauvoo limited his manual-writing time. The Church Educational System (CES) curriculum committee made adjustments and reassigned some of Lyon's courses to other teachers so he could focus on writing. Lyon did manage, however, to rewrite the manual for an advanced course on Church history from 1844 to 1895. For this manual, he incorporated new research from many scholars emerging during the 1960s, especially those with whom he was associated in the recently founded Mormon History Association. He submitted the lengthy manuscript in 1972. In a cover letter to the supervisor of new manuals, E. LV Richardson, Lyon noted,

> I'm positive this will never get by the Correlation Committee. I should have done it two years ago before they came into power, but other jobs made it impossible to squeeze it in. There are too many unorthodox views and interpretations, which are not of the "faith-promoting" style that is now so essential. I've tried to give source material—not warmed-over rehashes of a century or more of myth-making. So it is too shocking.[8]

And he was right. Previously, Lyon had to meet only the requirements of the CES curriculum committees, but now all published material had to pass through the Correlation Executive Committee. Lyon sensed that they would not accept it because of its academic approach. The manual never did appear in print, but completed drafts remain in the Church Archives. Following the rejection of this manual in 1972, Lyon ceased writing curriculum for the institutes. He understood the demands for institute teachers to conform to a standardized curriculum; after all, he had served as a temporary adviser to a correlation committee, and Hermana was a charter member of the Children's Committee. Lyon still yearned, though, for the days when teachers and administrators could sit down and discuss student needs as they wrote their lessons.[9] He felt that the new curriculum of the late 1960s was too subject-oriented and not student-directed. "I still write and tear up, write and tear up, as I'm not sure what is 'relevant' in the lives of those institute students."[10]

As an example of his concern for students more than subjects, Lyon confessed:

> I'm guilty of first introducing what had evolved (or degenerated) into course 45. It was a seminar type of course, and was oriented away from the presidents, and directed toward the lesser-known leaders—the Pratt brothers, Hyde, Rich, Lyman, etc. etc. Then I made it more student-centered, by asking those who had ancestry among pioneers to dig into family records and give reports of lesser-known people who had pioneered the West—thousands of them—who are never mentioned, but who actually did the hard work of establishing "Zion". . . . We uncovered a great deal of human nature type of material, original diaries that would probably have been destroyed, etc., as the students discovered their ancestors, and took a new sense of pride in the achievements of their ancestors.[11]

Lyon was the first institute instructor to prepare and teach a missionary training course. He based the curriculum on his experiences in the Netherlands, attempting to assist the future missionaries in acquiring "a life-long yearning on their part to be active in the Church." He observed that the then-present system of proselyting "was often destructive of the personalities of [some] young missionaries" and that some were literally exploited.[12]

For most of his career, Lyon directed his writing specifically at institute students and the general Latter-day Saint public. He found a new voice during the late 1960s when he began publishing in journals that were more academic—*BYU Studies, Dialogue,* the *Journal of the Illinois State Historical Society, Utah Historical Quarterly, Utah Humanities Review, Western Humanities Review,* and *Historical Quarterly.* In these outlets, Lyon published some of his most provocative and memorable articles, including "Church Historians I Have Known," "Doctrinal Development of the Church during the Nauvoo Sojourn," and "Recollections of 'Old Nauvooers.'"[13]

Another of those academic opportunities came in 1972 when Church Historian Leonard J. Arrington and his assistants James B. Allen and Davis Bitton decided to create a sixteen-volume professional history for the Church's sesquicentennial in 1980. They cast around searching for experts on specific periods or geographical areas. When they discussed Nauvoo, there "was only one logical choice—[T. Edgar Lyon] was the only one who knew enough to write it."[14] Arrington requested approval from the First Presidency and the Quorum of the Twelve for each writer. In a later interview, Arrington indicated that there had been problems with two or three of the names submitted, but Lyon "was a foregone conclusion by everyone in the Twelve. . . . There was absolutely no question at all."[15] Any negative residue from 1962 or conflicts regarding the Nauvoo Restoration project had apparently disappeared by 1972. Lyon was the oldest of the sixteen writers, so Arrington pushed to get him started immediately. Lyon devoted himself fully to the book, which would cover the period 1839 to 1846—the eight years Lyon considered most crucial in Church history due to the gospel understandings of the mature Joseph Smith.[16]

The fifteen to twenty thousand reference and research notes Lyon had written on Nauvoo would serve him well in the new project. Hermana's health was poor, and Ed spent much of his potential research time caring for her. The book developed slowly as Lyon struggled with some fundamental research questions. To his children he confided that he would have to write an honest, open, truth-filled chronicle of this dynamic period, yet keep it in the realm of faith-filled, affirming history.

While preparing the book, Lyon struggled with three basic problems: (1) the practice of plural marriage before public announcement of the doctrine; (2) the close relationship between Mormons and the Masonic Order in Nauvoo; and (3) the Church's involvement in politics. But he thought he could do it, and he jumped in with his usual energy. He planned to complete the writing in 1978 or early 1979, but sickness thwarted his goal.[17]

Still the Teacher

There were times during the 1960s and '70s when Lyon was working at least forty hours a week on Nauvoo research. Yet he was still teaching three to seven classes each quarter at the institute. He certainly missed Bennion but delighted in his association with Bennion's replacement, Joe J. Christensen. Lyon recognized the difficult task the new director faced in following Bennion. Christensen exhibited great tolerance and flexibility in juggling Lyon's schedule to meet the research needs of the Nauvoo Restoration project and in covering Lyon's classes when he was called away to Nauvoo.

Lyon continued to find energy in the classroom, and he, in turn, excited the students. J. Taylor Hollist recalled the historical insights that

Courtesy Church Archives

Illus. 13-1. Salt Lake institute faculty, March 1965. *Front row (left to right):* Bruce R. McConkie, Paul H. Dunn, Joe J. Christensen, T. Edgar Lyon, Fred Goldthorpe. *Middle row (left to right):* Marion D. (Duff) Hanks, Douglas Stott, A. C. Nielsen, Craig Bramwell, Carlisle Hunsaker. *Back row (left to right):* Don Colvin, Dale LeCheminant, L. Elmer Peterson, Albert L. Payne, Reed Durham.

Lyon presented.[18] Years later, his wife, Suzanne Parker Hollist, recalled that in 1965 Lyon had mentioned in class that "someday we won't have any Assistants to the Twelve—they'll all be Seventies. . . . He explained this because that is how the D&C explained it."[19] This predicted change was effected in the 1976 October general conference, under the direction of President Spencer W. Kimball.[20] Suzanne evaluated the "level of teaching and scholarship [in Lyon's class as] at least equal to what I was getting at the University [as a graduate student]. At the same time the teacher was deeply spiritual."[21]

For many years the Church Educational System called for mandatory retirement at age sixty-five. During spring quarter 1968, shortly before his sixty-fifth birthday, Lyon received and signed a contract to continue teaching as much as his Nauvoo Restoration project schedule allowed. In 1972, at age sixty-nine, he still taught seven sections of five different classes (illus. 13-1).[22] In his datebook, he casually noted that August 15, 1972, was his "last day of full contract employment at Institute," but records no emotion or other detail. The 1971–72 school year marked the

Courtesy Church Archives

Illus. 13-2. Elder Boyd K. Packer set Ed Lyon apart as a stake patriarch.

thirty-ninth year Lyon had taught in Church schools. But Lyon's career in the classroom was not over yet. He continued for three more years, until age seventy-two, on a part-time contract. "I remember the day [he] taught his last class," recalled colleague Dale LeCheminant. "He just looked around the room, turned, and walked out. Cal Rudd said regretfully, 'We didn't do anything for him! Ed Lyon just taught his *last* class and we didn't do anything!' We were both heartsick."[23] Lyon retired from teaching completely at the end of winter quarter on March 13, 1975, after a total of forty-eight years as a professional educator.[24]

Hermana's Activities

Lyon's energy, mind, and body were sufficiently strong and active that he could have continued teaching past 1975, but Hermana's health required his time and urgent care. In October 1967, she had discovered a large lump in her left breast. She underwent a radical mastectomy that month, followed by six weeks of radiation. In 1973 doctors discovered a lump in the other breast. It, too, was removed. Hermana tried to avoid even using the term "cancer," preferring to call it simply "my old enemy." Yet despite her denial, cancer returned in 1975, spreading throughout her body.[25] Childhood experiences and an ever-present fear of death kept her from going to the hospital at first, and she insisted that she was suffering only from arthritis. But the pain soon became unbearable. She submitted to further radiation treatments and chemotherapy, experienced serious side effects from medication, and was admitted to the hospital with pneumonia. For eight months, Ed filled his datebooks with reports on her condition. Hermana insisted on being cared for at home, and Ed was the full-time nurse. Ed and the children despaired for her life. Son Lynn, a medical doctor and cancer researcher, recorded that "most people with that extensive cancer do not survive more than a few months."[26]

Courtesy Church Archives

Illus. 13-3. Detail of a picture with Arta Hale *(standing)* and Hermana *(sitting)*.

When Elder Boyd K. Packer (illus. 13-2) came to the Lyon home in 1975 to set Ed apart as a stake patriarch, he recognized Hermana's serious condition and kindly offered to give her a blessing as well. "The blessing was remarkable in that [he] promised her she would be healed so that she could complete other work she [still] had to do [for the Church]," wrote Lynn.[27] She lived for five more "gift years," despite her doctors' view that she appeared to be very near death at that time.

During the past few decades, Hermana had also been working—hard. In addition to her everyday chores, she served on the Primary General Board (1944–64) and then was transferred to the Children's Correlation Committee, with a special assignment to the Family Home Evening Writing Committee (1965–73) and finally to the Instructional Development Committee (1973–75). This work had become so absorbing that her family often viewed it as equivalent to a full-time job. While on the Primary General Board, she established close ties with Arta Hale, a kindred spirit whose penetrating eyes and mind were complemented by a fearless tongue (illus. 13-3). Upon her release from the Primary General Board in 1964, Hermana, Arta, Erma Young Gardiner, Della Provost, Catherine Edwards, and Grant Hardy were called to be on the Children's Correlation Committee. Lynn Lyon recalled that "the committee members were brainstorming for ideas to increase parental support for Primary and Sunday School. Arta and [Hermana] took the position that we had it all wrong. We shouldn't be asking for the support of parents . . . [Church leaders] should be supporting the parents in teaching their own children."[28] They recalled counsel from past Church presidents about teaching the gospel in the home, especially the concept of a special night for families urged by President Joseph F. Smith in 1915. The committee also read the Christian magazine *Guideposts* and the works of various religious thinkers and child psychologists, trying to find practical programs to teach religious principles to children. They formulated a plan and took the idea of a regularized night, a "family home evening," to Elder Harold B. Lee, their supportive and involved overseer. He encouraged them to write sample lessons, and then he sought—and won—approval from President David O. McKay, who announced a formal Church program in October 1965. Within a few months, the Family Home Evening Writing Committee produced fifty-two lessons that were printed and distributed

Courtesy Church Archives

Illus. 13-4. Elder Gordon B. Hinckley, Primary General Board advisor, worked closely with Hermana in the 1950s and '60s.

throughout the Church. Arta Hale chaired the committee for the first year, and Hermana took over the task for several ensuing years.[29]

The program of family home evening prospered and grew as the committee produced some memorable Church lesson manuals. The Lyon sons were often surprised to find some incident from their childhood preserved for posterity, with appropriate name changes, in a lesson. Hermana and Arta Hale "were certainly the driving force in creating this much-needed Church program," wrote Elder Gordon B. Hinckley (illus. 13-4) in a letter expressing gratitude for their creative work.[30]

Teacher and lecturer George D. Durrant served with Hermana and Arta on the committee. He later stated that "it was Hermana who truly taught me to write—she taught me to develop my clever but under-developed ideas into a good lesson."[31] Hermana demanded excellence from the entire committee. During the writing of the first manual, George wrote to Ed Lyon, observing that "[Hermana] is able to convey her love and at the same time demand that others do their very best. She is completely honest and her judgment is unsurpassed . . . under her frank and yet kind direction I have grown greatly in my ability to write acceptable lessons."[32]

Despite her two bouts with cancer, Hermana continued her extensive Church service. In 1973 she accepted an assignment from the first Presidency to work on the Instructional Development Committee, reading lessons and planning future curricular changes (illus. 13-5). She was considered an expert on young children and tirelessly advocated their needs. Elder Thomas Fyans oversaw this committee work, but Hermana worked most closely with Wayne Lynn. In this capacity, as well as her previous calling, she participated in training sessions for Regional Representatives held prior to general conference. Her notes once again reveal her insistence on well-designed programs that were consistent with current educational research and the scriptures. She regularly asked, "How can we make [this program] better?" or "What is lacking here?"

Still the Scholar

While Hermana worked hard writing lessons and planning curriculum for the Church, Ed kept up his hectic pace, too. He continued to speak in church meetings and became a regular lecturer for various study groups (illus. 13-6). Once a month for eight years, he lectured to the Horne group about Nauvoo, though he often

Illus. 13-5. Hermana at typewriter, working on Primary lessons, c. 1960s.

included Church history in Utah as well.[33] Harriet Ann Horne Arrington, Dr. Horne's daughter, sat in on the discussions. According to Harriet, Lyon instilled in them the "integrity of history. . . . He was so precise and so very careful about what he gave us."[34]

Rarely do Lyon's datebooks include a notation that he sat down and relaxed. He did not enjoy television, except for an infrequent documentary or Church general conference. On only one occasion during the 1960s he mentions free time: "Hermana and I sat by front-room fire—read. first luxury of this kind during the holidays."[35] In the 1970s, when Hermana was often ill, he frequently records that they read together by the fire. Their reading selections included *The Arab Mind,* the New Testament, the Book of Mormon, *Those Who Love* (about Abigail and John Adams), *The Mind of Hitler, The Greek Treasure,* and *Love Is Eternal* (about Abraham Lincoln). The last book they read together, in August 1978, was *The Biography of Spencer W. Kimball,* by former student Edward L. Kimball and Andrew E. Kimball Jr. Lyon appreciated President Kimball's candor about his own struggles.

During the last fifteen years of his life, Lyon continued in his informal and unsolicited role as "answerer of gospel questions." As the number of

Illus. 13-6. Ed Lyon lectures at pioneer monument near Echo Canyon, 1978.

his former students grew each year, he received more and more inquiries. Lilie J. Boothe wrote requesting visual aids for an institute course on the history of religion. Lyon responded that "in my teaching I have tried to paint word-pictures of the early leaders. I have also tried to paint word-pictures of ideas," and he slightly chastised teachers who wanted to lean on visual aids as a crutch, asserting that college students ought to be interested in ideas, not pictures.[36] Political science professor J. D. Williams solicited his suggestions on a political-historical manuscript he was preparing. Former student and author Mary Bradford queried Lyon on a figure in Church history about whom she could write a biography. Senator Wallace F. Bennett requested help on the historical background to the bothersome topic of the "constitution hanging by a thread."[37] Lyon became involved in the controversy surrounding the rediscovered manuscripts of the book of Abraham and wrote an article affirming the authenticity of the find. He tried to assuage scores of upset Mormons, including his own sons, struggling with a conflict between scientific findings and Joseph Smith's translation of the book of Abraham. To one student he wrote that not all the answers were in yet and that, in the meantime, "the absence . . . of such information does not detract from the profound spiritual and religious truths taught by Joseph Smith."[38] He both hailed and cooperated with the dynamic new publication *Dialogue,* edited by former student and Bennion-devotee Eugene

England. After its appearance in 1966, Lyon began referring his correspondents to certain articles in the journal that would provide more detailed answers. Lyon's responses to letters of inquiry were often three pages long, single-spaced, indicating a tremendous amount of time devoted to former students, colleagues, and concerned Church members. Many times former students would call Lyon at home to talk about questions with Church history or gospel subjects, and he would be on the phone with them for a half hour or more (illus. 13-7).

Lyon continued to write to those who published articles that contained flagrant inaccuracies. And more than once, others corrected him in a healthy interplay of academic improvement through peer review. Elder Theodore M. Burton, president of the Church's Genealogical Society, responded to Lyon's article in *BYU Studies*[39] on doctrinal development in Nauvoo, suggesting that the sealing of children to parents was not carried out in the Salt Lake City Endowment House in 1855, as Lyon had written, and only began in 1877 in the St. George Temple. He then thanked Lyon for the valuable article and congratulated him for "the most interesting lecture [he] ever heard on the founding fathers and the constitution."[40] Richard L. Anderson, professor of religion and history at BYU, lauded Lyon for his service "in answering my questions. I could go to him any time. He would send a two or three page letter. And you always knew it was well-researched and thought out."[41]

Lyon's frequent association with teachers of religion and other historians interested in Church history naturally led to his participation in the creation of a scholarly organization dedicated to Latter-day Saint history. The initial planning committee met in Logan, Utah, on September 9, 1965, and its first annual meeting was held in San Francisco in December.[42] Leonard J. Arrington, one of the group's prime movers, was

Illus. 13-7. Ed talks on the phone to a former student.

selected as the first president of the Mormon History Association (MHA); Lyon was a charter member. Here Lyon found intellectual stimulation previously unknown. A newsletter held the group together until the *Journal of Mormon History* commenced publication in 1974. The organization grew from its few initial members to over 1,100 in 2001. Lyon functioned as the MHA's third president, during 1968–69, while also serving on the journal's board of editors for four years. He found great satisfaction in helping to develop new scholars.

Lyon was often honored for his historical research and teaching. James C. Fletcher, president of the University of Utah, appointed him as "Special Consultant for Utah History" in the university libraries, for which Lyon received one dollar a year compensation. In April 1976, Brigham Young University bestowed the David O. McKay Humanities Award on Lyon for his multiple contributions in writing, lecturing, and building ties with the Reorganized Church of Latter Day Saints as well as other groups. The next month the University of Utah Emeritus Club presented Lyon with the Merit of Honor Award (illus. 13-8). On January 24, 1978, by invitation of the Utah House of Representatives, he spoke in favor of a bill to restore the Deveraux House, in which Lyon's great aunt Jenny had lived and hosted many dignitaries who came to Utah Territory. Perhaps the most appropriate honor was the gift of an old-fashioned hand-held school bell, given by a group of students in the 1960s and inscribed with the simple words: "To T. Edgar Lyon, whose teachings ring true."

Courtesy Church Archives

Illus. 13-8. Ed Lyon receiving the Merit of Honor Award from the University of Utah Emeritus Club, May 1976.

Lyon offered further service through public speaking. He became a popular speaker at funerals, including those in his own Rosecrest Ward, as well as those of former Dutch Saints and missionaries, people who had participated on Holy Land or Hill Cumorah tours, and even his own students from the 1930s and 1940s. Among the funerals at which he spoke were those of his own siblings. Except for his brother Alan, who died in 1912, the Lyon siblings survived into their seventies and eighties. In 1970, Joe, the jovial, fun-loving owner-manager of the Magazine Printing Company, died of heart failure at age seventy-five, and Ed spoke at his funeral. Ed's oldest brother, Dave, a mining engineer, passed away ten months later, in October 1971, of heart failure at age eighty-four. Dave had served as Ed's model for missionary work and Church service. Ed's brother Kyle died sixteen months later (February 1973) of lung cancer at age seventy-two. In May 1974, Paul, the entrepreneurial rancher and insurance man, died of prostate cancer at age eighty-three. The deaths of four brothers in four years not only saddened Ed but emphasized his own mortality. Only he and his two sisters remained. Carol, the ever-loving older sister who had cared for "Teddy Boy" as a baby, died at age eighty-five, in February 1978, of kidney failure after an operation. His younger and beloved sister Janette outlived Ed, dying in 1994.

Health and Happiness

Lyon himself experienced relatively few health problems during his life. He had, however, suffered from cavity-prone teeth since his youth. For fifty years, his datebook records frequent visits to the dentist for extraction, extensive bridgework, cavity filling, and regular repair. When dentists began emphasizing flossing in the 1960s, he flossed regularly, frugally keeping some strands of used floss in the medicine cabinet to get a second use. But since his appendix operation shortly before his wedding in 1927, he was not hospitalized until the mid-1950s, at which time he checked in for minor hernia repair. His children recall that he often sported scrapes, cuts, and minor gouges on his balding head, usually the result of "conking his noggin" on a low branch in the family orchard or on the low-clearance basement stairs. At age sixty, while he was riding in the back of a truck helping son John move to a new house, a mattress came loose, flipped up, hit him in the head, and knocked him out of the moving truck. He rolled several times and hit the curb, but the driver of the vehicle was unaware of the accident. Lyon stopped a car for help and was eventually taken to Cottonwood Hospital, where he received stitches and had his knees and elbows bandaged. He was swollen and sore for weeks and had to cancel a few classes and speaking engagements because "[he] look[ed] too terrible to be in public."[43]

Lynn Lyon reflected, "I cannot recall ever seeing [Dad] in bed with even a cold all during the years I was growing up. From Dad I gained the impression that men never got sick when they were adults."[44] But in early 1968, the sixty-four-year-old Lyon entered the hospital for the second time in forty-one years. He had an enlarged prostate gland that had obstructed his bladder. Ed faced the operation calmly, even stoically, but it was hard for Hermana to see her husband in pain, confined to a hospital bed. Ed, on the other hand, worried more about Hermana and left detailed instructions about family finances. She had purposefully avoided the bill-paying, always leaving accounting entirely to him. The night before going into the hospital he also composed a hand-written will, after consultation with a lawyer friend. On January 3, 1968, Dr. Ned Mangelson removed part of the prostate and relieved the partial obstruction. After a few weeks, Lyon resumed his schedule of activities, but the painful operation had to be repeated in 1973.

As Ed was recovering in 1968, Hermana read *Aerobics,* a recently published book by Kenneth C. Cooper, which recommended regular exercise, especially jogging. In her usual pattern of assiduously applying what she read, Hermana sent copies of the book to each son and daughter-in-law, suggesting that they read it. Several of them began jogging as a result of her nudging. Ed took up jogging in summer 1968, at age sixty-five. For the next ten years he recorded in his datebook the precise amount of time it took him to jog. By December 12, 1970, he was jogging a mile and a half in thirteen minutes and five seconds.[45] He later increased the distance to two miles a day.

He was in sufficiently good shape that in 1973—shortly before turning seventy—he again began taking strenuous backpacking trips with his sons and grandchildren. They packed and carried all their gear for these camping trips up Stillwater Fork on the north slope of the Uinta Mountains, not far from the family cabin (illus. 13-9). The next summer Lyon, sons Ted and Lynn, and four grandchildren backpacked seven steep miles to isolated Toomset Lake, where they camped for four days (illus. 13-10). Here, Lyon applied skills from his days in the Jackson Hole area by helping the grandchildren build a raft, teaching them to carve wooden spoons, and constructing a usable camp table between two pine trees. Each evening around the campfire he recounted to wide-eyed grandchildren his famous "Uncle Nick stories," family tales

Illus. 13-9. Lynn, Ed, and Natalee Lyon at the family cabin, August 1970.

about his great-uncle Nicholas Crookston, a legendary sheriff in Cache County, Utah. He also told stories from Church history, giving vivid accounts from the life of Joseph Smith. The sunny, slow days were usually filled with delight, but once while her father was away fishing, Lyon had to spank Natalee because she "had a snit."[46] Such punishments were extremely rare, since he had never spanked his own children. He worried about the effect of the spanking on his relationship with Natalee, but noted that she forgivingly "cuddled on my lap as I told stories [that night]." After the children went to bed, father and sons stayed awake, talking for hours around the softly burning campfire, usually tapping into Lyon's vast pool of western and religious experiences.

Descending the steep, rocky trail back to the car, Lyon seriously twisted his knee, causing hemorrhaging into the joint. He recovered, without surgery, after a few months. He did not accompany the backpackers in 1975 because of Hermana's health, but in 1976, at age seventy-three, Lyon shouldered an awkward World War II surplus army pack, climbed the steep miles to the hidden lake, and spent four glorious days.[47] His only concession to modern equipment was borrowing a nephew's down-filled sleeping bag so he did not have to heat a rock to keep his feet warm.

In 1975 and 1976, caring for Hermana as she recovered from cancer absorbed almost all Ed's time. Hermana wrote on a stray piece of paper after Ed's death and tucked it in his 1975 datebook: "I have been reading parts of this diary—Ed [often] says I 'would not eat' or that I 'refused

Illus. 13-10. Lynn carrying Natalee and Ed carrying grandson Joseph on a hike.

to eat'—not so—*couldn't* eat." Then she added, "His great love and seldom-equaled devotion was probably the biggest factor in my pulling through this terrible illness. H.F.L."[48]

On November 1, 1975, during the depths of Hermana's illness, Elder Boyd K. Packer set Ed apart as a patriarch in the Canyon Rim Stake. Lyon was surprised when the call was extended to him, but he remembered that his grandfather and his father had also served in that sacred position. He read what he could to prepare and talked with other patriarchs, specifically Eldred G. Smith, the Patriarch to the Church. From December 20, 1975, through July 5, 1978, Lyon pronounced approximately forty blessings on the young people of his stake and a few for his own grandchildren.

In April 1977, Lyon developed a kidney infection and signs of urinary obstruction. On May 17, he underwent a cystoscopy. The doctor saw a tumor blocking the tube leading from the kidney to the bladder and concluded that surgical removal was not possible.[49] So Ed, like Hermana two years earlier, received irradiation, which appeared to completely arrest the cancerous cells. He recovered enough by August 16, 1977, that he and Hermana attended a celebration of their fiftieth wedding anniversary (illus. 13-11) in Brigham Young's restored Lion House. Their son Laurie planned a creative program of music and verbal tribute from their six sons, six daughters-in law, thirty-two grandchildren, and a host of friends. Despite her fragile health, Hermana glowed with gratitude and fulfillment. Ed recorded the details in his datebook, noting who arrived and at what times and that the bill for the meal was $273.50. But he also noted his emotions: "Each of the six sons gave a tribute—memories of their lives at home with us. I shed a few tears but held back many [more]. Very moving."[50] This type of emotional expression is rare in his diaries

Illus. 13-11. Ed and Hermana on their fiftieth wedding anniversary, August 16, 1977.

and datebooks. Curiously, on January 2, 1978, he confided in his new datebook, "I resolve to [not] write so much trivia—time of meals, food [eaten], etc.—*More comments*."

In April 1978, a detailed examination by doctors, several of them his former students, found no evidence of cancer.[51] But by early May, Lyon knew something was amiss. "My hips and ribs are sore—is this just the flu?"[52] A month later, he noted that Hermana's "cancer [was] active again," and he confessed that "I tried to work on Nauvoo, but was too upset [about her] to concentrate."[53]

On June 10, he recorded that "my left hip [is still] paining me. Aspirin won't help." He was still walking two miles, and as he scrupulously recorded his time each day, he noted that "something is wrong with me. . . . I tried to walk faster . . . can't take as long steps nor as rapid as formerly."[54] He measured the distance of each step and figured that they had decreased from thirty-nine to twenty-seven inches. In real pain, he finally visited former Lambda Delta Sigma interchapter president Dr. DuWayne Schmidt. He first suspected diverticulosis, a problem in the colon, but cancer was also a possibility. On July 18, surgeons performed an exploratory operation. Hermana was too weak to go to the hospital. She recorded: "David came soon after [the operation] and told me the terrible news—it is cancer—outside the colon. Could do nothing for him. Stunned[.] No words can describe my feelings. David is a great comfort, very great."[55] She visited Ed the next day and recorded that he "looked better than I expected . . . and [he] said 'I'm not through yet.'" He came home for three weeks and rallied a bit, but on August 9, his seventy-fifth birthday, the doctors again operated and began chemotherapy. His family fasted and prayed, and David pronounced a guarded blessing on August 13. Three days later, now at home but weakened from the second operation and the rapidly growing cancer in his abdomen and liver, Ed reviewed his fifty-one years of marriage. Hermana recorded, "We talked intimately and warmly. I read to Ed as he was in bed; then he asked when I was going to bed. When I was ready about 10 P.M. he got up, as sick as he is and came in and turned the bed down for me and said 'I want to put you to bed tonight.' Wonderful Ed!"[56]

A few nights later, disoriented, Lyon fell in the bedroom closet, mistaking it for the bathroom. On August 27, he was taken back to the hospital for an operation to remove "accumulations of fluid between his skull and the brain," but it was to no avail. "The muscles of his legs wasted away rapidly, as did his body fat. . . . He was often so nauseated he could tolerate no more than one or two mouthfuls of oatmeal mush, and a sip of milk."[57] On Wednesday afternoon, September 20, 1978, Hermana made her daily visit to the hospital room. A few hours later, Ed died suddenly, probably from a blood clot in his lungs. After returning home, Hermana wrote a single sentence in her diary: "Ed told me 'You're beautiful.'" These may have been his last words.

Less than two years after Ed's death, on June 8, 1980, Hermana died of cancer at her home in East Mill Creek, in the care of her family.

Notes

1. Mary Lythgoe Bradford, "Editor's Notes," *Dialogue: A Journal of Mormon Thought* 11 (Winter 1978): 8–10.

2. Dale LeCheminant, interview by Trent Lyon, July 9, 1992, Salt Lake City.

3. J. D. Williams to T. Edgar Lyon, November 23, 1964, T. Edgar Lyon Collection, Church Archives, Family and Church History Department, The Church of Jesus Christ of Latter-day Saints, Salt Lake City (hereafter cited as Church Archives). Unless otherwise noted, all citations for T. Edgar Lyon materials are located in the Lyon collection.

4. Bradford, "Editor's Notes," 8–10.

5. Alma P. Burton to T. Edgar Lyon, July 26, 1963, Church Archives.

6. Robert E. Parsons to T. Edgar Lyon, n.d., Church Archives.

7. Parsons to Lyon, n.d.

8. T. Edgar Lyon to E. LV Richardson, February 11, 1972, Church Archives.

9. By 1970, Ed felt that seminary and institute manuals had become too rigid and formulaic. He suggested:

> My personal impression is that a committee of Institute teachers ought to be called into a number of "brain-storming" sessions (such as we formerly had under Dr. West) and try to determine what the <u>Students</u> ought to be taught, not what the teachers think they need. Our Church history is too provincial—too Utah-centered, instead of world-centered. Such was our history in the early period, that is, a view of a world mission. Then we settled down out west and became narrow in our view. So we write and think. We need to decide just what is essential for a young person in our Church to learn about his historical foundations, and eliminate the entertaining window-dressing. I think we are scattering our shot too broadly. (T. Edgar Lyon to E. LV Richardson, January 9, 1970, Church Archives)

10. Lyon to Richardson, January 9, 1970. In 1972, Lyon's old colleague Albert L. Payne also complained about the "new curriculum." It "appears pretty rigid and structured to an ol' war horse like me. And anyway it takes much wiser heads than mine to program teachers into a lock-step process where they are told what questions to ask, what and when to write on the chalk board—and when to blow their noses and bear their testimonies." Albert L. Payne to T. Edgar Lyon, January 25, 1972, Church Archives.

11. Lyon to Richardson, January 9, 1970.

12. Lyon to Richardson, January 9, 1970. This concept of abuse or exploitation deals with a phenomena of the 1960s when missionaries were pushed so hard to baptize that they often performed the ordinance before conversion. In this letter to Richardson, Lyon explained the details of this missionary preparation course:

> I was [also] the guilty person who first introduced a missionary training course into the system. At Dr. West's direction I once wrote a student lesson manual (never heard of it again and probably thrown away by now). The Mission Home was functioning and giving a fairly good orientation, but there was a void—nowhere did the potential missionary get any help in understanding the personal problems of missionaries e.g., their dedication, their unselfishness, adjusting to living away from their homes, being on their own as financial managers of their allowances, learning to live with a variety of companions coming from homes with widely divergent backgrounds, the attitude they should take toward their converts, how much time they should put in tracting, etc. I had just come home from presiding over the Netherlands Mission, and had spent an unwarranted part of my time trying to get missionaries adjusted to missionary life—this was quite apart from the teaching of the gospel—and convert them to some Christian

idealism about living and applying the theories of the gospel they were teaching. I felt our system was often destructive of the personalities of the young missionaries, made hypocrites of many, and failed to create a life-long yearning on their part to be active in the Church. Then this expanded, until we had about a dozen missionary courses. (Bro. Widtsoe had worked with me on the course and felt it was a needful thing for missionary adjust-ment before, during, and after the mission). If anything like this is to be offered, I hardly see how it could be included in Course #231. I think we are wasting our time teaching "canned" missionary lessons. But personal interviews with many returned missionaries makes me sorry for them—so many have been literally "exploited" by their mission presidents (under pressure of the competitive system of the present day) and are resentful, never having been really "sold" on the idea of what the opportunity of real missionary work might be.

13. T. Edgar Lyon, "Church Historians I Have Known," *Dialogue: A Journal of Mormon Thought* 11 (Winter 1978): 14–22. In this article, Lyon gratefully acknowl-edges the stimulating role that Leonard J. Arrington played in prodding him into more serious academic scholarship.

14. Leonard J. Arrington, interview by Ted and Trent Lyon, July 2, 1992, Salt Lake City.

15. Arrington, interview.

16. In 1969, Lyon delivered an original speech at the Salt Lake City Institute of Religion entitled "The Development of Church Organization and Doctrine at Nauvoo, 1839–1846." He later reworked the talk into a twelve-page article for *BYU Studies* ("Doctrinal Development of the Church during the Nauvoo Sojourn, 1839–1846," *BYU Studies* 15 [summer 1975]: 435–46). Here he dealt with the chang-ing Latter-day Saint concepts of God and man, the newly preached doctrines of sal-vation for the dead, plural marriage, temple ordinances for the living (not practiced in the Kirtland temple), and the emerging ideas preached by Joseph Smith on eternal progression. Lyon reported to his family that the article was generally well received but had raised the ire of some who could not accept the basic premise that Church doctrines or practices would ever change or develop.

17. When it became apparent in September 1978 that Lyon would not recover from cancer, historians Leonard Arrington and Glen Leonard came to Lyon's home, discussed the unique research and scattered files he had accumulated, and reas-signed the project. Glen Leonard received all the research notes, rough outlines of the chapters Lyon had projected, and three nearly completed chapters.

18. J. Taylor Hollist and Suzanne P. Hollist, phone interview by Kaylynn Hollist, January 21, 1996.

19. Hollist and Hollist, phone interview.

20. Spencer W. Kimball, "The Reconstruction of the first Quorum of the Sev-enty," *Ensign* 6 (November 1976): 9.

21. Suzanne Parker Hollist to Kaylynn Hollist, January 22, 1996, in author's possession.

22. T. Edgar Lyon, Diary, January 9, 1972, Church Archives.

23. Dale LeCheminant, interview by Trent Lyon, July 9, 1992, Salt Lake City.

24. Lyon's work/teaching career included:

1 year—Idaho public schools

3 years—seminary in Idaho

1 year—graduate school, University of Chicago

1 year—Ricks College

4 years—mission president

35 years—Salt Lake institute, full-time

3 years—Salt Lake institute, part-time

48 years total, plus fourteen years with Nauvoo Restoration, Inc.

25. "A History of Laura Hermana Forsberg by Her Son Joseph Lynn Lyon," 1991, 143–44, L. Tom Perry Special Collections, Harold B. Lee Library, Brigham Young University, Provo, Utah.

26. "A History of Laura Hermana Forsberg," 143–44.

27. "History of Laura Hermana Forsberg," 143–44.

28. "History of Laura Hermana Forsberg," 134.

29. Joseph Lynn Lyon includes a discussion of the early functioning of the committee in "A History of Laura Hermana Forsberg," 134–38. Further first-hand insight appears in Hermana's personal papers on correlation, now in the Church Archives.

30. Gordon B. Hinckley to Hermana Lyon, December 6, 1965, Church Archives.

31. George D. Durrant, interview by author, July 10, 1992, Provo, Utah.

32. George D. Durrant to T. Edgar Lyon, June 22, 1965, Church Archives.

33. Harriet Horne Arrington, interview by author and Trent Lyon, July 2, 1992, Salt Lake City.

34. Arrington, interview.

35. T. Edgar Lyon, diary, January 1, 1966.

36. T. Edgar Lyon to Lilie J. Boothe, March 27, 1964, Church Archives.

37. J. D. Williams to T. Edgar Lyon, March 8, 1966, Church Archives; Mary Bradford to T. Edgar Lyon, March 10, 1966, Church Archives; and Wallace F. Bennett to T. Edgar Lyon, May 11, 1966, Church Archives.

38. T. Edgar Lyon to Hyrum Coon, October 31, 1966, Church Archives.

39. T. Edgar Lyon, "Doctrinal Development of the Church during the Nauvoo Sojourn, 1839–1846," *BYU Studies* 15 (1974): 435–46.

40. Theodore M. Burton to T. Edgar Lyon, January 9, 1964, Church Archives.

41. Richard L. Anderson, interview by author, April 4, 1996, Provo, Utah.

42. Patricia Lynn Scott, James E. Crooks, and Sharon G. Pugsley, "'Kinship of Interest': The Mormon History Association's Membership," *Journal of Mormon History* 18 (spring 1992): 153.

43. T. Edgar Lyon, Diary, December 3, 1963.

44. Joseph Lynn Lyon, "History of Laura Hermana Forsberg," 149–50.

45. T. Edgar Lyon, Diary, December 12, 1970.

46. T. Edgar Lyon, Diary, August 15, 1974.

47. T. Edgar Lyon, Diary, August 10–13, 1974.

48. Hermana's notes in T. Edgar Lyon's Diary, 1975.

49. T. Edgar Lyon, Diary, May 17, 1977.

50. T. Edgar Lyon, Diary, August 16, 1977.

51. Joseph Lynn Lyon, "History of Laura Hermana Forsberg," 147.

52. T. Edgar Lyon, Diary, May 9, 1978.

53. T. Edgar Lyon, Diary, June 8, 1978.

54. T. Edgar Lyon, Diary, June 10, 1978.

55. Hermana Forsberg Lyon, Diary, July 18, 1978, Church Archives.

56. Hermana Forsberg Lyon, Diary, August 13, 1978.

57. Joseph Lynn Lyon, "History of Laura Hermana Forsberg," 149.

Appendix 1

Imprint of the Man

In 1974 at a family gathering consisting of Edgar, Hermana, and their six sons and spouses, I suggested that each talk briefly about "a major frustration in [their] life." We went around the circle, revealing a little of ourselves as we discussed disappointments in our lives. As our father began, I thought, "What can a man who has it all together possibly be frustrated about?" Ed quickly admitted, in a sincere and almost sad tone, "I suppose the major frustration all my life has been my severe shyness." I was truly stunned. I had known him for thirty-five years and had never considered him shy. He continued, explaining that it was difficult for him to meet new people, speak up in public gatherings, and express a contrary point of view. I almost wanted to argue with him, tell him that he was not shy, that he was one of the most competent and confident people I had ever met. I wanted to remind him that he had delivered more than 4,500 talks in his adult life, that during more than forty years he had taught at least ten thousand high school and university students, encouraging them to think and ask questions. Ed had counseled with thousands of others, lending his insights to their most intimate problems. He had ably directed the work of a hundred diverse missionaries in the Netherlands. I wanted to tell him that all who knew him spoke of him in almost reverential, awe-filled terms, paying homage to his intellect and testimony. Though Ed had frequently walked with Apostles and prophets, he had not "lost the common touch." He could just as easily strike up a conversation with a husky corn farmer in Illinois as with a General Authority. "No, he couldn't possibly be shy," I said to myself. But he was. The research for this biography has confirmed this to me, but as his son, I never would have believed it without carefully examining his life.

Ever since his childhood, Lyon had felt overshadowed by the talents of his older brothers—their abilities to sing, dance, and play instruments. His high school mates performed on the debate team and the first string of the football team; he did not. He sat on the back rows of most classes at the University of Utah, rarely making comments or asking questions. During his mission and postmission travel he began to gain social confidence, but long before this he had already fashioned himself as shy. Circumstances later in life thrust him into frequent responsibility, public exposure, and debate; but he still felt bashful, even timid, in these situations. Ed's confession of shyness and insecurity during this adult family home evening caused me to reflect on how we may know a person well but still miss some of his or her basic character. Yet it was likely that Ed's self-image of shyness fostered humility and allowed him to accept changes in administrative policies, easily weathering conflicts with his superiors.

The Family Remembers

Ed's life has already been examined through his own diaries, letters, research, and writing. The following quotations and stories illustrate his life and character through the words of others—his children, colleagues, and acquaintances.

His oldest son David recalled:

Dad's family was his highest priority and mother was at the top of the list.

As a young man I thought he [sometimes] bowed down to mother's wishes too much—now I know the wisdom of his ways.[1]

John, Ed and Hermana's second son, wrote a Father's Day letter in 1977:

Fathers of teenage boys often get slighted by their sons because there seems to be an inherent force that . . . turns them to their mothers, which eventually is transferred to the girls they marry. . . . It was easier to talk with Mom, easier to kid her (such as untying apron strings), easier to ask for advice from her. . . .

Later, when I was on my mission, I grew again to appreciate you as a father through the kindly letters full of advice and information that you wrote me. This was a kind of growing back together stage for me as I began to realize that a son is only as great as his father lets him be by the time he spends with him when he is younger.[2]

In 1994, John jotted down some recollections:

Institute teachers did not earn very much money. He always seemed to be struggling to provide for his hungry family by working second and third jobs, i.e.: bookkeeping for Magazine Printing Co.; repairing the wooden pipeline that brought water to the electrical powerhouse at the mouth of East Mill Creek Canyon.

His frugal nature led him to always shop at Safeway, to manufacture home-made laundry soap, to get some of his existence from
the land (fruit trees, garden produce, milk, etc.).[3]

James recalled his father's character:

Dad gave me the unmistakable impression that his wife and his
children were his highest values. . . . The qualities that struck me
most were his wonderful ability to listen and his willingness to take
time for me.

His next highest value was the Gospel and serving the Lord.
I sensed that his work with students at the Institute was more than
a job—he viewed it as a calling. . . .

The remarkable thing I remember about Dad is that he never
seemed stressed, even when under pressure. . . . He just plugged
on. . . . [H]e bore . . . pressures more gracefully than any man I
ever knew.

. . . I never remember Dad getting angry at me. In fact, I only
remember seeing him get angry once (at one of my brothers), and
that lasted about fifteen seconds. He was the most even-tempered
man I've ever met in my life.

. . . He was always so positive, and his steady, warm, cheerful
way allowed the Spirit of the Lord to be present at times when Mom
was stressed or "down."[4]

Laurie observed a unique characteristic:

There are still a few people who never let fame and notoriety go
to their head, even when they become well-known and highly
respected authorities in their field. Dad Lyon was one of these
people. He never did feel he was all that important, which made him
a very important person in the eyes of others. It was dear Dad who
taught me that above all one ought to be honest and true to one's
true self. His integrity was always one of his great strengths. Even as
I stumble, I still have that model to cling to.[5]

Ted sent a late birthday letter to his father in 1975:

As I've seen you take care of Mom, with such a happy countenance, sacrificing your own time and needs and desires, I've been
very impressed. . . . Patience is not tried, I find out, until a man (or
a woman) has children. . . . I greatly admire the patience I've seen
in you since I was a child, and especially the patience you've shown in
the last weeks as you've lovingly cared for Mom. I'll try to follow
that model.[6]

When Ed received the David O. McKay Humanities Award from Brigham Young University, Ted observed:

> He taught us love, principally to love our mother as we saw him extending love to her. And he taught us to love Mormon and Western history. . . . The pioneer trail was not a line on a map but dust and mud under our feet as we scampered over its history, learning about the very practical realities of the trek. . . . History was never crammed down our throats but made tart and bubbly, sufficient that we, his sons and pupils, thirsted for more.[7]

A few days after Ed's death, Ted eased his grief by trying to capture some of his father's life in words:

> Dad once said, "I've never been bored a day in my life." He filled his life with so many things that were exciting that he never had time to feel sorry for himself, to dwell on negative feelings, to turn inward to anguish or boredom.
>
> He seemed to understand everything. Not only did he know facts and dates, but he knew why and how things worked. . . . Not only was he theoretical but so very practical. I could ask him questions about Church history, and with equal confidence ask about the care of fruit trees or types of stains or varnishes to use on cabinet doors. . . .
>
> Selflessness. . . . he always lived for others first. In this way I feel that he came so close to the ideal Christian life of service. . . . I recall many times, on Sunday evenings especially, when the phone would ring, and Dad would go on for 20 or 30 minutes answering the question of some upset student or old acquaintance who had been disturbed by a problem raised in class that day.
>
> Endurance. Dad seemed to be able to work endlessly, rarely tiring. . . . I'm sure that some of this endurance resulted merely from getting himself psyched up to not wear down or to keep going until the job was done. What an image of real manhood he conveyed to me!
>
> And he was happy. . . . He showed me that living the gospel does indeed fulfill the Lord's purpose that we might have joy.[8]

In a short narrative, "Dad as a Story Teller," son Lynn noted:

> Though Mother was the one who loved drama . . . it was Dad who had a gift for narrative storytelling that was unsurpassed. And because of this gift, he made history come alive for his students. His storytelling did not depend on the skills of the theater. . . . But he would relate a historical event as if it were a story. Dry historical facts were never boring with Dad. . . .

Dad's stories of the early Church leaders were always framed with the same sense of the dramatic and yet the practical. After he had done extensive research on Nauvoo, he would talk of the people who lived there. I can still see Wilford Woodruff sorting more than 14,000 bricks, fresh from the kiln, to be sure that those used for the front wall of his house were of the most uniform in color. Dad had found that interesting fact in Brother Woodruff's journal and incorporated into the account he told of the Woodruff home and its builder. . . . And as Dad talked about Brother Woodruff, I began to picture this man as someone with exceptional determination, someone who was remarkably careful about whatever he did. I could then imagine the intensity with which he preached the gospel and the dedication he brought to all of his Church callings.[9]

Colleagues and Friends Remember

Lyon's closest colleague from the Salt Lake Institute of Religion, Lowell Bennion, spoke at his funeral:

T. Edgar Lyon, a healthy and rugged man who had hardly known a sick day, died at age seventy-five after a short, losing battle with cancer. In his death, his wife, six sons, and thirty-two grandchildren lost a gentle, loving husband and father [and grandfather], and the Church a great historian and teacher.

Ed Lyon was a real Latter-day Saint, a worthy disciple of Jesus Christ. In him was a total absence of pretense. He never sought the honors of men. He never took the chief seats. His only interest was to serve, to give of himself, to lose his life in the interest of others. I was younger than Brother Lyon and much less prepared to teach religion than he was. However, because I was appointed the first director of the institute, I remained in that position. Ed Lyon was not envious nor resentful as my associate director, but wholly loyal and cooperative.

Ed exemplified the Beatitudes. He was humble, teachable, receptive of criticism without offense, meek, merciful, pure of heart, a peacemaker. I never saw him angry, deceitful, hypocritical, or selfish. In my memory, he will ever remain a Saint of Saints.[10]

Frederick S. Buchanan, a student and close friend who piped the mournful bagpipes at Lyon's burial, reflected on his former teacher:

I think I took every class taught by T. Edgar Lyon at the [Salt Lake] Institute of Religion during the late 1950s and later I attended the Sunday School class he taught in the University Ward. The things that I remember most about him as a teacher were his infectious enthusiasm for history, the twinkle in his eyes when he got students involved in thinking about difficult historical issues and his ability to communicate the human dimension of . . . divine events.

His treatment of the history of Christianity not only informed me about the Mormon perspective on the need for a restoration, but it communicated to me a deep personal appreciation for some of the early Catholic saints as well as the leaders of the Protestant reformation which I had never really sensed before. I don't think I had ever heard of St. Francis of Assisi until I learned about him from Ed Lyon and he became for me someone representing the very best of Medieval Christianity. Come to think of it, there was something of St. Francis in Ed himself, especially in his interpretation of the social gospel. Bro. Lyon pursued his subjects in the classroom with breathless enthusiasm and left us all amazed at the sheer amount of significant information and understanding that one person could possess. . . .

I suppose all this is to say that Ed Lyon taught in a way that promoted student growth—intellectually, morally and religiously. My own life was enriched, stimulated and made better for having had him as a teacher.[11]

Church historian Leonard J. Arrington admitted that he liked Lyon's historical articles, but there "just weren't enough [of them]. T. Edgar Lyon will live longer as a teacher than as a historian."[12]

Ronald K. Esplin, director of the Joseph Fielding Smith Institute for Church History at BYU, postulated that Lyon's "greatest impact was in the classroom or in Nauvoo, rather than in his publications."[13] Esplin recognized that Lyon's manuals influenced hundreds of thousands of faithful Church members, but to his mind

[Ed's] greatest contributions were as an enthusiastic, inspiring promoter and teacher of history with the capacity to fire up others to share the same passion (if not the same detailed knowledge) of Mormon history that he had. . . . He analyzed, integrated, interpreted, and shared his knowledge in a way that made it comprehensible and come alive for the rest of us. He made his students feel that he knew the people of whom he spoke—and more, he made us feel that we could too! He taught our heritage in a way that left all of us better informed and motivated many of us to want to learn more.[14]

Esplin was not the only one with this view. Scores of other Salt Lake institute students decided to make Mormon history and teaching a focus in their lives. Larry C. Porter, an emeritus professor of Church history and doctrine at BYU, picked up "many excellent ideas that [Ed Lyon] taught me [that] are employed in my teaching of Church history today."[15] Lyon's style and techniques were carried into the classes of Porter and many other former students. Richard L. Anderson, another prolific scholar of Church history, affirmed that

> Ed's trademark was responsive concern. Whenever I asked a question personally or jotted a note of inquiry, he took pride in giving a thorough answer. This cost him a lot of time, no doubt, but he was the constant teacher of those researching and thus made an undefinable but definite impact on Mormon studies, far beyond the articles that he himself produced.[16]

A few days after Lyon's death in September 1978, President Spencer W. Kimball wrote to Hermana:

Dear Sister Lyon:

> Deserved tributes have been paid to T. Edgar Lyon, a good and valiant servant of our Father in Heaven. And now come the lonely and contemplative hours when you who are dearest to him are left alone with your thoughts and memories. At this time, be assured that you do not mourn alone. Our prayers are with you.
>
> Looking back on a lifetime of service, how proud you must be of Ed Lyon, the husband, father, Church worker, teacher, historian, friend. We share this recognition and express our appreciation.
>
> Also, Sister Lyon, we recognize the importance of a supporting wife and children to the success of any man. We appreciate your individual contribution to Ed's outstanding accomplishments.
>
> May the knowledge that our Heavenly Father lives, and that life continues, comfort you and your stalwart sons, David, John, Lynn, Ted, Laurence, James and their families. May the calm, sweet assurance of eternal life with your worthy husband be yours. May his "thirst for historical accuracy" be satisfied.

> Faithfully yours,
> (Signed)
> Spencer W. Kimball
> President[17]

Notes

1. David Lyon to Ted Lyon, February 20, 1990, L. Tom Perry Special Collections, Harold B. Lee Library, Brigham Young University, Provo, Utah (hereafter cited as Perry Special Collections).

2. John Lyon to T. Edgar Lyon, June 1977, Perry Special Collections.

3. John Lyon to Ted Lyon, March 10, 1994, Perry Special Collections.

4. James Lyon to Ted Lyon, April 14, 1996, Perry Special Collections.

5. Laurie Lyon to brothers, March 5, 1995, Perry Special Collections.

6. Ted Lyon to T. Edgar Lyon, August 18, 1975, Perry Special Collections.

7. Ted Lyon, Introduction of T. Edgar Lyon, David O. McKay Humanities Award, April 23, 1976, Perry Special Collections.

8. Ted Lyon, "Dad the Camper," Perry Special Collections.

9. Lynn Lyon, "Dad as a Story Teller," Perry Special Collections.

10. Lowell L. Bennion, "Funeral Address," September 1978, tape and transcript in author's possession.

11. Fred S. Buchanan, "I Remember Brother Lyon," August 18, 1986, Perry Special Collections.

12. Leonard J. Arrington, interview by Ted and Trent Lyon, July 2, 1992, Salt Lake City.

13. Ronald K. Esplin to Ted Lyon, April 24, 1990, Perry Special Collections.

14. Ronald K. Esplin to Ted Lyon, April 24, 1990.

15. Larry C. Porter to Ted Lyon, March 7, 1990, Perry Special Collections.

16. Richard L. Anderson to Ted Lyon, "Questionnaire—T. Edgar Lyon," 1990, Perry Special Collections.

17. Spencer W. Kimball to Hermana F. Lyon, September 24, 1978, Perry Special Collections.

Appendix 2

Letter to New Missionaries from Elder Rudger G. Clawson, 1923

DEAR BROTHER:

Every missionary Elder of the Church of Jesus Christ of Latter-day Saints is endowed with the Holy Priesthood and is sent forth as a minister of the restored Gospel of our Lord and Savior. He is expected by those who send him to be of upright conduct and morally clean; and he should keep himself pure, sweet, and unspotted from the sins of the world. He should avoid the very appearance of evil, so that, when honorably released, he may return home with clean hands and a pure heart.

Among the items of counsel given by the authorities of the Church to missionaries before their departure for the mission field the following should be indelibly stamped upon the mind and a heart of every Elder:

TRAVELING TO MISSION FIELD

1. From the time that you are set apart for your missionary labors, ever bear in mind that you are a special representative of the Church and its work and never forget that the Church and its members will be judged by your actions. A thoughtless disregard of the simple rules of conduct is often responsible for positive injury to the missionary and the great cause he represents.

2. While in cars, ships, hotels, or other public places, never indulge in loud speaking, heated discussions, inappropriate singing, games of chance, vulgar stories or in any conduct whatsoever that is rowdy or boisterous and not becoming a gentleman.

3. The journey to the mission field often affords excellent opportunity for study. You will do well to avail yourself of this opportunity.

4. If you have the privilege of "sight seeing" within the larger cities, you should refrain from visiting the "districts" of bad reputation. If you cannot assist in correcting evil, avoid it entirely.

IN THE MISSION FIELD

5. When you reach your field of labor let all your talents, affections and powers be centered on the work of the ministry.

6. Carefully observe and perform all instructions given to you by those in authority.

7. Get an understanding of the Gospel through prayerful and careful study and teach it as the Spirit directs. Study the scriptures with care—the Jewish, the Nephite, and the latter-day revelations. Store you mind with knowledge of the truth, and the spirit of the Lord will bring it to your remembrance in due season.

8. Live near the Lord so that you can approach Him and appeal to Him on all occasions. Do all things with a prayerful heart; pray vocally morning and evening, oftener when necessary, and pray secretly every day. Prayer should be appropriate to the occasion, and the Spirit of the Lord will direct the one who prays if he be responsive to the divine influence.

9. Seek learning by faith as well as by study. Try to acquire proficiency in the use of the language, but do not depend upon fine words or upon the learning of the world for the effectiveness of your preaching.

10. Remember that you are sent out to preach the first principle of the Gospel and to call men to repentance; not to pose as expounders of mysteries, either spiritual or otherwise. Do not enter into debate with fellow missionaries nor with anyone else over obscure points and passages; and do not seek to advance beyond what the Lord has revealed.

11. Portray the excellencies of the Gospel, but never ridicule the religious beliefs of others. Impute sincerity of mind and purpose to other men as you claim it for yourself.

12. Do your best at all times. Your duty to yourself and to your God demands this constant effort.

13. Be appreciative of every act of kindness shown you and leave your blessing with the deserving.

14. Bless, but do not curse.

15. Be charitable to the unfortunate, and sympathize with the afflicted.

16. Lodge, eat and pray with the people as opportunity may allow and accept their hospitality with gratitude.

17. Seek to learn the will of the Lord and then do it. When success attends your labors give God the glory.

18. Observe the word of wisdom in all strictness, refraining from the use of tea, coffee tobacco, and intoxicants of every kind.

19. Care well for your health, remembering always that your life is

precious. All excesses are wrong and bring ill results. You should not walk too much, talk too much, fast too much, eat or drink too much, not attempt to do without needful things. Remember wisdom in all things is one of the greatest gifts, therefore, cultivate it.

20. Be cleanly in your person, clothing, and habits. Be of genteel deportment and pattern after the best manners. Do not engage in undignified games, sports, or pastimes.

21. Be candid and sincere; be pleasant and cheerful, but do not indulge in nonsense, ridicule, or unseemly jesting.

22. Guard against undue familiarity with persons of the opposite sex. Any departure from this rule may lead to immorality; and a fallen brother not only condemns himself but brings misery and woe to the kindred of both parties concerned. Sexual sin is a heinous offense; there are few sins more enticing and none more dangerous and deadly.

23. Keep a brief daily journal of your life's (missionary) labors. Elders should be especially careful to make a record of all their ministrations as bearers of the Priesthood, such as baptisms, confirmations, blessings and naming of children, ordinations, etc. Manifestations of the power of the Spirit in relief of suffering, healing, etc., should be recorded by missionaries who are witnesses thereto, and should be reported to the respective Mission Presidents.

24. Do not let your ambition to bring new members into the Church lead you to baptize those who are unworthy. Never baptize a married woman without the consent of her husband, nor minor children without the consent of their parents.

25. Be punctual in duty, that the Spirit of the Lord may not be grieved by the unseemliness of the tardy attendance.

26. Never say in public or in private that you do not know the Gospel is true.

27. Hold sacred and do not make common use of the names of Deity, or of such titles as Apostle, Prophet, Seer and Revelator. The ordinary titles for bearers of the Melchizedek Priesthood are Elder and Brother.

28. Honor the laws of the country, the state, and the community in which you labor.

29. Spend as little money as possible. Let the world and your fellow-members of the Church assist you in the things that are needful, thereby affording them opportunity to prove that they are disciples of the Lord.

30. Take good care of your money; guard against loss and robbery.

31. Do not borrow money from members of the Church or others.

32. Write your given name in full or abbreviate specifically, as "Geo."

for George, "Wm." for William. Initials fail to indicate the sex or to make clear which person is meant.

33. Do not engage in long sight-seeing trips during your mission.

34. Get the spirit of your mission and keep it. "Let your light so shine before men, that they may see your good works and glorify your Father which is in heaven."

RETURNING HOME

35. Upon your release, or prior thereto, do not make promises to write or render other personal service when you return home. Wait until you do return and then do all you reasonably can to keep alive the good and pure acquaintanceships you have formed in the mission field.

36. The conduct of missionaries on their homeward journey should be circumspect, and in every respect compatible with their high calling and their ministry. If there is opportunity for sight-seeing, it should be enjoyed in the spirit of learning and righteous pleasure. Let it be repeated that no good will come to you or others from witnessing evil sights.

37. Your ministry in God's service does not end with your missionary release.

38. In the zeal which comes of missionary experience caution should be observed not to obtrude your views on others. Every proper opportunity, however, should be sought to explain the Gospel.

39. Upon your arrival home and the resumption of your home associations, do not become discouraged in the service of the Lord, if you seemingly fail to find the same intense devotion to the work of the Gospel that you discovered among your missionary associates.

40. Be charitable in your judgment of others.

41. Be diligent in your Church duties at home. Accept willingly any appointment that may be given you which you can, in reason, perform, be it ever so humble. Let the beneficent spirit of your mission be infused into all your subsequent associations and work.

42. Remember that consistency, stability and fidelity to principle are qualities essential to a great character.

Rudger Clawson
In behalf of the Council of the Twelve Apostles

Note: *Keep the forgoing instructions with you for ready reference throughout your entire mission. Read and study them frequently.*

Appendix 3

T. Edgar Lyon's Poetry and Romantic Writings

[Four poems written by Ed between 1926 and 1927 while courting Hermana. By a touch, a kiss, a walk in the mountains, she awakens a never-before felt or even imagined emotion—love.]

Touch

An irresistible something drew me toward you; that night
Upon the doorstep. Unconsciously my hand reached out
And found its place on you. With greater speed than light
There moved from you to me through that embracing arm
A wondrous joy and thrill. I then experienced what Jesus said
He lost, for out of you, to me, there flowed a surging tide of virtue.
It reached my heart, then carried on to every body cell
Until my being tingled with its new born life and love.
Upon returning that night, (or morning had I better not admit),
My joy was too enriched to care for sleep.
I lay upon my bed and prayed and cried,
Because I had found you, and claimed you for my own.
May I ne'er act as though I had forgotten
That wondrous re-birth you gave me there that night,
When I your holy being so embraced.

The Kiss

The evening had been more than one could wish,
To o'er-flowing filled with all that love had taught,
Yet something lacked to make my prize secure.
I whispered to you, "I love you," and then,
As if that were the master-key of life,
Our lips in sweetest love each other met.

I have not words the wondrous joy to tell,
That through my being surged in countless waves,
Yet unto me that night a new love came,
That in eternity no dying out shall know.
With rapturous thrills my heart beat out its joy
Which could no longer its bounteous love contain,
Until my life has made itself a part
Of what I told you on that very night.

That kiss! It opened to my view and understanding,
New vistas of eternal life I had not e'er beheld.
It gave me the assurance that our love was true,
And from our God had come its fountain head of light.
Believe me now, my angel lover girl,
That though all earth against us turn,
My love shall for you e'er undying burn,
For truly shall I always say "I love you."

My Girl

There in the chair you sit, my angel Queen,
A picture of sweetest beauty rare. And I here
Of you think, and thrill to know that you are mine.
How blest and hallowed was that day
When God again you to me gave
My companion throughout eternity to be.
Each morn there comes with waking consciousness
Anew my unbounded love for you. Unlike the dawn,
Which merely brings for one more day the light
That with the eventide again shall disappear,
My love re-awakes possessing all its joy of yesterday
Added to that which still was earlier born.
This love for you, which springs as an eternal fountain,
Fed by the crystal pureness of your soul divine,
Again with each recurring dawn springs forth
To greater realms of ecstasy, and then is treasured up
Within my heart as safely as misers guard
Their worthless stores. It is from this great vault
Of gems so rare that come the many "streaks"

Which end so hopelessly and cause you disappointment,
Grief and pain. I mean these things to be of truest love
Unsullied by a mortal urge or care, yet fail I have and
Fail it seems I ever shall. Forgive me, Girl, I do love YOU!

The Spring

The day—not all that one could ask of Nature,
With threatening clouds and rain to interfere,
Yet these were all forgotten in the happiness you brought
To me throughout that most exquisite day.
That lark we took to higher mountain heights,
The rain, the trail, the rocks, the trees and flowers,
All served to form a frame of wondrous hue
In which was placed my new-born love for you.
Nor shall I e'er forget our rest beneath a tree
Which sheltered us, as your love shelters me.
Together o'er that rough and tangled road we journeyed on,
Each mindful of the other's presence near,
Until we reached the uplands dry, then paused,
And cast a glance back o'er the joyous road we'd climbed,
Serene, and happy, and in love with love.
Symbolic was that day of how I've lived—
Led on through tangled maze by you, Sweet Soul,
Until from narrow valleys I've emerged,
Unto the mountain-heights to view the whole
Of life and its eternal plans, with you, my guide.
And having reached the heights at end of day,
I shall look back o'er all we've done, and say,
"it has been sweet my life with you to live."

Reminiscences on Our Eleventh Wedding Anniversary—
August 16, 1938

[This was written while Ed was away from home at the University of Chicago.]

Meaningful life cannot be lived on level plains or in the valleys all the time. One must ascend to the rugged peaks from time to time in order to gain a better perspective of the whole of things. In prayer I ascended to the heights, drawing close to Our Father and caught a vision of the walk through life and the need of helpful companionship and joyous exhilaration coming from a life shared with a divine personage. There came a day when I saw this divinity embodied in human form and the Voice of God revealed my soul-half to me.

For several years, I'd treasured in my heart a Bible verse that was to be used to reveal my unending love and admiration for my treasured ideal. A Sunday night it was revealed beneath the stars and parting from her, I hoped she'd understand how I felt toward her.

Then followed another Sunday evening—a hand stretched forth across the space that intervened between earth and heaven, and as an electric current flows through a wire, there streamed a taste of virgin love from her to me, re-charging my soul with endless love for her sweet being.

A kiss came later, sealing all that we two had thought. No need to speak—the hearts knew and understood that marriage would the outcome be, uniting our souls in joyous felicity.

Rain and clouds all day. Toward evening the rain ceased. Clouds hung low. Grass and sage and bush and tree drenched. But nothing daunted, a lover of nature wanted to carry out his next act of devotional love midst the trails and the trees where his feet in childhood days of carefree life had often wandered. Dry wood and an axe and memories of yesteryear led the way to the spot and kindled a fire. There in the gleam of the blazing embers a ring came from my pocket and found its abiding place on her finger. Never can I forget the look on her face! She was not surprised, much to my regret, but she was pleased. And as the ring runs round and round without end, so was my undying love betrothed to her, to last forever.

There was an operation and she was there by me when I awakened, to give hope and solace to my soul, as she has done ever since. It made me love her all the more.

August 16th dawned clear and warm. She had arisen early and taken a last walk in singleness over the hills and vales of her girlhood—a last farewell to solitary life. Mine was a later arising, preparations, and then the temple. What a glorious day and what a thrilling memory! Through the veil she came-arrayed—an angel twice over—and offering herself to me with fullness of womanhood and beauty of girlhood and purity of soul. To the altar—yes, the altar in very deed, for there she sacrificed herself for me and not to be outdone, I sacrificed myself for her—where God, angels and witness were happy in our union. Heaven smiled and has continued so ever since, except for some brief moments when my lack of wisdom caused their light to be obscured by clouds of selfish will. Another ring upon her finger, binding the former one more securely, and doubly symbolic of our love that ne'er shall end. A kiss in the Temple— the ecstasy of it lingers on my lips and shall never cease to be a source of thrilling love and inspiration.

Wedding luncheon, resting, talking, a wedding dress—all parts of a busy afternoon. Reception, amid romantic music and a host of friends. Then off to Brighton—a thrilling and unexpected thing, for I did not want to be separated from her that night above all nights. Cold of early morning and high altitudes. A light before a cabin; wild columbine within—here was to be our honeymoon together. In childhood innocence we spent our nights and days together—mountain climbing, resting (for I was not strong), preparing meals together, reading to each other (except for her enrapturing book that shut me from close intimacy with her for many hours) and long nights of peaceful slumber 'neath whispering evergreens, an angelic being enclosed within my arms.

The ensuing years have been filled with adventures. Nothing monotonous about our life! Off to Idaho. And then started the gypsy life. Salt Lake, Idaho, Chicago, California, Holland and many parts of Europe. Move, move, move and more of it. Yet she did not complain. Babies—one two and then three-four at one fell blow! A staunch, sturdy soul throughout it all. A wonderful leader, and excellent organizer, a thrilling lover, a dear companion, a perfect wife, a model mother, a choice counselor, a wise girl, a gracious lady in all the vicissitudes of a school-teacher's life.

Not until this summer have I really known how dear she really is. Only when separated from her for a time did I really appreciate her sterling worth. Only from a distance did I see her high ideals to true advantage. Only through separation did I see how intimately our lives have been entwined. Without her near there is a definite vacancy within my soul that nothing else can fill. Part of me has gone away and makes me feel that I have lost a part of my very self—I do hope that she has it treasured within her soul, near her heart or else firmly embedded in the conscious recesses of her mind. Only separation from her made me realize what life without her would be. Only absence from her has driven home the vacuity that eternal life without her would be. This enforced living apart has made me realize how much I depend upon her for counsel. When the "dark night of the soul" came upon me, how I cried for her companionship and helpful advice. How I needed her near to give comfort and solace as only she can. She has taught me so much. I need her to teach me so much more.

And she will. It seems that our two souls are united in our four boys. I miss them, because in them is part of her and part of me, blended into one, and they bring her closer to me in thought, deed, love and admiration, yes, and adoration.

Eleven years! That isn't many. Just wait until eleven more have rolled onward toward eternity. Our souls will be closer together, our love nobler, our aspirations higher, and our understanding of each other greater than ever before. Dependence of each other will be even greater than now, for the two souls are on the highway of eternity, in which our personalities will develop into a perfect unity of love and ideals, while she will still retain her beauty of perpetual young-womanhood which she enjoys, and I will have attained impotent old age, in which our selves can live in harmony with each other, unmarred by any blemish of repugnance or misunderstanding.

Eternities? With her they will be all too short! For love as I have for her and she has for me must grow brighter and more thrilling and enduring with the passing of the years. God grant us peace and happiness in this world until we are satisfied to leave it, and in the world to come, life everlasting.

(Signed)
Ed

Chicago, Illinois

Appendix 4

Full-time Missionaries who Served under T. Edgar and Hermana Lyon (1933–37)

	Name	Arrived	Released	Birth Year	Other	Residence
1.	Carter E. Jones	10 July 1931	6 Nov 1933	1912		SLC
2.	James J. de Bry		6 Nov 1933			SLC
3.	Albert H. Bragonje	10 July 1931	2 Dec 1933	1910		Ogden
4.	Gabriel J. Neerings Jr.	2 Oct 1931	15 Feb 1934	1912		SLC
5.	Frederick Steenblik	2 Oct 1931	15 Feb 1934	1868	Married, older	SLC*
6.	Lowell J. van Dam	6 Nov 1931	12 Mar 1934	1912		Sandy
7.	Calton C. Kammerman	4 Dec 1931	20 Mar 1934	1910		SLC
8.	Morris H. Winward	4 Dec 1931	15 Mar 1934	1911		Whitney, ID
9.	Woodrow W. Winward	4 Dec 1931	15 Mar 1934	1913		Whitney, ID
10.	Walle Koster	29 Jan 1932	10 Apr 1934	1874	Married, older	SLC*
11.	Clyde A. Holdaway	29 Jan 1932	13 Jun 1934	1912		Vineyard
12.	Douwe J. van der Werff	29 Jan 1932	4 Jul 1934	1910		SLC
13.	Alma H. Dalebaut	29 Jan 1932	28 May 1934	1910		SLC
14.	William H. Timmerman	29 Jan 1932	12 Jun 1934	1910		SLC
15.	Martin L. de Korver	29 Jan 1932	31 Jul 1934			SLC
16.	John S. Lugt	14 Mar 1932	29 May 1934	1913		SLC
17.	Harold R. Williams	12 Nov 1932	9 May 1935	1912		SLC
18.	John W. Evertsen	15 Dec 1932	11 Mar 1935	1912		SLC
19.	Marvin H. Walton	15 Dec 1932	7 May 1935	1911		SLC
20.	Henry R. Stephenson	15 Dec 1932	12 Jun 1935	1911		SLC
21.	Kenneth E. Knapp	15 Dec 1932	12 Jun 1935	1911		SLC
22.	Raymond V. Kooyman	4 Feb 1933	1 Feb 1935	1909		SLC
23.	Lewis E. Whetman	4 Feb 1933	7 Jun 1935	1910		SLC
24.	Louis H. Hagen	4 Feb 1933	1 Feb 1935	1910	Married	SLC
25.	Cornelis J. Schaap	27 Jul 1933	9 May 1935	1879	Married, older	SLC*
26.	Johanna C. H. Schaap	27 Jul 1933	9 May 1935	1879	Married, older	SLC*
27.	Sterling K. Hixson	6 Oct 1933	26 Mar 1936	1913		SLC
28.	Clinton H. Esperson	6 Oct 1933	20 Apr 1936	1914		Midvale

Name	Arrived	Released	Birth Year	Other	Residence
29. Henry T. Sumsion	2 Nov 1933	26 Mar 1936	1912		Chester
30. Dale R. Curtis	14 Dec 1933	26 Mar 1936	1914		SLC
31. Arnold W. Miller	14 Dec 1933	20 Apr 1936	1913		Parker, ID
32. John M.C. Landwaard	25 Jan 1934	9 Jul 1936	1914		Sugar House*
33. Neil W. Kooyman	8 Mar 1934	30 Sep 1936	1915		SLC
34. Abraham Sieverts Jr.	31 May 1934	17 Feb 1936	1910		SLC*
35. Lee R. Ossmen	31 May 1934	10 Sep 1936	1911		Rigby, ID
36. Hugo Witt	17 Apr 1934	1 Feb 1935	1900	Older	Germany
37. Heber G. Bingham	4 Oct 1934	12 Apr 1937	1914		Weston,ID
38. Tracey G. Call	1 Nov 1934	19 Apr 1937	1915		Afton, WY
39. Platt D. L. Ward	29 Nov 1934	14 Apr 1937	1911		Preston, ID
40. Arthur E. Bingham	22 Dec 1934	20 May 1937	1914		Ogden
41. Dow T. Lewis	22 Dec 1934	8 May 1937	1916		Lewiston
42. John van Drimmelen	22 Dec 1934	20 May 1937	1914		Ogden
43. Harold B. Watkins	22 Dec 1934	8 Jun 1937	1914		Ogden
44. Roscoe J. Willey	3 Feb 1935	24 Jun 1937	1914		SLC
45. Leon R. de Korver	22 Feb 1935	19 Apr 1937	1914		SLC
46. Jules Dieu Jr.	21 Mar 1935	16 May 1937	1915		Ogden
47. La Mar T. Holt	21 Mar 1935	18 Jul 1937	1914		Clearfield
48. Henry Visser Sr.	21 Mar 1935	27 Oct 1936	1901	Married, older	Ogden*
49. Cornelis de Jong Sr.	2 May 1935	9 Feb 1937	1876	Married, older	SLC*
50. Jacobus J. van Langeveld	2 May 1935	8 Jul 1937	1875	Widower, older	SLC*
51. Aaron B. Vance	2 May 1935	8 Jul 1935	1912		Fairfield
52. Hendrick Winkel	2 May 1935	20 Apr 1936		Married	Richfield*
53. Everdina C.V.O. Winkel	2 May 1935	20 Apr 1936		Married	Richfield*
54. William Mulder	30 May 1935	28 Oct 1937	1914		SLC*
55. Thomas B. Ingram	3 Oct 1935	1 Feb 1938	1913		Nephi
56. Sebastiaan van Dongen	3 Oct 1935	24 Aug 1937	1906	Married, older	SLC*
57. Teda K. van Dongen	3 Oct 1935	24 Aug 1937	1901	Married, older	SLC*
58. Arthur B. Denhalter	31 Oct 1935	24 Aug 1937	1915		Provo
59. Alma R. Guthrie	31 Oct 1935	7 Apr 1938	1913		Alamosa, CO
60. Joseph D. Hodges	31 Oct 1935	7 Apr 1938	1916		Logan
61. Frank B. Jex	31 Oct 1935	7 Apr 1938	1915		SLC
62. Owen D. Clegg	28 Nov 1935	5 May 1938	1916		Grace, ID
63. John A. Roghaar	28 Nov 1935	24 May 1938	1916		Grace, ID
64. Franklin H. Hawkins	21 Feb 1936	24 May 1936	1913		Tremonton
65. Glenn H. Lybbert	21 Feb 1936	18 Aug 1938	1913		Vernal
66. William B. Carr	5 Mar 1936	29 May 1938	1917		Berkeley, CA

Name	Arrived	Released	Birth Year	Other	Residence
67. Joseph P. Lambert	5 Mar 1936	25 Jul 1938	1916		Burley, ID
68. Adriana V. de Jong	19 Feb 1936	9 Feb 1937	1875	Married, older	SLC*
69. Barney H. Hilton	28 May 1936	19 Sep 1938	1915		Pleasant Grove
70. Joseph P. Vorkink	28 May 1936	30 Jul 1938	1915		Los Angeles, CA
71. Lynn A. Argyle	25 Jun 1936	19 Sep 1938	1918		Spanish Fork
72. Melvin L. Neerings	25 Jun 1936	5 Jul 1938	1917		SLC
73. Richard S. Lewis	23 Jul 1936	26 Nov 1938	1918		Lewiston
74. Rex S. Gourley	1 Oct 1936	5 May 1938	1917		Pleasant Grove
75. Bert D. Isaac	1 Oct 1936	13 Mar 1939	1917		Spanish Fork
76. Gordon B. Swapp	1 Oct 1936	2 Feb 1939	1916		Enterprise
77. Martin de Waal Sr.	29 Oct 1936	13 Mar 1939	1917		SLC
78. Burnis R. Finlinson	29 Oct 1936	13 Mar 1939	1916		Oak City
79. Paul B. Clayton	26 Nov 1936	1 Jun 1939	1914		Los Angeles, CA
80. Garth G. Nebeker	26 Nov 1936	13 Mar 1939	1916		Richfield
81. Erwin Schick	26 Nov 1936	1 Nov 1938	1914		Kaysville
82. Elmo D. Buchanan	17 Dec 1936	13 Mar 1939	1915		Venice
83. Lorenzo C. de Haan	17 Dec 1936	1 Jun 1939	1915		Ogden
84. Walter H. Draper	17 Dec 1936	1 Jun 1939	1911		Wellington
85. Arie van Essen	17 Dec 1936	1 Nov 1938	1888	Widower, older	Los Angeles, CA*
86. Elmer S. van Boerum	17 Dec 1936	31 May 1937	1912		Ogden
87. Dean I. Nuttall	24 Dec 1936	2 Feb 1939	1916		Provo
88. Joseph O. Peterson	4 Feb 1937	1 May 1939	1910		Huntsville
89. Orme M. Jergonsen	4 Feb 1937	22 Aug 1939	1916		St. Anthony, ID
90. Clyde B. Beckstrom	1 Apr 1937	4 Apr 1939	1917		Spanish Fork
91. Judicus M. P. J. Verstegen	2 Apr 1937	1 Apr 1938	1876	Divorced, older	Netherlands*
92. Harry Kranendonk	29 Apr 1937	1 Apr 1938	1917		SLC
93. Joe H. de Long	27 May 1937	18 Apr 1939	1916		Escalante
94. Glen M. Bird	24 Jun 1937	22 Aug 1939	1918		Sandy

* Born in the Netherlands but living in the United States at time of mission call.

Note: Unless otherwise indicated, town of residence is in the state of Utah.

Part-time Dutch Missionaries who Served under T. Edgar and Hermana Lyon (1933–37)

Name	Branch	Date set apart
Cornelis Jacobus de Ronde	Schiedam	24 June 1934
Matthijs Johannes van Os	Schiedam	24 June 1934
Ana Kaper-Ohmacht	Amsterdam	26 June 1934
Hermanus J. Nieuwland	Rotterdam	8 Aug 1934
Pieter van der Meide Jr.	Rotterdam	8 Aug 1934
Cornelis Been	Rotterdam	8 Aug 1934
Leonie Louisa Pastijn	Rotterdam	8 Aug 1934
Cornelia Vriens van der Meide	Rotterdam	8 Aug 1934
Pieter Weggman	Rotterdam	15 Nov 1935
Adriana Johanna van Sleen	Rotterdam	15 Nov 1935
Adriaantje Dikgraaf Boekhout	Rotterdam	15 Nov 1935

Appendix 5

Publications of T. Edgar Lyon

BOOKS AND MANUALS

Apostasy to Restoration. Salt Lake City: Deseret Book Company, 1960. [Published as a lesson manual for Melchizedek Priesthood Quorums of the Church of Jesus Christ of Latter-day Saints.]

Contributions of Modern Scripture to Religious Living. [Twelve addresses given during the autumn quarter of 1948 over Station KSL in Salt Lake City as part of the Sunday Night L.D.S. Church Radio Broadcast. They were printed and distributed as a four-page pamphlet each week. Several were reprinted in the Deseret News.]

Contributions of Joseph Smith. Salt Lake City: Deseret Book Company, 1940. [Contains four published radio talks by T. Edgar Lyon.]

"Evangelical Protestant Missionary Activities in Mormon Dominated Areas: 1869–1900." Ph.D. dissertation. University of Utah, 1962.

Introduction to the Doctrine and Covenants and the Pearl of Great Price. Salt Lake City: Department of Education, The Church of Jesus Christ of Latter-day Saints, 1948. A revised edition appeared in 1955.

"Orson Pratt—Early Mormon Leader." M.A. Thesis, University of Chicago, 1932.

We Believe. Salt Lake City: The Church of Jesus Christ of Latter-day Saints, 1947. [Originally published as the manual for the M-Men and Gleaners of the Mutual Improvement Association of The Church of Jesus Christ of Latter-day Saints. A revised edition appeared in 1951 as a Junior M-Men and Junior Gleaners Manual. It was reviewed and issued again in 1959 as a manual for the Ensign and Laurel groups of the M.I.A. The original manual was translated and published in at least seven foreign languages.]

ARTICLES (in reverse chronological order)

"The Account Books of the Amos Davis Store at Commerce, Illinois." *BYU Studies* 19 (winter 1979): 241–43.

"Church Historians I Have Known." *Dialogue* 11 (winter 1978): 14–22.

"Recollections of 'Old Nauvooers,' Memories from Oral History." *BYU Studies* 18 (winter 1978): 143–50.

"From Solomon's Porch." *Ensign* 5 (September 1975): 24–29.

"Doctrinal Development of the Church during the Nauvoo Sojourn." *BYU Studies* 15 (summer 1975): 435–46.

"Greco-Roman Influences in the Holy Land." *Ensign* 4 (September 1974): 20–21.

"The City That Moved Itself 1400 Miles." *Ensign* 4 (March 1974): 30–35.

"Nauvoo and the Council of the Twelve." Chapter 6 in *The Restoration Movement: Essays in Mormon History*, ed. F. Mark McKiernan, Alma R. Blair, and Paul M. Edwards, 167–205. Lawrence, Kansas: Coronado Press, 1973.

"The New Testament—Why Read It?" *New Era* 3 (February 1973): 14–15.

"Independence, Missouri, and the Mormons, 1927–1933." *BYU Studies* 13 (autumn 1972): 10–19.

"Mormon Colonization in the Far West." *Improvement Era* 73 (July 1970): 10–14.

"The Current Restoration of Nauvoo." *Dialogue* 5 (spring 1970): 13–25.

"Some Uncommon Aspects of the Mormon Migration." *Improvement Era* 72 (September 1969): 33–34, 36, 38, 40.

"How Authentic are Mormon Historic Sites in Vermont and New York?" *BYU Studies* 9 (spring 1969): 341–50.

"The Sketches on the Papyri Backings." Improvement Era 71 (May 1968): 18–23.

"Religious Activities and Development in Utah, 1847–1910." *Utah Historical Quarterly* 35 (1967): 292–306.

"The Nauvoo Temple." *Instructor* 100 (March 1965), 97–99.

"Latter-Day Saint Teachers and the Evaluation of Historical Sources." *Improvement Era* 64 (February 1961): 94–96, 112–13.

"So You Have Been Called To Teach?" *Instructor* 95 (February 1960): 50–51.

"This Is the Place." *Utah Historical Quarterly* 27 (summer 1959): 203–7. Republished in *The Valley of the Great Salt Lake* (1959, 1963, 1967).

"Teaching the Apostasy." *Improvement Era* 61 (June 1958): 394–95, 470–71.

"Is It Hearsay or History?" *Instructor* 92 (April 1957): 116, 122.

"The Articles of Faith: How Were They Born." *Millennial Star* 119 (1957): 330–33, 338.

"Orson Pratt, Pioneer and Proselyter." *Utah Historical Quarterly* 24 (1956): 261–73.

"Let's Keep It Simple." *Instructor* 90 (March 1955): 96. Revised in *Instructor* 105 (November 1970): 440–41.

"Joseph Smith—The Wentworth Letter and Religious America of 1842." *Logan* (Utah) *Herald Journal*, December 26, 1954; also in *Joseph Smith Memorial*.

"Modern Scripture—the Doctrine and Covenants." *Instructor* 87 (June 1952): 171.

"The Articles of Faith." *Instructor* 87 (1952). [A series of three articles.]

"The Apostasy." *Instructor* 86 (1951). [A series of six articles.]

"Lorenzo Snow." *Instructor* 84 (March 1949): 109–10, 129.

"The Doctrine and Covenants and the Church." *Instructor* 84 (1949). [A series of twelve articles.]

"Reverence." *Children's Friend* 46 (1947): 536.

"Reading to Children." *Children's Friend* 46 (1947): 484.

"Family Prayers." *Children's Friend* 46 (1947): 443.

"The Latter-day Saint and the Sacrament." *Children's Friend* 46 (1947): 395.

"Orson Pratt, a Biographical Study." *Instructor* 82 (1947). [A series of twelve articles.]

"Christ, Christmas, and Santa Claus." *Improvement Era* 46 (December 1943): 756, 791–92.

"Recreation and the Mormon Church." *Character and Citizenship* (Chicago: National Council on Education for Character and Citizenship) 6 (September 1939): 28–30.

"Organization and Program of the L.D.S. Student Clubs at Institutes . . ." *Week-day Religious Education* 2, no. 1 (1938): 24, 31.

"Landmarks in the Netherlands Mission, 1861–1936." *Improvement Era* 39 (September 1936): 546–47, 573.

"A Blessing and Its Fulfillment." *Millennial Star* 98 (September 24, 1936): 613–15, 620–21.

PAMPHLETS AND PUBLISHED SPEECHES
(Available at Church Archives in the T. Edgar Lyon Collection, and at BYU's Perry Special Collections)

"This Is the Place Monument—Story and History" (Salt Lake City: Don Pearson, 1955). 24 pages.

"What Is a Prophet of God?" *BYU Selected Speeches*, November 2, 1960.

"History of the Salt Lake Institute of Religion, 1935–1965"—November 7, 1965, souvenir program.

Publications for Nauvoo Restoration
    A. Nine house and site leaflets.
    B. "Historic Nauvoo," 1967.
    C. "What Is Nauvoo, Inc.?" 1970.
    D. "Nauvoo Information Center Ground-breaking," 1969.
    E. "Dedication—Nauvoo Visitors Center," 1971.
    F. "Dedication, May 26, 1973" (houses and shops); 3–11.

"Will Ye Also Go Away?" "Lord, To Whom Shall We Go?" Salt Lake Institute of Religion, Devotional, March 14, 1975.

COURSES OF STUDY

A. Institute

1. *Nature and Content of the Doctrine and Covenants.* Fourteen chapters designed for a one-semester or two-quarter course in the Church schools and institutes; was multilithed as Scripture 124 (or 124–25); 1962–63.

2. "History and Doctrine of the Church, 1820–1844," teacher's manual for LDS Church History Course #141 (later course 441); multilithed in 1958 and 1960.

3. Revised edition of the above Church history course, "History and Doctrine of the Church (Interpretative History of the LDS Church, 1820–1844); Revised," 1967.

4. "History and Doctrine of the Church (Interpretative History of the LDS Church, 1844–1896) 1958" for course #142 (later course 442).

5. A manuscript edition of the above , enlarged, with a new format, and teachers' aids, was written during 1968 and 1969.

6. "History of Christianity—100 A.D. to 700 A.D." This manuscript was prepared during 1962–1963 as Institute Course #151 (later course 451).

B. Relief Society

1. "The Gospel as a Way of Life," nine lessons published for the use of small branches, new branches, and Relief Societies in the mission fields. They appeared for nine consecutive months . . . In August 1946 to May 1947 . . . In the Relief Society Monthly Bulletin.

2. "The Presidency—The Three Are One," a series of fifteen lessons and an introductory one, to be used two years, 1948–1950. They dealt with the counselors as well as the presidents of the Church.

3. "The Presidents of the Church." Joseph Smith through Heber J. Grant, plus an introductory lesson.

4. In addition to the above . . . two courses of study for the Relief Society. One on "The Articles of Faith" and the other on lesson interpretations for Talmage's *Jesus the Christ*. These were published in the 1950s and were sent out in the lesson bulletins.

C. Sunday School

Lessons in Sunday School Teachers' Manual

Adult Class, 1974–75. Four lessons for this course of study, dealing with the Four Gospels.

Adult Class, 1975–76. Three of the lessons . . . this manual, dealing with the Acts, the Epistles, and Revelation.

D. Unpublished Manuscripts

1. In 1939–1940 T. Edgar Lyon wrote a course of study, at the request of Franklin L. West, for a college course in the Institutes of Religion on the Doctrine and Covenants.

Manuscript lost in LDS Church Office Building; never published.

2. A Sunday School Lesson Manual for "Investigators' Class." On December 4, 1953, Lyon was authorized by the Executive Secretary of the Sunday School General Board to prepare a lesson manual for a new "Investigators' Class" in the Sunday Schools. It was to be entitled "The Revealed Gospel of Jesus Christ," and it was to be used during the calendar year 1955. Forty-four lessons were prepared, under the supervision of Carl J. Christensen of the Investigators' Class Committee. It was never printed, as there were fears that it would be disruptive of the other regular scheduled classes of the Sunday School for the same age groups.

3. A Doctrine and Covenants Lesson Course for college-age students. In August 1970, Dr. Thomas J. Parmley and Wayne Richards of the Sunday School General Board asked Lyon to prepare a course of study entitled "Distinctive Features of Mormonism," based on the Doctrine and Covenants. Several sessions were held and Lyon submitted an outline for a forty-four lesson course and prepared several sample lessons. These were read, suggestions made for improvement, and the go-ahead signal given. Before they were printed the Sunday School board

was reorganized and the Instructional Development Committee was placed in charge of the lessons and curriculum. The former board members were released and nothing more came of the lessons Lyon prepared.

E. Editorial work

1. James L. Barker, *Apostasy from the Divine Church* (Salt Lake City: Kate Montgomery Barker, 1960). At the request of Elder Henry D. Moyle, Lyon condensed Barker's extensive notes to a 780-page book.

2. James L. Barker, *The Restoration of the Divine Church* (Salt Lake City: Kate Montgomery Barker, 1960). Publication and organization of Barker's notes into a 140-page book.

3. From 1933 to 1937 Lyon authored at least eighty-five editorials and doctrinal and historical articles while serving as president of the Netherlands Mission. He also acted as general editor of the mission journal, the *Ster*.

OTHER

Approximately sixty-five book reviews published in seventeen different journals.

Index

*The numbers for pages with illustrations appear in **boldface**.*